Strategic Communication for Organizations

STRATEGIC COMMUNICATION FOR ORGANIZATIONS

Sara LaBelle and Jennifer H. Waldeck

UNIVERSITY OF CALIFORNIA PRESS

University of California Press

Oakland, California

Library of Congress Cataloging-in-Publication Data

Names: LaBelle, Sara, 1988- author. | Waldeck, Jennifer H., author.
Title: Strategic communication for organizations / Sara LaBelle
    and Jennifer H. Waldeck.
Description: Oakland, California : University of California Press,
    [2020] | Includes bibliographical references and index.
Identifiers: LCCN 2019021667 (print) | LCCN 2019980747 (ebook) |
    ISBN 9780520298521 (paperback) | ISBN 9780520970601 (ebook)
Subjects: LCSH: Business communication.
Classification: LCC HF5718 .L34 2020 (print) | LCC HF5718 (ebook) |
    DDC 658.4/5—dc23
LC record available at https://lccn.loc.gov/2019021667
LC ebook record available at https://lccn.loc.gov/2019980747

Manufactured in the United States of America

29   28   27   26   25   24   23   22   21   20
10   9   8   7   6   5   4   3   2   1

Contents

Acknowledgments   vii
Introduction: What to Expect from This Book   1

PART ONE:
Foundations of Strategic Communication   5

1. An Introduction to Strategic Communication   7
2. Organizational Types and Structures   37
3. Mission Statements, Organizational Identity and Image, and Branding   66
4. Communication Ethics   91

PART TWO:
Creating, Implementing, and Evaluating Strategic Messages   117

5. Organizational Goals and Objectives   119

6. Selecting and Understanding the Target Audience   152
7. Developing and Designing Messages: Using Persuasion Theory and Evidence-Based Principles   190
8. Selecting Channels   225
9. Cultural Diversity and Stakeholder Awareness   259
10. Implementing Campaigns   290
11. Evaluating Campaigns   318

Index   351

Acknowledgments

Strategic Communication for Organizations would not have been possible without the talented team at the University of California Press. Lyn Uhl, our executive editor, has been a tremendous source of support from our first discussions of writing a communication-centric textbook on the strategic communication campaign process. Her experience in the publishing industry and enthusiasm for this project encouraged us throughout the long process of bringing the book to fruition. She sought out the best possible willing and available reviewers and provided expert insight that assisted us in using those reviews to make the book better. We extend to her a great deal of appreciation for her continued support of this project.

Lisa Moore was a tremendous gift to us in her role as developmental editor. Her kind and constructive feedback was instrumental in the early phases of our writing process, and her comments and suggestions on the near-final versions of our chapters undoubtedly increased the value of this text. Some books are easier to conceptualize, organize, and write than others. This project was a challenge from the start, because it truly is the first of its kind. There were no competitors to assess and either model or seek to improve on. Working from a blank slate allows for innovation but requires focus and, often, an outside perspective on something that the authors are so intertwined with. Lisa provided both with professionalism and constant concern for student needs. Her suggestions helped us to articulate our ideas and clarify our

thinking. *Strategic Communication for Organizations* is better for her thoughtful, constructive, and insightful feedback.

We would also like to thank Enrique Ochoa-Kaup, who answered endless emails about the book preparation process with a kind and helpful attitude. We have appreciated you immensely. We are grateful to the production editors, graphic designers, and other technicians who made this book come alive beautifully. Thank you to Chris Jolly for doing the hard work of producing an instructor's manual—we are so grateful to have this accompany our text, and we know it will be of tremendous use to the instructors who adopt it. To all of those who work "behind the scenes" at the University of California Press—thank you for helping our vision become a reality.

A number of talented and insightful colleagues at various institutions gave generously of their time and wisdom in reviewing each and every chapter of this book. They challenged us, encouraged us, and provided their insights on a very interdisciplinary process—which in turn helped us to write a better book. Thank you to Katherine S. Thweatt (Oswego State University of New York), Janie Harden Fritz (Duquesne University), Patrice Buzzanell (University of South Florida), Scott W. Dunn (Radford University), Brad Van Alstyne (Dominican University of California), Joshua B. Barbour (The University of Texas at Austin), and Matthew Weber (University of Minnesota).

We would like to thank our students and colleagues in the School of Communication at

Chapman University for their support. Dr. Lisa Sparks, dean of the School of Communication, provided unconditional support for this project and believed deeply in its value. Her enthusiasm for a book of this nature was contagious and kept us focused and excited about our work.

To all of our colleagues and friends at Chapman, we appreciate your collegiality and support.

To our undergraduate students in strategic and corporate communication, a special thank you for inspiring the content and form of this work—we had you in mind when writing our chapters and creating content that would be interesting and applicable to you. Jennifer's graduate students in organizational communication and communication consulting provided functional support when they read unpublished drafts of several chapters. Their feedback and support for the value of a book on this topic were both helpful and encouraging.

Finally, it would have been nearly impossible to accomplish this endeavor without the loving support of friends and family. Your advice, mentorship, and friendship are not forgotten in acknowledging who has helped us achieve this goal. Sara would like to thank in particular Dr. Melissa Wanzer and Dr. Keith Weber—I doubt I will ever be able to express my gratitude for all that you have done for me, and for always ensuring that I have educators to aspire to be like. To my parents Tom and Carol LaBelle—thank you for always hearing me out, even when you do not entirely understand why I am stressed! To Nicole, for always being a model of what friendship entails. To Zac, who is the only other person who has listened to every thought, been a soundboard for every brainstorming session, who has heard every idea in every chapter of this book and provided insight, support, and advice along the way—no amount of thanks would ever be sufficient. Finally, to my coauthor Jennifer, you presented me with an opportunity that challenged me, that helped me grow, that gave me confidence, and that resulted in one heck of a book. Thank you.

Jennifer would like to thank dear friends and mentors Patricia Kearney, Tim Plax, Dave Seibold, Paul Nelson, and Judy Pearson. They taught me how to write about complex and sophisticated ideas in a fashion that undergraduate students and laypeople will learn something from. They also instilled in me the importance of mentoring and encouraging promising colleagues. Thank you to the most promising of all of them, Dr. Sara LaBelle, my coauthor, for giving me the opportunity to do just that.

Introduction: What to Expect from This Book

All organizations have to communicate to advance their mission and achieve their goals—but how can they do so successfully in a rapidly changing communication environment, with the endless options they have for how, when, and where to communicate, and with measures in place to evaluate their success? These are just a few of the challenges you will confront as a strategic communication professional. The purpose of *Strategic Communication for Organizations* is to provide you with an understanding of this emerging area of study, particularly as it operates in a variety of organizational settings. *Strategic Communication for Organizations* emphasizes how to use theory and research from the field of communication studies to support and advance the mission of all types of organizations, including for-profit, nonprofit, and government entities, across a variety of business sectors. Ultimately, you will determine how best to develop, implement, and evaluate messages that are consistent with an organization's identity and mission. You will decide how to effectively reach internal and external audiences. Communicating effectively as an organization is not guesswork or luck; it is a learned skill that can be improved with knowledge and practice.

WHAT IS A STRATEGIC APPROACH TO COMMUNICATION?

There are several reasons why an organization would want to use a strategic approach to communicate their mission. A strategic approach to communication considers an organization's unique type, identity, and mission in designing, implementing, and evaluating strategic communication campaigns aimed at realizing specific goals. Strategic communication relies on evidence-driven practices, theory- and research-based solutions, and systematic procedures to understand and analyze communication campaign opportunities for organizations. A strategic communication approach provides you with a number of distinct advantages for your personal, academic, and professional lives.

- **An emerging interdisciplinary perspective.** The world, and the organizations within it, are becoming more interdisciplinary. In fact, some have argued that a distinct strength of strategic communication is that it is a "transboundary" concept, meaning that it is not limited to one particular field or area of study but rather incorporates knowledge and practice from multiple related fields. As such, strategic communication is capable of accounting for the wide variety of organizational processes much more efficiently than the traditionally segregated fields of marketing, public relations, or human resources (Falkheimer and Heide 2014). To understand the world and the endless organizations within it from a strategic communication perspective is to understand, fundamentally and without limitations of academic discipline or field of study, what makes organizations function effectively.
- **Academic opportunities.** There are a number of emerging undergraduate programs across the country and world that focus on strategic communication. However, there is also a growing number of academic opportunities in graduate education. An increasing number of undergraduate and graduate programs are leaning toward the development of interdisciplinary strategic communication programs that encompass traditional majors such as advertising, marketing, organizational communication, and management. Learning how to think in this interdisciplinary way early can help you to succeed in graduate applications and programs. The expectation is no longer that you will succeed in one narrow aspect of organizational life, but rather that in your studies you will develop a well-rounded, interdisciplinary understanding of organizations—that is the strength of strategic communication.
- **Career opportunities.** At the time this chapter was written, a job search in "Strategic Communication" yielded over two thousand postings in the United States on the job search platform Idealist.org. With the growing number of academic opportunities in these areas already mentioned, employers are seeking graduates with interdisciplinary specializations and talents. Your abilities as a writer, speaker, and critical thinker will serve you well in pursuing these careers.

A strategic communication approach to organizations emphasizes research, analysis, critical thinking, planning, and insight in helping an organization to achieve its goals. In mastering a strategic approach to organizational processes, and communication in particular, you will benefit from a sound interdisciplinary base of knowledge and be well-prepared for cutting-edge academic opportunities and a growing job market.

HOW IS THIS BOOK ORGANIZED?

This book is divided into two main parts. The first part, "Foundations of Strategic Communication" (chapters 1 to 4), provides an understanding of the myriad organizational types and structures that engage in strategic communication as well as how organizations define and brand themselves to create a cohesive identity. Ethical communication is spotlighted in the first part as a key to maintaining organizational value and creating effective campaigns.

The second part, "Creating, Implementing, and Evaluating Strategic Messages" (chapters 5 to 11), lays out a step-by-step plan for creating strategic communication campaigns that align with the organization's identity and mission as well as for aligning campaigns with the needs of stakeholders and communication partners. In these chapters we discuss how organizations can organize and prepare for effective campaigns by having clear objectives, a thorough understanding of their target audience, an evidence-based approach to messaging, and by carefully selecting both traditional and new media platforms. Throughout this part, we attend to the cultural diversity that exists across campaign stakeholder groups and how that diversity should inform communication strategy. Finally, we address the importance of implementing and evaluating communication campaigns. You will learn a variety of strategies for assessing campaigns to identify successes and for adjusting your strategic communication plan moving forward.

REAL WORLD APPLICATIONS

One way to learn about effective strategic communication involves examining how actual organizations engage in these processes every day. Although this is an emerging area of study in higher education, organizations are already applying and using the theories, research, and practice of strategic communication to obtain impressive results. As you read through *Strategic Communication for Organizations,* you will have access to a number of features that leverage these real-world practices and that will help you contextualize and apply the content of this book.

- **Realistic Opening Vignettes.** Each chapter in this textbook starts with a vignette, or scenario, that depicts a typical situation you might confront as a strategic communication professional. Reading vignettes will help to put chapter content into context and get you to think critically about the role of strategic communication in organizations.

- **Strategic Communication Mentor.** To help illustrate the concepts discussed in each chapter, the **Strategic Communication Mentor** series featured in each chapter gives you insight from thought leaders in the strategic, corporate, or organizational fields. These features might include links to videos, online articles, or other interactive material that will help you connect the concepts in each chapter to "real" experiences and situations.
- **Interview with a Professional.** Throughout the text, look for these segments in which highly experienced and respected professionals in a variety of organizational types and structures offer their perspective.

RESOURCES FOR CRITICAL THINKING AND RESEARCH

Throughout this book, **Questions for Critical Thinking and Discussion** are included to help you summarize what you learned in a particular chapter, challenge your understanding of a particular concept, or help stimulate discussions with your peers about what you have read.

Keeping with our emphasis on real-world applications, the topics that are discussed throughout this book are based on research studies by professionals in a variety of academic fields. These topics have been chosen to deepen your understanding of the content presented in each chapter and are the focus of the **Further Readings and Resources** feature. Find the additional readings through your university's library catalog. When appropriate, you might also find links to online articles, web pages, or blogs that can help enhance your understanding of chapter content.

In summary, *Strategic Communication for Organizations* provides a theory- and research-based approach to the complex and sophisticated range of skills necessary for strategic organizational communication. We hope that this book serves as the backdrop for rich course discussions and interesting assignments that will help you grow and apply yourself as a communication professional. Internalizing the interdisciplinary, scholarly approach to practice that we advocate in this book will help you establish your unique professional value as you prepare for a competitive, exciting job market or graduate studies. We wish all the best for you as you embark on this journey, and welcome your feedback or questions about the content of our book or the field of strategic communication. Contact Sara at labelle@chapman.edu and Jennifer at waldeck@chapman.edu.

Reference
Falkheimer, J., and M. Heide. 2014. "From Public Relations to Strategic Communication in Sweden: The Emergence of a Transboundary Field of Knowledge." *Nordicom Review* 35, no. 2: 123–38.

FOUNDATIONS OF STRATEGIC COMMUNICATION

An Introduction to Strategic Communication

1

CHAPTER CONTENTS

1.1 The Need for Strategic Communication in Organizations   11

1.2 Laying the Groundwork: Communication as a Foundation for Organizational Success   16

    1.2.1 Defining Communication   17

    1.2.2 A Linear Model of Communication   20

    1.2.3 The Simultaneous Transactions Model of Communication   23

    1.2.4 The Study of Communication   27

1.3 A Strategic Communication Approach to Organizations   29

    1.3.1 All Organizations Engage in Strategic Communication   30

    1.3.2 Strategic Communication Is Mindful Communication   30

    1.3.3 Strategic Communication Is Inherently Interdisciplinary   31

    1.3.4 A Strategic Communication Approach to Organizations Focuses on Messaging   32

1.4 Tying It All Together: The Benefits of Applying a Strategic Communication Perspective to Organizational Processes   33

LEARNING OBJECTIVES

After reading this chapter, you should be able to do the following:

- ▶ Distinguish between strategic communication and communication more broadly.
- ▶ Explain why strategic communication is important in organizations.
- ▶ Identify common issues that both new and established organizations face in their internal and external communication efforts.
- ▶ Compare and contrast the linear and simultaneous transactions models of communication.
- ▶ Recall the four foundational assumptions of a strategic approach to communication.

Jacob is a recent college graduate. Armed with a degree in business and a passion for entrepreneurship, Jacob has developed an environmentally friendly home cleaning product, EcoCleanR. He is thrilled to finally pursue his passion by founding his own start-up company to manufacture and distribute the cleaner. At first, things are going great: Jacob has a small team of talented college friends who are helping him with design and manufacturing, and his family and friends are happy to help buy EcoCleanR and talk about it in their own social networks. After a few months, though, the excitement and energy levels are waning for Jacob and his small—and burned out—staff. Sales are also dropping; the friends and family that initially bought and used EcoCleanR are still supportive, but Jacob needs to reach new audiences if he wants to continue to sell this product. What makes matters worse is that a large manufacturer has just announced a new sustainability initiative and launched products that have similar ingredient profiles to EcoCleanR. The pressure of this announcement is causing stress on his staff, who are not sure how Jacob's product is unique or better than the competition.

Unfortunately for Jacob, the competition for EcoCleanR seems never ending . . . but the money and time are.

Facing pressures from both in and outside, Jacob realizes he needs a plan to help his start-up get back on track. He creates a list of things he needs to change for his company to succeed in an ever-changing market. First, he needs to get everyone in his company to agree on the identity and mission of their company, and the benefits EcoCleanR offers relative to the competition (both including and beyond the giant manufacturer initiative). Second, he needs to reach new audiences outside of his social and personal networks. Third, he needs to allocate funds for additional employees to lighten the current load on his overworked staff. All of these messages will require Jacob to communicate carefully and strategically to achieve his intended goals.

The stakes are high. If Jacob is successful, he can continue his passion for this product and seek investments to grow his company. If he isn't, it is back to the drawing board.

What would you do if you were in Jacob's situation? As you read about the challenges EcoCleanR faces, you may have had some ideas for how he can achieve his goals based on your own experiences, or experiences of friends and family. The truth is that the tasks that Jacob faces will require a complex understanding of his organization and the many people who are a part of it—or that he needs to be a part of it. Take a moment to think about the word *organization*. What comes to mind? Do you think of small organizations like Jacob's start-up, or larger corporations that dominate international retail markets? You might think of the various organizations you or your family and friends have worked for, like the local stores and restaurants in your hometown. You might think of governmental agencies that have affected you and the decisions you make, such as the Environmental Protection Agency or the Department of Education. You might even have a positive or negative bias toward the term *organization.* On the other hand, you might be considering organization to be a skill or act—one that you might be especially good (or bad) at performing! By definition, organization *is* both a noun and a verb:

- As a noun, an *organization* is an identifiable social structure consisting of members united toward meeting either an external or internal need or pursuing a collective goal. Typically, these structures have management or leadership processes in place to help coordinate members and direct their action as well as to determine roles and responsibilities.
- However, the term *organization* when used as a verb also implies a preventive and reactive process, in which individuals or groups of people anticipate and adapt to change to function effectively. Organizing in this sense is the act of breaking down a larger problem into a series of achievable tasks.

Together, both the noun and verb elements of organization imply a process. This process might including arranging various parts into a structured whole (as in the case of uniting employees toward a common goal) or coordinating various elements for an event or activity (as in planning a wedding party for a group of two hundred guests). Anyone with siblings knows that the process of organizing is rarely simple or quickly done. Think back to when you were a child and your parents tried to organize your family to get in the car to go to a family party. As "managers," your parents likely set time limits and boundaries ("we are leaving no later than 10:00 A.M." "you can take one toy!") that were perhaps followed by some "members," but not all. If you were the oldest, you may have been frustrated at these boundaries, or even at your younger siblings' inability to adhere to them. A number of complications likely arose in getting into the car, such as a misplaced shoe or a last-minute trip to the restroom. The process of organizing a group of children to get them from one location to the next is riddled with complications and requires complex orchestration of tasks and emotions. As defined by merriam-webster.com, this process of *organizing* ideally results in a coherent, united, whole product made of interrelated and interdependent parts—and as any communication scholar will add, this process is built on a complex set of interactions, both opposing and complementary needs among members, and an understanding that that organizing is an ongoing activity (Cooren, Taylor, and Van Every 2006).

Similar to families, organizations are not static entities. They must continually react to internal and external forces to survive (see Zorn 2010). Whereas for a family these forces might include anything from sibling rivalries to a visit from grandma and grandpa, for organizations these forces might include budget cuts, a changing economy, and a wide variety of emerging competitors. In fact, these continual alternations and modifications are as much a part of organizational life as stability and consistency (Weick 1995). In the modern

Figure 2 We engage in organizing throughout our lives, and for many different purposes.

world of globalization, big data, and rapidly evolving technology, flexibility and adaptability are essential requirements of organizational functioning. Organizations are not closed systems or isolated islands; they are highly affected by, and affect, their local, global, and even mediated environments. As Jacob's experience illustrates, organizations not only face political, social, environmental, and personal influences; they ARE political, social, environmental, and personal influences. With these influences and pressures, there are a number of continual stressors and challenges that face organizations and those working for them. How organizations choose to communicate with members both in and outside of their organization in addressing these challenges is often the difference between success and failure.

In this introductory chapter, we will discuss the many influences that inform a strategic approach to organizational communication. This will include a discussion of the field of communication studies as a whole as well as the principles that distinguish strategic communication from other areas of study. Ultimately, this chapter concludes by outlining four foundational assumptions of strategic communication approach to understanding organizations. We begin by discussing the need for strategic communication in organizational life.

1.1 THE NEED FOR STRATEGIC COMMUNICATION IN ORGANIZATIONS

Jacob's story might sound dramatic, but with nearly 500,000 new companies being introduced every year and an over 50 percent failure rate, it isn't common. New and established companies face a series of challenges, which commonly include competition; fast rates of growth that threaten stability; and inexperience in leadership, finances, and marketing. These issues are amplified within start-ups like Jacob's, which already typically work with fewer resources and smaller teams. As in Jacob's case, these problems can arise not only from expected outside competitors but also in how members of the company communicate with one another and understand their role in the organization. Such **internal challenges** are situated within the organization and relate to its structure or communication among its members.

Further, these challenges are far from being limited to profit or business ventures. Nonprofit organizations and governmental organizations face many of these same barriers in communication, and often with more far reaching implications than profit or personal success. Individuals working on governmental public health and environmental initiatives, for instance, face a host of external pressures that collectively have come to be known as "wicked" problems given their persistence, complexity, and lack of a singular solution: sustainable energy sources, climate change, land use decisions, and water quality and quantity (Burke et al. 2017). These **external challenges,** brought on by forces outside the organization's control, are compounded by the fact that individuals working in the government sector face a series of unique challenges given the nature of their work. Government work involves a complex understanding of communication with external publics, media scrutiny, legal boundaries, and budget constraints.

Despite the idiosyncrasies of working in the for-profit, nonprofit, and government sectors, there are challenges that are common to individuals working for any organization. These challenges are both influenced by and influence effective communication within the organization, and can include:

- **Internal Management and Leadership.** One of the most important aspects of organizational functioning is the relationships among its members, and how those in decision-making and leadership positions communicate with their peers and those whom they have authority over. The leadership and managerial styles that characterize individuals in power in organizations have a significant influence on employees' satisfaction, well-being, and intent to stay with an organization. For example, mutual liking, respect, and trust in relationships have been associated with managers' perceptions of employees as being invested and committed to team goals (Bakar, Mustaffa, and Mohamad 2009). In fact, some of the most successful types of leaders are **transformational leaders,** who create dynamic change among individuals and social systems. Such leaders focus on empowering their employees and helping them to achieve their best potential in the organization. The relationships fostered inside the organization are just as important as those outside it; positive relationships between all levels of organizational members are necessary but not sufficient criteria for organizational success.

- **Laws, Regulations, and Political Forces.** Organizations are directly and indirectly affected by legal, regulatory, and political forces surrounding them. **Regulatory laws,** which include federal and state laws that affect how organizations operate in specific situations, can have enormous effects on organizations of all sizes. Small organizations such as Jacob's, for instance, might be limited in their ability to take on new employees given regulatory laws mandating paid sick leave, health insurance provision, and minimum wage requirements. Taxes, trade policies, and the stability of the political environment can also directly affect organizational functioning. Conforming to the rules and regulations that come with running an organization, particularly a small business, can be extremely stressful, especially for those without much experience. In a 2015 survey conducted by the National Small Business Association, 67 percent of small business owners in the United States reported that federal taxes have a significant to moderate impact on the day-to-day operation of their business, with 59 percent reporting that credits and deductions have a significant to moderate influence over their decisions about their company and employees. The administrative and budgetary burdens that these (necessary and important) actions require can have a major impact on the communication within small organizations, which may be part of the reason why the overwhelming majority, 85 percent, of the 675 small business owners in the study paid an external practitioner or accountant to handle their taxes. In this case, clear and competent communication is imperative both within the organization and between the organization and various legal and regulatory entities.

- **Media.** Most organizations have a complex, ongoing, interdependent, and dynamic relationship with the media. In the case of **mass media** such as print, radio, or television, a message is being sent from one organization to a large audience. That message might comprise either praise or scrutiny for an organization and have far-reaching consequences. In many ways, a healthy relationship with the media can foster awareness and a positive public perception; however, the media is also a free entity that can represent an organization in potentially damaging ways. The coverage of scandals, controversies, or any form of crises in the organization might be largely out of control for the organization. For nonprofit organizations in particular, inexperience and wariness of the media can be a significant detriment to fostering these positive connections (Bonk et al. 2008).

• **Social media,** in which users (which includes individuals and organizations) generate and share content, can similarly be a strength or a weakness for an organization. Whereas companies can build a closer relationship with their clients and receive feedback via platforms such as Twitter and Yelp, they are largely not in control of negative feedback regarding their product. In this way, organizations are both creating and reacting to social media content. Organizations must be competent sources of information presented on varying media channels, including mass media and social media platforms and must be able to adapt and respond appropriately to positive and negative messages in the mediated environment.

• **Brand Recognition, Public Perception, and Client Relationships.** Related to the above, how stakeholders view the organization is of critical importance. Depending on the organization, those **stakeholders** may be investors, customers, employees, or any other person or persons affected by the well-being and actions of the organization. Organizations must communicate a consistent, clear branding message and maintain their public perception and client relationships. Think of tech giant and industry leader Apple: their successes have a great deal to do with consistent, clear branding and their treatment of customers in-store and online. Strategic messaging and a commitment to the mission of the organization are at the forefront of these successes.

• **Organizational Member Investment, Engagement, and Turnover.** Without its members, an organization does not exist. The relationships of members at the same hierarchical level, who have no authority over one another, is highly influential in organizational functioning. These **peer relationships** affect how quickly new members adapt and become socialized into the organization, learn their roles and tasks, and become more involved and satisfied with their work. If you have ever worked in an organization with multiple members, which most of us have, you know how much fun and enjoyment talking with peers can bring to an otherwise ordinary work environment. However, there is a dark side to peer communication in the workplace. Negative or hurtful communication among organizational members is also a significant communication issue.

• **Workplace bullying,** defined by the Workplace Bullying Institute as repeated, health-harming mistreatment of one or more persons (the targets) by one or more perpetrators, is something that nearly 40 percent of adult Americans have either direct or indirect experience with in the workplace, according to a 2017 survey by the Workplace Bullying Institute. This translates to approximately 60.3 million American workers—an "epidemic-level" phenomenon that is rooted in power dynamics, jealousy, and (most importantly) communication. The impact of negative workplace communication can be physical (40 percent of workplace bullying targets experience stress-related health problems), emotional, and career damaging. Just as successful

Figure 3 The communication among employees and superiors can have a very large impact on the success of not only individual members but also of the organization overall.

leadership is critical to organizational effectiveness, the types of relationships and communication that members have with one another should be a central concern.

- **Partnerships and Collaboration.** Perhaps now more than ever, organizations must rely on successful partnerships and collaborations to succeed. Whereas a **collaboration** involves an agreement to work with another organization or organizations to achieve a common goal, a **partnership** implies a more long-term and intimate shared investment of resources (usually accompanied by a legal contract, unlike a collaboration). Take for instance, the collaborations and partnerships of the National Coalition for Homeless Veterans (NCHV), a nonprofit organization dedicated to providing technical and resource assistance to our nation's nearly 1.4 million at-risk veterans. Whereas NCHV might collaborate with local homeless shelters to provide immediate housing for veterans, it might partner with local Veteran's Administration hospitals to ensure that veterans have access to their health insurance benefits at these shelters. The benefits of collaboration and partnerships can be enormous: access to greater resources, new ideas and greater audiences, and a shared excitement for a project or endeavor. However, in both cases frequent and clear communication is essential for these relationships to thrive and be mutually beneficial. Particularly in the case of partnerships, both the rewards and risks are shared between organizations and as such require careful planning and clear, thoroughly discussed expectations.
- **Growth, Change, and Flexibility.** Change is an inevitable aspect of organizational life. Whether it is welcomed, as in the case of innovation and growth, or dreaded, change is a part of the process of organizing. These changes might be internal to the organization, such as introducing new members or building a new product, or it might be external, in the form of new competition or changing trends. As written by scholars Charles Conrad

---

Strategic Communication Mentor: External and Internal Challenges and the National Coalition for Homeless Veterans

In the list of internal and external challenges, we mentioned an organization dedicated to providing resources to homeless veterans in the United States. Take a few minutes to research this topic using the information provided by the National Coalition for Homeless Veterans and your own research.

http://nchv.org

After reviewing this material, answer the following questions:

1. What would you say are the most significant challenges for this nonprofit? Would you characterize these as internal or external challenges?
2. How do these differ from those faced by Jacob in his start-up?

---

and Michael Sollitto (2017), communication is the element that links organizations to the societies, cultures, and economies around them. When these factors change, organizations are presented with new opportunities or barriers that they must choose to accept, reject, or adapt to. Whether accidental or planned, anticipated or surprising, alterations or modifications to organizational structures or processes (known as **organizational change**) are a part of organizational life. How organizations communicate these changes, and alter their communication with internal and external audiences related to the change, is key to organizational functioning.

- **Budget.** One thing most organizations share, of course, is an overall budget. This budget likely includes operating expenses, sales, assets, and income streams. For most organizations, the budget is and should be a primary concern; without revenue, most organizations cannot operate and pursue whatever their purpose might be. Perhaps surprisingly, there are many facets of communication that are included in the budgeting of organizations. For example, most companies produce operating budgets on weekly, monthly, or yearly bases to provide a forecast and analysis of projected income and expenses for the organization over a specified time period; the production of these budgets requires communication across multiple members of the organization, and the distribution from its producers to all organizational members must be clear and concise. Similarly, the production and distribution of cash flow budgets—or how and when money will come into and leave an organization in a given time period—might have a large impact on the decisions that organizations make. A real estate developer might, for instance, decide whether or not to take on a new construction project depending on the projections made from the cash flow budget. Misinformation or miscommunication here could mean a huge misstep for the company.

Common to many of these challenges is the need for effective, goal-directed, strategic communication. Fortunately, individuals and their organizations can learn to become strategic communicators. Employers consistently rate communication skills as one of the most sought after characteristics in new hires (Hart Research Associates 2013), and for good reason: communication is the foundation for successful organizational functioning. In fact, communication constitutes organizations; the boundaries, roles, relationships within, and purposes of organizations are created, sustained, and maintained through communication (Putnam and Nicotera 2009). As organizational communication scholars Linda Putnam and Dennis Mumby (2014) wrote, "organizations are products of the communication practices of their members" (12), adding that communication is the "essence" of both organizing activity and organizations themselves (15). Stated more simply, without communication there is no organization. By having a clear and strategic communication plan, organizations can handle the issues listed above more easily, although they might not be able to completely *avoid* them.

In this section, we have established a need for strategic communication across various types of organizations by outlining a series of internal and external challenges that these entities have in common—all of which emphasize the need for goal-directed, clear communication. With the importance of communication in organization and organizing established, let us now turn to defining communication and determining what distinguishes *strategic* communication. As you build an enhanced understanding of what communication and strategic communication are, you will have a better sense of why strategic communication is so critical within organizations.

1.2 LAYING THE GROUNDWORK: COMMUNICATION AS A FOUNDATION FOR ORGANIZATIONAL SUCCESS

Most people assume they are competent communicators, and that they understand what "communicating effectively" entails. Ask most people what they find important in a relational partner, and they will mention good and clear communication. Ask most people what they value in a leader, a boss, a teacher, a coworker, or nearly any other relationship, and you will see that being a good, clear communicator who gives articulate directions and useful feedback often rises to the top. But how many people truly are good communicators? How many of us perfectly convey what we feel or what we are thinking when we talk to others, every time? Further, how many of us know exactly why and when communication works best? The truth is: not that many! In organizations all over the globe, every day, people communicate in self-centered ways, don't listen fully, or choose the wrong place and time to say how they feel. They provide unclear directions and unhelpful feedback. They experience anxiety about communication, and, as a result, do it poorly—or avoid it entirely. They find it difficult to be sensitive to cultural differences. They experience stress, burnout, and information overload—and behave in overly emotional, unprofessional ways that are counterproductive to their strategic goals. As a result, meanings become unclear, and misunderstandings and conflicts ensue. Sound familiar? If so, you shouldn't feel bad. Misunderstandings and misinterpretations in communication are a part of life. However, knowing a bit more about the process of communication can facilitate the many steps involved in becoming a part of organizations as well as successful functioning within and for them.

Communication is a skill that we can improve over time, and with practice. If you are not a skilled communicator right now, that does not mean that you will never "get it." Sure, some of us are born with a knack for speaking in front of others, and others of us are very comfortable working with a team or collaborating one-on-one. But there are theories and evidence-based practices that can help all of us improve our communication skills. In fact, some communication professionals specialize in training people how to be better communicators (see Waldeck and Seibold 2016). This includes helping doctors to communicate treatments more effectively with their patients, helping teachers deliver content more effectively to their students, and of course helping students like you to be better public speakers and interpersonal communicators. Although learning and refining your communication skills is an effortful process, you will realize a return on your investment in your personal, academic, social, and professional experiences.

1.2.1 Defining Communication

Although we all likely have a rudimentary understanding of what communication is and how it affects our lives, at its most fundamental level **communication** is the process by which we stimulate meaning in the minds of others using verbal and nonverbal messages (McCroskey and Richmond 1996). When we communicate successfully and stimulate the meanings we intend in the minds of others, we achieve understanding. When communication is unsuccessful, others do not interpret our meanings as we intend, and a state of misunderstanding results.

Communication is a goal-directed process, and one that we are continually engaging in.[1] Organizations engage in goal directed communication for many reasons, including but not limited to branding their company, promoting their product, or maintaining relationships with their partners. Take a minute and list all of the reasons you have communicated with someone today, and how often you have done so. When you woke up to your phone alarm, you might

---

1. The following material is adapted from: Waldeck, J. 2014. *Communication Competence: Goals and Contexts.* San Diego: Bridgepoint Education.

Strategic Communication Mentor: Communication Competence Skills Assessment

How effective do you think you are as a communicator? What are your strengths in communicating with others? Weaknesses? Take the following assessment of your interpersonal communication competence, or your ability to manage relationships in interpersonal settings.

Instructions: Here are some statements about how people interact with other people. For each statement, write the number using the scale provided that best reflects YOUR communication with others. Be honest in your responses and reflect on your communication behavior very carefully.

For each of the following statements, use the scale provided to indicate if you never, seldom, sometimes, often, or almost always communicate this way.

1	2	3	4	5
Never	Seldom	Sometimes	Often	Almost Always

_____ 1. I allow friends to see who I really am.

_____ 2. I can put myself in others' shoes.

_____ 3. I am comfortable in social situations.

_____ 4. When I've been wronged, I confront the person who wronged me.

_____ 5. My conversations are usually not one-sided.

_____ 6. My conversations are characterized by smooth shifts from one topic to the next.

_____ 7. My friends can tell when I am happy or sad.

_____ 8. My communication is usually descriptive, not evaluative.

_____ 9. My friends believe that I truly care about them.

_____ 10. I accomplish my communication goals.

To score: Add up the number that you used for each of these items. You should have a score between 10 and 50. A lower score indicates lower interpersonal communication competence; a higher score indicates higher interpersonal communication competence.

After you have calculated your score, answer the following questions:

1. Did your score on this assessment surprise you? Was it higher or lower than what you would have expected?

2. Did any of the questions on this assessment surprise you? Are there aspects of interpersonal communication that you would add?

3. How do you think your own interpersonal communication competence translates to your communication at work?

Measure of interpersonal communication competence adapted from:[1]
Rubin, R.B., and M.M. Martin. 1994. "Development of a Measure of Interpersonal Communication Competence." *Communication Research Reports* 11, no. 1: 33–44. doi: 10.1080/08824099409359938.

---

1. Individuals' scores on the Interpersonal Communication Competence scale have been associated with a variety of outcomes, including the quality of their interpersonal relationships as well as their willingness and ability to adapt to changing communication situations. For more information on how ICC is related to relationships, see the following:
Martin, M.M., and C.M. Anderson. 1995. "Roommate Similarity: Are Roommates Who Are Similar in Their Communication Traits More Satisfied?" *Communication Research Reports* 12, no. 1: 46–52.

Strategic Communication Mentor: The Nature of Communication

Communication scholar Kathy Kellermann wrote the following argument in an essay published in *Communication Monographs* in 1992: "I hold two central beliefs about communication. First, I believe that *all* communication is strategic; that communication, by its very nature, cannot *not* be strategic. Second, I believe that communication is primarily automatic; that strategies are, for the most part tacitly acquired and tacitly deployed" (288). Sound contradictory? Kellermann goes on to explain that the inherent strategic nature of communication in essence becomes automatic; essentially, we learn to employ strategies for communicative purposes naturally and seamlessly in order to survive and thrive as social beings.

What do you think of these two beliefs? Are they consistent with how you communicate in your daily life, or how others communicate with you? Explain your argument for or against this point using specific examples. Do you have other beliefs about communication that you would add to Kellermann's?

---

have already had messages from others on social media or in texts, waiting for your response. You might have chatted with a roommate as you got ready for the day, or with the barista at your go-to coffee shop. You may have also been on the receiving end of communication, from morning talk show hosts on TV or your car radio on the way to school. We communicate with a wide variety of people and for a wide range of reasons. What themes do you see in these reasons? Although you likely use a wide variety of "new" communication channels throughout the day, the reasons you communicate were discussed by Greek philosopher and writer Aristotle nearly two thousand years ago: (1) to inform, (2) to persuade, (3) to entertain. How do all of the ways that you communicate throughout the day fit into these categories?

You also have to make a series of choices about how you communicate and through what medium. For instance, do we choose to communicate in person, via text, or through a phone application like Snapchat? Societally, we have a long list of unspoken rules about communication. Whereas email is an appropriate channel for sending a routine reminder to turn in time sheets at work, it is not an appropriate channel for a supervisor to inform someone that they are fired! These choices are also important for organizations and their members and can affect the messages they send as well as how they are received. How, as someone communicating *on behalf of* an organization, can we make competent choices about where and how we send messages?

When we think about how easily communicators misunderstand one another—whether due to the medium for the message, the culture of the communicators, or any number of other factors—we might find ourselves getting overwhelmed. What if we send the wrong message, or send the right message in the wrong way? Fortunately, understanding communication as a process as opposed to an event can help us to overcome, or at least to manage, some of the challenges that make human communication difficult. As communicators, if we begin with a clear goal in mind and outline a strategy for what we want to accomplish, we can avoid many pitfalls and challenges that come with thoughtless or rushed communication. Before we get too far into the planning and strategy of communicating, though, let's discuss a bit more thoroughly how communication scholars define and discus this process. To do so, we will discuss a simple model of communication between two people, or interactants, to lay the basic groundwork for the phenomenon we are discussing. Then, we will move to a more sophisticated model that can better account for the numerous factors that make communication a complex, and sometimes challenging, process.

1.2.2 A Linear Model of Communication

Models of communication are useful in helping to identify and understand the basic components of the communication process as well as how they are related; as such, early communication theorists focused on developing models that would provide structure to an emerging field of study (Nicotera 2009). Many of these early models are **linear** in that they depict a straightforward process in which an individual communicator transmits a **message** (i.e., a verbal or nonverbal series of signs or symbols used to depict meaning) to a receiving communicator. Perhaps the most influential of such models was actually developed to improve communication via telephone. In what became known as the Shannon Weaver Model of Communication (Shannon and Weaver 1949), the process of communication was depicted as consisting of five key components: a *sender* of information, a *transmitter* that converts a message into signals, a *channel* that conveys the message, a *receptor* that converts the signal back into a message, and a *receiver* that serves as the destination of the communication message (Shannon and Weaver 1949). Importantly, Shannon and Weaver noted that this process can be affected by (and less effective due to) *noise* in the communication channel. Noise in the context of telephone communication referred to factors that distorted the quality of the signal (e.g., static)—more broadly, we can understand noise to be anything that distracts our message from being received correctly by a receiver.

Although the original Shannon Weaver communication model was not designed to describe how we communicate with others face-to-face, communication scholar David Berlo (1960) developed a model that isolated elements that *all* communication situations have in common. In what has been termed the Sender-Message-Channel-Receiver (SMCR) model, Berlo (1960) describes the basic components of a communication exchange. This process, illustrated

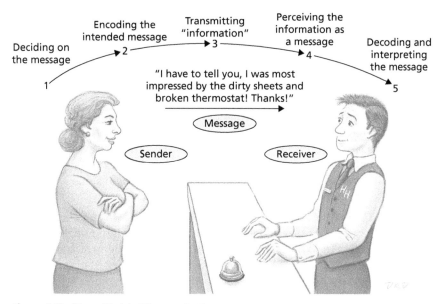

Figure 4 The Linear Model of Communication.

in figure 4, occurs in five stages. Let's take a closer look at each one in a common communication interaction for organizational members: the voicing of a complaint from a client to an employee. In this case, we have Carol (the sender) informing clerk at Harmony Hotels that she was not happy with her stay (the message). The hotel employee (the receiver) decodes this message.

This simple exchange has unfolded in five phases:

Phase 1: Deciding on the message. A sender selects a message to send to a receiver (or receivers) in order to achieve a desired outcome. The sender is also referred to as the source of the message. In our example, the unhappy hotel guest, Carol, is the sender. The message refers to either a verbal, written, or mediated (via TV, radio, computer, or other medium) message or a nonverbal expression sent from a sender to a receiver. The receiver is the intended recipient of the message (in our case, the Harmony Hotel clerk).

Phase 2: Encoding the message. Encoding refers to a psychological process in which the sender of a message assigns symbols, such as words, sounds, or gestures, to his or her thoughts and feelings. Effective communicators are able to translate their ideas into communication symbols appropriate for the message and the receiver. In our example, Carol has considered her hotel stay and determined what she considers to be an appropriate message given her stay at Harmony Hotels.

Phase 3: Transmitting the message. A message is "sent" from sender to receiver, using a particular channel that is selected by the sender. The channel is the medium that carries the message, such as email, telephone, face-to-face communication, or a written document. In our example, Carol chose to communicate her dissatisfaction with Harmony Hotels face-to-face on checking out of her stay.

Phase 4: Perception of the message. When a receiver detects that information has been communicated, he or she attends to it and perceives it in some fashion. Perceiving a message involves classifying it based on your knowledge and experience. The hotel clerk in our example perceives Carol's complaint from his perspective as a new employee.

Phase 5: Decoding and assigning meaning to the message. When a receiver assigns meaning to the message that has been communicated, he or she is engaging in a psychological process known as decoding. Decoding is the opposite of encoding (the activity that the sender engaged in at the beginning of the exchange). The receiver translates the symbols (words, sounds, and gestures) perceived into thoughts and feelings. The hotel clerk must interpret not only the content of Carol's message but also all of the "unspoken dialogue" (Burgoon, Guerrero, and Floyd 2016, 1) in their interaction, which includes her body language, tone of voice, insinuations, and eye contact (Burgoon, Guerrero, and Floyd 2016). This aspect of the decoding process is incredibly important; in fact, nonverbal scholars have produced an abundance of research on how elements of a message such as **kinesics,** or body language and gestures, and **vocalics,** including tone and pitch, have an impact on the communication process (see Burgoon, Guerrero, and Floyd 2016 for a comprehensive overview of this important research).

As this exchange indicates, communication can be deceptively complex. What on the surface appears to be a very simple exchange between a hotel guest and clerk can lead to a series of complications and opportunities for misunderstanding. In encoding her message, Carol chose a sarcastic tone and to smile as she delivered a negative message (i.e., a complaint). The young hotel clerk must attend to and respond to this message in a way that is appropriate and consistent with Harmony Hotel policy while also considering the other hotel guests that may overhear the interaction.

There are virtually limitless variations of such exchanges with clients that companies face each day. In addition to interpersonal interactions such as this, the staff of organizations such as Harmony Hotels might communicate with clients on online review sites or on social media. The functionality of some of these communication channels may pose a problem, hindering the ability to understand a sender's message accurately. For example, social media posts do not adequately convey nonverbal cues, such as facial expression or tone of voice, which in their absence cannot assist us in understanding the sender's intent. Further, although Carol is initially the sender of the message, isn't the hotel clerk acting as more than a receiver in this exchange? As Carol speaks, he is likely sending his own nonverbal communication messages and will be expected to provide a verbal response to her comment as well. Although the brief interaction between Carol and the Harmony Hotel manager has helped us to cover the basics of the communication process, we need to consider a model that more comprehensively describes what occurs in communication interactions to address our questions.

1.2.3 The Simultaneous Transactions Model of Communication

Although the linear model of communication outlined above is a useful tool for understanding the basic components of the communication process, it does not explain the numerous factors that affect our exchanges with others. As we decode messages, for example, we may have a difficult time doing so because the topic is new to us, complex, or sensitive; because we are distracted by something else going on in the physical environment or that happened earlier in the day; because of negative past experiences; or because we have anxiety or discomfort communicating with our particular partner. This is particularly true for our sample interaction between Carol and the Harmony Hotels clerk: as discussed by Gabbott and Hogg (2001), the nonverbal communication that occurs between individuals working in service industries and their clientele not only has a significant impact on communication outcomes, but this communication is also highly influenced by the characteristics of both the interactants and the organization. The gender, culture, and previous experiences of the service industry professional as well as the client affects the ways that messages are encoded and decoded by both parties, and the type of service industry, amount of employee training, and even elements of the environment will influence the nonverbal communication that is most likely to occur (Gabbott and Hogg 2001). For instance, whether the Harmony Hotel clerk is seated and the size of the counter space between him and Carol, might affect the nonverbal elements of both interactants' messages.

Additionally, communication is never a simple one-way activity in which the sender "tells" and the receiver "listens." Even in situations in which one "sender" is speaking to a group of receivers, as in a public speaking context, the receivers are actively sending messages. The receivers might smile, nod in agreement, frown with confusion or in disagreement, or they might even offer verbal responses to the sender and ask questions themselves. In fact, it is this wide array of possible responses that make public speaking so worrisome for most folks! These new messages represent **feedback,** the verbal or nonverbal message that a receiver provides to the sender as he or she perceives and assigns

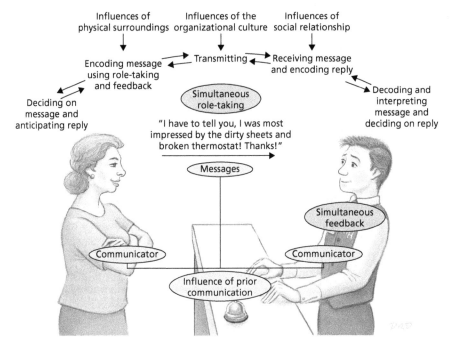

Figure 5 The Simultaneous Transactions Model of Communication.

meaning to the sender's message. The addition of feedback, along with consideration of the factors that make accurate decoding of messages difficult, transforms the linear model into the simultaneous transactions model (DeFleur et al. 2014) shown in figure 5.

A **simultaneous transactions model** illustrates how the sender and the receiver develop, share, shape, and *reshape* ideas at the same time. This more detailed model is ultimately more reflective of how communication actually occurs. Communication is more than merely telling someone else how we feel or what we think. We rarely create meanings and ideas independently of others, and we are more than passive, robotic recipients and processors of others' messages. Rather, communication is a simultaneous, interactive process. And, during interactions, communicators mutually influence one another—making the process a transaction in which all communicators are affected in some way. To illustrate this, let's consider the characteristics of the simultaneous transactions model more closely:

- Communicators are simultaneously encoding and decoding messages at all times during an interaction. Using our previous experiences, knowledge, expectations, and biases, we often begin to decode a message before a sender is through encoding and transmitting it. For example, volunteer coordinator Jodi has had years of experience in helping high school seniors to complete their service hours and is responsible for training incoming seniors on the requirements. When Adam raises his hand and starts to ask the question, "What should we wear?" Jodi starts with a list of unacceptable outfits she has seen in years past. Steeped in experience and, to some extent, biases, she is mostly highlighting mistakes NOT to make based on past experiences.

- Analysis of other communicators involved and feedback is key to communication. Because we decode messages and encode our responses simultaneously, communicators act as senders and receivers simultaneously. In other words, we are constantly analyzing and assessing our interaction partner(s) (the other communicator or communicators) during an interaction. When giving a presentation, you may be aware of the people in the audience who seem interested and alert through their nonverbal cues such as eye contact, nodding, or note taking; you are also aware of the people who are bored, confused, disinterested, or even hostile. Based on your reading of this feedback, you may modify your message by speeding it up, slowing it down, or asking whether anyone has any questions. In speaking with a customer about their complaints regarding an online purchase, a sales representative may notice the customer's voice rising and a defensive tone. Rather than mimicking their response and escalating the situation, the sales representative should be more amicable and keep the conversation as productive and positive as possible. This cycle of analyzing or reading your **audience** (the intended recipient or recipients of a message), whether it is a roomful of people or a single individual, helps the transaction to proceed. As you collect information from your audience in the form of verbal and nonverbal feedback cues, you are better able to provide them with what they want or need to more accurately understand your intended meaning and respond appropriately to your communication.

- Our previous interactions with one another influence our present communication. What people say during an interaction is highly dependent on any communication history people may have. If you groan when you have to make a call to your insurance company because in the past you have not found them helpful or polite, then you understand the influence of prior interactions on current communication. What has happened in the past, positively or negatively, significantly affects how we make sense of present interactions.

- Context is important. **Context** refers to the environment and situation in which communication occurs. Examples of communication contexts include the workplace, the classroom, the family, and intimate contexts such as close friendships or committed relationships. Context matters because inherent in any setting are prescribed, or normative, roles and rules. In other words, people have expectations for how others will behave that are highly dependent on the context. For example, in a health care context or setting, the patient has expectations for the role that the physician will assume. Typically, we expect physicians to be professional but warm, clear in their explanations, and credible in their knowledge of medical issues. We might also expect that our physician will see us later than our actual appointment time, have sloppy handwriting, use technical jargon that is hard to understand, or be abrupt, based on our previous experiences with communicating in the health care context. In another context, the roles we expect others to play will differ greatly; for example, we would not expect our relational partner to communicate the same way physicians do. The rules for interaction are also dependent on context. In our health-care-setting example, legal codes guide issues of patient confidentiality and appropriate physician behavior. We might expect a hug from a romantic partner when we do not feel well, but it would be unusual and in some cases inappropriate for a physician to engage in such intimate nonverbal communication. Context matters because it provides information about the roles communicators should assume and the rules they need to follow. Other contextual features that can affect communication include physical noise in the surroundings, temperatures that are too warm or too cold, poor lighting conditions, and personal distractions that we bring to the situation, such as hunger or fatigue.

- The channel we use affects the process and outcome of communication. People communicate differently based on the channel being used. For example, you may be much more formal in your written communication than in your verbal interactions. You may feel more comfortable expressing opinions in mediated contexts, such as email, text messages, or social network sites, than you would using face-to-face communication. Communication theorist Marshall McLuhan wrote extensively about the relationship between the medium and how messages are perceived, declaring that they are virtually inextricable. He argued persuasively that the medium selected for communication shapes the very nature of human association; "the medium is the message" (McLuhan 1964).

- Communication is influenced by the **sociocultural elements** of the situation. This refers to the social and cultural variables that affect human interaction, including gender and sex roles, race, ethnicity, religion, social class or socioeconomic status, power and influence, sexuality, or even the organization or field in which you work. These sociocultural elements have unique rules for behavior that may be more subtle and difficult to learn and follow than those of the physical context. For example, as you have probably already experienced, the norms for communication in the workplace are different from those related to your college classes. The sociocultural elements of your organization will inform anticipated gender roles regarding the work that you do, the value placed on expression of creativity and innovation, how you dress, and the hours that you keep at your workplace. Further, culture and religion will have a significant impact on the sociocultural situation and how workplace communication is conducted. For instance, an observant Orthodox Jewish colleague may feel left out or even discriminated against when work activities are planned for Friday evenings or Saturdays—an important period of ritual observance in Judaism and sacred restriction from work for observant members of the Jewish faith.

- The nature of the relationship between communicators should and does influence our communication behavior. The type of relationship that you share with your communication partner(s) matters. Whether you are strangers, acquaintances, or close friends will influence how you package and deliver the content of your message, and how it is received and transmitted. For example, you are more likely to disclose personal information with non-strangers than strangers. You may be less formal in communicating with coworkers with whom you have established ties than with a new supervisor. We interact differently with those individuals who have greater status or power compared to ourselves than we do with our peers and those with lesser status. For instance, you may be even less comfortable offering feedback on your manager's ideas than you would be offering similar feedback to a coworker or close friend.

As you probably realize now, the simultaneous transactions model of communication offers a more complete and accurate portrait of the complexities of the communication process than the linear model does. By drawing comparisons between these two models, it is easy to see the disconnect between "simple" ideas of communication and the reality of having to deliver an effective, appropriate message through the right channel, at the right time. Knowing how situations, relationships, and contexts both enable and interfere with effective communication equips us with an intellectual understanding of the communication process. However, knowledge is just the first step. The demands of an ever-changing market and world require leaders and members of organizations to hone their adaptability, flexibility, and skill sets to put this knowledge into practice.

1.2.4 The Study of Communication

Scholars who study communication examine these models and how they function in a variety of contexts. **Communication studies** is a rigorous academic area of inquiry with a rich history in the social sciences that seeks to answer questions regarding communication using systematic and scientific methods. A fundamental aspect of such research is that human communication can be understood, explained, and predicted through patterns (and eventually theories) identified through academic inquiry. Scholars examine communication in a wide variety of contexts, including the family, classroom, health care environment, and a wide variety of organizations.[2]

As communication scholar John Powers (1995) argued, however, messages are the cornerstone of the communication studies discipline. Communication scholars do not study situations or contexts as much as they study messages and how they affect individuals in a particular context. In fact, the roots of communication studies can be traced back to ancient Greek and Roman scholars, who explored the key elements of rhetoric and persuasion that we still refer to today. This is an important distinction of communication theorists and researchers, and one that frames the approach of this text: the message is always the most important element, from which all other concerns and inquiries radiate. As communication scholars Anita Vangelisti, John Daly, and Gustav Friedrich wrote (1999), "the field of communication was founded, in part, because of a felt need to make people better communicators" (xi). How the message is developed, how it is communicated, and what impact it has are all areas of concern for the communication scientist.

Scholars studying **organizational communication** focus not only on the communication that happens *in* organizations but also on how communication *creates* and *maintains* organizations (Putnam and Nicotera 2009). Initially, communication scholars focusing on organizations researched interpersonal aspects of organizational life, such as how employees and managers interact and influence one another. However, as the field (and world around it) changed, organizational scholars turned to more comprehensive understandings of organizational functioning: globalization, mergers, new technologies, and how the complex role of identity, gender, race, and culture has come to frame much of the work conducted by organizational communication scholars. In the attempt to understand more holistically how organizations communicate, some scholars have begun to explicitly focus on how organizations communicate to achieve their purpose, mission, or goals through strategic communication efforts.

In this section, we have laid the groundwork for understanding communication as a process and as an area of study. We have defined communication and discussed two approaches to understanding how this process affects and is affected by senders and receivers as well as the advantages of using a more complex, simultaneous model of communication. We have also provided a preliminary understanding of communication studies as a rigorous area of academic inquiry, the theory and research of which can be applied to understand organizational life and functioning. In the next section, we discuss how the

---

2. If you are interested in a much more thorough history of the field of communication, read: Rogers, E. M. 1994. *A History of Communication Study: A Biographical Approach.* New York: Free Press.

Table 1.1 Approaches to Examining Communication in Organizations

HUMAN RELATIONS

The process of training employees, addressing their needs, fostering a healthy and productive workplace culture, and resolving conflicts between different employees or between employees and management.

MARKETING

The systematic and planned activity of creating, communicating, delivering, and exchanging offerings that have value for customers, clients, partners, and society at large. Note: marketing efforts encompass both public relations and advertising efforts.

PUBLIC RELATIONS

A component of the overall marketing efforts of an organization. The establishment and maintenance of a favorable public image and mutually beneficial relationships between organizations and their publics.

ADVERTISING

A component of the overall marketing efforts of an organization. The paid, public, nonpersonal announcement of a persuasive message by an identified sponsor. The nonpersonal presentation or promotion by a firm of its products to its existing and potential customers.

ORGANIZATIONAL COMMUNICATION

The study of communication that happens in organizations as well as how communication creates and maintains organizations.

---

field of strategic communication has emerged out of these efforts as well as the foundational elements of a strategic communication approach to organizations

1.3 A STRATEGIC COMMUNICATION APPROACH TO ORGANIZATIONS

Organizational communication scholars are not the only ones concerned with how messages are sent within and outside of organizations. Review Table 1.1 for an overview of the various approaches to examining communication in organizations, each for a unique purpose by very different specialists.

So what is strategic communication, and how is it unique from other approaches to understanding organizational life? A quick internet search for strategic communication reveals that the term is used in a wide variety of fields and for a wide variety of purposes. At its simplest, **strategic communication** is the purposeful communication of an organization in order to advance its mission. This definition was first forwarded in the inaugural issue of the *International Journal of Strategic Communication* (Hallahan et al. 2007) in order to organize and provide identity to an emerging field of study in the social sciences. Strategic communication has since come to be understood as the practice and study of the deliberate and purposive communication that organizations engage in to reach their goals. Strategic communication scholars aim to describe, explain, and predict the practice of strategic communication and its impact on society, organizations, and individuals.

To understand this perspective more completely, let's turn to four foundational assumptions of a strategic communication approach to organizations.

1.3.1 All Organizations Engage in Strategic Communication

All organizations share a common need to manage and orchestrate the messages they send so they are consistent with their identity, and achieve their goals. Indeed, a strategic approach to understanding organizations considers that all organizations, from giant industry leaders to small start-up companies like Jacob's at the beginning of this chapter, engage in purposeful communication to achieve their goals. In the next chapter, we will distinguish between various organizational types and structures, including what determines and defines governmental entities and for-profit, nonprofit, corporate, and small businesses. The process of effective strategic communication is the same across all types of organizations.

1.3.2 Strategic Communication Is Mindful Communication

Does the word *strategic* have a negative connotation for you? If you are like most people, you might associate being *strategic* with being manipulative, calculating, or shrewd. However, this is not how *strategic* should be understood for organizations! The term *strategic* is used to explain the planned, systematic steps that organizations take to carry out their goals or aims. Naturally, these goals might be a little self-serving; corporate and for-profit organizations do want to make more money, after all. However, these goals can be incredibly altruistic, as in the case of nonprofit organizations seeking to raise funds for cancer research, or governmental organizations looking to affect the health and well-being of their constituents. Strategic communication is a catalyst for change in organizations, the process and decision-making of which are never entirely objective but rather driven by values, cultural assumptions, societal influences, and the identity of the organization (Gagliarde 1986). The consideration of ethics and corporate responsibility is paramount to ensuring that strategic communication is ethical and mindful—and not synonymous with manipulation or coercion. Strategic communication implies thoughtful, conscious, and mindful messaging and not manipulative intent. When you carefully consider what you wear to a job interview so that you are presenting your best self, this is strategic, mindful, and appropriate communication.

1.3.3 Strategic Communication Is Inherently Interdisciplinary

Importantly, although strategic communication is a relatively new area of formal study, it draws from a number of well-established fields including marketing, advertising, public relations, and organizational communication. There is some debate about how strategic communication "fits" in with these other fields. Some refer to strategic communication as an umbrella term that encompasses the persuasive efforts of each organizational process, for instance. This understanding is consistent with other efforts to consolidate resources and find commonalities among organizational activities, the perspective of **integrated communication** (alternately referred to as *integrated marketing* or *integrating marketing communication*). Such efforts, which blend the advertising and public relation functions of organizations in order to consolidate efforts and conserve resources, have recently become more popular. Notably, strategic communication is a broader area of study than integrated communication, the latter of which focuses much more on marketing initiatives and concerns of organizations.[3]

Others view strategic communication as a natural, integrated extension of more established academic and professional fields, such as the organizational communication scholarship mentioned earlier in this chapter. Whereas organizational communication research is concerned with the communication processes that occur among people within a dynamic system, across organizational boundaries for a wide range of purposes, strategic communication is solely focused on how the organization achieves its directives through the intentional actions of its members (Hallahan et al. 2007). In this way, how an organization builds and communicates its brand identity to its employees and to its customers would fall under the focus of *strategic* communication more clearly than the broader concerns of organizational communication.

Ironically, these two perspectives on strategic communication work well together. Broadly, strategic communication initiatives might include advertis-

---

3. For more information on how strategic communication and integrated communication are distinct, particularly from the perspective of a student, see www.mastersincommunications.com /faqs/strategic-communication-vs-imc-programs.

ing, marketing, public relations, public health and social marketing campaigns, diplomacy and international relations, political campaigns, risk and crisis communication, and various types of lobbying and negotiation efforts. To engage in these efforts effectively, organizations must use research and knowledge from a wide variety of academic and professional disciplines—which strategic communication scholars naturally draw from in their interdisciplinary work.

1.3.4 A Strategic Communication Approach to Organizations Focuses on Messaging

The myriad strategic communication efforts already mentioned often emerge in the form of campaigns. A **campaign** is a systematic, purposeful attempt to create change in a defined target audience over a specified time period. Campaigns include communication with audiences internal and external to an organization. Organizations often communicate to spread awareness of a product or to communicate their brand externally, but these efforts can also produce positive changes when communicated to internal audiences and members. Campaigns also occur through a wide variety of channels. As communication scholars Ronald Rice and Charles Atkin (2013, 526–27) indicate, campaigns are characterized by "purposive attempts to inform, persuade, or motivate behavior changes in a relatively well-defined and large audience . . . by means of organized communication activities involving mass and online /interactive media, and often complemented by interpersonal support." The purposeful communication, organization of various communication activities, and use of numerous channels to convey a unified message are all aspects of campaign work that clearly align with how strategic communication is understood in organizations.

Just as organizations vary widely in purpose, so too do strategic communication campaigns. Campaigns might include public health campaigns to encourage daily exercise, promoting a "revamped" brand image for a company, or advocating a specific piece of legislation. These campaigns might be for commercial or nonprofit entities, or for well-established organizations as well as start-ups looking to brand their product and reach new audiences. Regardless of the type of organization using the campaign strategies, or the outcomes sought in these efforts, the same tactics and principles lead to success.

In summary, there are four foundational assumptions of strategic communication:

- Strategic communication is enacted by individuals in all types of organizations, be they public or private, profit or nonprofit, small or large. Ultimately, strategic communication concerns the ability for all organizations— whether they be corporations, not-for-profit organizations, or governmental entities—to engage in purposeful communication attempts.

- Strategic communication is not negative or manipulative in nature, but rather planned, mindful, and thoughtful communication engaged in by various organizational members.
- Strategic communication is an inherently interdisciplinary endeavor. It has deep roots in various academic and applied fields, and it compiles knowledge from research and practice in a number of areas to approach messaging in organizations holistically and efficiently.
- Strategic communication focuses on messaging, which often takes form in a variety of campaign efforts conducted by the organization for both internal and external audiences.

In this section we have defined strategic communication and outlined it as a unique and emerging area of study. As the four foundational assumptions of strategic communication illustrate, strategic communication is not only widely practiced by organizations of all types, but is also examined by scholars and practitioners of many different backgrounds in both communication studies and other fields. Strategic communication is thoughtful, planned, and focuses on the communication messages that organizations send to internal and external audiences. A *strategic communication approach to organizations* therefore emphasizes communication theory and practice associated with the advancement of an organization's mission, services, and vision through persuasive messaging in the broad organizational context.

1.4 TYING IT ALL TOGETHER: THE BENEFITS OF APPLYING A STRATEGIC COMMUNICATION PERSPECTIVE TO ORGANIZATIONAL PROCESSES

In this chapter we have examined the need for strategic communication in organizations, particularly as it relates to the shared and varied internal and external issues that organizations face. We have examined organization and communication as processes, and we have outlined two models for understanding how communication messages are sent and received. We discussed the study of communication as a social science, and how from this field we have knowledge of both organizational and strategic communication. Strategic communication involves the purposeful communication of an organization in order to advance its mission, and consists of four foundational assumptions both as an area of academic inquiry and also as an applied science used by organizations every day.

In the beginning of this chapter, we met Jacob, a young business owner who was struggling to maintain sales of his environmentally friendly home cleaning product EcoCleanR. Declining sales stemmed from a lack of unity among his small staff as well as limited resources. The issues that Jacob faced, and the steps he needed to take to get his start-up back on track, are very common among organizations of all types, purposes, and structures. When he examines his business from a strategic communication lens, Jacob can develop a plan to create a more consistent vision for his company, reach new audiences (and potential consumers), and obtain further funding to support the manufacture and delivery of this product. Each of these steps should of course be informed by theory and evidence-based practices, which will be discussed in later chapters in this text.

The process of strategically communicating in an organization is ongoing and reflective. To communicate successfully with internal and external audiences, organizations must engage in a continual and dynamic planning process, ongoing evaluation of their successes and failures, and must be willing to reformulate their communication strategies and methods. This process requires flexibility, adaptation, and dedication from organizational members—this is just as true for small entrepreneurial start-ups like Jacob's as it is for international, well-established organizations. In the next chapter, we will discuss how this ongoing process of strategic communication differs across various organizational types as well as how it is affected by structural and cultural features that affect communication more broadly.

CHAPTER 1 REVIEW

Questions for Critical Thinking and Discussion

1. Jacob's start-up, which is described in the beginning of the chapter, is, by nature, a *small* organization. What are the benefits to being a small organization versus a large one? What does a small organization offer that a big organization can't? What are the limitations to being a small organization? How can a small organization offer the same things a big organization can?

2. As defined in this text, *organizing* is a process that results in a coherent, united, whole product made of interrelated and interdependent parts. How does this resonate with how you define organizing in your own life? Based on your experiences, is there more to this process than this definition accounts for? Come up with a personal definition for *organizing* as a process.

3. In this chapter, we provided a list of internal and external communication challenges that all organizations face. Read over this list and identify which are *internal* communication issues and which are *external*. Are some issues both internal and external? Explain your response.

4. As part of these communication issues, we discuss the importance of leadership and the influence of transformational leaders. Take a few minutes and read this *Harvard Business Review* letter on transformational leadership (https://hbr.org/2017/05/what-the-best-transformational-leaders-do). Based on this article, what is it that transformational leaders do or say that distinguishes them from other types of managers or leaders? Do you think this is a skill set that can be taught, or are some people just innately better leaders? Argue your point with specific examples either from your own experiences or from the article.

5. In Table 1.1 we present a number of approaches to communication in organizations. Create a visual diagram for how these aspects of organizational life and communication relate to one

another. Be sure to show not only where these concepts overlap but also how they are distinct in their approach to messages and communication in organizational life.

6. How would you explain that strategic communication is mindful in your own words? Can you think of a time when you engaged in strategic communication that was NOT manipulative or calculating? Were you successful in achieving your goal for that interaction? Why or why not?

Key Terms

audience: the intended recipient or recipients of a message.

campaign: a systematic, purposeful attempt to create change in a defined target audience over a specified time period.

collaboration: an agreement to work with another organization or organizations to achieve a common goal.

communication: the process by which we stimulate meaning in the minds of others using both verbal and nonverbal messages.

communication studies: A rigorous academic area of inquiry, with a rich history in the social sciences, that seeks to answer questions regarding communication using systematic and scientific methods.

context: the environment and situation in which communication occurs.

external challenges: challenges that are brought on by forces outside the organization's control.

feedback: the verbal or nonverbal message that a receiver provides to the sender as he or she perceives and assigns meaning to the sender's message.

integrated communication: efforts to consolidate resources and find commonalities among organizational activities.

internal challenges: challenges situated within the organization, relating to communication among its members or due to its structure.

kinesics: body language and gestures.

linear: a straightforward process with a clear beginning and end.

mass media: sending a message from one organization to a large audience, such as print, radio, or television.

message: a verbal or nonverbal series of signs or symbols used to depict meaning.

organizational change: alterations or modifications to organizational structures or processes.

partnership: a long-term and intimate shared investment of resources, usually accompanied by a legal contract.

peer relationships: the relationships of members at the same hierarchical level, who have no authority over one another.

regulatory laws: federal and state laws that affect how organizations operate in specific situations.

simultaneous transactions model: a model of communication that illustrates how the sender and the receiver develop, share, shape, and reshape ideas at the same time.

social media: a form of online communication in which users generate and share content.

sociocultural elements: the social and cultural variables that affect human interaction.

stakeholders: any person or persons affected by the well-being and actions of an organization.

strategic communication: the purposeful communication of an organization in order to advance its mission.

transformational leaders: leaders who create dynamic change among individuals and social systems.

vocalics: elements of speech, such as tone or pitch.

workplace bullying: repeated, health-harming mistreatment of one or more persons by one or more perpetrators.

Further Readings and Resources

American Marketing Association. 2017. "Definitions of Marketing." www.ama.org/AboutAMA/Pages/Definition-of-Marketing.aspx.

Argenti, P. A., R. A. Howell, and K. A. Beck. 2005. "The Strategic Communication Imperative." *MIT Sloan Management Review* 46, no. 3: 83–89.

Dulek, R. E., and K. S. Campbell. 2015. "On the Dark Side of Strategic Communication." *International Journal of Business Communication*, 52, no. 1: 122–42. doi: 10.1177/2329488414560107.

Holthausen, D., and A. Zerfass. 2014. "Strategic Communication: Opportunities and Challenges of the Research Area." In *The Routledge Handbook of Strategic Communication*, edited by D. Holthausen and A. Zerfass, 3–17. London: Routledge.

Men, R. L., and D. Stacks. "The Effects of Authentic Leadership on Strategic Internal Communication and Employee-Organization Relationships." *Journal of Public Relations Research*, 26, no. 4: 301–24. doi: 10.1080/1062726X.2014.908720.

Public Relations Society of America. 2017. "About Public Relations." http://apps.prsa.org/AboutPRSA/publicrelationsdefined/.

Werder, K. 2015. "The Integration of Domains: Multidisciplinary Approaches to Strategic Communication Campaigns." *International Journal of Strategic Communication,* 9, no. 2: 79–86. doi: 10.1080/1553118X.2015.1010829.

References

Bakar, H. A., C. S. Mustaffa, and B. Mohamad. 2009. "LMX Quality, Supervisory Communication and Team-Oriented Commitment: A Multilevel Analysis Approach." *Corporate Communications: An International Journal* 14, no. 1: 11–33. doi: 10.1108/ 3563280910931054.

Berlo, D. K. 1960. *The Process of Communication.* New York: Holt, Rinehart, and Winston.

Bonk, K., E. Tynes, H. Griggs, and P. Sparks. 2008. *Strategic Communications for Nonprofits,* 2nd ed. Hoboken, NJ: John Wiley and Sons.

Burgoon, J. K., L. K. Guerrero, and K. Floyd. 2016. *Nonverbal Communication.* New York: Routledge.

Burke, T. A., W. E. Burke, D. L. Cascio, K. D. Costa, K. Deener, T. D. Fontaine, F. A. Fulk, L. E. Jackson, W. R. Munns, Jr., J. Orme-Zavaleta, M. W. Slimak, and V. G. Zartarian. 2017. "Rethinking Environmental Protection: Meeting the Challenges of a Changing World." *Environmental Health Perspectives* 125, no. 3 (March): A43–A49.

Conrad, C., and M. Sollitto. 2017. "History of Organizational Communication." In *The International Encyclopedia of Organizational Communication,* edited by C. R. Scott and L. Lewis, 1–30. Hoboken, NJ: John Wiley and Sons. doi: 10.1002/9781118955567.wbieoc097.

Cooren, F., J. R. Taylor, and E. J. Van Every, eds. 2006. *Communication as Organizing: Empirical and Theoretical Explanations in the Dynamic of Text and Conversation.* Mahwah, NJ: Erlbaum.

DeFleur, M., P. Kearney, T. G. Plax, and M. DeFleur. 2014. *Fundamentals of Human Communication,* 4th ed. New York: McGraw-Hill.

Gabbott, M., and G. Hogg. 2001. "The Role of Nonverbal Communication in Service Encounters: A Conceptual Framework." *Journal of Marketing Management* 17, no. 1: 5–26.

Gagliarde, P. 1986. "The Creation and Change of Organizational Cultures: A Conceptual Framework." *Organization Studies* 7, no. 2: 117–34.

Hallahan, K., D. Holtzhausen, B. van Ruler, D. Verčič, and K. Sriramesh. 2007. "Defining Strategic Communication." *International Journal of Strategic Communication* 1, no. 1: 3–35.

Hart Research Associates. 2013. *It Takes More Than a Major: Employer Priorities for College Learning and Student Success.* An online survey among employers conducted on behalf of the Association of American Colleges and Universities. Washington, DC: Hart Research Associates.

Kellermann, K. 1992. "Communication: Inherently Strategic and Primarily Automatic." *Communication Monographs* 59, no. 3: 288–300. doi: 10.1080/03637759209376270.

McCroskey, J. C., and V. P. Richmond. 1996. *Fundamentals of Human Communication: An Interpersonal Perspective.* Prospect Heights, IL: Waveland Press.

McLuhan, M. 1964. *Understanding Media: The Extensions of Man.* New York: McGraw-Hill.

National Small Business Association. 2015. "2015 Small Business Taxation Survey." www.nsba.biz/wp-content/uploads/2015 /04/2015-Taxation-Survey.pdf.

Nicotera, A. M. 2009. "Constitutive View of Communication." In *Encyclopedia of Communication Theory,* edited by S. W. Littlejohn and K. A. Foss, 176–79. Thousand Oaks, CA: Sage. doi: 10.4135/9781412959384.n69.

Powers, J. H. 1995. "On the Intellectual Structure of the Human Communication Discipline." *Communication Education* 44, no. 3: 191–222.

Putnam, L., and D. Mumby. 2014. *The SAGE Handbook of Organizational Communication: Advances in Theory, Research, and Methods,* 3rd ed. Thousand Oaks, CA: Sage.

Putnam, L. L., and A. M. Nicotera. 2009. *Building Theories of Organization: The Constitutive Role of Communication.* London: Routledge.

Rice, R. E., and C. K. Atkin, eds. 2013. *Public Communication Campaigns,* 4th ed. Los Angeles: Sage.

Shannon, C. E., and W. Weaver. 1949. *A Mathematical Model of Communication.* Urbana: University of Illinois Press.

Vangelisti, A., J. Daly, and G. Friedrich, eds. 1999. *Teaching Communication: Theory, Research, and Methods.* 2nd ed. Mahwah, NJ: Lawrence Erlbaum.

Waldeck, J. H., and D. R. Seibold, eds. 2016. *Consulting That Matters: A Handbook for Scholars and Practitioners.* New York: Peter Lang.

Weick, K. E. 1995. *Sensemaking in Organizations.* Thousand Oaks, CA: Sage.

Workplace Bullying Institute. 2017. Workplace Bullying Institute US Workplace Bullying Survey. www.workplacebullying .org/wbiresearch/wbi-2017-survey/.

Zorn, T. E. 2010. "Organizational Change Processes." In *The International Encyclopedia of Communication,* ed. W. Donsbach. Hoboken, NJ: Wiley Blackwell / ICA International. doi: 10.1002/9781405186407.wbieco017.

Organizational Types and Structures

CHAPTER CONTENTS

2.1. Organizations and Organizational Communication   40
    2.1.1 Four Identifiable Dimensions of All Organizations   40
    2.1.2 Organizational Communication and Its Relationship to Strategic Communication   44
    2.1.3 Three Broad Types of Organizations   44

2.2 Organizational Structural Features That Influence Communication   52
    2.2.1 Complexity   53
    2.2.2 Centralization   55
    2.2.3 Formalization   55

2.3 Organizational Culture and Its Impact on Communication   56
    2.3.1 How Culture Is Created Affects Organizational Life   56
    2.3.2 Analyzing Organizational Culture   58

2.4 Tying It All Together: Organizational Features and Their Relationship to Communication   62

LEARNING OBJECTIVES

After reading this chapter, you should be able to do the following:
- ▶ Define organizations and organizational communication.
- ▶ Distinguish between organizational and strategic communication.
- ▶ Explain the characteristics of for-profit, nonprofit, and government organizations.
- ▶ Analyze how the dimensions of organizational structure and organizational culture influence communication strategy and message design.

Kim works for the United States government in the Department of Defense. She works from a home office three days a week and in an office in Columbus, Ohio, two days a week as part of a virtual team with members operating out of four countries. Kim has a high-level security clearance, and her communication with vendors and clients outside of her agency is highly regulated. Her interactions with her teammates and other coworkers is informally, but strictly, influenced by the political dynamics of the agency and the nature of government work. Kim's family knows very little about the day-to-day nature of her job, because it is confidential. One of the most important rules of engagement at work for Kim is to follow the orders and directives of her superiors. Questioning or ignoring higher-ranked employees would be a dangerous professional mistake.

Kwan is a human resources executive with a global oil company. Influenced by the formality of this corporate structure and culture, Kwan is strategic in every aspect of his communication—what he wears, with whom he shakes hands, what kinds of humor he uses, who he talks to, how long he talks, what communication channel he selects, and the topics he discusses. How he represents his company with external stakeholders, such as prospective employees or clients, is highly scripted. Kwan recalls being coached by senior members of the executive team early on about how to communicate the image of the company to the public, and he is passing the same information on to the younger employees he is mentoring. He has learned an important rule for internal and external communication: "Be polite, but don't get too close. Never reveal too much of yourself or too much of our internal work."

Keisha is the chief executive officer of a community food bank in a small city of 45,000 people. The food bank relies on a tiny staff of just three employees and an army of 150 volunteers. Whether she is fund-raising in the community, working side by side with volunteers packing food for delivery to homeless shelters, or visiting with the needy of the community who are fed by the food bank, Keisha's communication style and strategy can best be described as "warm" and "open." Keisha's primary mission is to connect with people and to show appreciation and compassion for them. She sets a tone that employees and volunteers all try to model. Keisha "lives and breathes" her work and takes every opportunity to promote the food bank and its mission in their personal and professional relationships.

Mike is a white American college student working in a small family-run Thai restaurant part-time to help pay his school-related expenses. Mike quickly discovered after he started work that he was the only employee at the restaurant who was not part of the owner's family. This also meant he was the only non-Thai employee. He realized how disorganized and arbitrary decision-making, problem solving, and general communication was within this small family business.

Mike observed a lot of marketing, advertising, and public relations problems that he felt he could help the owner with since he had a lot of college coursework in these areas. The owner immediately dismissed Mike's attempts to offer feedback because of Mike's young age, cultural dissimilarity, and low status within the organization.

Zachary is a mid-level manager in a small, start-up tech company. The company is owned by a creative entrepreneur. When Zachary first accepted the job, he was excited about the potential for innovation and advancement within the company. The open floor plan of the office, the near-constant collaboration among employees, and the array of technologies were impressive. Over time, Zachary became disillusioned. No sooner would he get excited about a project, than his boss would decide to change direction. The boss couldn't stay focused and often abandoned projects that his employees were passionate about. On the plus side, Zachary found his boss very open to feedback. He maintained an open-door policy and was a good listener. He allocated resources freely and was willing to spend money to make money. But the constant change and lack of goals and strategy resulted in a company-wide feeling of chaos that made work very difficult to accomplish. Just as challenging was the task of communicating a clear brand identity for the firm to prospective clients.

As revealed in their stories, Kim, Kwan, Keisha, Mike, and Zachary have professional lives that are very different from one another. The primary reason for this is that they belong to and work within different *types* of organizations that are characterized by varied structures, norms for communication, and organizational cultures. Their work, and therefore their communication, is organized around very different missions, processes, and formal and informal rules. Organizations have unique characteristics that help define how things get done, regulate the norms for communication both inside and outside of the organization, and script the culture of what life is like for members and other stakeholders. For example, consider Kim's job. The confidentiality associated with working in the agency charged with US national defense, in addition to the bureaucratic and political dynamics of working for the government, dictate the norms for how she communicates while doing her work and how she talks about her job and her employer with outsiders. In contrast, Keisha's work with the nonprofit food bank requires her to be as open and responsive as possible. She could not succeed if she did not speak often and candidly about her organization's mission and day-to-day work. And the nature of Kwan's corporate work even defines his communication networks and the depth of his professional relationships. Although many factors influence communication style and strategy for organizational communicators, organization type is a significant one.

Organization type also influences an organization's mission and vision—important foundations on which strategic messages are built. In this chapter, we will explain in greater detail what we mean by the concept of *organization* introduced in chapter 1, and we will explore the concept of organizational communication. We will discuss some of the most prevalent types of organizations as a starting point for understanding how the unique properties of an organization influence its communication. Further, we will identify some of the most important features of an organization's structure and culture that affect the design and enactment of strategic communication.

2.1 ORGANIZATIONS AND ORGANIZATIONAL COMMUNICATION

Recall in chapter 1 that we introduced you to the formal concept of organization (an identifiable social structure consisting of members united toward meeting internal and external goals). You are already probably part of numerous organizations on campus and in your community. If you have a job, you belong to an organization. If you are involved in Greek life, you belong to an organization. If you volunteer, belong to a service club, or perform community service, you are part of an organization. The college or university you attend is an organization, as is the department that houses your major. You or your family may be regulated in some way by a neighborhood or homeowner association that sets rules about the appearance of yards and houses. You interact with organizations when you pay your bills, file your income taxes, apply for student loans, get a license plate for your car, attend church, shop for food and clothing, and on and on. In other words, organizations are a ubiquitous presence in our lives, without which we would have just the opposite of *organization:* chaos. But what are they?

2.1.1 Four Identifiable Dimensions of All Organizations

If we think about the kinds of organizations referenced in the examples above, they all have at least four things in common.

ORGANIZATIONS ARE MADE UP OF PEOPLE WHO MUST INTERACT WITH ONE ANOTHER These people may have an internal or an external affiliation with the organization. For example, when you pay your taxes, you are an external stakeholder relative to the IRS. However, thousands of people work within the IRS. When you are a patient in a health care facility, you have an external relationship to that organization, but you are very much a part of it. The health care professionals who work there are internal members of the organization. Members of the Gamma Phi Beta sorority are the internal mechanism through which goals are pursued and accomplished, but Gamma Phi Beta's philanthropic work benefits nonmembers all over the globe.

All internal members of an organization must communicate with other members to some extent. For instance, Kim, whom you met in the introduction to this chapter, communicates frequently with her virtual team on her telework days and interacts closely with her supervisor on days she is in the office. The extent to which they interact with others outside the organization is highly dependent on their role, or job function (concepts we will explore later in this chapter). Kim's role involves very little external communication. Keisha, however, communicates as much or maybe more with potential donors and volunteers as she does with people already working on the "inside" of the community food bank. The bottom line? Organizations are made up of people who create social relationships with one another and communicate in ways relevant to the organization.

ORGANIZATIONS ARE EMBEDDED WITHIN EXTERNAL ENVIRONMENTS THAT EXTEND BEYOND THEIR OWN BOUNDARIES   Without a dynamic interdependence with that environment, an organization cannot succeed. An example of this emerges from Kwan's story. As a human resources executive with his corporation, he is responsible for the recruiting and hiring strategy. He must cultivate relationships with educational institutions graduating qualified talent for his company to hire. Kwan must make sure that his company is represented at job and recruitment fairs all over the globe and ensure that the company's social media plan is executed and evaluated. He is ultimately responsible for the quality and results of the hiring interviews conducted within the corporation.

Another example of organizational embeddedness and interdependence with the environment is the relationship that an organization has with its customers and the communities in which it exists. Recently, your authors noticed that a new ice cream shop was opening near their campus, and the message that alerted them to this new business is a good illustration of the interdependence an organization needs to create with its environment. Rather than through traditional advertising channels, such as TV or radio, our first news of this business came via a Facebook notification of a grand opening event. The shop was wisely using social media to create a communication connection with its customer base near a college campus. We also noticed some of the activities planned for the grand opening, including an appearance by the city's mayor to welcome the business to town, giveaways designed to build customer loyalty and affinity, and entertainment for adults and children. All of these planned events illustrate the interdependence between organizations and the environments or communities in which they are embedded. Finally, the shop advertised that they make their ice cream in house each day. This led us to conclude that the organization will rely on local sources for their ingredients—requiring the shop to build relationships not only with their own prospective customers but also with the vendors they will depend on for the resources they need to conduct their business.

Figure 7 This local business's grand opening event notification illustrates the principle that organizations are embedded within, and interdependent with, their environments.

ORGANIZATIONS AFFECT THEIR INTERNAL AND EXTERNAL ENVIRONMENTS   The third aspect of an organization is closely related to the second. Not only are they embedded within an environment that extends beyond their boundaries, but organizations also affect their internal and external environments. Ideally, this impact is positive. Organizations strive to make some contribution of value to their stakeholders (i.e., individuals who have some interest or concern in them such as employees, customers, prospective customers, shareholders, donors, community members). Keyton (2011) wrote that "each type of organization contributes to our collective economic, civic, community, and social lives in some fundamental way" (1). For example, an organization most of you are probably familiar with, Target, affects its consumers with the goods that they purchase there, at what many consider to be a fair price. Many customers report enjoying Target's generally clean, organized store appearance. In addition, this organization generates sales tax revenue for communities and provides access to necessary supplies and food. Target endeavors to benefit its employee team members and the communities in which it has stores through wellness programs, diversity and inclusion policies, civic activity, and volunteerism. As Target illustrates, through the pursuit of their collective goals, organizations provide a variety of fundamental benefits to a wide range of internal and external stakeholders.

ORGANIZATIONS HAVE A GOAL THAT BINDS THEIR MEMBERS TOGETHER   Perhaps the goal is to serve the most cups of coffee, create the most frequently used social media platform, provide efficient and effective customer service, or unite members around a social or philanthropic cause. Let's look at a specific example. According to its website, the service club Rotary International's goal is to "bring together professional and business leaders in order to provide humanitarian services, encourage high ethical standards in all vocations, and to advance

Strategic Communication Mentor: Target's Commitment to Corporate Responsibility

Organizations that fail to affect their internal and external environments in positive ways are likely to fail in their missions. Target is well known for its commitment to contributing to the collective economic, community, and social concerns of the places it does business. Target has corporate responsibility policies that address employee well-being, customer satisfaction, and local community quality of life. Take a few minutes to explore Target's Corporate Responsibility website and answer the questions that follow.

https://corporate.target.com/corporate-responsibility

1. After reviewing Target's practices, how do you define corporate responsibility?
2. What does Target teach you about why organizations need to have an impact on something other than their own bank accounts to be successful? In other words, after reviewing Target's practices, why do you think organizations have a responsibility to provide something of value to both their internal and external stakeholders?
3. What methods could an organization use to determine what its internal and external stakeholders perceive as valuable? In other words, how do organizations go about finding out what employees, consumers, local community members, and other stakeholders will value in terms of organizational impact?
4. Thinking about the organizations that you belong to, identify two to three ways that one of them contributes to something "larger than itself."

goodwill and peace around the world." Within any organization, under these sorts of umbrella goals are numerous specific objectives and agendas belonging to groups and individuals. If the organization has engaged in the necessary activities to create member buy-in relative to organizational goals, those group and individual agendas should be in alignment with the larger organizational goals. Extending our Rotary International example, local clubs pursue unique initiatives that contribute to the larger organization's goal. Some raise funds for students interested in studying abroad, others may prioritize the repair and maintenance of parks and playgrounds, and still others are focused on health concerns in underserved areas. For example, one chapter in India created an educational campaign aimed at early cancer detection.

So, we can say in summary that an **organization** is a communicative, social enterprise with shared goals that is interdependently linked with its external environment. The box on page 44 summarizes the four primary defining dimensions of organizations.

Four Primary Dimensions of Organization

- Organizations are made up of people who interact with one another.
- Organizations are embedded within an environment that extends beyond their boundaries.
- Organizations affect their internal and external environments in some way.
- Organizations have one or more overarching goals that bind their members together.

2.1.2 Organizational Communication and Its Relationship to Strategic Communication

Without communication, organization is not possible. Whether at a micro, or internal, level (e.g., with supervisors, peers, subordinates) or at the macro, external, level (e.g., with the public, customers, other organizations, or other external target audiences), communication facilitates organizational activity and outcomes. It is a critical and necessary condition for effective organizational functioning. Communication is the resource that allows the individuals who constitute organizations to design work processes, build relationships, set goals and create strategies, create and innovate, collaborate with others, market and sell products and ideas, establish and enforce policies, provide feedback, and more. Organizational communication, you will recall, is the use of oral, written, and nonverbal messages among people working within an organization to accomplish shared goals. However, not all communication within an organization is aimed at goals and objectives. Organizational members gossip, engage in conflict, talk about their personal lives, and communicate about any number of issues unrelated to their shared goals. Thus, as we discussed in chapter 1, communication focused on organizational objectives and advancing an organization's mission is the purview of this book—strategic communication. Strategic communication is shaped, planned, designed, and executed in specific ways that are heavily influenced by organization type, structure, and culture.

2.1.3 Three Broad Types of Organizations

When you consider the range of organizations that you interact with, the list is probably quite long and diverse. We purchase clothes and household goods from retail establishments; we vacation and dine in hospitality businesses; we deposit and withdraw funds from institutions in the financial services sector; we volunteer with and make donations to animal-related charities, human services organizations, and religious institutions. We get driver's and business licenses, pay taxes, and send our children to public schools by interacting with federal, state, and local government agencies. We obtain health care by going to clinics and hospitals, and for many of us, that health care is subsidized by an insurance plan that we have access to through an employer or the government, or a policy that we purchase independently. In terms of employment, some of you are servers in restaurants, others sell real estate, and still others create social media strategies and content for a variety of different businesses. There are many ways to categorize or label organization types, but that list could become very long if we organized it around specific goals, products, or services. In this book, we classify organizations into three broad categories and provide diverse examples of each type throughout (Miller 2015):

- for-profit, such as retail, hospitality, agriculture, manufacturing, real estate, information technology, and financial services
- nonprofit, such as charities, often including health care
- local, state, and federal government entities, like public schools, the Department of Motor Vehicles (DMV), or the armed services

These classifications provide some beginning insight into appropriate communication strategy. In later sections of this chapter, we examine additional features of an organization's structure that should inform its strategic communication practices.

FOR-PROFIT ORGANIZATIONS   A **for-profit organization** is designed for the primary purpose of generating a profit for the owner or owners of the entity. The ownership of a for-profit organization then decides what to do with that profit: keep it for themselves, or invest it back into the organization. There are several ownership models for for-profit organizations. For instance, they might be owned by a sole proprietor or a group (i.e., a partnership). For-profit organizations are sometimes publicly traded on the stock market, meaning that interest in the company is made available for sale to the public. Individuals who purchase this interest are known as shareholders. Yet other for-profits are employee owned through a profit-sharing plan. Most companies that you think of as "businesses" are for-profit organizations. Examples include:

- Retail businesses where you shop (either in person or online) for new clothes, food, and household supplies
- Tech brands from which you purchase your phones, laptops, and tablets (and the service providers that enable you to use them)
- Restaurants you eat in
- Hotels and resorts where you vacation, spend the night while on a road trip, or attend business meetings
- Real estate firms that facilitate your purchase, sale, or lease of a residential or commercial property
- Banks and investment firms where you make deposits or borrow money

Figure 8 When you shop retail (either brick-and-mortar or online), you are dealing with a for-profit organization.

In addition, some hospitals and educational institutions, which are typically nonprofit organizations, are actually for-profit. We will discuss nonprofit organizations later in this chapter. However, the litmus test for determining whether an organization is for-profit or nonprofit lies in the answer to two questions. If the answer to these questions is "yes," then the organization is for-profit. First, does this organization seek to make more money than it spends? For instance, Dick's Sporting Goods is a Fortune 500 publicly traded retail company. Dick's had total revenue of nearly $9 million, costs of about $6 million, and a gross profit of over $2.4 million in 2018 (Yahoo! Finance 2019). Second, is this organization's primary duty and obligation to itself (rather than to the welfare of society, or some charitable, social, or educational cause)? Although Dick's sponsors youth athletic leagues all over the country through its "Sports Matters" initiative (*Philanthropy News Digest* 2014) the company's primary objective is to generate a profit through the sales of sporting goods. With these profits, Dick's pays bonuses to employees, dividends to shareholders, reinvests in the company to open and remodel stores, and contributes to its charitable foundation.

For-profit organizations are concerned with their own interests, such as bringing new products to market and maximizing sales of those products, driving traffic to their physical or virtual business space, generating clicks on website links, expanding their geographic footprint or customer base, or reaching goals related to their financial bottom line of making a profit. However, in contemporary society, very few, if any, successful organizations thrive based solely on their motivation to generate revenue and profit. According to research reported in *Business News Daily* (Post 2017), nine of ten consumers expect for-

Strategic Communication Mentor: Ben & Jerry's
Corporate Social Responsibility

Ben & Jerry's is a for-profit company well known for its commitment to **corporate social responsibility.** Examine some of the initiatives it has promoted over the years and read about the owners' commitment to social outreach in the *New York Times* article linked below and then respond to the questions that follow.
www.benjerry.com/whats-new/2014/corporate-social-responsibility-history
www.nytimes.com/2015/08/23/business/how-ben-jerrys-social-mission-survived-being-gobbled-up.html?mcubz=0

1. Define CSR in your own words based on the understanding you have developed from Ben & Jerry's practices. To what extent do you believe that organizations have an ethical responsibility to engage in CSR?
2. Do you believe that a commitment to CSR can enhance an organization's profit-generating goals? In other words, are the commitments to profit and social responsibility at odds, or can they be compatible and even synergistic? Explain your answer.
3. Why do you believe 90 percent of respondents to a national survey reported that they believe for-profit companies should be involved in philanthropic activity?
4. What other examples of corporate social responsibility are you familiar with or can identify in a quick internet search? List and briefly describe them.

profit organizations to operate in responsible ways that benefit society. Recall that in defining the characteristics of an organization, we established that successful organizations recognize that they are embedded in a larger community and seek to affect that environment in positive ways. Just as Dick's Sporting Goods supports youth sports, Apple, Microsoft, Starbucks, and virtually all brands you could quickly bring to mind have a strong philanthropic orientation. However, they are organized as for-profit companies. Ideally, companies balance the requirements for generating profit with their responsibilities to the external environment and avoid doing harm with their business practices. As an extension of for-profit organizations' commitment to philanthropy, many are dedicated to **corporate social responsibility (CSR),** which involves policies and practices that enhance the company's impact on environmental and social well-being. Read the case of Ben & Jerry's above to learn more about CSR and to see some examples.

Within this category of for-profit organizations, many unique characteristics shape an organization's goals and define its work and communication processes. Here are some examples to consider. For-profits might be classified as small businesses (using the size and revenue guidelines established by the US Small Business Administration) that serve their local communities, or they might be very large global enterprises. Internal communication strategy should be very different for small organizations than larger ones. In addition, for-profit organizations exist in every business sector and provide a long and diverse list of products and services. External communication strategy, such as sales and marketing messages, will differ for companies selling cars and those selling food. For-profit organizations may be well-established, or newer start-up businesses. In a start-up business, internal communication strategy might focus on brainstorming and establishing efficient work design and flow, and external communication strategy might seek to build consumer brand awareness. Once an organization is established and recognized, internal communication shifts from an emphasis on design to a focus on feedback and refining products, ideas, and processes for maximum effectiveness. External communication efforts might be aimed at building loyalty among the customer base or getting new customers to switch from another brand. In addition, for-profit organizations are characterized by a number of diverse cultural features that make their work and communication unique. We will examine the cultural and structural properties of organizations later in this chapter. For now, it is important to understand that identifying an organization as a for-profit entity is only a starting point for understanding the goals that should inform its communication strategy.

NONPROFIT ORGANIZATIONS   The primary purpose of a **nonprofit organization** is to promote a particular cause; advocate a viewpoint; or advance a political, social, or philanthropic mission. These organizations are often interested in health care, education, environmental conservation, wildlife protection, and providing basic needs like food and water. Rather than distribute surplus revenue (profit) to owners, a **nonprofit** reinvests it to advance its mission. Nonprofit organizations often rely heavily on a volunteer workforce, but they may include the expense of salaries for employees and administration in their operating budgets. Examples of **nonprofit** organizations you might be familiar with include the United Nations Children's Fund (UNICEF), Human Rights Campaign (HRC), Doctors without Borders, the Metropolitan Museum of Art, the YWCA/YMCA, Planned Parenthood Federation of America, Oxfam, Greenpeace, Red Cross, the World Wildlife Federation, American Cancer Society, and the Heritage Foundation. Most libraries and churches, and many colleges, universities, and hospitals, are **nonprofit** organizations as well.

Nonprofits require revenue and must engage in fund-raising and development to raise money and other tangible and intangible goods necessary for their work. Recall Keisha from the opening of this chapter, the CEO of a community foodbank. A great deal of her time and effort is dedicated to cultivating relationships with potential donors and building partnerships with prospective

Figure 9 YWCA is an example of a nonprofit organization.

corporate sponsors in the community. The money she raises is used for food, supplies, space, and staffing related to the food bank's primary mission of feeding the needy. Although a for-profit organization's success is based largely on its profit, a nonprofit's success is measured by the extent to which it fulfills its mission and meets its goals. For instance, one of the benchmarks for the food bank's success is the number of pounds of food distributed throughout the year.

The target external audience for nonprofit strategic communication tends to be much broader than that for for-profit organizations. Primarily, for-profit businesses seek to reach consumers who will purchase their products and services, enhancing their revenue and allowing them to expand their business and reach new target consumer bases. Without successfully reaching this target audience—prospective customers and consumers—the for-profit business could not succeed. Nonprofit organizations, alternatively, depend on strategic communication with a much longer list of stakeholders in order to succeed. For example, nonprofit organizations must interact with volunteers, donors, corporate sponsors, the target audience(s) for their work (e.g., in the case of the food bank, people without the resources to provide nourishing food for themselves and their families), corporate sponsors, and the general public.

GOVERNMENT ORGANIZATIONS   A **government** is the means through which a community, state, or country is organized and regulated. Local, state, and federal governments employ millions of people in the United States in hundreds of agencies. These people perform professional, administrative, technical, clerical, and a host of both white-collar (i.e., knowledge-intensive, nonroutinized, nonmanual work) and blue-collar (i.e., manual, routine work) job functions (United States Office of Personnel Management 2013) in all geographic regions of the country. To see a complete list of US government agencies and departments, go to this website: www.usa.gov/federal-agencies/a. At the state level, examples of government agencies include those responsible for registering motor vehicles and licensing drivers and collecting state income taxes. At the local level, governments oversee public schools, parks and recreation activities, issue business licenses, collect property taxes, and maintain roads.

The primary purpose of government agencies is to deliver goods and services that benefit their external stakeholders (e.g., beneficiaries of Medicare, members of the armed forces, citizens of the area governed), rather than to generate profit. For example, the Defense Logistics Agency (DLA), a branch of the United States Department of Defense, provides combat support to the military services by acquiring and managing everything from tanks and weaponry to office supplies. In addition, DLA provides humanitarian assistance to people from war-affected regions and supports natural disaster relief efforts in the United States. The funding for government activities like these is generated through taxes paid by citizens.

Several features of government organizations distinguish them from for-profit and nonprofit organizations. First, government systems tend to be large and highly bureaucratic, meaning that they have a unique organizing structure typically used in very large, multiunit systems. German sociologist Max Weber (1947) created a theory of **bureaucratic organizations** in which he delineated the characteristics of bureaucracies like government:

1. *Bureaucracies require hierarchical structure with most communication flowing from the top down.* In government, decision-making power is concentrated among a relatively small number of people in comparison to the number of people employed. Communication often takes the form of directives that are disseminated from the more powerful to the less powerful. As a result, organizational communication in many government agencies can resemble the linear model discussed in chapter 1, rather than the simultaneous transaction model. For instance, members of the military take orders from their commanding officers without questions or the opportunity for feedback.

2. *The division of labor should be clear, and tasks highly specialized.* In government organizations, job descriptions are clear and specific. Members of a particular agency that one of your authors has worked with on a consulting basis have a saying: "We stay in our own lanes." By this, they mean that they tend to their own job requirements and assigned tasks and rarely concern themselves with learning about other job functions that don't affect their own roles and responsibilities. This is very much unlike a nonprofit organization or most for-profits, where members must be adaptive and flexible in the requirements of their jobs. In very few organizations other than government can members remain of high value if they do not understand job functions other than their own—in other words, if they always stay in their own lanes.

3. *The organization should operate in a relatively closed fashion.* Bureaucracies such as governments arrive at a set of unique working principles that

enable the organization to function smoothly, and Weber argued that outside influences could unnecessarily disrupt the process. Modern literature emphasizes *open* organizational systems as a means of learning best practices adopted by other organizations and new innovations. However, Weber believed that the best practice was the one that you develop internally—and that looking at what your competitors do and trying to copy those practices might be a detriment to performance. A completely closed system is unrealistic and ill-advised for most organizations. The best nonprofit and for-profit organizations look to the best practices of similar organizations. Even some government employees attend conferences with their counterparts from other agencies to network and share ideas. Many might argue that government organizations could improve their processes, strategies, and outcomes by creating a more open system for communication and operation. However, many government organizations, such as the Defense Logistics Agency, are by necessity highly closed systems characterized by an extreme degree of confidentiality and protection from outside influences.

4. *Written rules are essential.* Weber believed that a system of rules should address all possible **contingencies,** or unexpected but possible deviations from standard operating procedures. Municipal, state, and federal codes provide the laws and regulations that govern activities and behavior.

5. *Bureaucracies must be guided by strict authority.* Government employees like Kim, whom we met in the introduction to this chapter, are highly sensitive to the power and importance of rank in the workplace. Weber wrote about three types of bureaucratic authority. First, **charismatic authority** is based on a manager or leader's communication style, personality, and ability to relate on an interpersonal level to those around him or her. Charismatic leaders attract people with their vision, warmth, likeability, and relatability. Weber called the second type of power **traditional authority.** This kind of authority is based on an individual's title or position in the hierarchy; it may or may not reflect his or her actual talents and abilities. As an illustration, Kim is not always very confident in her supervisor's competence or credibility. She often questions his ability to manage the essential functions of her team. Nonetheless, he is Kim's superior, and by virtue of his rank, he has immense influence on Kim and her peers. Finally, Weber wrote about a third type of authority known as **rational-legal authority,** which is the basis for management and leadership in bureaucratic organizations such as government. Rational-legal authority does not reside in a person or people but rather in the rules, laws, norms, and policies that characterize the organization. Weber argued that when the rules were clear and strictly enforced, a traditional hierarchy with power centralized at the top was in place, and labor was divided within a closed organizational system, there was little

need for charisma or traditional authority. Rather, in government bureaucracies, there is a clear, codified set of rules, policies, and procedures that establishes how things work. There is little to no room for deviation from this code.

For example, consider the task of filing a return with the Internal Revenue Service. The print version of the US tax code is an astonishing 75,000 pages! (Russell 2016). Every possible tax situation is addressed in the document, and it contains an answer to every question. Luckily, there are professionals who can assist taxpayers in interpreting these rules and policies—but as a bureaucracy, the IRS established this code as a rational-legal authority over our behavior. No IRS agent, regardless of his or her title or charisma, has the authority to override the rules for any of us.

In this section, we have established three broad categories into which all organizations can be classified: for-profit, nonprofit, and government. We have discussed the characteristics of each and what bearing these three types of organizations may have on the communication that characterizes them. However, we have emphasized the point that within each of these three broad categories, there is a diversity of organizations that will exhibit different missions, structures, and cultures—and consequently, communication strategies. Therefore, we next turn to a discussion of additional features of organizations that influence the nature of communication within them and their strategies for communicating with external stakeholders.

2.2 ORGANIZATIONAL STRUCTURAL FEATURES THAT INFLUENCE COMMUNICATION

Organizational structure refers to the overall pattern according to which work gets done and objectives are pursued and accomplished (Jablin 1987). Structure is the template or guide for how roles are assigned and work allocated, and how power and control are distributed. Other structural features of an organization include its size, degree of formality, and its configuration (e.g., the degree to which an organization relies on teamwork and collaboration or individual accountability, and whether work is distributed across geographic locations, virtual, centralized in a primary location, or some hybrid combination of these arrangements). Let's discuss the traditional dimensions of organizational structure (complexity, centralization, and formalization) and how they influence communication, and specifically, strategic communication. We draw on some of the classic scholarship on organizational communication, behavior, and structure in this section (cf. Galbraith 1973; Mintzberg 1980; Oldham and Hackman 1981; Porter and Lawler 1964) and offer you some contemporary examples.

2.2.1 Complexity

Organizational complexity refers to a series of interrelated structural features that describe the tangible ways people and practices relate to one another within an organization (McPhee and Poole 2001). Complexity influences communication in substantial ways, as evidenced by research going back to the 1960s conducted in the organizational behavior, industrial and organizational psychology, management, and communication fields. There are three aspects of complexity to consider when analyzing an organization: horizontal differentiation, size, and vertical hierarchy.

HORIZONTAL DIFFERENTIATION   The first facet of complexity refers to how individual roles are defined and work allocated across the organization. In older literature, this was called *division of labor*. Specific job descriptions and clear roles that rigidly distinguish one person's responsibilities from another's tend to promote managerial control and oversight over work processes and heightened clarity among organizational members regarding what is expected of them. That sounds good, but consider that strict horizontal role differentiation also results in lowered creativity, innovation, communication satisfaction, and general work satisfaction. These conditions strain organizational communication and make strategic communication that supports organizational objectives almost impossible. At the organization level, strategic objectives become hard to accomplish when organizational structure features strict horizontal differentiation, as it tends to create communication and cooperation problems that result in high levels of internal conflict. Overall, a rigid division of tasks and responsibilities is viewed as a negative structural feature by contemporary organizing standards that favor shared responsibility, teamwork, and the ability to adapt and "pinch hit" for other organizational members who perform diverse kinds of tasks. Strategic communication and the pursuit of collective team and organizational goals requires cross-functional understanding of what goes on in other parts of the system.

SIZE   A second feature of an organization's complexity is its relative size. Simply put, communication is very different in larger organizations than in smaller ones. Communication becomes more formal, mechanistic, and even bureaucratic the larger an organization is, primarily because large organizations require strict systems of coordination and control to avoid chaos (Jablin 1987). Coordination and control over communication and work processes, then, preclude members from engaging in the kinds of informal organizing processes that promote creativity and so-called outside-the-box thinking that is necessary to flourish in today's environment. Organization size also influences the way strategic decisions are made and how members are involved in developing strategy. Although more people participate in decision-making and strategic planning in larger organizations, it may be more difficult to incorporate a large number of voices into the plan that is created. Employees may report feeling like they had the opportunity to contribute, but that their ideas ultimately were not incorporated into the strategy. Some research also indicates that in larger organizations, managers make decisions and establish goals and strategy based on their own division (or unit, or team, or department) needs rather than integrating their thinking with the bigger picture of the organization. In smaller organizations, more communication occurs across teams, units, and departments, so strategy may be more comprehensive and the resulting communication in better alignment with the organization's mission than individual or team needs and agendas.

VERTICAL HIERARCHY   The third and final element of organizational complexity is **vertical hierarchy.** This refers to how "tall" the organization's structure is. More top-down, or vertical, hierarchies have a number of layers of management between front-line employees and leaders at the top level. "Shorter" or "flatter" hierarchies have fewer levels. In tall organizations, managers have fewer direct reports and provide closer supervision than in flatter ones. As a result, flatter organizations allow, and in fact require, individuals to take heightened initiative and to be self-directed to some degree in their work. In taller hierarchies, top management and executives, who are often responsible for creating the strategy that defines an organization's communication efforts, have less communication with those of lower rank. As a result, unless they familiarize themselves with the perspectives of others, their strategy might be out of sync with the reality of those "in the trenches" doing the work of research and design, sales, marketing, external relations, and so on. When they do collect "data" from front-line employees, it is usually filtered through the layers of management that exist between the top and bottom of the organizational pyramid. In flatter organizational structures, there are fewer rigid prescriptions of who talks to whom; thus, in flat hierarchies, people tend to collaborate more and have a greater understanding of organizational objectives and strategy than in tall ones. Further, in tall structures, those lower in status are dependent on higher-ranked individuals for information. Thus, unless managers are "communication minded" and have processes in place to ensure the flow of necessary information, some members might become information deprived while others are overloaded. These issues can create a range of obstacles to effective, strategic communication.

Complexity manifests in very practical ways for contemporary organizations. Companies operate globally in many different countries; leaders manage numerous people and brands. Complexity often results in poor processes, confusing role definitions, and unclear expectations. However, strategic communication aimed at creating useful, effective internal processes, roles, and standards can make the business of dynamic contemporary global organizing less difficult. By extension, then, resources are available to focus on external strategic messaging.

2.2.2 Centralization

Centralization, the second facet of organizational structure, refers to the degree to which the power to make decisions and chart strategy is concentrated at higher levels within the organization. In decentralized environments, employees at all levels of the organization are charged with decision-making and strategic planning that results in action, such as communication, that is relevant and useful because it is performed by those closest to the issue in question. Decentralization has clear benefits, but an organization can suffer drawbacks if it does not implement distributed, or decentralized, power thoughtfully. In such cases, local decisions might not reflect organizational strategy.

To better understand why careful attention to decentralization is important, consider a large organization such as Walmart's efforts to expand globally. Walmart has over eight thousand stores in fifteen countries but has struggled to succeed in all of them. One reason is the centralized nature of organizing and organizational strategy that Walmart has historically implemented. After attempting to expand its presence in Germany for over a decade and failing, Walmart finally pulled out in 2006 (Berfield 2013; Landler and Barbaro 2006). Analysts attribute the failure to Walmart's centralized corporate insistence on imposing business practices that are effective in the United States on a country with a very different set of cultural business and communication values. For example, Walmart now acknowledges that the names of their stores in foreign countries should be left up to local management, as the founder's name (Walton) and the Walmart brand name carry little cultural significance in other countries. In the United States, Walmart employees are trained to smile at customers. In Germany, employees and customers were uncomfortable with this practice of forced smiling at strangers. Both of these examples illustrate the lesson that Walmart learned through its failure to thrive in Germany: to be strategic, decentralized, rather than centralized, decision-making processes are important. However, organizations must be careful to implement an efficient decentralization plan that ensures decentralized decisions and solutions are aligned with overall organizational objectives.

2.2.3 Formalization

Formality refers to the extent to which rules, processes, and procedures are explicitly stated in writing. The more formalized an organization is, the less freedom individual members have to make case-by-case decisions about the best way to act. By virtue of the bureaucratic characteristics we discussed earlier in this chapter, government is an example of highly formalized organizational environment. Although formalized organizations offer members a clear picture of what is expected of them, they tend to become stagnant rather than strategic and innovative. Consider how long Congress takes to propose, debate, and vote on changes to federal law. The process of change in formalized organizations is similarly long and painful. Formalization is in direct opposition to the kinds of organic, collaborative communication and work processes that characterize successful contemporary organizations. For example, consider an organization's customer service responsibilities. In a highly formalized organization, if a customer's particular complaint or problem isn't addressed in the "handbook," employees are disempowered from doing much—resulting in an even more disgruntled customer. If you have ever had a customer service experience in which the employee used creative solutions and took actions to satisfy you, chances are, the organization has a low to moderate degree of formalization as it relates to customer service.

All organizations need formal rules and processes. We would be concerned if you were to take a job with an employer that did not provide you with some written account of what is expected of you. Organization would be impossible without some degree of formalization. However, when an organization becomes overburdened by formalized regulation, it becomes constrained from engaging in the kinds of strategic thinking, planning, and communication needed for growth.

2.3 ORGANIZATIONAL CULTURE AND ITS IMPACT ON COMMUNICATION

Every organization has a unique culture that is created by the interactions its stakeholders have and that has a substantial impact on subsequent communication. Communication scholar Joann Keyton defines **organizational culture** as "the set of artifacts, values, and assumptions that emerge from the interactions of organizational members" (2011, 21) and Edgar Schein, MIT Sloan Management Professor Emeritus and noted organizational culture scholar, adds that culture is "taught to members as the correct way to perceive, think, and feel in relation [to the organization and its problems]" (2004, 17)

2.3.1 How Culture Is Created Affects Organizational Life

There is considerable disagreement among authors writing on the topic of culture about the extent to which organizational members produce culture through their communication and other actions (as Keyton's definition suggests), and the extent to which the culture is determined by the leaders of the organization and taught to employees who are expected to adapt (as Schein argues). Based on our experience as researchers studying organizational communication behavior and consultants working directly with practitioners in business settings, we believe that culture develops both ways. In many organizations, experienced veterans and leaders with power and influence have more input into what life is like than newcomers and those with less power. In these organizations, the leadership and/or executive team establishes the parameters of the culture, and members are expected to learn what is culturally expected of them and comply. Over time, employees in these more formal, hierarchical organizations may be able to create change. But they will face obstacles if their ideas are at odds with tradition or senior members' vision.

However, other organizational cultures are quite open to employee input, regardless of that individual's status or time with the organization. In these organizations, teams and units may develop their own informal climates and cultures as a by-product of how they communicate and work together, and those have an impact on the organization at large. In organizations with less rigid hierarchies, communication flows easily and newcomers and those with less status are able to imprint the organization with the fruits of their knowledge, skills, and experience. For example, despite Zachary's frustrations working for a boss with a short attention span for challenging projects, the boss's open-door policy and the interactive, informal culture of this start-up allows Zachary to have an influence on the direction of the company. The owner of the company is open to newcomers' ideas and encourages frequent input. Most organizations are somewhere in the middle; in them, culture neither comes solely from the top, nor do newer members or those with relatively little amounts of authority or responsibility have an excessive amount of influence over what the organization values.

The nature of an organization's culture helps distinguish it from other organizations, including its competitors. It defines just what life and work and relationships are like within that organization. Culture reflects an organization's mission and vision, and simultaneously influences the kinds of goals and objectives an organization pursues. Therefore, culture both informs and reflects communication strategy. An organization with a strong culture is going to practice the values and behaviors of that culture both internally and externally. For that organization, culture is not just a way of working together, but an ethos for how it interacts with its external stakeholders as well. That's why you can probably almost immediately identify many organizations with strong cultures, such as Nordstrom, whose cultural value of customer service is well known, or Disney, famous for its emphasis on creating a memorable guest experience.

When you think of culture, you probably first think of geographic or ethnic cultures. For example, most people have some idea about the differences between living in a large city such as New York or Los Angeles and a midsize midwestern city like Columbus, Ohio, or Indianapolis, Indiana—or between life in any city and life on a rural farm. Most adults can name at least a few cultural traditions that characterize life in the United States (e.g., eating hamburgers and hotdogs at summer barbecues, fireworks on July 4, decorating pumpkins in the fall) and in another country (e.g., the cultural value placed on taking time for afternoon tea in Great Britain, or removing one's shoes when entering an Asian home). You should also be able to identify some of the core values of your own cultures (e.g., freedom as an American value, regular attendance at weekly Mass as a Catholic value, or reverence for your elders as an Asian value). You can begin to think about the concept of *organizational* culture by contemplating questions like: "What is the identity of an Apple user, and how is it different from that of a Microsoft user?" "What makes working at IBM different from working at Facebook?" "How is life at (the school you decided to attend) different from life at (the other schools you applied to or considered attending)?"

2.3.2 Analyzing Organizational Culture

Just how can we analyze an organization's culture and discover what characterizes "life" as it is in any particular organization? The thinking on organizational cultures was largely influenced by seminal books on this topic titled *Corporate Cultures: The Rites and Rituals of Corporate Life* by Terrence Deal and Adam Kennedy and *In Search of Excellence: Lessons from America's Best-Run Companies* by Tom Peters and Robert Waterman. Both of these perspectives suggest several key features we can use to analyze organizational culture and the extent to which it enhances the organization's strategic ability to accomplish its objectives. Further, companies can become successful by intentionally, strategically building cultures with attention to the characteristics of strong cultures. What follow are the eight key features of organizational cultures and some representative examples. You can find a summary of these cultural features in the box on page 59.

VALUES   **Values** are defined by the more or less shared set of beliefs about appropriate behavior, the organization's goals, and the ideals that the organization collectively views as important. Examples include innovation, stability, conservativism, risk taking, or strong customer orientation. For example, at Disney theme parks, employees (referred to as "cast members") have a single priority regardless of their job description: to make guests happy.

METAPHORS   **Metaphors** are words or phrases used within the organization to define something abstract in terms of something more familiar to members. For example, members might say, "This organization is like a family"; "We're like a football team: Sheryl is the quarterback who gets us all in position, and I'm a receiver—I take her ideas and run with them"; "These men are like

---

Eight Features for Analyzing Organizational Culture

- Values
- Metaphors
- Artifacts
- Rituals
- Heroes
- Stories
- Norms
- Communication

---

brothers to me"; or "We are like a well-oiled machine!" Sometimes people use more negative metaphors to describe their organizational experience, such as "This place is like a prison." The metaphors people use to describe their experiences say a lot about their organization's culture. They reflect attitudes that permeate both internal and external communication.

ARTIFACTS **Artifacts** are tangible, physical features of the organization. Examples of cultural artifacts include the office decor aesthetic, how the physical space is arranged (e.g., are there offices with doors, or open cubicles? Or perhaps the organization uses a "hotel" workspace model—no permanent territory for employees), and the dress code. For example, Jennifer Waldeck, one of the authors of this book, and Sean Ross, an organizational consultant, wrote about a project they worked on together in which rank-and-file police officers in one department complained about a power imbalance and an "us versus them" divide between them and their commanding officers. The negative feelings emanating from this perceived imbalance was even beginning to affect the officers' interactions with the general public they were sworn to serve. They pointed out that even the dress code created division: officers wore blue shirts and the upper-level ranks wore white shirts. As Waldeck and Ross helped this department redefine its culture, one change they agreed on was that all officers would wear the same color shirts as a strategic symbol of solidarity and equality.

RITUALS **Rituals** are traditional activities that highlight what the organization considers to be important. Common examples include an annual holiday party or summer picnic, a quarterly earnings call, or a fall retreat. Some organizations practice less positive rituals, such as the practice of hazing newcomers. At Chapman University, where the authors of this book are professors, a number of positive rituals highlight what is culturally important. These include the opening convocation held every fall to mark the new academic year, homecoming weekend, the state of university address, and of course, graduation. More unique to Chapman's culture is the 5K that was held for many years as part of the school's homecoming festivities, championed by the university's past president, who is an elite distance runner who enjoys physical accomplishment, competition, and personal achievements. The 5K was an example of a cultural ritual, but also an illustration of how those in leadership positions influence what an organization's culture is like. Public-facing rituals—those that involve external stakeholders or are performed for the public to see—make strategic statements. What public perceptions might an event like a community 5K race cultivate?

HEROES   **Heroes** are members (past or present) who have been successful and made the company what it is today and who serve as role models to present and future members. Most often, heroes achieve their status by acting consistently with the culture or having a strong influence on it. Prominent examples of organizational heroes are Steve Jobs (Apple), Ray Kroc (McDonalds), Walt Disney (Disney), Howard Schultz (Starbucks), Carly Fiorina (Hewlett-Packard), Oprah Winfrey (OWN), and Sheryl Sandberg (Facebook). Heroes are often one of the public faces of an organization. That is, external stakeholders become familiar with them either through the media or through direct contact. Thus, an organization's heroes can serve as a very strategic element of an organization's narrative.

STORIES   **Stories** are narratives that are told and retold to communicate cultural values, important events in the history of the organization, and the consequences of complying or deviating from cultural norms. Stories may be true, hyperbolic, or mythical. Any conversation at work that begins with "remember that time . . . ?" is probably going to be a good example of a story. Another example would be the famous story of Facebook's birth in Mark Zuckerberg's dorm room at Harvard, or the story told by a billionaire of how he and his wife would alter their voices when taking phone calls during the early, lean years of their company—to give the impression that they had multiple employees and departments. These stories reflect perseverance, strong work ethic, creativity, and other values important to their organizations. Stories can reflect harmful, dysfunctional qualities of organizational life, too. Recall Zachary from the introduction to our chapter. As he gained experience working in the start-up company, he was surprised that his coworkers already told stories about the company owner's lack of focus and commitment to projects. From these narratives and his own experiences, Zachary realized that life in this entrepreneurial, start-up organization was already characterized by some negative cultural values that had not been discernable during the interview process.

NORMS   **Norms** are the everyday ways of getting things done successfully within the organization—what is acceptable and unacceptable behavior.

Strategic Communication Mentor: Stories as Strategy

In this blog found at

https://ceplan.com/art-of-the-tell-indentifying-the-heroes-in-your-organizations-story,

nonprofit fund-raising expert Eddie Thompson discusses how he strategically leverages cultural stories in his work.

Why is it important to be able to construct and tell good stories as a form of strategic communication?

What are some of the elements of a good story that can help an organization accomplish its strategic objectives?

Examples of organizational norms might include whether you refer to managers and executives by their first names or formal titles; respecting peoples' "turf" and territory within the workplace (e.g., "we never enter without knocking," or "we never talk to one another's customers"); understanding who has the formal and informal power to help you; knowing how to avoid stepping on the toes of the "good old boys" and the "good old girls"—i.e., those who have been around the longest and have the most influence; and even something as basic as how long of a lunch break you can take. Mike, the college student working in the Thai restaurant in our introduction, violated an organizational norm as well as the owner's cultural norm when he attempted to provide feedback about the business's marketing strategy.

COMMUNICATION   What people talk about, with whom, and how are very revealing aspects of organizational culture. An organization's **communication culture** involves things like the chain of command, the informal and formal communication networks, when face-to-face communication is preferred over technologically mediated interactions, and what topics are taboo for discussion and with whom. In Kim's work with the Department of Defense, we saw that chain of command is very influential on communication. When people in power talk (or email or text), their subordinates listen and act. Kim and her coworkers follow a strict policy articulated by the government that regulates all aspects of communication when they work from home (known as the "telework agreement"), including how long they take to respond to a teammate's message, how to secure information, and what communication technologies to use for what purposes.

Examining an organization for these eight elements can give us some insight into the nature and strength of its culture. In practice, identifying cultural elements like values, heroes, stories, and communication can help to identify aspects of the culture that are weak or missing and provide direction on what areas of communication and development the organization should be focusing on to enhance its effectiveness.

The research on organizational culture also provides some guidance for strategically building successful communication cultures. For example, Peters and Waterman's (1982) study of excellent organizations revealed they tend to be characterized by:

1. A preference for action rather than an overabundance of planning and discussing. In other words, excellent cultures just do it!
2. A focus on customers and clients.
3. Empowered employees who are trusted to make decisions, take risks, and be creative.
4. Positive, open, friendly relationships among management and employees.
5. A clear understanding of and emphasis on the organization's core values.
6. A focus on what the organization does best, without becoming distracted by unrealistic or irrelevant new ideas.
7. Simple structure.
8. Similar members who share dedication to the goals of the organization, but enough diversity among employees to be able to innovate and try new things.

This line of thinking suggests that strong organizational cultures with these features are best-suited for strategic communication. They are in a position, thanks to their structure, leadership style, hiring practices, values, goals, and objectives, to place their focus on strategically communicating in ways that will support their mission.

2.4 TYING IT ALL TOGETHER: ORGANIZATIONAL FEATURES AND THEIR RELATIONSHIP TO COMMUNICATION

In this chapter, we have examined the meaning of organization and explored the roles of organizational and strategic communication in organizing. We have discussed three primary types of organizations and considered how organization type influences internal and external communication strategy and action. Because within each broad type of organization there are many unique examples, we have further clarified the kinds of organizational features that affect communication: structural and cultural characteristics. After reading chapters 1 and 2, one thing should be clear to you—organizing is a dynamic, increasingly challenging activity that requires goal setting, strategy, flexibility, and adaptation by organizational members in order to be successful. The nature of an organization—its type, structure, people, and culture—are both influenced by and highly influential on the nature of its communication. One helpful framework for understanding this rather abstract idea is the theory of structuration advanced by Anthony Giddens (1979). Structuration theory suggests that the nature of organizing and organizational communication is constituted by the actions and interactions of members. To ensure the effectiveness and efficiency of member behavior, organizations need structures such as rules, resources, standards and criteria, feedback processes, leadership, technology, space, and so on. But if, in the course of interaction and organizing, these structures need to be adapted or changed to meet the needs of an organization attempting to strategically accomplish its goals, then these adaptions must be allowed to occur. Organizational communication scholars Eisenberg, Trethewey, LeGreco, and Goodall (2017) refer to this as an organization's ability to balance creativity (practices critical for strategic communication such as innovation, introspection, and willingness to change) and constraints (often-necessary obstacles to strategic communication such as budgetary limitations, deadlines, and rules). Further chapters in this book will address just how organizations do that in their efforts to create strategic messages that advance their missions.

CHAPTER 2 REVIEW

Questions for Critical Thinking and Discussion

1. Select an organization you are or have been a part of. Analyze it in terms of the facets of organizational structure discussed in this chapter. For example, is its vertical hierarchy tall or flat?

2. How do organizational heroes influence the nature of communication and communication strategy within an organization? Explain your answer and be as specific as possible, using examples.

3. Based on what you learned about the three broad types of organizational types discussed in this chapter, which type would you most prefer working for? Why?

4. As a new member, what are some ways you might go about learning the characteristics of an organization's culture?

5. Do you perform better when rules, policies, procedures, and processes are clearly and rigidly defined? Or do you prefer a less formalized environment? Why? Explain your answer.

Key Terms

artifacts: tangible, physical features of the organization.

bureaucratic organization: a unique organizing structure typically used in very large, multiunit systems and the focus of sociologist Max Weber's theory of bureaucratic organizations.

charismatic authority: a form of organizational power that is based on a manager or leader's communication style, personality, and ability to relate on an interpersonal level to those around him or her.

communication culture: what people within an organization talk about, with whom, and how.

contingencies: unexpected but possible deviations from standard operating procedures.

corporate social responsibility: self-regulating business model that helps a company be *socially* accountable to itself, its stakeholders, and the public.

for-profit organization: an organization designed for the primary purpose of generating a profit for the owner or owners of the entity.

government: the organizing means through which a community, state, or country is organized and regulated.

heroes: members (past or present) who have been successful and made an organization what it is presently, and who serve as role models to present and future members.

metaphors: words or phrases used within the organization to define something abstract in terms of something more familiar to members.

nonprofit organization: an organization that exists to promote a particular cause; advocate a viewpoint; or advance a political, social, or philanthropic mission.

norms: the everyday ways of getting things done successfully within the organization; what is acceptable and unacceptable behavior.

organization: a communicative, social enterprise with shared goals that is interdependently linked with its external environment.

organizational culture: the specific set of artifacts, values, and assumptions that emerge from the interactions of organizational members.

rational-legal authority: a form of organizational authority derived from rules, laws, and norms; the basis for management and leadership in bureaucratic organizations such as government.

rituals: traditional activities that highlight what the organization considers to be important.

stories: narratives that are told and retold to communicate cultural values, important events in the history of the organization, and the consequences of complying or deviating from cultural norms.

traditional authority: a form of organizational power based on an individual's title or position in the hierarchy that may or may not reflect his or her actual talents and abilities.

values: the more or less shared set of beliefs about appropriate behavior, the organization's goals, and the ideals that the organization collectively views as important.

vertical hierarchy: the height of an organization's structure. More top-down, or vertical, hierarchies have a number of layers of management between front-line employees and leaders at the top level. "Shorter" or "flatter" hierarchies have fewer levels.

Further Readings and Resources

Birkinshaw, J., and S. Heywood. 2010, May. "Putting Organizational Complexity in Its Place." *McKinsey.* www.mckinsey.com/business-functions/organization/our-insights/putting-organizational-complexity-in-its-place.

Denning, S. 2011, July 23. "How Do You Change an Organizational Culture?" *Forbes.* www.forbes.com/sites/stevedenning/2011/07/23/how-do-you-change-an-organizational-culture/#7c198da439dc.

Green, E. 2013, December 19. "Why It Can Be Tough to Work for the Government." *The Atlantic.* www.theatlantic.com/politics/archive/2013/12/why-it-can-be-tough-to-work-for-the-government/282497/.

Hamm, J. 2006, May. "The Five Messages Leaders Must Manage." *Harvard Business Review.* https://hbr.org/2006/05/the-five-messages-leaders-must-manage.

Morgan, J. 2015, July 5. "The 5 Types of Organizational Structures." *Forbes.* www.forbes.com/sites/jacobmorgan/2015/07/06/the-5-types-of-organizational-structures-part-1-the-hierarchy/#12b358245252.

Teegarden, P. H., D. R. Hinden, and P. Sturm. 2010. *The Nonprofit Organizational Culture Guide: Revealing the Hidden Truths That Impact Performance.* San Francisco: Jossey-Bass.

Viki, T. 2017, August 8. "The 10 Characteristics of a Future-Facing Company." *Forbes.* www.forbes.com/sites/tendayiviki/2017/08/08/the-10-characteristics-of-a-future-facing-company/#5e0d1de418b5.

Watkins, M. D. 2013, May 15. "What Is Organizational Culture? And Why Should We Care?" *Harvard Business Review.* https://hbr.org/2013/05/what-is-organizational-culture.

References

Berfield, S. 2013, October 11. "Where Wal-Mart Isn't: Four Countries the Retailer Can't Conquer." *Bloomberg.* www.bloomberg.com/news/articles/2013–10–10/where-wal-mart-isnt-four-countries-the-retailer-cant-conquer.

Eisenberg, E. M., A. Tretheway, M. LeGreco, and H. L. Goodall. 2017. *Organizational Communication: Balancing Creativity and Constraint,* 8th ed. Boston: Bedford St. Martin's.

Galbraith, J. R. 1973. *Designing Complex Organizations.* Redding, MA: Addison-Wesley.

Giddens, Anthony. 1979. *Central Problems in Social Theory: Action, Structure, and Contradiction in Social Analysis.* Berkeley: University of California Press.

Jablin, F. M. 1987. "Formal Organizational Structure." In *Handbook of Organizational Communication: An Interdisciplinary Perspective,* edited by F. M. Jablin, L. L. Putnam, K. H. Roberts, and L. W. Porter, 389–419. Newbury Park, CA: Sage.

Keyton, J. 2011. *Communication and Organizational Culture,* 2nd ed. Thousand Oaks, CA: Sage.

Landler, M., and M. Barbaro. 2006, August 2. "Wal-Mart Finds Its Formula Doesn't Fit Every Culture." *New York Times.* www.nytimes.com/2006/08/02/business/worldbusiness/02walmart.html?mcubz=0.

McPhee, R. D., and M. S. Poole. 2001. "Organizational Structures and Configurations." In *The New Handbook of Organizational Communication,* edited by F. M. Jablin and L. L. Putnam, 503–43. Newbury Park, CA: Sage.

Miller, K. 2015. *Organizational Communication: Approaches and Processes.* Boston: Cengage.

Mintzberg, H. 1980. "Structure in 5s: A Synthesis of the Research on Organizational Design." *Management Science* 26, no. 3: 322–41.

Oldham, G. R., and R. J. Hackman. 1981. "Relationships between Organizational Structure and Employee Reactions: Comparing Alternative Frameworks." *Administrative Science Quarterly* 26, no. 1: 66–83.

Peters, T. J., and R. J. Waterman. 1982. *In Search of Excellence.* New York: Harper and Row.

Philanthropy News Digest. 2014, March 12. "Dick's Sporting Goods Foundation Launches $25 Million Youth Sports Initiative." http://philanthropynewsdigest.org/news/dick-s-sporting-goods-foundation-launches-25-million-youth-sports-initiative.

Porter, L. W., and E. E. Lawler. 1964. "The Effects of Tall versus Flat Organizational Structures on Managerial Job Satisfaction." *Personnel Psychology* 17: 135–48.

Post, J. 2017, April 3. "What Is Corporate Social Responsibility?" *Business News Daily.* www.businessnewsdaily.com/4679-corporate-social-responsibility.html.

Ross, S., and J. H. Waldeck. 2016. "White Shirts, Blue Shirts." In *Consulting That Matters: A Handbook for Scholars and Prac-titioners,* edited by J. H. Waldeck and D. R. Seibold, 319–30. New York: Peter Lang.

Russell, J. 2016, April 15. "Look at How Many Pages Are in the Federal Tax Code." *Washington Examiner.* www.washington examiner.com/look-at-how-many-pages-are-in-the-federal-tax-code/article/2563032.

Schein, E. H. 2004. *Organizational Culture and Leadership,* 3rd ed. San Francisco: Jossey-Bass.

United States Office of Personnel Management. 2013, March. "Common Characteristics of the Government." www.opm.gov/policy-data-oversight/data-analysis-documentation/federal-employment-reports/common-characteristics-of-the-government/common-characteristics-of-the-government-2012.pdf.

Weber, M. 1947. *The Theory of Social and Economic Organization.* Edited by T. Parsons. Translated by A. M. Henderson and T. Parsons. New York: Free Press.

Yahoo! Finance. 2019. "Dick's Sporting Goods." https://finance.yahoo.com/quote/DKS/financials?p = DKS.

Mission Statements, Organizational Identity and Image, and Branding

CHAPTER CONTENTS

3.1 Mission Statements and Their Role in Strategic Communication Campaigns 68
    3.1.1 The Benefits of a Good Mission Statement 70
    3.1.2 Six Principles of Effective Mission Statements 72

3.2 How the Organization Sees Itself and How It Is Seen: Organizational Identity and Image 77
    3.2.1 The Distinctions between Organizational Identity and Image 78
    3.2.2 Influencing Organizational Image and Identity: The Role of Public Relations and Workplace Structure 80

3.3 Communicating the Organization's Identity: Organizational Branding 81
    3.3.1 Branding and Visibility, Memorability, and Credibility 82
    3.3.2 Branding: Nonprofits and Governmental Organizations 82
    3.3.3 How to Build Your Brand: The IDEA Framework 83

3.4 Tying It All Together: How Mission Statements, Corporate Culture, Identity, Image, and Branding Can Be Used to Evaluate Strategic Communication 87

LEARNING OBJECTIVES

After reading this chapter, you should be able to do the following:
- ▶ Describe the benefits of mission statements.
- ▶ Identify the six principles of writing effective mission statements.
- ▶ Explain the distinctions between organizational image and identity.
- ▶ Analyze how the concepts of brand and branding are used to create credibility and loyalty.
- ▶ Apply the IDEA framework to analyze brand equity.

Sharda is a corporate communications director for a large PR company in her hometown of Seattle, Washington. After years of working long hours and weekends, she needs inspiration and an all-around "break" from work. A lifelong dog lover, Sharda signs up to volunteer for a nonprofit dog rescue organization. The organization has only been established for a year. The founder, after learning about Sharda's skill set and career, asks Sharda to run the group's website and social media accounts. Sharda, thinking this will be an easy task, quickly learns that there is a lot of work to be done for the rescue group—the website has no information about the actual organization, just pictures of available dogs for adoption. Before she can even begin to work on these accounts, Sharda asks Martha, the founder and director, to go to lunch. She has one goal for their meeting: to figure out the mission statement of this organization. From there, she is confident she can help the group develop a better online presence that will support its mission and goals.

Dominic has worked in the airline industry for over thirty years. He started out with an entry-level position as a flight attendant for a well-established international airline, and after many years decided to enter the corporate side of this field. He obtained a degree in marketing and after four years of college and internships worked as a data analyst for the same airline where he used to work as a flight attendant. His current position is the strategic campaign manager of this airline, which makes him responsible for directing all advertising and public relations efforts that the airline pursues on its multiple platforms (television, radio, print, and social media). He loves his job and enjoys the challenge of a large and competitive market. Recently, though, the airline has been experiencing a lot of challenges with its public perception. A few days ago, a frustrated flight attendant had a particularly heated argument with a passenger about the passenger's large (and not altogether well-behaved) service dog. The controversial argument, in which the flight attendant said more than a few things out of line with the company's customer service policy and legal requirements regarding service animals, was recorded by several passengers. The resulting video was the fodder for national morning talk shows the next day, and stock in the company dropped significantly. In defense of the service dog and its owner, hundreds of Twitter users have left comments on the airline's posts, and even created a hashtag (#supportdogs) to show their disagreement with the flight attendant's behavior. The incident has also caused instability within the organization—the decision to fire the troublesome flight attendant has not been a universally supported decision by its employees, many of whom have expressed to management that they feel unsupported by the company, who apparently cares more about its public image than ensuring its staff are prepared for such an incident. As the head of strategic campaign messages, this controversy and its fallout—both inside and outside the organization—are Dominic's problem. He needs to come up with a plan to restore the public's faith in the customer-service orientation while reassuring its employees of their worth . . . and he needs to think quickly.

As you learned in chapter 1, part of being a successful communicator is not only being an attentive listener but also having an awareness of oneself. As communicators, we must make a series of choices to encode and deliver the messages we intend for our receivers effectively. We must also continually analyze their feedback and adjust our messaging if necessary. To communicate effectively is to have a continual and reflective awareness of internal and external factors affecting the accuracy of the communication process.

The same is true for organizations and the people who communicate on their behalf. An in-depth understanding of what the organization is, and how its messages are perceived by others, is key to its members communicating strategically and effectively. The purpose of this chapter is to introduce you to the concepts of organizational identity and image and explain how each of these can contribute to strategic communication initiatives for organizations. We will end with a discussion of branding and how organizations strive to communicate their mission and purpose to those outside of it. We begin by discussing the organizational mission statement and its effect on organizational members and outcomes.

3.1 MISSION STATEMENTS AND THEIR ROLE IN STRATEGIC COMMUNICATION CAMPAIGNS

A **mission statement** is a formal, stable declaration of an organization's purpose. The mission statement is formal in that it is officially recognized and sanctioned by the organization; it is stable in that mission statements are not frequently altered. A mission statement describes the central reason your organization exists and serves as a representation of its "voice" to its members and to those external to it (Heath 1994, 22; Leuthesser and Kohli 1997). These declarations can be as short as a few words to a full paragraph, and likewise may be public or private documents (see the box on page 69 for sample mission statements from real for-profit, nonprofit, and governmental organizations). Regardless of its length or the degree to which it is shared with others, every type of organization can and should have a mission statement. A good mission statement gives meaning and purpose to organizational activities. It lays the foundation for how the organization markets itself, distinguishes itself from competitors, and plans its future. It helps to bring together those internal to the organization, uniting them with a common purpose and vision. In such a way, it can motivate and inspire organizational members at all levels.

Sample Mission Statements from Real Organizations

SAMPLE MISSION STATEMENTS OF FOR-PROFIT ORGANIZATIONS

The Walt Disney Company. The mission of the Walt Disney Company is to be one of the world's leading producers and providers of entertainment and information. Using our portfolio of brands to differentiate our content, services, and consumer products, we seek to develop the most creative, innovative, and profitable entertainment experiences and related products in the world.

Alder BioPharmaceuticals Inc. Alder's mission is to help alleviate human suffering by generating better and safer antibody therapeutics through novel technologies.

Kraft Foods Inc. Our mission is to be THE best investment in the industry.

Patagonia. Build the best product, cause no unnecessary harm, use business to inspire, and implement solutions to the environmental crisis.

Arby's. To provide an exceptional dining experience that satisfies our guests' grown-up tastes by being a "Cut-Above" in everything we do.

Tyner Construction Company Inc. Our mission is to provide our employees with an honest and helpful working environment, where every employee, individually and collectively, can dedicate themselves to providing our customers with exceptional workmanship, extraordinary service, and professional integrity. Our commitment to this mission will allow Tyner Construction to become not only a premier construction company, but the premier construction company in western North Carolina.

SAMPLE MISSION STATEMENTS OF NONPROFIT ORGANIZATIONS

TED. Spread ideas.

Best Friends Animal Society. A better world through kindness to animals.

National Parks Conservation Association. To protect and enhance America's National Park System for present and future generations.

Public Broadcasting Service (PBS). To create content that educates, informs, and inspires.

USO lifts the spirits of America's troops and their families.

Wounded Warrior Project. To honor and empower wounded warriors.

SAMPLE MISSION STATEMENTS OF GOVERNMENT ORGANIZATIONS

Buffalo Municipal Housing Authority. To assist our residents in attaining and maintaining a high standard for their quality of life. The Buffalo Municipal Housing Authority will provide services and opportunities associated with affordable, desirable, and secure housing to individuals and families. We will provide customer service, programs, and amenities that are the best possible.

Central Intelligence Agency. Preempt threats and further US national security objectives by collecting intelligence that matters, producing objective all-source analysis, conducting effective covert action as directed by the President, and safeguarding the secrets that help keep our Nation safe.

Federal Highway Administration. To improve mobility on our nation's highways through national leadership, innovation, and program delivery.

Occupational Safety and Health Administration. To assure safe and healthful working conditions for working men and women by setting and enforcing standards and by providing training, outreach, education, and assistance.

Pittsburgh Chamber of Commerce. The mission of the Greater Pittsburgh Chamber of Commerce is to conduct activities and solve problems to create a more competitive business climate for the firms located in this region. Simply stated your Chamber is business and professional people working together to make your community a better place for everyone.

US Army. The US Army's mission is to fight and win our nation's wars by providing prompt, sustained land dominance across the full range of military operations and spectrum of conflict in support of combatant commanders.

3.1.1 The Benefits of a Good Mission Statement

As summarized in an article on mission statements, "Are They Smoke and Mirrors," Bartkus, Glassman, and McAfee (2000) note that a sound mission statement benefits an organization in four primary ways:

1. To communicate the organization's direction and purpose.
2. To provide boundaries for what the organization does and does not do.
3. To help make everyday decisions.
4. To inspire and motivate organizational members.

The benefits of a mission statement, then, give meaning and purpose to the everyday activities of all members of the organization. One of the first jobs an author of this book had was with aerie by American Eagle Outfitters (AEO). Aerie is an extension of the larger AEO retail outfitters that specializes in bras, underwear, and sleepwear for young women ages fifteen to twenty. One of the author's most memorable experiences of this job was the orientation meeting. At this meeting, with six new fresh-faced employees, the store manager explained the mission and brand of aerie. The emphasis on treating every customer with care and tailoring the shopping experience to *her* needs was paramount. Distinct from its competitors, aerie targeted a younger demographic and emphasized making each customer feel comfortable, special, and confident in wearing her aerie clothing. At the time, aerie was new on the market and still establishing itself as a regular stop for mall shoppers. This emphasis on the mission statement, vision, and brand of aerie had an impact on not only your textbook author but on all of the young women who worked at this location during her four years with the company. Each employee considered herself a representative of the brand and was proud to exemplify it in how she treated customers. This was due in large part to the clear, concise mission statement the organization had crafted. Years later, the mission has been adapted to reflect its new focus on responsible modeling practices in its #AerieREAL campaign (no retouching of images of

---

Effective Mission Statement: Aerie by AEO

"aerie is bras, undies, and more for every girl. We want to make our girls feel good about who they are inside and out. It's time to think real. It's time to get real. No retouching. No supermodels. Because the real you is sexy."

---

women in aerie ads) (Krupnick 2014), but the core dedication to making every girl feel special is still present. As this example illustrates, an effective mission statement is capable of guiding the efforts of everyone in an organization, from its corporate office to its retail associates.

To further understand how mission statements function in the overall life of an organization, let's explore Heath's (1994) concept of an organizational voice. As you recall from chapter 1, the study of organizational communication is not only about the communication that happens in organizations, but also how communication helps to create and maintain the organization. As people communicate within and outside the organization, they help to define it and how it exists and is perceived in the world. In this way, an organization exists only through the nonverbal and verbal communication of its members. This is where Heath's concept of **organizational voice** helps us to understand organizational life; the voice of an organization is all of the communication that makes it meaningful to itself and to others. The organization's voice can therefore include the quality of its products, the dedication of its employees, the failure and successes the organization shares, and any beneficial or harmful effect an organization has on its environment. Importantly, an organization's voice is not created or enacted solely by upper management or those who write the company mission statement. Rather, the mission and the organizational voice that it represents are demonstrated (or not demonstrated) by the everyday actions and reactions of its members.

Because an organization's mission statement is so important, the process of creating one can be intimidating and difficult. Suppose you are crafting the mission statement for an organization, as Sharda is in the beginning of this chapter. Where do you start? What information should you include? What is important to say about your organization?

The following four questions are also a good starting place for developing your organization's mission statement (Hull 2013):

1. What do we do as an organization?
2. How do we do it?
3. Who do we do it for?
4. What value do we bring as an organization?

The responses to these four questions should form the basis of your mission statement. Let's revisit the effective mission statement from aerie we mentioned earlier. Can you answer these four questions from reading their mission statement? If the answer is yes, then their mission statement is doing its job to identify the purpose of the organization.

Some general information that could be provided in this statement includes: (1) the people you intend to serve; (2) your central product or products; (3) your geographic domain; (4) expressions of growth, innovation, and/or profit; and (5) key elements of the organization's values, philosophy, and desired image. Although some may argue that a mission statement needs to cover all of these bases (see Pearce and David 1987), we contend that you should select one or two of these foci in developing your mission statement. How the mission statement is ultimately framed is up to the organization. The same organization could have a mission statement based on profit, customers, or its impact on the environment: the focal point of the mission statement is an important decision.

3.1.2 Six Principles of Effective Mission Statements

Management scholar Romauld Stone (1996) offered the characteristics of an effective mission statement. This list, which has been echoed in other literature on the topic, remains valid in today's digital, interdisciplinary, and dynamic organizational environment.

1. **Keep it short.** A company's mission statement should not be longer than fifteen to twenty words. In compiling a list of fifty mission statements from top nonprofit organizations, web source TopNonprofits.com found that mission statements on average were just 15.3 words, with some mission statements as short as two words! Remember that you want people both internal and external to the organization to remember this statement—this will be easier if the statement is short and to the point.

   If you cannot condense the company purpose to a brief fifteen- to twenty-word statement, consider a shorter **mission tagline** to accompany the formal mission statement. Consider the following mission statement and accompanying tagline from the Estee Lauder Company, a skin care, cosmetic, and fragrance company.

   > *Mission Statement:* The guiding vision of The Estee Lauder Companies is "Bringing the best to everyone we touch." By "The best," we mean the best products, the best people, and the best ideas. These three pillars have been the hallmarks of our Company since it was founded by Mrs. Estee Lauder in 1946. They remain the foundation upon which we continue to build our success today.
   > *Mission Tagline:* "Bringing the best to everyone we touch."

The mission statement identifies what makes Estee Lauder's products unique and gives a sense of the history of the company; the accompanying tagline is more of a mantra for the company's nearly fifty thousand employees.

2. **Be transparent.** Be sure to avoid clichés, buzzwords, and jargon. Anyone should be able to read your mission statement and understand your organization's purpose. Clarity is important for internal audiences as well. When employees perceive a mission statement as being clear, they are more likely to perceive it as significant or meaningful to their work (Desmidt 2016). Consider the following mission statement from Zenefits, a cloud-based human resources software program: "To help businesses thrive by creating a complete HR platform that empowers employees and manages change." In one sentence, Zenefits conveys its purpose and whom it serves. There is no need to discuss the complex mechanisms that allow it do so, or the ways in which a company might sign up to use it—the mission statement contains only the information that is necessary without jargon. One way to assess the clarity of a mission statement is to subject it to a readability assessment, which is available in most writing software programs (see the related Strategic Communication Mentor box in this chapter, Conducting a Readability Assessment).

   In addition to being clear, the mission statement should also be transparent and visible to its target audiences. For members of an organization to remember and reference the mission statement in their daily work, the organization must emphasize its importance (Desmidt, Prinzie, and Heene 2008). Upper-level administrators and management in organizations should make sure that the mission statement and its importance are clearly communicated to new and even longtime members.

   For external audiences, online webpages are a cost effective, easy means of maintaining relationships with stakeholders and others involved in the organization, and organizations should take advantage of this platform as a means of presenting themselves to the world. After all, the mission statement available online may very well serve as the "digital handshake" that introduces the organization to new members, donors, and supporters (Craig, Ngondo, and Flynn 2016, 693). As argued by Bartkus, Glassman, and McAfee (2000), a mission statement should communicate a description of the organization that allows current and future members "to determine whether they want to be involved with it" (27). By having a clear mission statement, an organization is more likely to have more interest from people who would like to be a part of it. Think of the implications for a nonprofit organization dependent on donations and volunteer help! Thus, the importance of a clearly written and clearly presented mission statement cannot be understated.

3. **Be specific to your organization.** A mission statement should reflect the values, shared history, and other indicators of an organization's culture (Campbell and Nash 1992). As president of brand consultant company Taylor Brand Company, David Taylor (2011) advises, if you can switch your organization's name with another in the same industry in

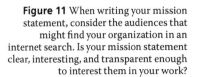

Figure 11 When writing your mission statement, consider the audiences that might find your organization in an internet search. Is your mission statement clear, interesting, and transparent enough to interest them in your work?

Strategic Communication Mentor: Conducting a Readability Assessment

As we discuss in the tips for writing an effective mission statement, it is important to write your organization's mission statement without jargon and at an appropriate reading level. But what is an appropriate reading level, and how can you really assess your mission statement to make sure it isn't too difficult to comprehend? After all, we tend to have a bias in thinking that our own writing is clear.

Fortunately, the popular writing software program Microsoft Word has a quick and easy readability formula that you can use to assess the clarity of your mission statement. Following the steps below, we will assess the readability of a mission statement of an organization in which you are a stakeholder: your academic institution.

To try it, first find the mission statement of your academic institution online. Most institutions will have this information easily accessible on their web page, or easily searchable from the school's home page.

Once you have identified the mission statement, do the following:

1. Paste this mission statement into a blank Microsoft Word document.
2. Check the spelling and grammar of the document using the Tools function.
3. When the spelling and grammar check is complete, a window will open that displays information including word count, characters, and other information. At the bottom, you should see a Flesch-Kincaid reading level displayed (if not, you can easily troubleshoot online or in Word's Help menu to figure out how to get these numbers to be displayed).

Note that this number rates text on a US school grade level. For example, a score of 7.0 means that a seventh grader can understand the document. You should aim for a score of approximately 7.0 to 8.0.

What was the reading level of your institution's mission statement?

How do you think this reading level could affect your institution? Who might be important audiences to consider in evaluating academic mission statements for their readability?

your mission statement and it still makes sense, you do not have a compelling mission statement. In other words, if your competitors could use the exact same statement to describe what they do, your mission statement needs work.

4. **Consider your audience.** Who will ultimately be reading your mission statement should be a factor in determining its content, tone, and length. The extent to which stakeholders are included in the development of the mission statement has an impact on its effectiveness (Bart and Tabone 2000). For example, Sebastian Desmidt's research on the value of mission statements, "Looking for the Value in Mission Statements" (2016) found that employee's perceptions of the quality of organizational mission statements had much to do with how well the statement aligned with their own goals and values; this perception, in turn, affected employee's intent to actually carry out the mission statement in their own daily work. Participants in the study, who were members at all levels of a Belgian public organization, also perceived the mission statement more positively when they believed their superiors acted in accordance with it and "practiced what they preached." In seeking a diversity of opinions and feedback on the mission statement, the organization has a better opportunity to see what is critically important to all of its stakeholders versus in just one small group or groups. Who these stakeholders are will depend on the organization; in some cases, it may be a board of directors, customers, or investors who are asked to contribute to the mission statement. In any case, an organization's mission statement should be developed with the individuals who are a part of its everyday functioning in mind (Bart and Tabone 2000).

   Take for instance IBM's reformulation of its mission statement in 2003, as part of a comprehensive, top-to-bottom review of the organization and its future. Rather than dictating the values and mission of the organization from the top down, IBM held a seventy-two-hour online "values jam" for its 319,000 members. The result of this interactive discussion was a set of three core values that the organization continues to use as its driving mission today (see www.ibm.com/ibm/values/us/). By inviting all of its members to express what they believe the organization valued, IBM communicated to its employees that their voices mattered. It was a transformational (and needed) moment in the company's history, which has been credited by some to be its saving grace in a competitive technological environment that, until that moment, had been leaving IBM behind (Bower 2012).

5. **Update when necessary.** Although a mission statement should be a relatively enduring mantra for an organization, it should be revisited regularly to ensure it is current and still reflects the purpose and goals of the company. In certain industries—technology, health care, and education,

to name a few—change is constant. Does your organization's mission statement reflect what is currently important? Has your organization changed significantly since the mission statement was written?

6. **Think (and write) positively!** A mission statement should be encouraging and inspiring. It should not be boring, mundane, or routine (see figure 12). If you are an internal member of the organization, reading the mission statement should invoke a sense of pride, identity, and motivation. For external members, the mission statement should evoke the sense that the organization is worth their time, support, and investment. As Stone (1996) writes, a clear and concise mission statement is more able to achieve positive reactions than one that drags on. Consider the mission statement of Ford Motor Company: "We go further to make our cars better, our employees happier, and our planet a better place to be." This mission statement is short, clear (and transparent—it is easily accessed on the company's website), value-driven, inclusive, and inspiring.

In summary, a good mission statement should read like a strategy. It should be succinct, clear, inspiring, and continually revisited. The shorter a mission statement is and the more clearly it is communicated to employees, the more helpful and practical it actually can be. A mission statement should in some way touch on what the organization does for its customers, employees, organizational leaders, communities, and any other person or persons that come in contact with it, so it should be developed with and by its various stakeholders. If you are not responsible for writing an organization's mission statement, then these principles can be used to evaluate or improve existing statements. Perhaps you are in a similar position as Dominic in the opening of our chapter and need to help a company get back on track. Visiting and evaluating the mission statement is a good first step in communicating strategically on behalf of an organization.

A clear, purposeful mission statement provides organizational leaders and their employees with a framework for action. Every move that the organization makes should be evaluated in accordance with its mission statement. It is also helpful for those outside the organization; potential donors, investors, volunteers, employees, and students will look to the mission statement to understand the organization and how it compares to its competition. For nonprofit organizations, the mission statement has a somewhat weightier purpose in its legal implications; a nonprofit that does not execute its stated mission could lose funding or its tax exempt status.

An organization's mission statement forms the foundation from which all messaging and future strategic plans should emerge. In the next section, we discuss two more characteristics of organizations that might drastically affect how and why they pursue strategic communication campaigns: organizational identity and image.

Figure 12 How NOT to write a mission statement.

Strategic Communication Mentor: Hometown Mission Statements

Did you know that most towns and cities have a mission statement? Using your favorite internet search engine (e.g., Google) see if you can find yours!

If you can't find yours, use the city of Orange, California, as an example: http://www.cityoforange.org/177/Strategic-Plan

Once you have a city mission statement to read, answer the following questions:

1. How does the mission statement "stack up" against the criteria for evaluating mission statements we discussed in this chapter? Would you say this is an effective mission statement? Why or why not?
2. How important do you think it is for a city or town to have a mission statement? How might it be useful, and who might it be useful to?

3.2 HOW THE ORGANIZATION SEES ITSELF AND HOW IT IS SEEN: ORGANIZATIONAL IDENTITY AND IMAGE

Mission statements are integral to organizational functioning for a very important reason: they connect the organization's internal culture with its external environment (Hatch and Schultz 1997). Specifically, a mission statement reflects and influences two key aspects of how organizations communicate and

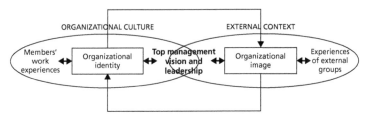

Figure 13 The Relationship of Organizational Identity and Image.

exist in the world around them: organizational identity and organizational image. As can be seen in figure 13, the concepts of organizational identity and culture are related yet distinct factors that affect an organization's functioning. In the next few sections, we define each in more detail and discuss why these factors are important to understand and examine from a strategic communication perspective.

3.2.1 The Distinctions between Organizational Identity and Image

You might recognize a familiar term in figure 13—organizational culture. As we discussed in chapter 2, an organization's culture is composed of the values, assumptions, and rituals emerging from interactions among organizational members. This culture is influenced by upper level managers and leaders as well as by an organization's everyday employees, as indicated in figure 13. Embedded in this overall organizational culture is its **organizational identity,** or what members perceive, think, and feel about the organization. It is the collective, commonly shared understanding of the organization's values and characteristics (Albert and Whetten 1985; Hatch and Schultz 1997). This includes those factors that are central, enduring, and distinctive about an organization (Albert and Whetten 1985). In other words, what events have framed the history of the organization (i.e., its central attributes)? What characteristics are deeply embedded in the organization (i.e., its enduring attributes)? Finally, what sets this organization apart from organizations like it (i.e., its distinctive attributes)? The answers to these questions form a narrative of "who we are" among its employees—this is the organization's identity. As a part of the culture, identity therefore also emerges from its employees and their communication with one another and the organization.

Alternatively, **organizational image** is the way that the organization is viewed and perceived by external audiences. It reflects the organizational communication practices that occur within it, but also the carefully constructed presentation of the organization that it projects outwardly in its marketing and public relations efforts. An organization's image is influenced by not only these polished, refined, and tested messages (perhaps those delivered by spokespersons or

Figure 14 How an organization's employees feel about going to work will ultimately affect how customers perceive the organization. Has your attitude toward an organization ever been affected by your sense of how happy the employees are to work there?

CEOs) but also by the everyday interactions its members have with those who encounter it. Have you ever had a negative experience with an employee that forever affected your perception of an organization? Perhaps you were not greeted by a sales associate in a retail store and did not feel welcome, or a ticket agent was rude as you sought help for your missed flight. Although apathetic or rude employees might not be typical of the organization, their actions in the moment can have a very strong and lasting impact on customers. This is the reason customer reviews are so influential in the lives of restaurants, entertainment, and retail companies. The organizational image is a fluid, ever-changing construct that is influenced by every member who is a part of it.

As we see in figure 13, organizational image is also influenced by and influences organizational identity. Have you ever worked for an organization that you know is perceived negatively by external members? Perhaps it is a "big box" organization known to have less-than-ideal conditions for its workers overseas, or perhaps its product is not well made or is contributing negatively in some way to the well-being of its consumers. These negative outside perceptions affected how you felt about working there, right? It can be hard to take pride in your work when you receive a lot of negative messages about your employer. In fact, most employees in such a situation would either have to practice indifference (e.g., "They give me a paycheck, that is all I care about!") or develop their own set of rationalizations for the employer (e.g., "They actually are a better company than people think") even to continue to go to work. On the other hand, it is easier to be excited about and motivated by your work when everyone you talk to about it is supportive ("I love that brand!" "I hear that is a great company to work for"). This is the interconnectedness of organizational identity and image; although they represent the internal and external perceptions of an organization, they are inextricably linked.

Communication from the top management and leadership, such as the mission statements discussed previously in this chapter, foster this mutual

influence. A mission statement is a written extension of an organization's identity (and therefore culture), and so influences the image it has in the eyes of
external audiences. Other facets of communication from an organization's top
management, such as how it treats its employees and structures decision-
making, are clearly part of both organizational culture and organizational
image. Organizations that treat their employees well become known as "good"
organizations to work for.

3.2.2 Influencing Organizational Image and Identity: The Role of Public Relations and Workplace Structure

Organizational image is different from identity, however, in the sense that it
can be manipulated by its internal members (Hatch and Schultz 1997) and is
more fleeting and easily affected. A negative image, for instance, is viewed as
something that should and can be rectified. In fact, many organizations employ
full-time members to manage its public perception; this is the role of **public
relations** in strategic communication. Public relations refers to the professional maintenance of a favorable public image. Although public relations professionals are continually working to establish favorable relationships and perceptions with external member of organizations, we tend to see their work
more when something goes wrong. In fact, when an organization has a negative
public image, it is the job of public relations personnel to correct it.

Of course, in addition to being a reactive process, public relations professionals seek to proactively maintain a positive image. Those working in public relations write press releases, contact media, and organize community-centered
programs and events to promote the idea that an organization is involved and
dedicated to its clientele. Further, the role of public relations personnel continues to become more interdisciplinary as technology and social media influence
how organizations are perceived and interact with external members. Consider
Dominic's dilemma at the beginning of this chapter. The internal and external
crises he is facing in the fallout of the #supportdogs incident is something that
needs to be addressed from multiple perspectives beyond public relations,
including management, human resources, and crisis communication.

In an in-depth examination of how natural foods retailer Whole Foods
presents its image via various online platforms, public relations scholar Dawn
Gilpin (2010) found two exemplary practices that we can learn from. First, the
retailer uses a wide variety of platforms (e.g., press releases, Twitter, and blogs).
Second, the messages were clearly differentiated in their language and intended
impact on organizational image, depending on the channel being employed.
That is, although Whole Foods is determined to have a strong central image,
there appear to be clear themes across each channel used in their public relations strategy. For instance, news releases are used to address conflicts or relevant news stories affecting the company. The blog space is used almost exclu-

sively to deliver recipe and product-based information. Even further, Twitter is used to interact with customers and had a noticeably less formal tone (e.g., the use of acronyms).

Although organizational identity cannot be manipulated in the same way as image, organizations do exert energy in fostering positive identity perceptions among their members. In fact, some organizations take a lot of pride in the work they do to achieve a positive workplace identity. The multinational tech giant Google has become well known for its creativity-encouraging, collaborative, innovative "open office plans." Treadmill desks, basketball courts, nap pods, and video game rooms are regular sights in Google's international offices. Why? To foster a workplace culture of creativity, and to have happy, motivated, and more loyal employees. In an interview with a digital architecture and design magazine, Stefan Camenzind, the executive director of Evolution Design Ltd., a Swiss architectural firm responsible for many of Google's international offices, summarized Google's approach: "Google has such a strong company culture, which is all about open communication and collaboration, creativity and innovation, food and fun. Once you are designing the 'look and feel,' the offices start having a similar language, which naturally connects them all." In their focus on how employees think, feel, and work, Google is heavily concentrated on organizational culture and identity.

A strategic communication approach to organizations must consider organizational identity and image. As we have indicated with the discussion of negative image and identity, these perceptions might be the reason that strategic communication campaigns are needed. Maintaining the loyalty of these members often involves maintaining identity and image, the direct reflections of how those internal and external to the organization perceive it. A campaign, as we discussed in chapter 1, is a systematic and purposeful attempt to influence a target audience. That target audience often includes those external to the organization but can also include those internal to it. As the lines between organizational culture and external environments become more blurred, the potential receivers of an organization's messages increase in number. Organizations must be sure to communicate in ways that are consistent with how an organization views itself and wishes to be viewed. The manifestation of these perceptions, which can and should be used to guide campaign development, often comes in the form of organizational branding.

3.3 COMMUNICATING THE ORGANIZATION'S IDENTITY: ORGANIZATIONAL BRANDING

So far in this chapter we have discussed the internal and external processes of knowing your organization and presenting it to its various stakeholders. We have discussed the importance of mission statements, organizational identity, and organizational image in how an organization functions and presents itself to the outside world. In the next section, we discuss perhaps the most visible aspect of how an organization presents itself: its brand. In many ways, the brand becomes the visual representation of many of the things that we have discussed so far in this chapter. As organizations consider strategic communication approaches, a critical examination of the brand and how it is perceived by relevant audiences is an important first step toward campaign and message development. In the space below, we will unpack many of the terms used in conjunction with brands and branding. We will then discuss a framework for developing your brand as part of the strategic communication planning process.

3.3.1 Branding and Visibility, Memorability, and Credibility

The word "brand" alone most likely brings to mind a few images or organizations. Nike, Apple, Target, McDonalds, and Starbucks are all organizations that have very distinct brands. In fact, just hearing their name most likely calls to mind an image, slogan, or product. A **brand** is a name, term, design, symbol, or other artifact (or a collection of these) used to distinguish an organization from its competitors (Common Language Marketing Dictionary 2018). A brand often includes specific logos, color schemes, fonts, imagery, and even sounds carefully selected to represent the organization (think of the Nike *swoosh* or McDonald's iconic golden arches). Used heavily in business and commercial marketing, **branding** is therefore the process of creating a brand that will distinguish an organization from others.

A brand helps you to create visibility and memorability in competitive markets and to establish credibility. If you have ever been shopping and decided to purchase one item over another because of its label or because you recognized the product's name, you have been influenced by branding. In a world where we have to make dozens, if not hundreds, of decisions each day, isn't it comforting to trust a brand we are familiar with? From our Kellogg's cereal in the morning, to commuting to work in our Subaru, to watching Netflix on our Apple MacBook Air at night, we are continually selecting and interacting with brands. Marketers refer to the quantifiable trends in consumer knowledge and awareness of the brand as **brand awareness,** and they strive to increase it for their brands to drive purchasing and consumer loyalty (Common Language Marketing Dictionary 2018).

3.3.2 Branding: Nonprofits and Governmental Organizations

While the importance of branding seems obvious in the profit sector, you might not associate the concept with nonprofit and governmental organizations. However, all types of organizations can benefit from a consistent, well-respected brand. Nonprofit organizations, for instance, are in constant competition for donations and recognition. According to the National Center for Charitable Statistics, as of 2016 there were over 1.5 million tax-exempt organizations in the United States, including public charities, private foundations, and other types of nonprofit organizations. Further, these organizations received approximately $390.05 billion in 2016, with 72 percent of these funds coming from individual donors (Giving USA 2017). Smaller nonprofits are therefore competing to establish their legitimacy against an environment with multiple competitors. Having a clear brand will help potential donors to remember the "product" of your organization and contribute to the nonprofit's mission.

Perhaps the best illustration of how corporate branding can benefit a nonprofit is the trajectory of the Susan G. Komen Breast Cancer Foundation. Do you know what color ribbon signifies breast cancer awareness? (pink). Do you know what month is breast cancer awareness month? (October). More than likely, you could answer at least one of these questions without hesitation. This is largely attributable to the popularity and near ubiquity of Susan G. Komen's advertising and branding efforts. During the month of October, think of all of the pink products that you see or those with a pink ribbon: from kitchen supplies, to food items, to players in the National Football League wearing pink shoes, it is clear that the month of October is dedicated to raising awareness of breast cancer. In these ways, Susan G. Komen has established itself as a highly recognized brand with a clear purpose. This approach to branding pays off, literally. To date, Susan G. Komen has funded more research than any other nonprofit—over $956 million—second only to the US government, and has invested over $2.9 billion in its research, community health outreach, advocacy, and programs (Susan G. Komen 2018). There is a lesson to be learned here for even the smallest local nonprofit: make your mission clear, partner with organizations that can do more than you can, and brand yourself accordingly. When people are looking to donate money, they take comfort in a recognized, consistent, clear brand (Katz 2018; Michel and Rieunier 2012).

3.3.3 How to Build Your Brand: The IDEA Framework

Ultimately, your brand can be used to do much more than solicit donations and sell t-shirts or mugs with your logo on it. Any type of organization can use its brand identity to drive decisions about the long-term goals and objectives it strives for. Similar to an organization's mission statement, the brand helps to clarify what the organization does and does not do. If undertaking a specific action could threaten the brand image that you currently have, you may not want to pursue it. To use your brand strategically in this way as an organization, you want to achieve a favorable and consistent brand equity. **Brand equity** refers to the overall value of the brand (Common Language Marketing

Dictionary 2018) and is often marked by how widespread the awareness is of the brand, how credible the brand is perceived to be, and how loyal internal and external members are to the brand (Lassar, Mittal, and Sharma 1995).

So what practical branding advice can be given to organizations that want to stay true to their organization's mission and values while considering both their organizational identity and image? Researchers at Harvard University sought to answer that question in a series of structured interviews with seventy-three nonprofit executives, communication directors, consultants, and donors in forty-one organizations. As a result of these conversations, Kylander and Stone (2012) developed the IDEA framework. Originally developed for use in the nonprofit sector, the IDEA framework presents a succinct step-by-step approach to approaching the branding process based on four key principles: integrity, democracy, ethics, and affinity.

INTEGRITY   The **integrity** of the brand is the extent to which the organization's internal identity and external image align with each other as well as with the organization's mission. In this way, the brand integrity of the organization is the "glue" that holds each of the aspects of this chapter together. Kylander and Stone are not referring to integrity in a moral sense with this term, but instead are referring to the strength of the organization in a conceptual sense: "Internally, a brand with high structural integrity connects the mission to the identity of the organization, giving members, staff, volunteers, and trustees a common sense of why the organization does what it does and why it matters in the world. Externally, a brand with high structural integrity captures the mission in its public image and deploys that image in service of its mission at every step of a clearly articulated strategy" (Kylander and Stone 2012, 40). In other words, an organization that is consistent across its mission statement, identity, and image would be said to have a high degree of structural integrity.

DEMOCRACY   The **democracy** of a brand refers to the extent to which the organization trusts its members to communicate their own (similar) understanding of the organization's mission and identity. The stronger the democracy of the brand, the less the organization needs to worry about controlling its image. As noted by Kylander and Stone, the ubiquitous nature of social media has rendered complete control of brand exposure impossible. One way to achieve democracy in the modern media environment is to provide sample images and text that all staff can access and adapt for their own messaging channels and purposes (Kylander and Stone 2012). Another way to create wider participation in the brand's maintenance is to employ **brand ambassadors,** or individuals hired to promote a brand or product publicly. You might be familiar with a number of celebrity brand ambassadors for products ranging from travel credit cards to makeup companies, but brand ambassadors can also be college

The Principles of the IDEA Framework

- Integrity
- Democracy
- Ethics
- Affinity

students like you. Take for instance the "Rep Program" by retail company Pura Vida—which encourages its target audience to become brand ambassadors in exchange for discounted merchandise and a percentage of all sales credited to them (watch video on this program here: www.puravidabracelets.com/pages /pura-vida-reps). By allowing consumers of the product to be a part of the brand and create their own content, Pura Vida is demonstrating what Kylander and Stone (2012) would call high brand democracy.

ETHICS   The **brand ethics** refers to the extent to which the brand portrayed reflects the core values of the organization. Similar to brand integrity, brand ethics concerns the alignment between internal identity and external image but goes further by focusing on the incorporation of core values into the overall branding process. Does the organization ensure that the brand reflects its values and what it believes to be important?

AFFINITY   The **brand affinity** is the extent to which the brand is well liked and respected, particularly as it pertains to working alongside and partnering with other organizations. Organizations with high brand affinity will attract partners and collaborators in part because they promote the brands of their partners as much as they promote their own agenda (Kylander and Stone 2012). Note that this might be more important in the nonprofit sector, where **coalitions** in which multiple organizations work collectively to resolve a common problem are more common (National Council of Nonprofits 2007). For example, a nonprofit organization addressing media literacy among youth would benefit from working with local elementary schools and community centers. In working together these organizations can pool resources and share strengths, but this process is much more effective if the organizations seek to help—and not exploit—one another in the process. A for-profit organization likely would not have a reason to promote or share information on other for-profits; that said, being a "team player" is respected in any sector of organizational life.

Together, the four key principles of the IDEA framework can assist organizational leaders in any sector to assess the strengths and weaknesses in their branding strategy. Brands are not just about revenue, whether it be profits or donations. Rather, branding should be a process in which the mission, values, and identity of the organization are reflected and support a positive organizational image. For global organizations, which may have to change logos or visuals for customization to varying languages and cultures, having a branding process rooted in the IDEA framework can help to ensure consistency despite these cultural adjustments.

An organization's brand is strongest when its organizational identity and image are aligned. These internal and external forces, when in sync, support cohesion across all organizational activities. In fact, the process of rebranding and re-examining mission statements often emerges out of a misalignment between these internal and external perceptions (Kylander and Stone 2012). An organization with a clear brand encourages heightened levels of cohesion among its members and perceptions of credibility and trust from external audiences. This cohesion and trust, as Kylander and Stone (2012) write, lead to "more efficient and focused use of existing resources, and high external trust attracts additional talent, financing, and authority. . . . By leveraging the trust of partners, beneficiaries, and policy makers, an organization can make greater strides toward achieving its mission" (39). Indeed, research by Cheung and Chan (2000) on intentions to donate to international relief organizations indicated that individuals' consideration of their trust in the organization and how well they think the organization can actually address the issue are significant predictors of intention to donate. The perceived ethics and morality of an organization are also significant predictors of intention to donate both money and time to it (Michaelidou, Micevski, and Cadogan 2015). For nonprofit organizations, it is therefore imperative for their campaigns to communicate that they are useful, efficient, ethical, and reliable (Michaelidou, Micevski, and Cadogan 2015).

From a communication perspective, much of the work on branding can be understood to address the credibility of the organization. **Source credibility** refers to the message receiver's perception that the source is competent, trustworthy, and caring (McCroskey and Teven 1999). The outcomes associated with these perceptions of a source are well documented in the literature on communication; research on college professors, advertising, mass media, and organizational relationships all suggest that perceptions of source credibility drastically affect the way in which a message is received and processed (e.g., McCroskey and Teven 1999; Richmond and McCroskey 2000). Research suggests that source credibility even affects our behavior toward religious organizations. According to a study by Horan and Raposo (2013), parishioners' perceptions of Catholic priests' credibility affect their own interest and engagement in church. Much of how organizations communicate to their various publics will be affected by how credible that organization is perceived to be.

Strategic Communication Mentor: Assessing Source Credibility

Instructions: On the scales below, indicate your feelings about your manager (or, if not currently employed, your most recent supervisor). Numbers 1 and 7 indicate a very strong feeling. Numbers 2 and 6 indicate a strong feeling. Numbers 3 and 5 indicate a fairly weak feeling. Number 4 indicates you are undecided.

1. Intelligent 1 2 3 4 5 6 7 Unintelligent*
2. Untrained 1 2 3 4 5 6 7 Trained
3. Cares about me 1 2 3 4 5 6 7 Doesn't care about me*
4. Honest 1 2 3 4 5 6 7 Dishonest*
5. Has my interests at heart 1 2 3 4 5 6 7 Doesn't have my interests at heart*
6. Untrustworthy 1 2 3 4 5 6 7 Trustworthy
7. Inexpert 1 2 3 4 5 6 7 Expert
8. Self-centered 1 2 3 4 5 6 7 Not self-centered
9. Concerned with me 1 2 3 4 5 6 7 Not concerned with me*
10. Honorable 1 2 3 4 5 6 7 Dishonorable*
11. Informed 1 2 3 4 5 6 7 Uninformed*
12. Moral 1 2 3 4 5 6 7 Immoral*
13. Incompetent 1 2 3 4 5 6 7 Competent
14. Unethical 1 2 3 4 5 6 7 Ethical
15. Insensitive 1 2 3 4 5 6 7 Sensitive
16. Bright 1 2 3 4 5 6 7 Stupid*
17. Phony 1 2 3 4 5 6 7 Genuine
18. Not understanding 1 2 3 4 5 6 7 Understanding

SCORING: To compute your scores, add your scores for each item as indicated below. For items with an *, flip the scoring such that:

1 = 7
2 = 6
3 = 5
4 = 4
5 = 3
6 = 2
7 = 1

Competence Factor (1, 2, 7, 11, 13, and 16)_____

Caring/Goodwill Factor (3, 5, 8, 9, 15, and 18)_____

Trustworthiness Factor (4, 6, 10, 12, 14, and 17)_____

Source: McCroskey, J.C., and J.J. Teven. 1999. "Goodwill: A Reexamination of the Construct and Its Measurement." *Communication Monographs* 66, no. 1: 90–103.

REFLECTION:

1. How did answering these questions affect your perception of your manager, if at all?
2. Which of the three components of credibility—competence, caring, or trust—do you think is most important in a manager?
3. How would these questions be different if the source was an entire organization as opposed to an individual manager?

3.4 TYING IT ALL TOGETHER: HOW MISSION STATEMENTS, CORPORATE CULTURE, IDENTITY, IMAGE, AND BRANDING CAN BE USED TO EVALUATE STRATEGIC COMMUNICATION

In this chapter, we have taken a closer look at the internal and external environments that affect how organizations act in and react to the worlds around them. We have expanded our understanding of organizational types and structures offered in chapter 2 by discussing the communication elements that frame an organization's purpose and identity. We have taken an in-depth look at organizational mission statements from profit, not-for-profit, and governmental organizations and discussed how and why mission statements can be so effective for strategic communication campaigns. We have examined the reflexive, interactive constructs of organizational identity and image and how each of these might be manipulated and maintained by the organization to its benefit. We will expand on these ideas in later chapters, where we will discuss the long-term goals that might emerge out of a critical reflection of an organization's current identity and image. Finally, we explored how an organization's branding is most effective when it aligns with its mission statement, identity, and image. The power of a clear, consistent brand for all three major types of organizations should now be evident. You should now have a clear understanding of what a strategic approach to understanding organizations means as well as how complicated and intricate the various facets of organizational communication can be.

CHAPTER 3 REVIEW

Questions for Critical Thinking and Discussion

1. How have you encountered the concept of organizational voice in your own experiences? Is there an organization that you have been a part of that had a distinct voice? How would you describe it, and how was that voice communicated?

2. Consider this quote from Heath (1994): "What we think an organization is, what we perceive it to be, is the result of persons—individual and collective—who enact it" (31). What do you think of this statement? How have you experienced this principle with organizations in your life? To what extent do you agree with Heath's claim about the centrality of communication to how organizations are perceived?

3. Using the box on page 69 as your guide, evaluate a mission statement from each sector (nonprofit, for-profit, and government) using the six tips we outlined for writing effective mission statements. How did each sector compare? What were consistently enacted tips? Were there tips that you did not see enacted?

4. The emphasis on open and creative workspaces, as demonstrated in our discussion of Google's headquarters and international offices, is not universally recognized as being "good for business." For context, read the following *Washington Post* article critiquing these spaces as well as a response to the critique by design website Work Design. After reading each, and in the context of this chapter, what are your thoughts? Do you think organizations should spend this much time and effort on promoting positive cultures and identities among their employees?
Critique: www.washingtonpost.com/postevery thing/wp/2014/12/30/google-got-it-wrong-the-open-office-trend-is-destroying-the-workplace/?utm_term=.85cdb6745a12
Response: https://workdesign.com/2015/01/google-didnt-get-wrong-deeper-look-recent-wapo-piece-open-offices/

5. How could the IDEA framework help Sharda develop a strong brand identity for Kings of Washington? What other advice would you give Sharda based on your reading of this chapter?

Key Terms

brand: a name, term, design, symbol, or other artifact (or a collection of these) used to distinguish an organization from its competitors.

brand affinity: the extent to which the brand is well liked and respected, particularly as it pertains to working alongside and partnering with other organizations.

brand ambassadors: individuals hired to promote a brand or product publicly.

brand awareness: the quantifiable trends in consumer knowledge and awareness of a brand.

brand equity: the overall value of the brand.

brand ethics: the extent to which an organization's portrayal of its brand reflects the core values of the organization.

branding: the process of creating a brand that will distinguish an organization from others.

coalitions: multiple organizations working collectively to resolve a common problem.

democracy: the extent to which the organization trusts its members to communicate their own (similar) understanding of the organization's mission and identity.

integrity: the extent to which the organization's internal identity and external image align with each other as well as with the organization's mission.

mission statement: a formal, stable declaration of an organization's purpose.

mission tagline: a shortened version of the mission statement, which typically accompanies the formal mission statement.

organizational identity: what organizational members collectively perceive, think, and feel about the organization's values and characteristics.

organizational image: the way that the organization is viewed and perceived by external audiences.

organizational voice: all of the communication that makes it meaningful to itself and to others.

public relations: the professional maintenance of a favorable public image.

source credibility: a message receiver's perception that the message source is competent, trustworthy, and caring.

Further Readings and Resources

Chin, A. 2015. "Interview with Evolution Design, the Firm behind Many of Google's Offices." www.designboom.com /design/camenzind-evolution-google-08-06-2015/.

Evans, S. K. 2015. "Defining Distinctiveness: The Connections between Organizational Identity, Competition, and Strategy in Public Radio Organizations." *International Journal of Business Communication* 52, no. 1: 42–67. doi: 10.1177/2329488414560280.

Groza, M. P., and G. L. Gordon. 2016. "The Effects of Nonprofit Brand Personality and Self-Brand Congruity on Brand Relationships." *Marketing Management Journal* 26, no. 2: 117–29.

Kim, L. 2015. "30 Inspiring Billion-Dollar Startup Company Mission Statements." www.inc.com/larry-kim/30-inspiring-billion-dollar-startup-company-mission-statements.html.

Top Nonprofits. 2017. "50 Example Mission Statements." https://topnonprofits.com/examples/nonprofit-mission-statements/.

Wymer, W., H. P. Gross, and B. Helmig. 2016. "Nonprofit Brand Strength: What Is It? How Is It Measured? What Are Its Outcomes?" *International Journal of Voluntary and Nonprofit Organizations* 27, no. 3: 1448–71.

References

Albert, S., and D. A. Whetten. 1985. "Organizational Identity." *Research in Organizational Behavior* 7: 263–95.

Bart, C. K., and J. C. Tabone. 2000. "Mission Statements in Canadian Not-for-Profit Hospitals: Does Process Matter?" *Health Care Management Review* 25, no. 2: 45–63.

Bartkus, B., M. Glassman, and B. McAfee. 2000. "Mission Statements: Are They Smoke and Mirrors?" *Business Horizons* 43, no. 6: 23–28. doi: 10.1016/S0007–6813(00)80018-X.

Bower, J. L. 2012. "Sam Palmisano's Transformation of IBM." *Harvard Business Review.* https://hbr.org/2012/01 /sam-palmisanos-transformation.html.

Campbell, A., and L. L. Nash. 1992. *A Sense of Mission.* Reading, MA: Addison-Wesley.

Cheung, C. K., and C. M. Chan. 2000. "Social-Cognitive Factors of Donating Money to Charity, with Special Attention to an International Relief Organization." *Evaluation and Event Planning* 23, no. 2: 241–53.

Common Language Marketing Dictionary. 2018. https://marketing-dictionary.org.

Craig, C., P. S. Ngondo, and M. A. Flynn. 2016. "How Firm Is Your Digital Handshake? Mission Statements and Transparency." *Public Relations Review* 42, no. 4: 692–94.

Desmidt, S. 2016. "The Relevance of Mission Statements: Analysing the Antecedents of Perceived Message Quality and Its Relationship to Employee Mission Engagement." *Public Management Review* 18, no. 6: 894–917.

Desmidt, S., A. Prinzie, and A. Heene. 2008. "The Level and Determinants of Mission Statement Use: A Questionnaire Survey." *International Journal of Nursing Studies* 45, no. 10: 1433–41.

Gilpin, D. 2010. "Organizational Image Construction in a Fragmented Online Media Environment." *Journal of Public Relations Research* 22, no. 3: 265–87. doi: 10.1080 /10627261003614393.

Giving USA. 2017. "See the Numbers—Giving USA 2017 Infographic." https://givingusa.org/see-the-numbers-giving-usa-2017-infographic/.

Hatch, M., and M. Schultz. 1997. "Relations between Organizational Culture, Identity, and Image." *European Journal of Marketing* 31, no. 5/6: 356–65.

Heath, R. L. 1994. *Management of Corporate Communication: From Interpersonal Contacts to External Affairs.* Hillsdale, NJ: Lawrence Erlbaum.

Horan, S. M., and P. C. Raposo. 2013. "Priest as Teacher I: Understanding Source Credibility." *Journal of Communication and Religion* 36, no. 2: 73–91.

Hull, P. 2013. "Answer 4 Questions to Get a Great Mission Statement." www.forbes.com/sites/patrickhull/2013/01/10/answer-4-questions-to-get-a-great-mission-statement/amp/.

Katz, H. 2018. "The Impact of Familiarity and Perceived Trustworthiness and Influence on Donations to Nonprofits: An Unaided Recall Study." *Journal of Nonprofit and Public Sector Marketing* 30, no. 2: 187–99. doi: 10.1080/10495142.2017.1326874

Krupnick, E. 2014. "Aerie's Unretouched Ads 'Challenge Supermodel Standards' for Young Women." www.huffingtonpost.com/2014/01/17/aerie-unretouched-ads-photos_n_4618139.html.

Kylander, N., and C. Stone,. 2012. "The Role of Brand in the Nonprofit Sector." *Stanford Social Innovation Review.* https://ssir.org/articles/entry/the_role_of_brand_in_the_nonprofit_sector.

Lassar, W., B. Mittal, and A. Sharma. 1995. "Measuring Customer-Based Brand Equity." *Journal of Consumer Marketing* 12, no. 4: 11–19. doi: 10.1108/07363769510095270.

Leuthesser, L., and C. Kohli. 1997. "Corporate Identity: The Role of Mission Statements." *Business Horizons* 40, no. 3: 59–67.

McCroskey, J. C., and J. J. Teven. 1999. "Goodwill: A Reexamination of the Construct and Its Measurement." *Communications Monographs* 66, no. 1: 90–103.

Michaelidou, N., M. Micevski, and J. W. Cadogan. 2015. "An Evaluation of Nonprofit Brand Image: Towards a Better Conceptualization and Measurement." *Journal of Business Research* 68, no 8: 1657–66.

Michel, G., and S. Rieunier. 2012. "Nonprofit Brand Image and Typicality Influences on Charitable Giving." *Journal of Business Research,* 65, no 5: 701–7. doi: 10.1016/j.jbusres.2011.04.002.

National Council of Nonprofits. 2007. "Working in Coalitions." *Center for Lobbying in the Public Interest.* www.councilofnonprofits.org/sites/default/files/documents/07_coalitions.pdf.

Olden, P. C., S. D. Roggenkamp, and R. D. Luke. 2002. "A Post-1990s Assessment of Strategic Hospital Alliances and Their Marketplace Orientations: Time to Refocus." *Health Care Management Review* 27, no. 2: 33–49.

Pearce, J. A., and F. David. 1987. "Corporate Mission Statements: The Bottom Line." *Academy of Management Executive* 1, no. 2: 109–16.

Richmond, V. P., and J. C. McCroskey. 2000. "The Impact of Supervisor and Subordinate Immediacy on Relational and Organizational Outcomes." *Communication Monographs* 67, no. 1: 85–95.

Shocker, A. D., R. K. Srivastava, and R. W. Ruekert. 1994. "Challenges and Opportunities Facing Brand Management: An Introduction to the Special Issue." *Journal of Marketing Research* 31, no. 2: 149–58.

Stone, R. A. 1996. "Mission Statements Revisited." *Advanced Management Journal* 61, no. 1: 31–37.

Susan G. Komen Breast Cancer Foundation. 2018. "About Us." https://ww5.komen.org/AboutUs/AboutUs.html.

Taylor, D. 2011. "On a Mission to Make Mission Statements Relevant to the Brand." *Central Penn Business Journal* 27, no. 39: 17.

Communication
Ethics

CHAPTER CONTENTS

4.1 Defining Ethics and Ethical Communication   94
   4.1.1 The National Communication Association's Ethical
   Credo: A Foundation for Practicing Ethics in Strategic
   Communication Work   95
   4.1.2 What Practitioners Have to Say: Professional Society
   Codes of Ethics   101

4.2 Putting Professional Ethics into Practice   108

4.3 Summarizing Ethical Considerations for Strategic
Communication Practitioners   113

4.4 Tying It All Together: Being an Ethical, Responsible
Communicator Will Help You Accomplish Program Goals   115

LEARNING OBJECTIVES

After reading this chapter, you should be able to do the following:
- ▶ Explain the concept of ethics as they relate to strategic communication.
- ▶ Apply the tenets of established codes of ethics associated with the practice of strategic communication as a means of accomplishing program goals.
- ▶ Create an approach for communicating strategically based on ethical principles.

*Bryan was employed in the marketing department of a medical device manu-
facturer that specialized in assistive breathing apparatuses for people with mus-
cular dystrophy. These devices were made available to people who need them by
prescriptions issued by physicians. Bryan's job function involved creating visual
marketing materials for sales representatives to present to physicians and other
medical practitioners who could prescribe the device. A little over a year ago,
Bryan began to hear rumors within the company of quality control problems
with several devices. He hadn't heard anything official from his company about
defects in any of their products, but rumors continued to swirl until several
weeks later, he learned of a massive recall being issued. A part within the breathing devices was flawed and prone to cracking. The cracks caused leaks in the system and reduced the volume of oxygen the device delivered to the patient. Bryan
was then tasked with creating strategic messaging materials explaining and
educating health care practitioners about the recall. Above all, Bryan's boss told
him that the goal was to maintain the trust of the company's customer base. He
was to do so by being informative, transparent, and sincere. Bryan had a lot of
concerns about his boss's requests. Notably, he was almost certain that the company's leadership knew about the problems long before it issued a recall. Second,
as a professional communicator, Bryan needed to have confidence that his
employer was taking the appropriate steps to correct all quality control problems before he could credibly engage in the work of rebuilding the company's
image and repairing public trust in the company and its products.*

Like all strategic communication professionals, Bryan's work required careful
attention to the ethical dimensions of his messages. Ethics are always important to consider when communicating, but some situations will test your ethical boundaries and your ability to communicate clearly, accurately, and honestly. Of course, some of the most obvious ethical aspects of communication
involve telling the truth, not misleading people with your communication, and
presenting information in understandable ways for your audience so that they
can make well-informed decisions. Consider some high-profile corporate ethics scandals that have made the news:

- In late 2008, stockbroker and investment banker Bernard Madoff admitted
  to turning his investment business into a massive Ponzi scheme (a fraudu-
  lent investment operation that pays returns to investors from their own
  money or money paid into the fund by subsequent investors, rather than
  from any actual profit earned. The Ponzi scheme attracts new investors by
  offering returns other investments cannot guarantee, such as abnormally
  high short-term gains. The perpetuation of the returns that a Ponzi scheme
  promises requires a constantly increasing flow of money from new investors
  to keep the scheme going). He defrauded thousands of investors of about
  $65 billion (Bray 2009).

- A survey of workers on the Deepwater Horizon oil rig in the weeks before it exploded in the Gulf of Mexico in April 2010, indicated that many were concerned about the safety practices and feared reprisals if they reported problems. In the survey, they revealed that drilling took priority over maintenance that could have ensured safety. The explosion killed eleven workers and led to an oil spill that lasted for weeks, killing large numbers of ocean life and damaging local economies (Urbina 2010).
- In 2017, United Airlines security personnel forcibly removed sixty-nine-year-old passenger David Dao from an aircraft after an altercation with a member of the flight crew. Cell phone video footage shows the passenger's head being smacked against an armrest and him ultimately being dragged on his back violently off the aircraft. In an essay on the "biggest business scandals of 2017," *Fortune* noted that public outcry was loud, but United Airlines' response was unsatisfactory: "United CEO Oscar Munoz apologized for the incident in rather sanitized corporate speak, saying 'this is an upsetting event for all of us here at United'—underestimating just how viscerally disturbing the video footage had been, and how dissatisfied fliers were with the airline industry" (Shen 2017). In a second statement widely perceived as even more insensitive than the first, Munoz criticized Mr. Dao harshly as "disruptive and belligerent" (Wattles and Ostrower 2017). Consumer complaints against the industry skyrocketed in response to this incident, and CEO Munoz, who was seeking chairmanship of the board, was denied the new position.

In varied ways, Bryan's hypothetical work situation and the other high-profile real-life examples we just presented all highlight the importance of ethics when communicating internally and externally relative to your job. Ethical lapses by communication professionals lead to a long list of negative outcomes with broad impact. No one wins when individuals choose to communicate or act unethically.

Strategic communication is, as you undoubtedly now understand, a process of influencing an audience. Influence, or persuasion, can be used to enhance people and their communities, but can often be used in unethical ways that may be in one stakeholder's best interests but not the target audience's (Frymier and Nadler 2013). We don't doubt that each reader of this book is an honest person with earnest intentions, but you will likely encounter the kinds of ethical challenges that confront good people every day. This chapter is designed to get you thinking about the kinds of ethical dilemmas you are likely to face in each phase of the strategic communication process we will be discussing in this book. This chapter will provide you with an understanding of what ethics mean relative to organizational and strategic communication, and with an overview of standard acceptable ethics practices for communication professionals. In addition, the content of this chapter will guide you in applying ethical frameworks as you plan, implement, and evaluate strategic campaigns.

4.1 DEFINING ETHICS AND ETHICAL COMMUNICATION

Broadly, the term **ethics** refers to criteria or guidelines for what is right and what is wrong. We use those ethical criteria to guide what to do and what to say in communication situations and to define what constitutes ethical communication. When working on a strategic message project, your ethics are as important, and in some cases even more important, than your skills and knowledge. In the authors' campaign and messaging work on prescription stimulant abuse, financial literacy/debt management, workplace safety in the landscaping and tool-forging industries, nutrition literacy for non-native English speakers, environmental protection and electric vehicles, and other arenas, we learned a lot about issues and industries that were previously unfamiliar to us (and had the opportunity to apply our expertise about strategic communication across a variety of contexts and settings). That knowledge was necessary, but insufficient, for designing and implementing a set of messages that would help us accomplish our goals and those of our key stakeholders. Common to all of these projects and the ones you will encounter, however, was the foundational importance of ethics and doing the right thing. In a chapter on communication consulting in organizations, Keyton noted "ethics are the bedrock of . . . practice and process" (2016, 43). A message campaign that reaches its intended audience with dazzling professional visuals or a fun and engaging social media presence will fail, despite its innovativeness, unless it is ethical in every way.

One of the difficulties of communicating ethically is the reality that truthful, good people operate from different ethical frameworks and may view "right" and "wrong" as arbitrary and subjective labels when the focus of communication is not factual (i.e., when the messaging isn't dealing with verifiable facts). For instance, although research evidence suggests that fear appeals are effective influence strategies in some circumstances, people vary in their beliefs about the ethicality of frightening people (especially vulnerable groups such as previously victimized people, children, or the elderly) into thinking or behaving a certain way. You don't have to be the CEO of United Airlines to face ethical challenges and dilemmas: all professionals, and communication professionals in particular, must be sensitive to the importance of using ethical frameworks to guide their activities and manage the organization's image.

Take a few minutes to complete this Strategic Communication Mentor to begin thinking about the role of ethics in internal and external workplace communication. Then, we will discuss a general framework for ethical communication articulated by the National Communication Association, a scholarly society dedicated to the study of communication across contexts.

Strategic Communication Mentor

www.youtube.com/watch?v=D3YFkecPShw

   As you saw in the video you just watched, regular people in regular jobs face ethical challenges every day.

1. In what ways was the salesman's communication in the first scenario unethical? Who could be harmed by his response to the unhappy customer?
2. Rewrite the salesperson's response to the angry client based on the lessons his boss reminded him of in the second half of the video.

4.1.1 The National Communication Association's Ethical Credo: A Foundation for Practicing Ethics in Strategic Communication Work

The National Communication Association (NCA) is the primary professional association for scholars, teachers, and practitioners of communication in the United States. NCA (known as SCA, or the Speech Communication Association, prior to 1997) serves its members and the communication field by publishing and disseminating scholarship and creative work relevant to human communication, hosting an annual convention and other professional development meetings, advocating for public policy related to communication and expression, and promoting ethical communication in all of its initiatives. In 1984, an informal group of association members interested in ethics formed a sanctioned unit within SCA that hosted conferences, promoted teaching and scholarship related to ethics, and ultimately created a formal document on ethics and communication. This "Credo for Ethical Communication" (see the box on page 100) is a broad statement that applies to "all forms and settings of communication" and functions "as a social contract" for ethical and fair communication "in a democratic society" (Smitter 2004, 2). This document serves as a general foundation for thinking about ethical communication and suggests specific ethical considerations for strategic communication professionals.

The framework established in NCA's "Credo" begins by pointing out that "questions of right and wrong arise whenever people communicate." Although you may believe that "right and wrong" can be arbitrary distinctions, the ability to determine what is right and wrong is critical to competent thinking, planning, communicating, and decision making; forming sound relationships; and building communities. What are the basic values underlying the National Communication Association's statement on ethics that are particularly relevant to providing strategic organizational communicators with direction on how to handle the inevitable questions of right and wrong?

First, and perhaps most obviously, *communication must rely on accurate and truthful information.* Accuracy and truth relate to facts, or statements that are verifiably right or wrong, true or false. However, sometimes, what is true or false is not exactly black and white, and these situations require transparency. For example, if you are responsible for developing a workplace wellness campaign, you would have access to a large body of valid and reliable research literature documenting the benefits of exercise for a healthy life characterized by physical fitness and lowered stress. You would also have access to other sources, such as social media, where so-called (and often self-identified) experts (often with financial interests in the products and programs they endorse) make all kinds of recommendations about specific exercise programs backed by little or no evidence beyond their own questionable source credibility. Ethically, you are responsible for recommending what the most credible, valid, and reliable evidence suggests will be effective, and for explaining the evidence in a fashion that will be understandable to your audience. If you refer to other approaches, you are responsible for ensuring that your audience understands that they have not undergone the same rigorous screening or testing as those backed by scientific literature. When it comes to being truthful and accurate, you also have the responsibility of recognizing that not all audience members will have the training, skills, or experience to evaluate claims themselves. As message design professionals, we must always be cognizant of our audience's ability to understand the nature of the information we present and the recommendations we make—and to choose language and influence strategies appropriate for our audience's level of understanding. In summary, this ethical principle admonishes us always to tell the truth, be transparent when there is gray area between truth and falsity, and never deceive a campaign stakeholder with dubious claims or sources lacking in credibility. Do your due diligence in investigating the sources and evidence you rely on to support your campaign messages and be sure that they are accurate, trustworthy, and in the audiences' best interests.

Second, NCA suggests that *communicators should consider a diversity of perspectives* when creating their messages, selecting message channels, and designing an overall approach to their communication task. What does this mean for strategic communication? In order to reach the target audience in ethical ways, the campaign team needs to understand the audience's current level of knowledge and set of present beliefs about the subject. Related questions you should consider: Who are their trusted sources about this issue? Why do they believe what they believe? In what ways are they served, and perhaps limited, by their beliefs? How could changing those beliefs possibly make their lives better? What needs could a change meet; what problems could a shift in their attitudes or behaviors help solve? Why and how might the audience resist change?

Assuming a position of superiority—that you or other campaign stakeholders "know better" than your target audience—and proceeding to force messages about change on the audience is not only an unfriendly and alienating approach to interaction, it is unethical by NCA standards. Ethical communication involves taking the time to get to know your audience. Ask, who are these people, relative to my program's topic? Doing so will enable you to honor their beliefs, but suggest realistic, desirable change in a manner that will establish trust with your target audience.

In a project detailed later in this book, George Mason University professor and researcher Gary Kreps developed a message campaign related to African American health and beliefs about the health care profession. Based on a large body of documented evidence, Kreps knew that the African American community was characterized by some degree of mistrust in the medical field and its recommendations. If he were to ignore this and go the traditional route of using trained medical experts as spokespeople in a health-related campaign, he would have missed a critical opportunity to influence his audience in positive ways. Instead, he considered the *diversity of perspectives* inherent in his audience on this topic in the design of his campaign. In other words, to reach its target audience, the campaign team needed to understand that audience's perspective on medical information and trusted message sources and proceed accordingly with an appropriate design. In sum, this ethical principle reminds us that we need to understand our audience and be tolerant of its diverse views on the subject(s) we are attempting to influence them about—and recognize that we will only be successful in influencing positive change when an audience trusts us and understands our messages.

Third, in ethical strategic communication work, professionals must *respect participant privacy and anonymity, and protect confidential information entrusted to them.* Throughout this book, we provide many examples of opportunities we have had to interact with campaign stakeholders both formally and informally for the purposes of learning about their needs, testing messages, evaluating their responses to campaigns, and more. The rich data we obtain through these conversations benefits campaigns, their stakeholders, and target audiences. Your work will be valuably audience-centered, satisfy your external stakeholders, and overall, highly effective when you base it on these types of conversations. But you must always keep in mind that revealing the identities of the individuals who share this information, or associating them with their responses to your questions, would be potentially damaging to them and therefore unethical. Related to the principle of privacy is the proprietary nature of most organizational work, a topic that is addressed in greater depth by professional societies focused specifically on public relations and business communication and that we will discuss later in this chapter. Simply put, the work you do for your employer or a client is typically private and should not be discussed or written about outside of the organization without permission. This ethical principle reminds us of important components of the trust we must establish to do effective strategic communication work: privacy and confidentiality.

Fourth, the NCA document suggests that *to be ethical, communicators must always keep in mind that they have the potential to make something better.* You may have heard the saying that *with great power comes great responsibility.* In terms of how this ethical principle relates to strategic communication, a communication campaign is a powerful tool for change and influence. And with it comes the responsibility of campaign personnel to provide their audience with information resources that will enhance their lives. Campaigns related to disease prevention and screening or drug misuse and abuse prevention are particularly critical venues for understanding this ethical value. In these types of programs, the stakes are high, and the outcome could literally mean the difference between life and death for a receiver. Thus, the campaign is tasked with both great power and great responsibility to use that power for good.

To illustrate, the second author of this textbook had an important lesson in the power of communication and her responsibilities to use it well when she worked on a campaign designed to promote enhanced safety in an industrial setting. When consulting, Jennifer always encourages client involvement, because after all, clients have important insider insights on organizational dynamics. However, in this particular message design project, she found the client to be somewhat overbearing in his desire to manage the process. The client asked to listen in on focus group discussions with the target audience and insisted on "interpreting" for her what employees said about current safety practices, standards, and training. Jennifer quickly determined that the client's interpretation of what employees reported was consistent with his desire to minimize the costs associated with the safety campaign, rather than the employees' actual safety. In this scenario, Jennifer had to pause and ethically consider her responsibilities and duties not just to her client but also to his employees and the greater good relative to workplace safety.

Regardless of whether the campaign is aimed at altering the audience's health, workplace behaviors, driving habits, energy consumption, grocery buying decisions, or any other beliefs or behaviors, to be ethical, the professionals behind it must be aware of the influence the campaign carries. We are not in the business of brainwashing or coercing audiences but of providing them with valid and reliable information packaged appropriately for unique consumers, and allowing them to critically evaluate our messages and decide for themselves.

Finally, consistent with the great power and responsibility that accompanies a strategic communication campaign professional's work, is the importance of *accepting short- and long-term consequences of our messages.* Be aware that messages have consequences, and that by design, strategic communication is intended to shape the nature of those consequences. For example, a campaign aimed at encouraging sunscreen use by people who work outdoors is designed strategically to get the target audience to use sunscreen, not just believe that they should use sunscreen or understand why they should use sunscreen. In ethical ways (i.e., by being truthful and attendant to your audience's diverse beliefs and behaviors), you will develop messages you hope will shape the outcomes intended by your campaign.

Importantly, the goals of your campaign must be in the best interests of your target audience, while still satisfying the requirements of other stakeholders. The target audiences' best interests must be at the forefront of your work at all times. For instance, a colleague of ours once shared a consulting experience he had working with a food service company that produced premade, reheatable meals for consumption by children in school lunchrooms. He was hired as a freelance contract consultant to lead a multiphase project that involved investigating perceptions of the company's (not very nutritious or tasty) food, making change recommendations, and then developing a marketing and public relations strategy for the new and improved offerings. When he found out that certain company executives insisted on concealing and continuing some cost effective manufacturing processes that were detrimental to the overall nutrition value of the product (a practice he determined was legal, but by his standards, not ethical), he resigned from the project. In his assessment, certain stakeholder interests were in conflict with the best interest of the young people who were counting on nutritious meals, and despite his efforts to reason with them, they would not alter their stance. Similarly, your authors have learned that stakeholder interests are sometimes in conflict with one another, or even with the objective of the project. Organizations can be highly political places, and campaigns can become challenging. We have learned through experience the importance of sensitively managing stakeholder demands, but never at the expense of the target audience and its needs relative to our campaign focus.

These five core values serve as the backdrop to the NCA "Credo" and represent those most relevant to strategic communication work. Take a moment to review the statement found in the box on page 100 in its entirety. Do you see any other elements that are especially applicable to strategic communication? Using the section you have just read along with the entire statement to direct your thinking, as directed by your instructor, be prepared to discuss the specific ways the NCA document can be applied to strategic communication in organizations. Whether you are marketing a product, asking organizational members to accept a change, designing a messaging campaign to encourage a behavior such as voting or recycling, shaping citizens' attitudes toward a candidate for public office, or educating a target audience about an important health practice, ethical communication is important. Considering this section and your own reading of the document, think through ways the NCA "Credo" can help you communicate ethically in organizational settings.

The NCA "Credo" is an extremely broad document that is useful across communication contexts and in interacting with any type of stakeholder using

National Communication Association Credo for Ethical Communication

Questions of right and wrong arise whenever people communicate. Ethical communication is fundamental to responsible thinking, decision making, and the development of relationships and communities within and across contexts, cultures, channels, and media. Moreover, ethical communication enhances human worth and dignity by fostering truthfulness, fairness, responsibility, personal integrity, and respect for self and others. We believe that unethical communication threatens the quality of all communication and consequently the well-being of individuals and the society in which we live. Therefore, we, the members of the National Communication Association, endorse and are committed to practicing the following principles of ethical communication:

- We advocate truthfulness, accuracy, honesty, and reason as essential to the integrity of communication.
- We endorse freedom of expression, diversity of perspective, and tolerance of dissent to achieve the informed and responsible decision making fundamental to a civil society.
- We strive to understand and respect other communicators before evaluating and responding to their messages.
- We promote access to communication resources and opportunities as necessary to fulfill human potential and contribute to the well-being of families, communities, and society.
- We promote communication climates of caring and mutual understanding that respect the unique needs and characteristics of individual communicators.
- We condemn communication that degrades individuals and humanity through distortion, intimidation, coercion, and violence, and through the expression of intolerance and hatred.
- We are committed to the courageous expression of personal convictions in pursuit of fairness and justice.
- We advocate sharing information, opinions, and feelings when facing significant choices while also respecting privacy and confidentiality.
- We accept responsibility for the short- and long-term consequences of our own communication and expect the same of others.

Source: www.natcom.org/sites/default/files/pages
/1999_Public_Statements_NCA_Credo_for_Ethical_
Communication_November.pdf.

any medium. Other professional societies offer ethics guidelines specific to the professional practice of communication in business, corporate, and other organizational settings. Let's explore those next.

4.1.2 What Practitioners Have to Say: Professional Society Codes of Ethics

Whereas the NCA "Credo" is a useful guide for thinking about ethical communication, it remains a theoretical set of criteria developed mostly by scholars. Practitioners working in fields focused on aspects of strategic communication, such as marketing, business communication, and public relations, have adapted theories of ethical communication to define the ethical principles that guide their daily work in applied settings. Professional societies in these areas may require that members sign and adhere to their respective ethical code, and they typically have sanctions in place for anyone found in violation of the code. In this section, we provide a summary and analysis of some of the key issues addressed in these codes, written especially for practitioners working in professional settings. We selected and analyzed professional codes of ethics based on their relevance to the kinds of work described in this book; specifically, we reviewed the codes of ethics developed by the International Association of Business Communicators (ABC) (see the box on page 105 for the complete code), the Public Relations Society of America (PRSA) (see the box on page 106), and the American Marketing Association (AMA) (see the box on page 109). These associations' ethical principles overlap with NCA's to a great extent, but they also address specific issues relevant to the actual professional practice of communication.

What are some of the specialized concerns beyond the general principles addressed by NCA that these practitioner-oriented ethical codes emphasize? We identified the following:

- Adherence to corporate policies and laws, conflicts of interest, and gifts and remuneration
- Trade secrets, intellectual property, copyright, trademarks
- The ability to guarantee results
- Collegiality (both within an organization and across the industry)

First, in determining what is ethical and unethical within a professional settings, your primary source of guidance should be your contract, the employee manual, training content, and any documents that specify what work-related practices are acceptable and unacceptable. These documents, typically found online and provided to you when you are hired, can clarify what otherwise is unknown or unclear to you. For example, many communication professionals work on a contract basis; that is, they do not have permanent, full-time employment with any single organization. However, their clients may request in writing that they not provide services for competitors, or for any other project, for the duration of their contract. Full-time employees may have provisions in their agreements with their employees governing the kinds of freelance work that they may engage in, as well. For example, as college professors, we are encouraged to provide consulting services based on our scholarly area of expertise (that can enhance our research and creative activity in return), but our employee manual specifies a percentage of time that we are permitted to dedicate to these outside activities. You may be required to abide by noncompete policies that prohibit you from working for a direct competitor of your employer for a certain period of time after your relationship with the organization ends. The kinds of policies we refer to in this paragraph prevent **conflicts of interest,** or situations in which the objectives of two parties compete, or are incompatible with one another.

Your employer might similarly have written policies regarding the kinds of gifts and remuneration (payment) you are permitted to accept from clients and vendors. Is it ethical to accept those World Series tickets from your client? Maybe, but maybe not. Your employer's policies should be your first source of decision-making guidance in the event that an external stakeholder offers you something beyond your typical salary or payment for services rendered.

Ethical principles should govern your work habits as well. For example, are you surprised to learn that one of the leading forms of corporate theft in the United States is time theft? (Ahmed 2018). Time theft occurs when you are being paid to work but take extended breaks, use excessive work time to deal with personal or family matters without employer authorization, or use technology (e.g., the internet and social media) for non-work-related purposes. Similarly, overreporting hours spent on hourly work, not showing up for meetings, and logging in to web conferences but doing other work during them constitute forms of theft and fraud that are as unethical as stealing money or tangible items from the workplace. It's beyond the scope of this book to cover the myriad forms of company policy that exist, but to summarize, your employer's rules and regulations should be a primary source of information to help you apply ethical values at work.

In addition to company policy, local, state, and federal laws may govern your work. Your employer and the professional associations you belong to should help you interpret these. For example, government work is guided by strict federal laws that govern how much you can be paid, what kinds of gifts you can accept, how much overtime you can work, permitted uses of technology and email addresses, and more. Laws may prohibit **bribery** (directly or indirectly receiving something of value in exchange for awarding business). Earlier, we mentioned following employer policy when making decisions about accepting outside work. If you are employed by the federal government (and some state and local governments), the law prohibits you from supplementing your income. Legal code similarly governs aspects of employment in professions such as medicine, law, and accounting. Again, a comprehensive review of laws governing ethical behavior across business sectors and fields is impossible here, but the bottom line is that you are responsible for understanding how both employer policy and legal code govern your behavior.

The second theme that we found across professional ethics codes is related to protection of trade secrets and proprietary information. This concept builds on the value of confidentiality we discussed earlier in this chapter. To behave ethically, you must obey your employer's policies relevant to confidentiality and **trade secrets** (formulae, practices, processes, designs, concepts, and/or methods that are owned by an organization and that, if leaked, would give other organizations unfair competitive advantage). This principle also applies to how you handle what you know about your clients as well. Whether you work for a (marketing, public relations, advertising) firm or operate as an independent consultant, you must protect your knowledge about your client's business plans and practices so as not to give their competitors unfair advantage. Often, these secrets are legally protected by **trademarks** (a legally registered name, symbol, or design that distinguishes an entity from others), **patents** (the exclusive legal right to make or sell an original invention for a specified period of time), and **copyrights** (a legal right to determine if, and how, others may use some aspect of your work). For example, companies trademark their names and logos for their exclusive use. They obtain patents for innovations (e.g., IBM obtained a patent in 2015 for a fact-checking technology used by journalists). Authors obtain copyrights for their written, published work. Using a trademarked image, infringing on a patent, or using another's written work without permission and citation are all examples of ethical violations in professional practice.

Over the years, the second author of your book has been involved in a number of interesting training and consulting projects with unique organizations. Often, she has recognized opportunities to write about these engagements in scholarly journals or as case studies in books like these. Sometimes her clients are enthusiastic about these ideas, but often, they are not. When they are willing to let Jennifer write or speak about some aspect of their organization's functioning, they usually set strict parameters for how she may do it. For example, they may request that she not reveal the identity of the organization, or that she change details of the case to make the organization and its employees unrecognizable. Generally, when you are employed either full-time or on a contract basis by a private organization, the dynamics that you observe, the projects that you work on, the organization's strategic plans, and the details of how work is done are private. It is unethical to reveal them to outsiders without approval and a clear understanding of the entity's guidelines for how **proprietary information** (data that are not public knowledge and that represent an organization's property) may be shared.

A third theme across professional ethics codes involves the ethicality of guaranteeing results from a communication program or campaign.

Commonly, for-profit organizational decision makers are concerned with the potential return on their investments. Investment in marketing, public relations, and other communication activities is no exception in that if the organization expends resources, executives want to know what will come back in return. However, the outcomes of a human behavior such as communication can be difficult to predict. Thus, communication professionals must be very cautious in guaranteeing specific results tied to their programs. This book will cover a range of activities that will help you ethically promise your client or employer how a campaign will unfold and what he or she can reasonably expect will happen. Specifically, we emphasize rigorous formative, process, and summative evaluations that will help ensure that your messages have their intended effects on audiences. You will learn how to evaluate what your audience needs relative to the subject of your campaign in order to design it appropriately, assess a campaign's effectiveness as it unfolds (and make necessary changes), and evaluate the outcomes of the campaign after it concludes in order to demonstrate to your client what worked and what didn't work (and what still needs to be done). Ethically, you can assure a client that you have the knowledge and skills to design and evaluate an effective campaign that are likely to have a positive impact. You can reasonably predict how many people your messages will reach, and that because your messages were designed using theory- and research-backed evidence, that they will have their intended effects. But generally, we recommend that you avoid making precise quantitative promises about the expected results of your work. Ethically, you should always avoid finding yourself in the unprofessional position of overpromising and underdelivering results.

The fourth theme across the three professional communicator's codes of ethics that we have chosen to focus on here is related to collegiality. **Collegiality,** broadly speaking, refers to your ability to relate to, work with, and cooperate with people professionally, productively, and in a prosocial manner. Collegiality is based on the mutual respect that people must have for one another in order to get along and be supportive of one another professionally. Admittedly, collegiality is a difficult concept to think about objectively. Organizations cannot really mandate that you like your coworkers, or that people behave interpersonally in particular ways. Some people are more aggressive, abrasive, or argumentative communicators than others—but they may bring valuable skills and knowledge to a project. Others may be passive, reticent, and hesitant to contribute to discussions and work sessions—and therefore may be perceived as being just as uncooperative as the argumentative jerk albeit behaving in a very different way. But there are some basic standards for collegial behavior that define what is ethical and potentially unethical in professional practice. These are safe rules of thumb for building and maintaining helpful, collegial relationships and ensuring that others have a positive perception of you, your employer, and your profession. For instance:

The International Association of Business Communicator's Code of Ethics

1. I am honest: My actions bring respect for and trust in the communication profession.
2. I communicate accurate information and promptly correct any errors.
3. I obey laws and public policies; if I violate any law or public policy, I act promptly to correct the situation.
4. I protect confidential information while acting within the law.
5. I support the ideals of free speech, freedom of assembly, and access to an open marketplace of ideas.
6. I am sensitive to others' cultural values and beliefs.
7. I give credit to others for their work and cite my sources.
8. I do not use confidential information for personal benefit.
9. I do not represent conflicting or competing interests without full disclosure and written consent of those involved.
10. I do not accept undisclosed gifts or payments for professional services from anyone other than a client or employer.
11. I do not guarantee results that are beyond my power to deliver.

Source: www.iabc.com/about-us/governance
/code-of-ethics/.

- Always give credit to others for the work they have done, and never take credit for work or ideas that you are not responsible for.
- Bullying, harassment, and abusive communication behavior related to professional activities is always unethical. Although what constitutes these types of behavior may be difficult to objectively define, you should be familiar with your employer's policies on workplace bullying and harassment. You should avoid words, actions, or even tone of voice that may contribute to the perception that you are engaging in these forms of antisocial communication. Consider seeking mentoring or other professional advice on your workplace communication style, and look for positive role models that will help you develop a collegial approach to work.
- Avoid badmouthing coworkers, clients, and competitors. Avoid potentially damaging gossip or participating in the spread of unfounded rumors.
- Report violations of ethical principles, policies, and codes.
- Mentor subordinates relative to collegial behavior and ethical communication.
- Engage in professional development opportunities that will help enhance you as a skilled colleague with current knowledge of the field.
- Practice the Golden Rule in your interactions with clients, vendors, and coworkers, as suggested in the American Marketing Association's Statement of Ethics: Treat others as you want to be treated.

PRSA Ethics Code Provisions of Conduct

FREE FLOW OF INFORMATION

Core Principle: Protecting and advancing the free flow of accurate and truthful information is essential to serving the public interest and contributing to informed decision making in a democratic society.

Intent:

- To maintain the integrity of relationships with the media, government officials, and the public.
- To aid informed decision-making.

Guidelines:

A member shall:

- Preserve the integrity of the process of communication.
- Be honest and accurate in all communications.
- Act promptly to correct erroneous communications for which the practitioner is responsible.
- Preserve the free flow of unprejudiced information when giving or receiving gifts by ensuring that gifts are nominal, legal, and infrequent.

Examples of Improper Conduct under This Provision:

- A member representing a ski manufacturer gives a pair of expensive racing skis to a sports magazine columnist to influence the columnist to write favorable articles about the product.
- A member entertains a government official beyond legal limits and/or in violation of government reporting requirements.

COMPETITION

Core Principle: Promoting healthy and fair competition among professionals preserves an ethical climate while fostering a robust business environment.

Intent:

- To promote respect and fair competition among public relations professionals.
- To serve the public interest by providing the widest choice of practitioner options.

Guidelines:

A member shall:

- Follow ethical hiring practices designed to respect free and open competition without deliberately undermining a competitor.
- Preserve intellectual property rights in the marketplace.

Examples of Improper Conduct under This Provision:

- A member employed by a "client organization" shares helpful information with a counseling firm that is competing with others for the organization's business.
- A member spreads malicious and unfounded rumors about a competitor in order to alienate the competitor's clients and employees in a ploy to recruit people and business.

DISCLOSURE OF INFORMATION

Core Principle: Open communication fosters informed decision making in a democratic society.

Intent:

To build trust with the public by revealing all information needed for responsible decision making.

Guidelines:

A member shall:

- Be honest and accurate in all communications.
- Act promptly to correct erroneous communications for which the member is responsible.

- Investigate the truthfulness and accuracy of information released on behalf of those represented.
- Reveal the sponsors for causes and interests represented.
- Disclose financial interest (such as stock ownership) in a client's organization.
- Avoid deceptive practices.

Examples of Improper Conduct under This Provision:

- Front groups: A member implements grassroots campaigns or letter-writing campaigns to legislators on behalf of undisclosed interest groups.
- Lying by omission: A practitioner for a corporation knowingly fails to release financial information, giving a misleading impression of the corporation's performance.
- A member discovers inaccurate information disseminated via a website or media kit and does not correct the information.
- A member deceives the public by employing people to pose as volunteers to speak at public hearings and participate in grassroots campaigns.

SAFEGUARDING CONFIDENCES

Core Principle: Client trust requires appropriate protection of confidential and private information.

Intent:

To protect the privacy rights of clients, organizations, and individuals by safeguarding confidential information.

Guidelines:

- A member shall: Safeguard the confidences and privacy rights of present, former, and prospective clients and employees.

- Protect privileged, confidential, or insider information gained from a client or organization.
- Immediately advise an appropriate authority if a member discovers that confidential information is being divulged by an employee of a client company or organization.

Examples of Improper Conduct under This Provision:

- A member changes jobs, takes confidential information, and uses that information in the new position to the detriment of the former employer.
- A member intentionally leaks proprietary information to the detriment of some other party.

CONFLICTS OF INTEREST

Core Principle: Avoiding real, potential, or perceived conflicts of interest builds the trust of clients, employers, and the publics.

Intent:

- To earn trust and mutual respect with clients or employers.
- To build trust with the public by avoiding or ending situations that put one's personal or professional interests in conflict with society's interests.

Guidelines:

A member shall:

- Act in the best interests of the client or employer, even subordinating the member's personal interests.
- Avoid actions and circumstances that may appear to compromise good business judgment or create a conflict between personal and professional interests.

- Disclose promptly any existing or potential conflict of interest to affected clients or organizations.
- Encourage clients and customers to determine if a conflict exists after notifying all affected parties.

Examples of Improper Conduct under This Provision:

- The member fails to disclose that he or she has a strong financial interest in a client's chief competitor.
- The member represents a "competitor company" or a "conflicting interest" without informing a prospective client.

ENHANCING THE PROFESSION

Core Principle: Public relations professionals work constantly to strengthen the public's trust in the profession.

Intent:

- To build respect and credibility with the public for the profession of public relations.
- To improve, adapt, and expand professional practices.

Guidelines:

A member shall:

- Acknowledge that there is an obligation to protect and enhance the profession.

- Keep informed and educated about practices in the profession to ensure ethical conduct.
- Actively pursue personal professional development.
- Decline representation of clients or organizations that urge or require actions contrary to this Code.
- Accurately define what public relations activities can accomplish.
- Counsel subordinates in proper ethical decision making.
- Require that subordinates adhere to the ethical requirements of the Code.
- Report practices that fail to comply with the Code, whether committed by PRSA members or not, to the appropriate authority.

Examples of Improper Conduct under This Provision:

- A PRSA member declares publicly that a product the client sells is safe, without disclosing evidence to the contrary.
- A member initially assigns some questionable client work to a nonmember practitioner to avoid the ethical obligation of PRSA membership.

Source: www.prsa.org/wp-content/uploads/2018/04/PRSACodeofEthics.pdf.

4.2 PUTTING PROFESSIONAL ETHICS INTO PRACTICE

Putting professional ethical principles into practice in your work as a strategic communication is made easier by the guidelines and codes created by various associations that we have just explored. These vary in their degree of specificity and the kinds of example behaviors they include. Some are targeted at message

American Marketing Association Statement of Ethics

STATEMENT OF ETHICS

Preamble

The American Marketing Association commits itself to promoting the highest standard of professional ethical norms and values for its members (practitioners, academics, and students). Norms are established standards of conduct that are expected and maintained by society and/or professional organizations. Values represent the collective conception of what communities find desirable, important, and morally proper. Values also serve as the criteria for evaluating our own personal actions and the actions of others. As marketers, we recognize that we not only serve our organizations but also act as stewards of society in creating, facilitating, and executing the transactions that are part of the greater economy. In this role, marketers are expected to embrace the highest professional ethical norms and the ethical values implied by our responsibility toward multiple stakeholders (e.g., customers, employees, investors, peers, channel members, regulators and the host community).

Ethical Norms

As Marketers, we must:

1. Do no harm. This means consciously avoiding harmful actions or omissions by embodying high ethical standards and adhering to all applicable laws and regulations in the choices we make.
2. Foster trust in the marketing system. This means striving for good faith and fair dealing so as to contribute toward the efficacy of the exchange process as well as avoiding deception in product design, pricing, communication, and delivery of distribution.
3. Embrace ethical values. This means building relationships and enhancing consumer confidence in the integrity of marketing by affirming these core values: honesty, responsibility, fairness, respect, transparency, and citizenship.

Ethical Values

Honesty—to be forthright in dealings with customers and stakeholders. To this end, we will:

- Strive to be truthful in all situations and at all times.
- Offer products of value that do what we claim in our communications.
- Stand behind our products if they fail to deliver their claimed benefits.
- Honor our explicit and implicit commitments and promises.

Responsibility—to accept the consequences of our marketing decisions and strategies. To this end, we will:

- Strive to serve the needs of customers.
- Avoid using coercion with all stakeholders.
- Acknowledge the social obligations to stakeholders that come with increased marketing and economic power.
- Recognize our special commitments to vulnerable market segments such as children, seniors, the economically impoverished, market illiterates and others who may be substantially disadvantaged.
- Consider environmental stewardship in our decision-making.

Fairness—to balance justly the needs of the buyer with the interests of the seller. To this end, we will:

- Represent products in a clear way in selling, advertising and other forms of communication; this includes the avoidance of false, misleading and deceptive promotion.

- Reject manipulations and sales tactics that harm customer trust.
- Refuse to engage in price fixing, predatory pricing, price gouging or "bait-and-switch" tactics.
- Avoid knowing participation in conflicts of interest.
- Seek to protect the private information of customers, employees and partners.

Respect—to acknowledge the basic human dignity of all stakeholders. To this end, we will:

- Value individual differences and avoid stereotyping customers or depicting demographic groups (e.g., gender, race, sexual orientation) in a negative or dehumanizing way.
- Listen to the needs of customers and make all reasonable efforts to monitor and improve their satisfaction on an ongoing basis.
- Make every effort to understand and respectfully treat buyers, suppliers, intermediaries and distributors from all cultures.
- Acknowledge the contributions of others, such as consultants, employees and coworkers, to marketing endeavors.
- Treat everyone, including our competitors, as we would wish to be treated.

Transparency—to create a spirit of openness in marketing operations. To this end, we will:

- Strive to communicate clearly with all constituencies.
- Accept constructive criticism from customers and other stakeholders.
- Explain and take appropriate action regarding significant product or service risks, component substitutions or other foreseeable eventualities that could affect customers or their perception of the purchase decision.
- Disclose list prices and terms of financing as well as available price deals and adjustments.

Citizenship—to fulfill the economic, legal, philanthropic and societal responsibilities that serve stakeholders. To this end, we will:

- Strive to protect the ecological environment in the execution of marketing campaigns.
- Give back to the community through volunteerism and charitable donations.
- Contribute to the overall betterment of marketing and its reputation.
- Urge supply chain members to ensure that trade is fair for all participants, including producers in developing countries.

In addition, the AMA has created formal statements about sexual harassment and conflicts of interest within the marketing industry that you can review, along with the ethical statement, on their website: www.ama.org/codes-of-conduct.

design and dissemination work and others are general criteria for human interaction of any kind. But they all require interpretation and the ability to select and apply them critically in various situations, considering:

- The goals of the campaign or message
- The intended audience
- The channels available to the communicator
- The nature of the relationship among the communicators and their history, trust, and perceived credibility

Chapter 2 introduced you to a variety of organizational types. Strategic messages associated with for-profit, nonprofit, and government organizations will vary in terms of the ethical principles that communicators emphasize. For example, nonprofit organizations and for-profits with strong commitments to environmental sustainability may rely more on ethical principles that emphasize sustainability and environmental stewardship than others. Within those three major categories of organizational types, organizations have different purposes, missions, and corresponding values. For example, health care and banking institutions will operate very differently in terms of their communication priorities and ethical values. Even within a single industry, ethical emphases will vary (e.g., nurses will operate based on different values and ethical principles than accountants in the same hospital). In a 2008 study, Lieber used a valid and reliable measure of moral development to assess how public relations professionals make ethical decisions, and found statistically significant differences based on the practitioner's unique job and employer characteristics. Thus, the use of ethical codes and their individual values and tenets is dependent on the organization's values and the perspectives of its stakeholders.

Further, situation matters. Recall United Airlines CEO Oscar Munoz and his widely criticized response to a passenger being violently dragged from an aircraft. The CEO of a major international airline probably does not encounter frequent situations where "human dignity" is an ethical priority. His day-to-day job responsibilities are focused primarily on enhancing his company's financial profits while other company leaders focus on the employee and passenger experience. Yet, in this high-profile situation, the CEO was called on to make an explanation and an apology for behavior that most of the public viewed as inhumane.

In addition, as you will learn in greater depth later in this book, individual differences among target audiences will influence how receivers selectively attend to, process, and act on strategic messages. Individual differences, including cultural and co-cultural identifications, will affect communication professionals' ethical judgments. For instance, in one study, marketing students evaluated the ethics of a number of sales tactics, including offering gifts, entertaining clients, overpromising to close a sale, and withholding negative information from clients. Females scored higher on a morality scale than males and thus rated these strategies as less ethical than males (Donoho, Heinze, and Kondo 2012). In addition to receiver and sender or message designer characteristics, research indicates that the communication medium used can make a difference in the ethical choices communicators make. In an experimental study, Xu, Cenfetelli, and Aquino (2012) found, for example, that people engaged in face-to-face negotiations were less likely to be deceptive than those using text messaging. Elsewhere, Langett (2013) suggests that digital media must be used ethically for strategic communication purposes, emphasizing

Figure 16 Corporate leaders often need coaching on ethical strategic communication. United Airlines CEO Oscar Munoz damaged his career with what much of the public perceived as unethical messages that disregarded the human dignity of a passenger.

dialogue (i.e., using blogs and social media to interact with stakeholders, rather than simply transmitting information to them), civility and truthfulness, and relationship building.

Making an ethical choice requires both sensitivity and communication competence. Ethical communication isn't always an easy task. For example, recall Bryan from the opening vignette to this chapter. Consider the workers on the Deepwater Horizon rig who noted unsafe conditions and practices but didn't speak up. We might not all have the courage to challenge an employer or client asking us to incorporate a misleading or exaggerated claim into a campaign. Behaving ethically when others around you aren't doing so, or challenging other people about their behavior, requires a lot of motivation and skill. Calling others out isn't always practical—after all, you won't want to end up being labeled a whiner or troublemaker and possibly experience harm to your career. Although doing the "right thing" every time sounds good in theory, there may not always be *one* "right thing." When is it acceptable to put our self-interest first? It's a tough question, not unlike most ethical dilemmas.

Thus, people apply ethical principles when deciding how to act. Our own guiding ethical principles may be based on our culture, religious beliefs, profession, political values, or other individual differences. Rather than apply a strict set of ethical criteria, however, some people assess the unique characteristics of the situation and then decide what to do. Those who subscribe to this code of situational ethics do not believe certain behavior is always wrong; instead, they examine behavior for its appropriateness in a given situation. In the organizational setting, using religious beliefs, politics, or even interpretations of the law to determine what is right and wrong can be arbitrary and subjective. What one individual views as unethical may seem perfectly acceptable to another. Although there will be a number of influences on what ethical principles parties choose to rely on in strategic communication, the ethical codes—and the values on which they are based—discussed in this section should serve as important starting points for your work.

4.3 SUMMARIZING ETHICAL CONSIDERATIONS FOR STRATEGIC COMMUNICATION PRACTITIONERS

In this section of our chapter on ethics, we leave you with a final list of ethical considerations relevant to strategic communication work. We began the chapter with the general principles for ethical communication articulated by the National Communication Association, and then explored themes that emerged from several specific frameworks applicable to business communicators, public relations professionals, and marketers. In this section, we revert to a general set of principles that encompasses communication ethics as well as the business ethics that communication professionals need to be concerned with. To do so, we turned to the work of Montgomery, Heald, MacNamara, and Pincus (1995) and Stolle and Studebacher (2011) who wrote about business consulting ethics and adapted their thinking to address both consulting and full-time work in communication. In your professional work beyond message design, we believe the following ethical positions are very important.

First, *your professional responsibilities require you to be faithfully committed to your project's purpose.* You must understand and commit to the goals and objectives of your project, and to some extent, "pledge allegiance" to the overall mission of your organization and the message design projects you work on. You might not always have a choice in the projects that you commit to, but you must make that commitment. If your personal values, beliefs, or interests create a barrier to your identification with your organization's work, you should consider searching for another job. Halfhearted work reflects an unethical level of commitment.

Second, as each of the codes of ethics previously reviewed in this chapter state, you have a *responsibility to be truthful in your communication with all stakeholders:* your client, sponsor, or employer; your colleagues; the individuals and communities to which your strategic communication is aimed. You must provide all parties with complete, accurate, and reliable information.

Third, as a professional, *you must be committed to benefiting, and not harming, the intended audience for your message(s), while protecting the interests of other stakeholders.* That is, in all of your actions, you must protect the well-being of your target audience and the organization(s) you serve. Your messaging efforts should not harm anyone or pose risks to any stakeholders (even if they promise benefits to others).

Fourth, you have a *duty not to benefit beyond the agreed-on compensation for your work* (e.g., contract fee, salary, or hourly rate). You should be paid fairly for your work, but you should not knowingly take or otherwise receive additional monetary or nonmonetary benefits that are not permitted by your employment contract or other employer policies. This would include intimate relationships with project sponsors or supervisors.

Fifth, you must always *protect proprietary information belonging to your employer or client.* Recall that proprietary information refers to data that are not public knowledge. It is the organization's property. Do not reveal trade secrets or discuss confidential aspects of your work with unauthorized individuals. Do not speak to the media or use your personal social media accounts to mention your work unless you have received permission to do so (and received situation-specific guidance and training on how to do it effectively). If you attend conferences or professional meetings where you will encounter employees of competing organizations, be very cautious in your communication with them not to reveal proprietary data or other information.

Sixth, *use the best communication practices (that you learn in this book and in your course) to establish trusting relationships with stakeholders and to enhance others' favorable perceptions of your organization.* Communicate in ways that influence program stakeholders to view you as a credible, trustworthy professional. This proactive approach will serve you and your organization well in times of stability as well as during times of organizational crisis when you will need to manage and refine or revise stakeholder impressions. In their analysis of the 1993 Jack in the Box fast food chain *E. coli* outbreak crisis, Ulmer and Sellnow (2000) concluded that the public viewed the company's formal response as ethically questionable because it was ambiguous and seemed to privilege financial stakeholders over other groups, including victims. They noted that to build trust and credibility during times of "complex, painful, damaging, and stressful" (153) organizational crisis, communication professionals must examine the diversity of stakeholder needs and address them in unique ways. In addition, recall that people generalize their initial impressions; if they initially view you as a positive, trustworthy, and credible communicator, they will revert to those perceptions quickly if problems arise and be more likely to give you the benefit of the doubt than if their initial impressions were unfavorable.

Finally, *you are responsible for ensuring the acceptability and legality of your messaging activities.* Ensure the accuracy of all claims and that recommended behaviors (such as health recommendations, educational practices, or financial advice) have an ethical basis in scientific research, industry best practices, or credible and expert testimony. Be transparent about your message's claims and the evidence that supports them. Always apply relevant legal standards and abide by any ethical code you have agreed to as a contingency for employment or membership in a professional society. Montgomery and colleagues (1995) explain that the acceptability and legality principle is contextual and that "techniques, methods, and even language acceptable in one setting may be unacceptable in another" (378). Thus, you should maintain continuous awareness of your organization's and industry's standards.

4.4 TYING IT ALL TOGETHER: BEING AN ETHICAL, RESPONSIBLE COMMUNICATOR WILL HELP YOU ACCOMPLISH PROGRAM GOALS

In an essay on the ethics of strategic communication campaigns, Botan (1997) wrote that "the more successful a campaign is at influencing others, and hence the greater its reach or impact, the more significant its ethical questions become" (189). In this chapter, we have encouraged you to consider the wide range of ethical values undergirding professional communication and the specific ethical principles that guide competent strategic communication work. Bryan, whom we met in the introduction to this chapter, represented someone with a serious ethical dilemma that had the potential to affect consumers' well-being and required him to balance his concern for ethics with his vested interest in his company. Throughout the chapter, we have discussed a range of ethical situations with consequences more or less as serious as Bryan's case—but that are common to campaigns. Without careful attention to relevant ethical frameworks, even the most masterfully planned, designed, and implemented communication strategy will be ineffective at accomplishing its goals. On the other hand, ethical behavior and ethical messaging strategies will serve a communication campaign or program very well. Ethical decision making will enhance stakeholder confidence in you and your messages and serve as the foundation for a program that meets organizational objectives.

CHAPTER 4 REVIEW

Questions for Critical Thinking and Discussion

1. Identify an ethical principle mentioned in this chapter that guides your own communication behavior. Ask three classmates to do the same. Compare your responses. How similar or different are your ethical principles and the values they reflect? As a group, discuss what factors you believe account for these differences and similarities.

2. Review the Public Relations Society of America Code of Ethics in this chapter. Then focus on the "examples of improper conduct" under each ethical guideline. Select three to five examples and give a brief interpretation of how and why these examples illustrate unethical behavior.

3. Review the IABC, PRSA, and AMA codes provided in this chapter. Can you identify any additional themes across these frameworks that are relevant to strategic communication work that

perhaps we did not address in this chapter? Explain and be prepared to discuss with your teacher and classmates.

4. Why do you believe company executives, such as those with United Airlines and Jack in the Box in this chapter, have a difficult time responding to organizational problems or crises in ethical ways that satisfy most stakeholders?

5. Ethics are important when communicating with both internal and external stakeholders of an organization. Do you believe one or the other is more important, or are they equally important? Explain your response.

6. Describe a situation in which you have experienced an ethical challenge when communicating. After reading this chapter, how would you have handled the situation more competently? What would you have done differently?

Key Terms

bribery: directly or indirectly receiving something of value in exchange for awarding business.

collegiality: a broad term that refers to one's ability to relate to, work with, and cooperate with people professionally, productively, and in a prosocial manner.

conflicts of interest: situations in which the objectives of two parties compete, or are incompatible with each other.

copyright: a legal right to determine if, and how, others may use some aspect of your work.

ethics: criteria or guidelines for what is right and what is wrong.

patent: the exclusive legal right to make or sell an original invention for a specified period of time.

proprietary information: data that are not public knowledge and that represent an organization's property.

trade secrets: formulae, practices, processes, designs, concepts, and/or methods that are owned by an organization and that, if leaked, would give other organizations unfair competitive advantage.

trademark: a legally registered name, symbol, or design that distinguishes an entity from others.

Further Readings and Resources

Arnett, R. C., A. M. Holba, and S. Mancino. 2018. *An Encyclopedia of Communication Ethics: Goods in Contention.* New York: Peter Lang.

Day, L. A. 1991. *Ethics in Media Communications: Cases and Controversies.* Belmont, CA: Wadsworth.

Jaska, J. A., and M. S. Pritchard. 1994. *Communication Ethics: Methods of Analysis.* 2nd ed. Belmont, CA: Wadsworth.

Johannesen, R. L., K. S. Valde, and K. E. Whedbee. 1996. *Ethics in Human Communication.* 6th ed. Long Grove, IL: Waveland.

Martin, D., and D. K. Wright. 2016. *Public Relations Ethics: How to Practice PR without Losing Your Soul.* New York: Business Expert Press.

References

Ahmed, A. 2018, January 19. "How to Insure against Time Theft." *Forbes.* www.forbes.com/sites/ashikahmed/2018/01/19/how-to-insure-against-time-theft/#2a5430a75ac8.

Botan, C. 1997. "Ethics in Strategic Communication Campaigns: The Case for a New Approach to Public Relations." *Journal of Business Communication* 34, no. 2: 188–202.

Bray, C. 2009, March 12. "Madoff Pleads Guilty to Massive Fraud." *Wall Street Journal.* http://online.wsj.com/article/SB123685693449906551.html?mod = djemalertNEWS.

Donoho, C., T. Heinze, and C. Kondo. 2012. "Gender Differences in Personal Selling Ethics Evaluations: Do They Exist and What Does Their Existence Mean for Teaching Sales Ethics?" *Journal of Marketing Education* 34, no. 1: 55–66.

Frymier, A. B., and M. K. Nadler. 2013. *Persuasion: Integrating Theory, Research, and Practice.* 3rd ed. Dubuque, IA: Kendall Hunt.

Keyton, J. 2016. "Many Paths: The Role of the Consultant's Paradigms, Values, and Ethics." In *Consulting That Matters: A Handbook for Scholars and Practitioners,* edited by J. H. Waldeck and D. R. Seibold , 33–48. New York: Peter Lang.

Langett, J. 2013. "Blogger Engagement Ethics: Dialogic Civility in a Digital Era." *Journal of Mass Media Ethics* 28, no. 2: 79–90.

Lieber, P. S. 2008. "Moral Development in Public Relations: Measuring Duty to Society in Strategic Communication." *Public Relations Review* 34, no. 3: 244–51.

Montgomery, D. J., G. R. Heald, S. R. MacNamara, and L. B. Pincus. 1995. "Malpractice and the Communication Consultant: A Proactive Approach." *Management Communication Quarterly* 8, no. 3: 368–84.

Shen, L. 2017, December 31. "The 10 Biggest Business Scandals of 2017." *Fortune.* http://fortune.com/2017/12/31/biggest-corporate-scandals-misconduct-2017-pr/.

Smitter, R. 2004. "The Development of the NCA Credo for Ethical Communication." *Free Speech Yearbook* 41, no. 1: 1–2.

Stolle, D. P., and C. A. Studebacher. 2011. "Trial Consulting and Conflicts of Interest: An Introduction." In *Handbook of Trial Consulting,* edited by R. L. Wiener and B. H. Bornstein, 351–69. Boston: Springer.

Ulmer, R. R., and T. L. Sellnow. 2000. "Consistent Questions of Ambiguity in Organizational Crisis Communication: Jack in the Box as a Case Study." *Journal of Business Ethics* 25, no. 2: 143–55.

Urbina, I. 2010, July 22. "Workers on Doomed Rig Voiced Concern about Safety." *New York Times.* www.nytimes.com/2010/07/22/us/22transocean.html?_r=1&th&emc=th.

Wattles, J., and J. Ostrower. 2017, April 17. "United Airlines CEO Oscar Munoz Won't Be Promoted to Chairman." money.cnn.com/2017/04/21/news/companies/united-airlines-oscar-munoz-chairman-board/index.html.

Xu, D. J., R. T. Cenfetelli, and K. Aquino. 2012. "The Influence of Media Cue Multiplicity on Deceivers and Those Who Are Deceived." *Journal of Business Ethics* 106, no. 3: 337–52.

CREATING, IMPLEMENTING, AND EVALUATING STRATEGIC MESSAGES

Organizational Goals and Objectives

CHAPTER CONTENTS

5.1 The Importance of Planning   121

5.2 The Nine Steps of Planning a Strategic Communication Campaign   123

5.3 Conducting Background Research and Evaluating Sources   125

     5.3.1 Primary and Secondary Sources   126

     5.3.2 Four Criteria for Evaluating Sources   127

     5.3.3 The Importance of Research in Decision-Making   127

5.4 Setting Organizational Goals and Objectives   128

     5.4.1 Types of Organizational Objectives   130

     5.4.2 Setting SMART Objectives   134

     5.4.3 Synthesizing Goals and Objectives: The Role of Organizational Strategic Plans   137

5.5 Analyzing the Organization's Ability to Meet Its Goals: The Importance of SWOT Analysis   140

     5.5.1 Internal Assessment: Organizational Strengths and Weaknesses   140

     Factors That Affect Internal Assessment: Identity   141

     Factors That Affect Internal Assessment: Groupthink   142

     5.5.2 External Assessment: Organizational Opportunities and Threats   144

     5.5.3 Conducting a SWOT Analysis: Best Practices for Success   146

     5.5.4 Making SWOT Strategic   147

5.6 Tying It All Together: Connecting Your Organizational Goals, SMART Objectives, and SWOT Analyses into a Formal Strategic Plan   148

LEARNING OBJECTIVES

After reading this chapter, you should be able to do the following:

▶ Discuss the importance of strategic planning for organizations.

▶ Identify the nine steps in developing a strategic plan.

▶ Distinguish between organizational goals and objectives.

▶ Identify the types of organizational objectives.

▶ Analyze organizational objectives using the SMART criteria.

▶ Conduct a SWOT Analysis to achieve organizational goals.

Childhood obesity has reached epidemic proportions in the United States. According to the Center for Disease Control (CDC), the number of children affected by obesity has more than tripled since the 1970s, with nearly 1 in 5 US children age six to nineteen having a BMI above at or above the eighty-fifth percentile. There are many factors that affect childhood obesity rates, including genetics, metabolism, sleep, diet, and exercise, and environmental influences such as neighborhood design and access to parks. Further, children's perceptions and behaviors are influenced by family members, peers, members of their local, religious, and cultural communities, schools and after-school programs, government agencies, the media, food and beverage manufacturers, and the entertainment industry (CDC 2018). Reversing the trend of childhood obesity in the United States will require action from several if not all of these parties.

Jasmine is the principal of a large public elementary school just outside of Chicago, Illinois. In addition to ensuring the academic integrity of her school's programs, a major part of Jasmine's job is to ensure that district, state, and federal regulations are being met regarding students' physical well-being. Her job therefore includes monitoring and shaping the school's lunch and after-school programs. Jasmine has decided to limit students' access to junk food by prohibiting vending machines on school property and requiring that parents have any "shared" snacks approved by teachers before allowing their children to bring them to class. Given all of the time that she spends making sure that the school is following regulations and taking active steps to ensure the health of its students, she is stunned when the school nurse reports no change in the average BMI of its students over the past year—despite all of her efforts, nearly 30 percent of the students at the school still qualify as overweight.

Andre has just been hired as creative director for an international advertising agency. One of the agency's major clients is Knack, a food manufacturer that specializes in easy, nutritious family meals for the average American home. In his new position, Andre has been tasked to lead a corporate responsibility initiative on healthy eating for children and their families. Andre jumps right in to the task and creates a hashtag that families can use on social media called #KnackSnacks. He immediately creates a post for all of Knack's social media platforms, asking families to use the hashtag when they share pictures of their healthy family meals. Extremely proud of how quickly he handled this initiative for Knack, Andre is shocked when the CEO bluntly asks, "Okay, what's the point of this?" at their weekly board meeting.

Liam is the community outreach coordinator for a minor league baseball team in Southern California, the Rancho Cucamonga Quakes. For years, Liam has been coordinating a "Shake with the Quakes" workout event, where children from the community are invited to come play field games with the players in their ballpark. Every year, hundreds of kids show up for this free event and leave happy and worn out from running around outside. Liam has also worked with a number of local and national food manufacturers to provide free samples of healthy snacks and beverages at the event, along with education on the importance of diet and exercise—especially if you want to grow up to be a professional baseball player. Liam thinks the work he has done with the Quakes should be able to get him a position on the staff of a major league baseball team—but how can he provide evidence of the impact of the "Shake with the Quakes" event to help him make this next step?

In each of these examples, we see an organization that is addressing a common issue—childhood obesity—through three very distinct methods. These organizations not only vary in their type and structure—from Jasmine's local public school system to Andre's international advertising agency—but also in the clarity of the actions they are taking to address the national childhood obesity epidemic. While some organizations are measuring their successes, others don't even seem sure of what to measure. There are also various motivations for tracking these successes—as individuals working in organizations, Jasmine, Andre, and Liam have both personal and professional reasons for wanting to show that they are doing well. In each of these three scenarios, the organizational members were acting as leaders to carry out the mission and vision of the organization—but were they doing so in a way that was accurate? Measurable? Effective? The purpose of this chapter is to help individuals like Jasmine, Andre, and Liam improve the work they are already doing for their organization by setting realistic, measurable, and effective goals and objectives in line with their organization's unique capabilities, limitations, and brand. In this chapter, we discuss nine steps for achieving a strategic communication campaign. We then examine several of these steps more closely, including how an organization should identify its goals and objectives, how these objectives should be approached for optimal success, and finally how an organization can assess its own ability to meet these objectives. We begin with a discussion of the importance of detailed planning in this aspect of organizational strategy.

5.1 THE IMPORTANCE OF PLANNING

People who set goals tend to be more successful than those who do not. This seems like an obvious statement, right? Of course the Steve Jobses and Oprah Winfreys of the world set goals—to grow their companies, to establish their brand, to achieve continual improvement. Goal setting also relates to success on a smaller level: the goals that we set for our relationships, our teams, and ourselves affect our everyday lives. For these reasons, the nature of goals and their impact on messaging has been a focus of communication scholars for decades. We know from this research that individuals who are goal oriented tend to be more motivated and efficacious than those who are not (Huang, Jin, and Zhang 2017; Tolli and Schmidt 2008). Whether it is in school, at work, or at the gym, there is a mentality to goal-setting that simply helps us to be better. However, goals become meaningless if they are not pursued and ultimately achieved.

Just as individuals who set goals tend to achieve more, organizations that engage in purposeful activities tend to be more effective (Berger 2008; Peralta et al. 2015). As we have established in previous chapters, much, if not all, of organizational functioning is strategic. To be strategic, however, an organization must engage in careful, detailed planning. Without clear vision and a path forward, organizational activities will be scattered, without purpose, and (at worst) harmful to the organization and its members. An organization must always think of the past, present, and the future: what have we done in the past that has worked? What has not worked? What are we doing right now and how is that helping us to achieve our mission? What do we want to be doing next year? In five years? How can we make sure that this will happen? This process of reflecting on the organization, identifying where the organization should be headed, and outlining how the organization will get there is known as **strategic planning.**

What would be the reason for failing to set a clear strategic plan? Have you ever started a group project with your peers and suggested in the first meeting to create a detailed schedule of responsibilities and tasks? If so, you can probably guess what a lot of organizational leaders would say about strategic planning—"Sure, that sounds great . . . but who has that kind of time? We need to just get to work" or "I don't see the point of spending time on this." As the US Department of Health and Human Services (2002) writes in its classic health communication program guide *Making Health Communication Programs Work,* effective planning can help determine appropriate roles, establish logical processes, set priorities, assign responsibilities, and perhaps most importantly, avoid disasters. Therefore, this process of carefully planning actually ultimately saves the organization time and effort. An organization's strategic plan should serve as a framework for decision making, stimulate and guide change and growth in the organization, and serve as a benchmark and assessment tool for organizational activities. An organization with a well-defined strategic plan will have a clear idea of what it is, what it wants to be, and what it needs to be doing. As a result, organizations with clear strategic plans act with purpose and waste no effort in achieving their goals. Think of our case studies in the beginning of this chapter—how would Jasmine, Andre, and Liam each be in a different situation if they had a detailed, deliberate plan of action and evaluation for their campaigns? In the next section, we overview the nine steps that any organization should undertake to plan a strategic communication campaign.

5.2 THE NINE STEPS OF PLANNING A STRATEGIC COMMUNICATION CAMPAIGN

As we discussed in chapter 1, the myriad strategic efforts that an organization engages in often emerge in the form of communication *campaigns,* or systematic, purposeful attempts to create change in a defined target audience over a specified time period. In developing a strategic communication campaign, there are nine overall steps that an organization should engage in. A brief description for each step follows, with a few expanded in later sections of this chapter on organizational goals and objectives. Other steps are explored in the following chapters 6 to 11. Together these chapters provide a blueprint for the type of deliberate action necessary in creating campaigns on behalf of an organization, whether it is in the for-profit, nonprofit, or government context.

1. **Conduct background research.** An organization developing a strategic plan should fully understand the problem or issue that it addresses. This background research might include the extent or prevalence of an issue, who is being affected, and what the potential preventative measures or alternatives are. For for-profit companies, research should be completed to understand the competition and new trends in product development. We will discuss ways to research the problem or issue your organization addresses, as well as the organization itself, more in this chapter.
2. **Identify long-term goals.** Before an organization can develop a strategic plan, it must identify what it would like to achieve long term. These long-term goals might be look forward six months, one year, or even ten years. The length of time for these goals, as well as the goals themselves, will depend on the type and size of the organization. A newly opened restaurant owner's long-term goal might be to survive the first year, and so her strategic plan will be based around that (realistic) goal; however, a one-year strategic plan isn't as realistic for a national restaurant chain. We will discuss a few common types of long-term goals for organizations in this chapter, but these can and do vary widely.
3. **Select short-term objectives.** As we will discuss more in this chapter, strategic planning is not just about the big picture dreams of an organization. Rather, much of the planning efforts are and should be focused on the day-to-day activities that will help the organization to succeed. If the goal of the restaurant owner is to survive the first year in business, what will that take from the executive chef, sous chefs, line cooks, servers, busboys, and hostesses every day? What will be the nightly and weekly goals that will get the restaurant to its 365th day in business? These are the short-term objectives, which are no less important than the long-term goals. We will discuss a few common organizational objective types in this chapter.

4. **Conduct a SWOT analysis.** In addition to researching the problem or issue that your organization addresses (and the people it serves), part of developing a strategic plan should be thoroughly examining and researching the organization itself. In order to determine an organization's ability to achieve its goals and objectives, an analysis of both internal and external environments is necessary. A SWOT analysis, as we discuss in later sections of this chapter, allows an organization to take an in-depth look at its own strengths, weaknesses, opportunities, and threats. This analysis allows an organization to look inward before moving forward and ultimately to pursue realistic but progressive goals.

5. **Analyze your target audience.** Who an organization is serving should be at the forefront of any strategic plan. The intended receivers of organizational messages should be consulted, analyzed, and understood before organizations make any attempts to pursue organizational goals and objectives. An organization and its intended audiences—whether internal or external, local or international—should have an ongoing, mutually beneficial relationship.

6. **Develop messages.** Once background research is conducted, goals are set, and target audiences are carefully considered, an organization can begin to develop and test the effectiveness of its intended messages. These messages should be developed in accordance with theoretical and evidence-based principles of message design. These messages are central to the strategic plan, as they become the "face" of the organization for its recipients. Ultimately, the goal is that these messages will influence the target audience to change their behavior in accordance with the established goals and objectives of the organization's strategic plan.

7. **Select channels.** In tandem with or closely after developing messages, an organization must consider how it can best reach its target audience. This will include decisions on which type of media to use to convey messages. There are many choices of media for communicating your message to your target audience. From traditional mass media efforts like radio and television, to more immersive, user-generated content experiences on social media platforms, organizations have much to consider at this stage in the process. Ultimately, the channel should reflect the organization's mission, its target audience, and the purpose of the messaging.

8. **Consider community relationships, stakeholders, and partnerships.** An organization can often increase its influence, credibility, and effectiveness by partnering with individuals or groups in its community. If you are working on an antidrug campaign funded by the government, for instance, you will probably have a much higher rate of success by partnering with local schools, where youth spend six to eight hours of their day, five days a week. Partnership can be risky, though—so clear partnership plans are key to mutually beneficial relationships.

9. **Develop implementation and evaluation plans.** The final step in planning is to set a path for success when your strategic communication plan actually launches and to decide how you will evaluate your progress and successes. When planning an event with multiple people involved, distributing tasks and setting clearly defined roles is key. Although unpredictable events will undoubtedly occur, going in to your campaign with a clear plan of how events will unfold can only help your organization. You should also be as prepared as possible for the unexpected. What will you do if a crisis emerges? Who will be responsible for setting the organization back on track? Are you willing to make changes to your plan as the campaign is in progress? These aspects of the strategic communication campaign plan are not to be overlooked.

Clearly, these nine steps involve a lot of research, discussion, revision, and reflection. There is a reason the planning phase of strategic communication campaigns is so important: it takes a lot of effort! For now, let's focus on the first and arguably most important step in developing a strategic plan: conducting background research.

5.3 CONDUCTING BACKGROUND RESEARCH AND EVALUATING SOURCES

Regardless of the type of organization (for-profit, nonprofit, or government), the first step in developing a strategic plan should always be to do your research. How you investigate the problem or issue that your organization addresses, and what type of information you are looking for, will vary considerably depending on whether you are a for-profit, nonprofit, or government organization.

- *For-Profit Organization:* Investigating the issue for a for-profit organization might involve researching the best materials to use to create your product, what your potential consumers are interested in, and what your competition is currently doing.
- *Nonprofit Organization:* For a nonprofit, background research likely includes the scope or extent of the problem you are addressing and what potential solutions might be. If you are a nonprofit working to address homelessness in your area, for instance, your background research will involve not only determining the number of individuals who are homeless in your community, but also what factors led to this homelessness rate and how they can be reduced.
- *Government Organization.* If you are a government organization, you are likely working with larger databases to uncover the prevalence and percentage of the population engaged in your issue.

Regardless of the type of information you seek, there is one truth to conducting background research: The more you understand the background of the issue your organization addresses, the better you can address it.

5.3.1 Primary and Secondary Sources

So, how is background research conducted? When we refer to "background research," we don't necessarily mean research conducted by white-coat-wearing scientists in research labs (although this might be the case for organizations in the medical or pharmaceutical fields). More often, to understand the problem or issue addressed by your organization, you will conduct research by reviewing available data sources. This process of reviewing and summarizing existing data is known as **secondary research** and typically involves a number of sources. Sometimes referred to as "desk research," this process can be as simple as browsing the results of an internet search but can also include using library resources to read academic articles, online government databases, popular press articles like magazines and blogs, and even information on other organizations or entities addressing the same problem. If you are addressing childhood obesity like our organizational members in the beginning of this chapter, for instance, you might use information from the Centers for Disease Control (CDC) to learn about national obesity trends, the current measures available to track obesity rates, or its current programs to address this issue in schools nationwide. Establishing information on national obesity rates on your own or working to address obesity in schools without researching what schools are currently doing would not only be creating more work than is necessary but also could fatally undermine the success of your campaign efforts.

As indicated earlier in the chapter, conducting secondary research is therefore important for several reasons. First, there is a lot of information available out there! You should avoid having to collect your own data, known as **primary research,** if it isn't necessary. Conducting your own research can be expensive and time consuming and requires training to do well. Further, there is simply some research you cannot do yourself: compiling national, state, and local databases on health information such as the Youth Risk Behavior Surveillance System used by the CDC is beyond the scope of most researchers. Second, conducting secondary research might help you define your problem or issue more clearly. As you learn more about your topic, your organization's unique focus will likely evolve. Third, reading and researching allows you to see what is being prioritized in your topic area. What do others in your area find to be important? What types of projects are being funded or prioritized? Spending time conducting secondary research might seem tedious, but the right background research will only strengthen your strategic campaign plan.

5.3.2 Four Criteria for Evaluating Sources

Of course, there is a range of quality to the secondary research that is available to you as a researcher. Whether you are a novice or an experienced researcher, it is always important to engage in critical evaluation of the resources you find. Generally, there are four criteria that you can use to evaluate the quality of the secondary research resources you are using.

- **Accuracy.** Can you cross-check the facts that are being stated in this resource? What are the references they provide for their research? If it is primary research, how was the data collected and from whom? Do you trust that their research was conducted ethically and with rigor?
- **Expertise.** What are the credentials of this source? Who is the person or persons who authored this information? Are the authors credible in this area?
- **Timeliness.** How recent is this information? Generally, you don't want to use information that is more than five years old. In some contexts, like social media research, you don't want to use information that is more than one year old. Does this information seem to be up to date, based on the most recent research or information that is available?
- **Objectivity.** Is there any bias to this source? Are the authors presenting both sides of an argument? If it is primary research, who is funding it? Do you think there could be any conflict of interest with this funding?

You might not always be able to assess each of these four criteria fully, but you should always think critically about your sources. If you are using information from a blog or web page, for instance, check closely to make sure that information is cited—and if scholarly sources are referenced, find those sources yourself and read them. It is not uncommon for academic research to be misquoted, or for writers to pick and choose the facts that they want to include to support their own points. Remember, this information is the first step in your overall plans to develop a strategic communication campaign, so you want to make sure the information that you have is accurate, based on expert knowledge, timely, and not biased.

5.3.3 The Importance of Research in Decision-Making

At this point you might be wondering who in an organization is responsible for these sorts of tasks, and the not-so-simple answer is that it will depend on the organization, its structure, and the goals at hand. In a family business, for instance, the decision-making for both long- and short-term goals might be determined by one or two leaders. In other organizations, the decision-making might be more lateral and involve more stakeholders. Recall from chapter 2 that such horizontal differentiation and vertical hierarchy are key characteristics that set organizations apart in terms of their complexity and decision-making; these qualities undoubtedly affect the background research element of developing a strategic campaign plan. Regardless of who is conducting the background research, the researcher must clearly summarize and present the data for the next two steps of strategic campaign planning: setting organizational goals and objectives.

5.4 SETTING ORGANIZATIONAL GOALS AND OBJECTIVES

Consider each of the following words: goals, objectives, strategy. What do they have in common? How are they different? When you are being goal-driven, is it the same as being strategic? Understanding these words, their meanings, and their differences is crucial to understanding organizational strategic planning. Indeed, all of these words are central to the process of narrowing in on an organizational plan and deciding how to achieve it. To help you understand their similarities and differences, we will define and consider each in the context of planning a strategic communication campaign. We will start with the impetus for any strategic communication campaign: the organization's goals.

A **goal** is a long-term outcome desired by the organization. An organization's goal or goals should be directly in line with the mission of an organization. In chapter 1, we discussed the three reasons we communicate in our everyday lives: to inform, to persuade, and to entertain. How do these goals translate to organizational functioning? Do organizations have similar communication goals as individuals do in *their* everyday lives? Organizations do need to seek information (and also to provide it), build and maintain relationships, persuade others, and in some cases do provide entertainment. However, the ways in which an organization must communicate (and to whom it must communicate) are much more complex than those of individual people. As we discussed in chapter 2, a central characteristic of organizations is that they have some type of overarching goal that binds members together. So what are these goals?

Although it would be nearly impossible to list every goal that for-profit, non-profit, and government organizations could have, there are few common goals that most of these organizations would share. These include to:

- increase stakeholder awareness and/or commitment
- enhance name recognition
- improve team productivity
- improve team efficiency
- obtain new partners
- recruit more members, volunteers, or staff

- improve team culture
- increase brand loyalty
- increase sales, donations, or funding
- reduce prevalence of a particular health, social justice, or environmental issue
- achieve public reform
- improve service delivery
- improve public perceptions of the organization

Although the types of goals that an organization might have are truly limitless, there are two general categories of goals that can be used to understand them further. The first type of goal is related to the organization achieving its core mission or purpose. These *task management* goals might help the organization to sell its product, increase its consumer base, increase the individual or community wellness of its target audience, or affect policy decisions. The specific goal might vary widely, but all goals in this category directly help the organization to fulfill its purpose. The second type of goal is *relationship and identity management* goals, which are goals centered on the identity and perception of the organization. Most commonly aligned with public relations initiatives, goals centered on reputation management concern how the organization is perceived by its own members and by the people it serves. An organization's relationship with stakeholders, community members, investors, donors, and consumers is crucial to its success. For small entrepreneurial organizations, keeping the team of ten employees satisfied in their positions and motivated to continue working and striving to grow is paramount to organizational success. For high schools and universities, maintaining a positive image and good relationship with alumni as they become successful is a key factor in maintaining donations, support, and reputations. Given their influence, there may be a number of long-term goals centered on these endeavors.

Whereas goals are long-term visions of what the organization needs to achieve, **objectives** are the smaller, incremental steps needed to achieve them. Objectives quantify the goals and state more specifically how they will be met. Whereas goals are "big picture" ideas, objectives are the small, precise actions that will be necessary to accomplish to get there. Think of a goal you might have in your personal life. It might be to graduate with your degree in four years. To run a marathon. To get accepted to graduate school. To buy your dream car. These are the "big picture" things that you desire, and they will take time, hard work, and dedication to achieve. Now, think of the things you need to do to achieve those goals. Let's take running a marathon as an example. To run 26.2 miles, most of us likely need to outline a series of objectives. For most runners, these objectives will come in the form of a training plan. Training plans typically include a complex schedule of short, quick runs to increase speed, longer slow runs to help with conditioning, cross-training to increase strength, and rest time

Figure 18 What do you think are some of the long-term goals of your university? What task management and/or relationship identity management goals do you think your university has?

to allow the body to recover. If you follow a formal training plan, the amount of time you spend in each of these activities will be strictly dictated: cross-train for thirty minutes on Monday, run a quick three miles on Tuesday, cross-train for thirty minutes on Wednesday, run five miles on Thursday, etc. With each week, a runner builds toward longer and faster running times. In this way, looking at a six-month plan at the start of your training might seem overwhelming, and perhaps even overly tedious, but without taking these small incremental steps you will likely not achieve your goal (or achieve it and still be able to walk after the marathon!). This is the relationship between goals and objectives for organizations. The overall goal should be something to strive for, but achievable. The objectives are incremental, measurable, realistic steps that help that goal come to life. Each objective should be treated as a small contract; just as skipping a few long runs can lead to disastrous results in marathon training, treating objectives as "minor" could lead to major problems for an organization.

Of course, everyone's strategy will look different based on a number of unique factors: if you are a beginning, intermediate, or advanced runner, if you have any injuries, how fast you would like to finish the race, and how much time you have to train will affect your training plan. Given our individual strengths, weaknesses, and overall goals, our strategies will look different. This difference in strategy is also true for organizations, and it certainly affects their planning. We will discuss the idea of different organizational strategies in more detail later in this chapter when we discuss the importance of conducting situational analyses in light of organizational goals and objectives. For now, let's turn to a discussion of the various types of objectives an organization might undertake to achieve its goals.

5.4.1. Types of Organizational Objectives

Your organization's objectives likely fall into one of three main categories in terms of their intended impact on the organization's target audience, or individuals whom you intend to influence with your message. These categories are informational objectives, attitudinal objectives, and behavioral objectives.

- **Informational** objectives aim to inform or educate people about some relevant topic, event, issue, or product. The Truth Campaign was launched in 1999 with the broad goal of eliminating teen smoking in the United States, with the apparent objective of informing youth about the tobacco industry and its marketing techniques. If you check out their "Facts" page (www .thetruth.com/the-facts), you will see numerous examples of such informational objectives. By translating academic and government research into short, easily digestible and shareable facts about smoking, the Truth campaign is seeking to achieve its long-term goal by having its target audience know something that they did not know before. Other examples of informational objectives might be to educate target audiences about the benefits of a product or the drawbacks of a competitor's product. Information objectives might also include the work of political activists or lobbyists who attempt to educate voters on important issues prior to elections.

- **Attitudinal** objectives attempt to alter existing attitudes and underlying beliefs regarding a topic, event, issue, or product. Sometimes our target audience *knows* they should be engaging in a good behavior, avoiding a bad behavior, or buying a certain product—but they still don't! Our **attitudes** are positive or negative evaluations of an idea, behavior, or product. Decades of research on persuasion support that attitudes have a significant impact on individual's behavior (Petty and Cacioppo 1986). Therefore, sometimes the objectives of an organization are aimed solely at changing these attitudes and their underlying beliefs. If we continue with the Truth Campaign as our example, one attitudinal objective they clearly have, according to their messages, is to change the perception that smoking is popular among teens. As they cite on their website, less than 6 percent of teens still smoke, and cigarette use is declining. Why would an antitobacco campaign advertise this fact? Doesn't it show that their work isn't needed? Quite the opposite. The Truth Campaign, in sharing these statistics, is attempting to lessen the **descriptive norm,** or perception of what similar others are doing. Their hope is that teens will realize smoking isn't nearly as popular or "cool" as it once was and not be tempted to pick up a pack of cigarettes. Other attitudinal or belief objectives might be to increase perceptions of risk, convince people that a product or service will actually help them, and convince target audiences that taking the recommended action or buying the recommended product is worth the cost.

- **Behavioral** objectives attempt to change what people are doing or saying. Last but not least, organizations can have behavioral objectives in which they want their target audience to DO something. This might be to start a new behavior, modify an existing behavior, or stop engaging in a behavior. What is the apparent behavioral objective of the Truth Campaign? To quit smoking, right? If you check out their website, do you see other behaviors that are being promoted? Often, organizations have many behavioral objectives, and some might be more obvious than others. Without influencing behavior, most organizations would not have a reason to exist. Whether it is encouraging shopping, voting, eating, adopting, or any other limitless number of behaviors, most organizations would cease to exist without a behavioral objective for a target audience.

An organization might have any combination of informational, attitudinal, or behavioral objectives. However, you should always aim to have at least one behavioral objective in your strategic campaign plan. If you don't ask your audience to DO something, your messages might seem unclear and your success difficult to evaluate. With for-profit organizations, the behavioral objective is typically pretty straightforward: buy this product or use our services. The objective might be less clear for nonprofit organizations, many of which aim to increase awareness of social or health-related issues. This is not to say that an informational or attitudinal goal is not important; rather, it is imperative to consider *how* you will assess whether your goal has been reached. Often, this assessment requires a behavioral element that can be measured.

As we already noted, goals and objectives are not interchangeable terms. They are interdependent and should inform each other but should be treated as unique entities. Outlining your objectives closely is very important for your strategic communication plan. The objectives that you select will have a significant impact on the direction of your campaign, the messages you develop, and how you will ultimately assess your effectiveness.

Perhaps one of the best illustrations of how goals and objectives are used to frame strategic communication campaigns differentially is that outlined by the Office of Disease Prevention and Health Promotion in their Healthy People initiative. The Healthy People initiative provides evidence-based ten-year national initiatives for individuals working in all sectors of public health. These initiatives are focused on a number of topics and help to identify national health priorities, increase awareness of health needs, and provide measurable objectives for health care at the local, state, and national level (US Department of Health and Human Services 2018). Within each topic area, health professionals can find a number of long-term goals and corresponding objectives to strive for until the next evaluation period.

Let's take the topic of "Occupational Safety and Health" as an example. As seen in "Long-Term Goals to SMART Objectives: An Example from Healthy People 2020," Healthy People notes the long-term goal for 2020 is to "Promote the health and safety of people at work through prevention and early intervention" (US Department of Health and Human Services 2018; SMART stands for Specific, Measurable, Attainable/Achievable, Relevant, Time sensitive, see page 133). This fairly broad goal is then broken down into ten smaller objectives,

Long-Term Goals to SMART Objectives:
An example from Healthy People 2020

**GOAL: PROMOTE THE HEALTH AND SAFETY OF PEOPLE AT WORK THROUGH PREVENTION
AND EARLY INTERVENTION**

List of All Overall Objectives to Achieve Goal

OSH-1 Reduce deaths from work-related injuries
OSH-2 Reduce nonfatal work-related injuries
OSH-3 Reduce the rate of injury and illness cases involving days away from
work due to overexertion or repetitive motion
OSH-4 Reduce pneumoconiosis deaths
OSH-5 Reduce deaths from work-related homicides
OSH-6 Reduce work-related assaults
OSH-7 Reduce the proportion of people who have elevated blood lead con-
centrations from work exposures
OSH-8 Reduce occupational skin diseases or disorders among full-time
workers
OSH-9 Increase the proportion of employees who have access to workplace
programs that prevent or reduce employee stress
OSH-10 Reduce new cases of work-related, noise-induced hearing loss

Subcategories of Objectives to Achieve OSH-1

OSH-1.1 Reduce deaths from work-related injuries in all industries
OSH-1.2 Reduce deaths from work-related injuries in mining
OSH-1.3 Reduce deaths from work-related injuries in construction
OSH-1.4 Reduce deaths from work-related injuries in transportation and
warehousing
OSH-1.5 Reduce deaths from work-related injuries in agriculture, forestry,
fishing, and hunting

MEASURABLE SMART OBJECTIVE

To reduce the number of work-related injury deaths to 3.6 per 100,000 full-time
workers ages sixteen years and older from 4.0 per 100,000 (a 10 percent
improvement) in the 2020 Census of Fatal Occupational Injuries and Current Population Survey.

> For more information on how this data will be measured,
> visit www.healthypeople.gov/node/5035/data_details.

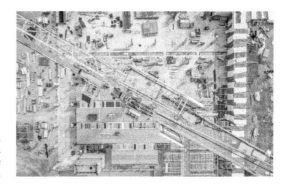

Figure 19 The goal of reducing workplace injuries in high-risk work environments might seem overwhelming, but it becomes manageable with a series of smaller, achievable objectives.

including *to reduce deaths from work-related injuries.* As this example indicates, this is just one of many ways to promote occupational health and safety. Yet reducing workplace deaths from injuries is still quite broad and can be further classified into a series of five smaller objectives, including addressing workplace injuries across several particular areas of work. The ultimate objective is to reduce the number of work-related injury deaths to 3.6 per 100,000 full-time workers ages sixteen years and older from 4.0 per 100,000 (a 10 percent improvement) in the 2020 Census of Fatal Occupational Injuries and Current Population Survey. This is much more specific than the overarching "Goal" for Occupational Safety and Health, right? As this example illustrates, with background research and the right resources, a seemingly intangible large goal can be addressed through a series of well-researched, measurable, and achievable objectives.

Regardless of the type of objective, the objective must be relevant to the overall goal you (or the organization) aspire to reach as well as providing a clear path forward toward that goal. Fortunately, organizations and their employees can use the SMART method to design objectives that will be an asset to organizational strategic planning.

5.4.2 Setting SMART Objectives

The first known use of the SMART acronym was in 1981 by consultant George T. Doran in an article titled "There's a S.M.A.R.T. Way to Write Management's Goals and Objectives" in *Management Review.* A former corporate planner, Doran recognized not only the importance of objective setting for organizations but also the difficulty most mid- and upper-level managers faced in conducting this task. The resulting SMART method has become widely used by campaign designers in public relations, advertising, health communication, and a number of other fields that employ campaigns or strategic plans. So what does SMART stand for?

• **Specific.** The objectives for the strategic plan must be precise, clear, and detailed. In some cases, being specific will be easy: perhaps you want to increase the number of followers your organization has on social media by two hundred. In other cases, it might be more complex, such as increasing brand equity as we discussed in chapter 3. In these cases, it is imperative to turn the abstract, fuzzy ideas into tangible, clear statements. In addition, it will be important to think about how these statements can be measured.

- **Measurable.** It is imperative that organizations measure their success in strategic planning. To ensure that long-term success can be identified, each individual objective in a strategic plan must be measurable given the organization's resources. This measurement might be **quantitative,** in which results are discussed in terms of numerical values such as percentages or ratios, or **qualitative,** in which results are non-numerical and based on words or text. The type of measurement used will depend on the goal and context of the objective.

- **Attainable/Achievable.** Objectives must be considered doable by the organization and its members. Keep in mind that expecting 100 percent change is unreasonable; most marketers and campaign designers achieve about 2–3 percent change in the population they target! Consider the marathon example we used earlier in this chapter—if the first task in a marathon training plan was to run twenty miles without stopping, most marathon hopefuls would shrug their shoulders and say, "Ah well, that's not for me." It is important to set realistic objectives that can be systemically achieved. Being realistic is beneficial for morale purposes as well; if an organization's members feel that the objectives are out of reach, they will lose confidence or (even worse) not even try. If you need help figuring out what is reasonable for your context, consider consulting with a data expert in statistics, economics, epidemiology, or a field related to the purpose of your organization.

- **Relevant.** Brainstorming goals and objectives for strategic planning can be fun and can lead to a host of creative ideas. However, it is always important to evaluate objectives in light of the major goal at hand. Does this objective help the organization to eventually achieve its overall goal, or fulfill its mission? Is it beneficial to the organization and its employees? Is it in line with the identity and branding of the organization? Are there enough resources in place to support this objective? If not, it might be important to forgo even the most exciting objectives.

- **Time sensitive.** Finally, objectives should have an "expiration" date. In other words, there should be a set date (even time, if applicable) that an objective will be evaluated for its success. This keeps the organization accountable and on track.

By following the SMART method for developing objectives, organizations will develop a series of steps that will lead them actively toward achieving their goals. As a note, it is possible that not all aspects of the SMART system will work for each objective; it might not be reasonable to place a time frame on a given activity, for instance. That is okay—but to whatever extent possible,

Strategic Communication Mentor: Applying the SMART Method to Organizational Objectives

Use the SMART method to evaluate each of the following sample objectives. For each objective, use the scoring system to rank it as either 1 = Not Adequate, 2 = Adequate, or 3 = More than Adequate for each element of the SMART system (Specific, Measurable, Attainable, Relevant, Time sensitive).

OBJECTIVE 1: INCREASE LIKES ON SOCIAL MEDIA POSTS

Criteria	Score (1–3)
Specific	
Measurable	
Attainable	
Relevant	
Time sensitive	

OBJECTIVE 2: DECREASE THE NUMBER OF CAR ACCIDENTS DUE TO DISTRACTED DRIVING IN ERIE COUNTY BY 50 PERCENT IN THE NEXT FIVE YEARS

Criteria	Score (1–3)
Specific	
Measurable	
Attainable	
Relevant	
Time sensitive	

OBJECTIVE 3: INCREASE OVERALL CUSTOMER SATISFACTION SCORES ON POST-SERVICE-CALL SURVEYS TO 4.5 OR HIGHER ON A 5 POINT SCALE

Criteria	Score (1–3)
Specific	
Measurable	
Attainable	
Relevant	
Time sensitive	

Which objective had the highest score? What is it about this objective that caused you to rate it the highest?

If you rank an objective as 1 on any one of the SMART criteria, how could you revise it to improve?

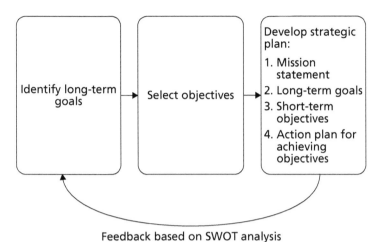

Feedback based on SWOT analysis

Figure 20 Strategic Plan Development.

organizations should use this acronym to evaluate their plans before engaging in any strategic activities. To summarize: These objectives should be specific, measurable steps that can be reasonably achieved by the organization in a given time period and help it to achieve its goals. These SMART objectives will make writing an overall strategic plan for a communication campaign a much smoother and clearer process.

5.4.3 Synthesizing Goals and Objectives: The Role of Organizational Strategic Plans

Once long-term goals are identified and SMART objectives are selected, an organization can start to put together a **strategic plan,** or the sum of the objectives an organization intends to undertake to achieve its long-term goals. A strategic plan is a written document that would typically be distributed among organizational members for informational, motivational, and feedback purposes. It can be as short as one page or as long as a full binder, depending on the level of detail needed to communicate the goals and objectives being pursued to organizational members. As can be seen in figure 20, the development of a strategic plan based on goals and objectives is a fairly linear process. Goals are first needed to inform objectives, which are then incorporated into an overall strategy or action plan. If multiple goals and objectives have been identified, part of developing this strategic plan will be to select particular goals and corresponding objectives to focus on.

As seen in figure 20, a strategic plan should be driven by and consistent with the mission of the organization as communicated in its mission statement. Therefore, once you have your background research in place and your goals and

Interview with a Professional: JoAnna Jacob, the American Cancer Society

The following interview is with JoAnna Jacob, a senior manager in community development for the American Cancer Society. As you read, think about how JoAnna's experiences relate to what you have read so far in this chapter about the strategic planning process. Does any of this information surprise you? How do you think these responses might be different for individuals working in the for-profit or government sectors?

Could you describe your job duties as senior manager of community development? What does your day-to-day activity look like?

As senior manager of community development with the American Cancer Society, I lead a team of community development execution staff that manages a portfolio of community-based fundraising events in Buffalo, New York.

Along with managing, coaching, and developing our community development team members, I maintain accountability for significant income performance targets and am responsible for profits and loss management for the community development revenue activities in the market.

On a regular basis, I engage, mobilize, and steward relationships with community influencers who significantly contribute to the success of the society.

In our text we define goals as the long-term outcomes desired by an organization. What does the process of goal setting look like in your organization? Who decides what goals need to be set and how they will be achieved?

A 501(c)(3) nonprofit corporation[1], the American Cancer Society is governed by a single board of directors that, among other responsibilities, sets long-term goals.

Our top staff executives set the organization's strategic direction accordingly, and staff members across the organization work with their respective management teams to develop individual goals that support shared organizational objectives.

Staff members collaborate with their managers to identify the primary activities—and corresponding targets and measures—needed to attain their goals.

What are some long-term goals that you are currently working on as senior manager of community development? What are more immediate, short-term objectives, or steps needed to achieve these goals?

As senior manager of community development, I am currently charged with achieving approximately $1 million in net community development revenue.

To achieve this annual revenue target, several steps are needed. Among other steps, I need to work with my team to identify and quantify existing and potential revenue streams. From there, our team must determine if it is feasible to pursue the identified streams. If it is feasible, how will our team pursue these streams? If it is not feasible, what other streams do we need to target and materialize to support the attainment of our annual revenue goal?

What are some of the challenges you face in achieving these goals and objectives?

A—perhaps surprising—challenge that my team members and I face while attempting to attain our annual revenue goal is weather.

Most of our annual community development revenue is drawn from a one-day, outdoor fundraising event. While a significant amount of event revenue is generated prior to event day, on-site activities such as product and food sales contribute to the event's overall proceeds.

Inclement weather may deter society constituents from attending the referenced outdoor fundraising event. In turn, our team may see an unanticipated year-over-year decline in event-day revenue.

While this scenario presents a challenge to our team as we attempt to attain our goal, we may course-correct and stay on the track to achieving our goal by adding or modifying identified objectives.

In this text, we refer to strategic planning as the process of reflecting on the organization, identifying where the organization should be headed, and outlining how the organization will get there. Is this something that you do in your position for the American Cancer Society? How important is setting a plan like this?

In my role, I am not involved in the society's strategic planning process, but I am responsible for ensuring that the organization-wide strategic plan is translated into my team's long- and short-term work.

For instance, one of the society's strategic goals is to achieve 80 percent of adults age fifty and older being screened for colorectal cancer. As senior manager of community development, I work with my team to acknowledge our part in achieving that shared goal and identify customized supporting objectives that we can materialize within our sphere of influence.

I see strategic planning as vital to organizational success. Within the society, specifically, the organization's strategic plan informs and directs staff members' day-to-day work and long-term goals. Our maintenance of a shared mission, vision, and plan of work only strengthens our organization's ability to do what is most important: save lives.

Finally, do you have any advice or suggestions on this topic for the readers of our textbook? What would you like to say about long-term goals and objectives based on your experience in the non-profit sector?

Strategic planning, goal-setting, and objective-setting are integral to achieving success, especially in the nonprofit sector.

Having worked in the nonprofit sector for nearly seven years, I've become acutely aware of my—like other nonprofit employees'—limited capacity, which is mainly due to nonprofit organizations' need to allocate essential resources to the execution of the work at hand.

Accordingly, I need to allocate my limited time and resources as efficiently as possible to maximize our organization's mission impact. That can occur most effectively when I am aware of my organization's mission, vision, and strategic direction and when I have defined short- and long-term goals as well as a plan around how I will attain them.

For more information on community development near you, as well as volunteer and internship opportunities, visit the American Cancer Society's website at www.cancer.org.

1. A 501(c)(3) is a tax-exempt designation by the Internal Revenue Service. To qualify, an organization must meet certain criteria, including that none of its earnings may directly benefit any private shareholder or individual. In addition, a 501(c)(3) may not attempt to influence legislation as a substantial part of its activities, and it may not participate in any campaign activity for or against political candidates. For more information on 501(c)(3) designations, and the other nonprofit organization designations according to the IRS, see www.irs.gov.

objectives set for your organization, it is a good time to step back and evaluate not only your organization in more depth but also its unique capabilities, barriers, and internal and external factors that might affect its success in achieving long-term goals. As indicated by the feedback loop in Figure 20, this highly important process might be cause to revise goals and objectives. To engage in this process, an organization should conduct a situation analysis, or SWOT analysis (Strengths, Weaknesses, Opportunities, and Threats), of its ability to enact its strategic plan.

5.5 ANALYZING THE ORGANIZATION'S ABILITY TO MEET ITS GOALS: THE IMPORTANCE OF SWOT ANALYSIS

Part of outlining goals in organizational life is to examine the organization itself with a critical eye. *What* is it that you need to achieve? Why it is important that this is achieved? A good starting place for this sort of internal reflection is the content that we discussed in chapter 3: mission statements, identity, image, and branding. How your organization wants to be viewed, and how it is actually viewed, are typical starting places for organizational agenda setting. However, when developing strategic communication campaigns, a more thorough and critical examination of the organization is often necessary. This is why so many organizations incorporate the simple yet effective SWOT analysis into their planning (Fallon 2018). A **SWOT Analysis** is an in-depth examination of an organizations' strengths, weaknesses, opportunities, and threats. Although an organization can conduct a SWOT analysis at any point in time, this practice is more useful when it is directed at some particular goal or objective, which is why it is helpful to think of it as coming after your strategic plan development (Lee and Kotler 2016).

In conducting a SWOT analysis, there are two main areas of interest to consider: internal and external factors. Internal factors are those directly related to the organization, such as its employees, revenue, structure, or any other factor it has some control over. External factors, on the other hand, exist outside of the organization or its influence, including current social events, economic or environmental forces, and technological or market trends. An evaluation of strengths and weaknesses falls under the internal assessment of the organization, whereas opportunities and threats are evaluations of external factors (Fallon 2018; Lee and Kotler 2016).

5.5.1 Internal Assessment: Organizational Strengths and Weaknesses

An organization's **strengths** are the benefits it has relative to the competition. This might include funding, the quality of its products and services, the commitment of its staff, past successes, and current partnerships. Such strengths are aspects of the organization that should be highlighted or maximized. Key questions to ask in a strengths assessment are:

1. What are the best qualities we have as an organization?
2. What does our organization do better than other organizations?
3. What is our organization's **unique selling proposition,** or thing that we offer that our competitors cannot offer?

An organization's **weaknesses** are drawbacks the organization faces. The same elements discussed above, if not in support of the organization achieving its goals, might be considered: funding, product and service quality, internal support, partnerships, and past efforts at achieving goals. Weaknesses are areas that should be addressed if possible, and minimized if not. Being aware of weaknesses in these early stages of strategic planning will help organizations to be realistic in pursuing their long-term goals and short-term objectives. Key questions to ask here include:

1. What is something that we could improve on as an organization?
2. What would outsiders say is a weakness of our organization?
3. What do our competitors do better than we?
4. What would be a reason not to use our organization for this purpose?

Consider school principal Jasmine from the beginning of this chapter. In evaluating her organization's (a large public elementary school) ability to address childhood obesity, what are some strengths she can identify? She might consider the amount of time that students spend at the organization (six to eight hours a day, five days a week), the support of faculty members and school administrators, and the amount of control the school has in determining what food is allowed on its campus all as strengths. Weaknesses might include limited prioritization by teachers who need to focus on educational goals rather than student health, and a lack of consistency in disseminating messages about healthy eating. These elements are either helping or hindering Jasmine's long-term goals and are all aspects of the organization that she has some degree of control over. Although SWOT analyses are extremely common for organizations of all types, conducting this sort of honest reflection is very difficult. In the space below, we discuss two factors that might affect how well organizational members can conduct internal assessments: identity and groupthink.

Factors That Affect Internal Assessment: Identity

Of course, identifying weaknesses is harder than it seems when you are a part of the organization. Think of the organizations to which you have belonged: your family, sports teams, your first job, your current job. If you sat down all of the members of this organization and asked, "What is our greatest weakness?" what sort of response do you think you would get? Would it be easy or even realistic to expect that the members could identify their shortcomings? Often, when we are a part of an organization, it is challenging to critique how it functions. We invest a lot of time, effort, and passion into the organizations to which we belong, and our **personal identity,** or sense of self, might be intricately tied to it. As psychologists Tajfel and Turner maintain in "Social Identity Theory" (1986), persons' sense of self is largely determined by the groups to which they belong. More specifically, our various **social identities,** or memberships in various groups and how those groups are evaluated, influence our overall personal identity or sense of self. Those group memberships might include our gender, ethnicity, sexual orientation, religion, age group, and our occupation. As such, our social and personal identities are closely linked; we continually strive to maintain a positive personal identity by making continual comparisons between the groups to which we belong and other groups.

Favorable social comparisons with such out-groups enhance the membership associated with the group, which in turn determines a positive self-concept (Tajfel and Turner 1986). Any sports fan knows this to be a common phenomenon. We continually make comparisons to rival team fan bases to enhance our self-concept—we are more dedicated, more respectful, and all around better fans than "they"! The same sort of thinking comes in to play when we are evaluating organizations for which we might work or contribute to. If I critique my employer, my company, or my university, I am critiquing myself. This can make honest internal assessment very difficult.

Factors That Affect Internal Assessment: Groupthink

Another reason that identifying weaknesses might be difficult is due to **groupthink,** or a process of group decision-making that diminishes group creativity and individual thinking (Janis 1972). When groupthink occurs, members of an organization strive for cohesion and harmony within the group, at the cost of critical thinking and evaluating alternative courses of action in a decision, situation, or on a particular issue. Notably, a group is more susceptible to groupthink when its members are similar in background, when the group is insulated from outside opinions, and when there are no clear rules for decision-making (Janis 1972). Groupthink also tends to occur when there is pressure to make a quick decision.

Fortunately, groupthink is avoidable even in the smallest and most cohesive groups. To avoid groupthink, a group can take the following simple actions:

- **Appoint roles.** A good strategy to approach a decision is to appoint various roles or "hats" within the group. Communication researchers who specialize in small-group decision-making agree that minimally three **formal,** meaning-appointed, or elected, roles should be assigned to help the group function. These roles are a formal leader, a recorder, and a critical advisor (Myers and Anderson 2008). The **leader** keeps the group on task toward

Figure 21 Fortunately, there are a series of steps you can take in organizing group meetings in order to avoid groupthink. This includes setting clear roles and taking your time in coming to a decision.

achieving its goals and represents the group to external audiences (e.g., providing a report of the group's progress to a superior; Myers and Anderson 2008). The **recorder** serves an important function in the group by taking minutes of group meetings and notes of any progress or issues that need to be permanently recorded. The **critical advisor** challenges the group in a constructive manner and encourages the group to thoroughly consider their thinking and decision-making (Myers and Anderson 2008). Of course there are a variety of other formal and **informal** (e.g., those that emerge naturally from group interactions; Myers and Anderson 2008) roles that small-group communication scholars examine in terms of their impact on group functioning and outcomes; for an overview see Myers and Anderson (2008).

- **Change roles.** Roles should not be stagnant. The frequency with which roles will be switched depends on the length of the group's meeting, but roles should be changed at least once.
- **Encourage active involvement from all members.** For various reasons, individuals might be apprehensive about participating in the SWOT analysis. Maybe you are new to the organization and are uncomfortable sharing your thoughts on weaknesses and threats as a new member. Perhaps you are high in **communication apprehension,** meaning that you have high amounts of fear or anxiety when considering communication with other people (McCroskey and Richmond 1979). Given the variety of contextual and individual factors that might affect a member's willingness to participate in the SWOT, it is important to set a series of ground rules for discussion. We discuss this a bit more in the sections that follow, but key to avoiding groupthink is to ensure that all members feel free to share their opinions without fear of retribution or judgment.
- **Invite outside critique.** Involving an external evaluator, someone who is not a part of the organization, is perhaps the best way to avoid making a decision colored by groupthink.

- **Take your time.** Decision-making as an organization takes time, and a SWOT analysis can be an even lengthier process. By allotting enough time, you can alleviate the pressures that tend to lead to rushed, groupthink-tainted decisions.

Interestingly, research indicates that the two factors we have discussed as affecting the assessment of weaknesses—identity and groupthink—are related to and affect each other. Specifically, Haslam and colleagues (2006) found that as individuals' social identification with an organization increased, so too did their commitment to a project over time—even when that project is faltering and becoming detrimental to the organization's goals. When the task at hand might affect the way that the group is perceived by outsiders, which is often the case for both for-profit and nonprofit entities, protecting the group might be an attempt to protect one's one identity within it (Turner and Pratkanis 1998). This connection emphasizes the importance of proactively avoiding group-think. Organizational members who are highly committed and identify strongly with the organization might struggle to objectively evaluate it, a necessary task in the development of a strategic communication campaign. For these reasons, following the best practices for conducting a SWOT analysis discussed later in this chapter are critical to avoiding biases and ego-involved decision-making that might affect the strategic plan development process.

5.5.2 External Assessment: Organizational Opportunities and Threats

An external assessment of an organization is a careful consideration of existing opportunities and threats, which are essentially factors outside of the organization's control. Although it might seem counterproductive to spend time considering these factors for that reason, being aware of what is going on *around* an organization can be just as important as what is going on *inside* of it.

An organization's **opportunities** include events, trends, or factors outside of the organization that can be drawn on to help it succeed. These opportunities should be taken advantage of to help bring awareness or visibility to the organization and to otherwise help it achieve its goals with less effort than altering internal factors would require. This might include trends in entertainment, cultural and technological trends, economic or political factors, and even new laws. Key questions that an organization can ask to assess opportunities include:

1. Who are potential organizations we can partner with?
2. Are there any political, economic, technological, or social trends existing that support our cause?
3. Are there any policy changes that support what our organization does?

Strategic Communication Mentor: The Nature of Groupthink

Irvin Janis described groupthink as a group making faulty decisions because of a pressure to conform and come to consensus. As we discuss in this chapter, this might occur because the group has little time to come to a decision, and the group is both cohesive and isolated.

Take a moment to think about the decisions you have made in groups. This might have been at home, with friends, in school projects, on teams, or at work. Have you ever experienced anything similar to what Janis coined " groupthink"?

What was the outcome of that decision? Was it positive or negative?
Were there any elements of your situation that did not resonate with Janis's definition?
Are there any situations when groupthink would be a good thing for organizational decision-making?

Read the following article on consensus in the modern business world, then answer the following questions:

www.psychologytoday.com/blog/are-you-persuadable/201801/difficult-decisions-the-costs-consensus

The author argues that there are times when consensus should be the goal: Do you agree? Why or why not?

Similarly, an organization's **threats** include events, trends, or factors outside of the organization that threaten the success of the organization. There may be changes in public dialogue surrounding issues central to your organization, new regulations or laws that affect the creation and distribution of your product, or economic limitations among your target audience members that affect spending and buying power. Key questions that might be asked to assess threats include:

1. What are barriers to our organization's achieving its goals?
2. Are there any political, economic, technological, or social trends that exist that do not support our cause?
3. Are there any policy changes that prevent our organization from achieving its goals?

If we continue to consider Jasmine's position as a school principal, what are opportunities that might exist for her in addressing childhood obesity? The changing dialogue surrounding children's eating and exercise habits, with increased awareness of the long-term implications of obesity in childhood, certainly supports her cause. The introduction of new regulations and government-sponsored programs to reduce childhood obesity give her efforts not only credibility but also financial support and resources. However, in terms of threats, there are plenty: the popularity of video games encourages a sedentary lifestyle, and the tremendous advertising power of snack food companies and the perception that eating healthy is "too expensive" among children's parents all threaten her success at reducing obesity at her school. These external factors, although outside of Jasmine's control, are crucial to consider before she moves forward with a strategic communication plan.

5.5.3 Conducting a SWOT Analysis: Best Practices for Success

Conducting a comprehensive analysis of all of these factors might sound overwhelming, but there are five tips you can use to set up and conduct your SWOT analysis. The first is to make sure you allot enough time for a SWOT analysis. If you are planning one for your organization, dedicate at least one to two hours to this activity if you can (though a comprehensive SWOT might take even more time and research than that!). Second, think carefully about who to involve in the SWOT analysis process. You should include representatives from each level of your organization, if possible. For instance, a SWOT analysis at a university should involve representatives of the faculty, students, staff, and administrators (and even community members from the area around the university, if applicable). Third, be sure to have the right amount of people for the SWOT analysis session. You want this group to be about five to seven people—too much smaller or too much larger can affect the quality and quantity of ideas raised. If you need to have a particularly large group (more than seven people) due to the nature of your organization or because you simply want more members involved, consider breaking up your SWOT analyses into smaller **buzz groups.** These smaller subgroups can work on the entire SWOT analysis or components of the SWOT analysis and then report back to the larger group; this method has been successful in multiple organizational contexts in helping to bring new energy and increased involvement in decision-making processes (Siebold and Krikorian 1997).

Fourth, carefully organize the SWOT analysis session. You should think of this time as a **brainstorming** session, in that it allows the group to generate more ideas than they would as individuals, but that shouldn't mean it is unorganized or haphazard. There should be one person leading the discussion, and one person taking notes (i.e., a leader and a recorder). A good SWOT analysis will involve ample conversation and ideas—the leader might record general themes that arise on a white board in front of the room, while the recorder takes more extensive notes. You can use the template in table 5.1 as a visual to help organize participants' thoughts and the resulting conversation. This

Table 5.1   SWOT Analysis Template

SWOT Analysis	Strengths (Internal, Positive)	Weaknesses (Internal, Negative)
Opportunities (External, Positive)		
Threats (External, Negative)		

template will be important in prioritizing the thoughts that come out of the SWOT analysis, which we discuss in more detail below.

Last but not least, the leader should set a series of ground rules for discussion. These can be modified to the particular group, but in general should include the following:

- ✔ the idea is to get as many ideas out as possible, so all ideas are welcome,
- ✔ you do not need to "justify" your responses,
- ✔ you should build on other's ideas when you can, and
- ✔ you should not criticize other's ideas either verbally or nonverbally

These effective brainstorming rules (Osborn 1953) will lead to a more productive use of group members' time and energy.

Who conducts SWOT analyses? Fortunately, your skills in SWOT analyses can transfer to nearly every organizational environment—government, for-profit, and nonprofit organizations all engage in SWOT analyses. Further, conducting a SWOT analysis isn't limited to organizations. SWOT analyses can be conducted for individuals, teams, products, or any other goal-directed venture.

5.5.4 Making SWOT Strategic

At the end of your SWOT analysis, you will have four lists of organizational members' perceptions of internal and external factors affecting your organization's ability to achieve its goals. This information should be carefully reviewed and refined to be as precise as possible. Then, the individual pieces of information in each list should be prioritized. Which strengths are most important to focus on? What threats are the most pressing? In this way, the information from your SWOT is being used for more than just awareness and reflection. Some questions you might ask at the end of the brainstorming process include:

- How can we use our strengths to take advantages of the opportunities we have identified?
- How can we use our strengths to avoid or overcome the threats we face?
- What can we do to minimize the weaknesses we have identified?

Table 5.2   Using your SWOT Strategically: The TOWS Analysis

TOWS Analysis	Strengths (Internal, Positive)	Weaknesses (Internal, Negative)
Opportunities (External, Positive)	**Strength-Opportunity (SO) Strategies** Which of the company's strengths can be used to maximize the opportunities you identified?	**Weakness-Opportunity (WO) Strategies** What action(s) can you take to minimize the company's weaknesses using the opportunities you identified?
Threats (External, Negative)	**Strength-Threat (ST) Strategies** How can you use the company's strengths to minimize the threats you identified?	**Weakness-Threat (WT) Strategies** How can you minimize the company's weaknesses to avoid the threats you identified?

This strategic process of linking internal and external factors in order to develop a plan of action has been coined a TOWS analysis (Weihrich 1982). As you can see in table 5.2, the questions in a TOWS analysis are linking the strengths and opportunities (SO), weaknesses and opportunities (WO), strengths and threats (ST), and weaknesses and threats (WT) directly to one another. In doing so, organizational members can look forward to new goals and opportunities—the heart of a strategic plan.

In sum, you should conduct a comprehensive SWOT analysis so that the resulting information can be used to hone and refine organizational goals. This will take time, research on your organization and the people within it, and a good deal of self-awareness as an organization. This effort, and potential discomfort, is worth the outcome. Think of Jasmine, Andre, and Liam from the beginning of this chapter. How might each of their stories have been different had they used SWOT analyses this way?

5.6 TYING IT ALL TOGETHER: CONNECTING YOUR ORGANIZATIONAL GOALS, SMART OBJECTIVES, AND SWOT ANALYSES INTO A FORMAL STRATEGIC PLAN

We began this chapter with the stories of three individuals addressing the same topic (childhood obesity) from three distinct perspectives. Jasmine, Andre, and Liam were each in need of setting a strategic plan to structure and evaluate their efforts, for both personal and professional reasons. Throughout this chapter, we have discussed how these individuals—despite their very different backgrounds and day-to-day work—can approach this task from a strategic communication perspective. We discussed the importance of outlining a clear strategic plan for organizational growth and development, and we provided an overview of the nine steps that an organization must engage in to develop a strategic communication campaign. As an organization's long-term goals can vary so widely, we discussed two types of goals for for-profit, nonprofit, and governmental organizations—*task management* goals and *relationship and identity management* goals. These long-term goals should then be translated to SMART objectives, whether they be informational, attitudinal, or behavioral in nature. Finally, as part of developing a strategic plan to reflect critically on your abilities as an organization, we discussed the importance of conducting a thorough and unbiased SWOT analysis of an organization's ability to meet its objectives. The importance and implications of the SWOT analysis emphasize the reflective and adaptive process of developing a strategic plan for communication campaigns. Although the process appears very linear on the surface, organizational members should be prepared to continually make revisions and adjustments based on each of these steps.

After reading this chapter, the importance of researching not only your environment but also your own organization should be clear, as the answers that you find in your research might change your course of action. If this seems like a lot of information for an organization to consider, it is! The planning stage is often regarded as the most tedious and time-consuming part of developing a communication or marketing campaign (US Department of Health and Human Services 2002). However, the work done at this stage is crucial to achieving success in later stages of the campaign development process. In the coming chapters, we will discuss the next few steps in developing a strategic communication plan, but we will continually come back to the questions raise in this chapter: What does our organization want to achieve and how will we know if we succeed?

CHAPTER 5 REVIEW

Questions for Critical Thinking and Discussion

1. How do the goals of for-profit, nonprofit, and governmental organizations differ? How do you think each type of organization differs in their prioritization of task management and relationship and identity management goals?

2. Using your secondary research skills, find three facts about the problem being addressed by Jasmine, Andre, and Liam in the beginning of this chapter: childhood obesity in the United States. How are your three facts similar or different from a peer in your class? Using the four criteria for evaluating secondary sources, how would you rate the quality of the sources you used?

3. In this chapter, we argue that both the long-term goals and short-term objectives of organizations should be realistic and achievable for organizations. Does this contrast with advice you hear about "dreaming big" or "shooting for the stars"? How do you feel about the idea of setting realistic (and therefore potentially smaller) goals? What is your perspective on goal setting in organizations?

4. In this chapter we presented five tips for conducting a SWOT analysis effectively. How might these tips change if a team needs to meet virtually? What other tips would need to be added?

5. Write a SMART objective on increasing diversity for your university. Then, conduct a SWOT analysis for your university's ability to achieve this objective. How do you think this process might be helpful to the university administration? Who should be included in a SWOT analysis on this topic?

Key Terms

attitudes: positive or negative evaluations of an idea, behavior, or product.

attitudinal: objectives that attempt to alter existing attitudes and underlying beliefs regarding a topic, event, issue, or product.

behavioral: objectives that attempt to change what people are doing or saying.

brainstorming: in group work, a session that allows the group to generate more ideas than they would as individuals.

buzz groups: in group work, subgroups that are formed to work on smaller tasks and report back to the larger group.

communication apprehension: fear or anxiety experienced when considering communication with other people.

critical advisor: in group work, this role is responsible for challenging the group in a constructive manner and encouraging the group to thoroughly consider their thinking and decision-making.

descriptive norm: perception of what similar others are doing.

formal: an appointed or elected role.

goal: a long-term outcome desired by an organization.

groupthink: a process of group decision-making that diminishes group creativity and individual thinking.

informal: a role that emerges naturally from group interactions.

informational: objectives that aim to inform or educate people about some relevant topic, event, issue, or product.

leader: in group work, this role is responsible for keeping the group on task toward achieving its goals and representing the group to external audiences.

objectives: the smaller, incremental steps needed to achieve larger organizational goals.

opportunities: the events, trends, or factors outside of the organization that can be drawn on to help it succeed.

personal identity: one's sense of self.

primary research: research conducted in which the researcher collects original data.

quantitative: an approach to research in which results are discussed in terms of numerical values such as percentages or ratios.

qualitative: an approach to research in which results are non-numerical and based on words or text.

recorder: in group work, this role takes minutes of group meetings as well as notes of any progress or issues that need to be permanently recorded.

secondary research: the process of reviewing and summarizing existing data.

social identities: memberships in various groups and how those groups are evaluated.

strategic plan: the sum of the objectives an organization intends to undertake to achieve its long-term goals.

strategic planning: the process of reflecting on an organization, identifying where it should be headed, and outlining how it will get there.

strengths: the benefits an organization has relative to its competition.

SWOT analysis: an in-depth examination of an organizations' strengths, weaknesses, opportunities, and threats.

threats: the events, trends, or factors outside the organization that might threaten its success.

unique selling proposition: the thing or things that an organization offers that its competitors do not.

weaknesses: drawbacks of the organization.

Further Readings and Resources

Bryson, J. M. 2018. Strategic Planning for Public and Nonprofit Organizations: A Guide to Strengthening and Sustaining Organizational Achievement. Hoboken, NJ: John Wiley and Sons.

Centers for Disease Control and Prevention. 2016. "Communities of Practice: Resource Kit." www.cdc.gov/phcommunities /resourcekit/evaluate/index.html.

Esser, J. K. 1998. "Alive and Well after Twenty-Five Years: A Review of Groupthink Research." *Organizational Behavior and Human Decision Processes* 73, no. 2–3: 116–41.

Hallahan, K. 2014. "Organizational Goals and Objectives in Strategic Communication." In *The Routledge Handbook of Strategic Communication,* edited by D. Holtzhausen and A. Zerfass, 244–66. New York: Routledge.

Metzger, M. J. 2007. "Making Sense of Credibility on the Web: Models for Evaluating Online Information and Recommendations for Future Research." *Journal of the American Society for Information Science and Technology* 58, no. 13: 2078–91.

References

Berger, C. R. 2008. *Planning Strategic Interaction: Attaining Goals through Communicative Action.* New York: Routledge.

Center for Disease Control and Prevention (CDC). 2018. "Childhood Obesity Facts." www.cdc.gov/healthyschools/obesity /facts.htm.

Doran, G. T. 1981. "There's a S.M.A.R.T. Way to Write Managements' Goals and Objectives." *Management Review* 70, no. 11: 35–36.

Fallon, N. 2018. "SWOT Analysis: What It Is and When to Use It." www.businessnewsdaily.com/4245-swot-analysis.html.

Haslam, S. A., M. K. Ryan, T. Postmes, R. Spears, J. Jetten, and P. Webley. 2006. "Sticking to Our Guns: Social Identity as a Basis for the Maintenance of Commitment to Faltering Organizational Projects." *Journal of Organizational Behavior* 27, no. 5: 607–28. doi: 10.1002/job.370.

Huang, S., L. Jin, and Y. Zhang. 2017. "Step by Step: Sub-Goals as a Source of Motivation." *Organizational Behavior and Human Decision Processes* 141: 1–15. doi: 10.1016/j.obhdp .2017.05.001.

Janis, I. L. 1972. *Victims of Groupthink.* Boston: Houghton Mifflin.

Lee, N. R., and P. Kotler. 2016. *Social Marketing: Changing Behaviors for Good.* 5th ed. Los Angeles: Sage.

McCroskey, J. P., and V. A. Richmond. 1979. "The Impact of Communication Apprehension on Individuals in Organizations." *Communication Quarterly* 27, no. 3: 55–61. doi: 10.1080/01463377909369343.

Myers, S. A., and C. M. Anderson. 2008. *The Fundamentals of Small Group Communication.* Thousand Oaks, CA: Sage.

Osborn, A. F. 1953. *Applied Imagination.* New York: Scribner.

Peralta, C. F., P. N. Lopes, L. L. Gilson, P. R. Lourenco, and L. Pais. 2015. "Innovation Processes and Team Effectiveness: The Role of Goal Clarity and Commitment, and Team Affective Tone." *Journal of Occupational and Organizational Psychology* 88, no. 1: 80–107. doi:10.1111/joop.12079.

Petty, R. E., and J. T. Cacioppo. 1986. *Communication and Persuasion: Central and Peripheral Routes to Attitude Change.* New York: Springer Verlag.

Siebold, D. R., and D. H. Krikorian. 1997. "Planning and Facilitating Group Meetings." In *Managing Group Life: Communication in Decision-Making Groups,* edited by L. R. Frey and J. K. Barge, 270–305. Boston: Houghton Mifflin.

Tajfel, H., and J. C. Turner. 1986. "The Social Identity Theory of Intergroup Behavior." In *Psychology of Intergroup Relations,* edited by S. Worchel and W. G. Austin, 7–24. Chicago: Nelson Hall.

Tolli, A. P., and A. M. Schmidt. 2008. "The Role of Feedback, Causal Attributions, and Self-Efficacy in Goal Revision." *Journal of Applied Psychology* 93, no. 3: 692–701. doi: 10.1037/0021–9010.93.3.692.

Turner, M. E., and A. R. Pratkanis. 1998. "A Social Identity Maintenance Model of Groupthink." *Organizational Behavior and Human Decision Processes* 73, no. 2–3: 210–35.

US Department of Health and Human Services. 2002. *Making Health Communication Programs Work: A Planner's Guide.* Bethesda, MD: National Cancer Institute.

———. 2018. "About Healthy People." www.healthypeople .gov/2020/About-Healthy-People.

Weihrich, H. 1982. "The TOWS Matrix: A Tool for Situational Analysis." *Long Range Planning* 15, no. 2: 54–66.

Selecting and Understanding the Target Audience

CHAPTER CONTENTS

6.1 What Is a Target Audience? 154
    6.1.1 Three Overall Steps to Selecting Your Target Audience 155
    6.1.2 The Four Types of People in Your Target Audience 156

6.2 The Process of Segmentation: Key Characteristics and Theoretical Approaches 160
    6.2.1 The Transtheoretical Model as a Target Audience Segmentation Tool 162
    6.2.2 The Benefits of Segmentation 167

6.3 Message Dissemination Approaches 168
    6.3.1 The Mass Communication Approach 169
    6.3.2 The Targeted Communication Approach 169
    6.3.3 The Tailored Communication Approach 171

6.4 The Single Person Method 173

6.5 Understanding Your Target Audience: The Role of Formative Research 176
    6.5.1 Survey Research 182
    6.5.2 Focus Group Research 184
    6.5.3 Social Network Analytic and Content Analytic Research 185

6.6 Tying It All Together: Selecting and Understanding Your Target Audience 186

LEARNING OBJECTIVES

After reading this chapter you should be able to do the following:

- ▶ Define target audience.
- ▶ Discuss the four groups of people in the target audience.
- ▶ Identify the three steps to selecting a target audience.
- ▶ Apply segmentation characteristics to an intended target population.
- ▶ Discuss the benefits of segmentation.
- ▶ Recognize and evaluate the three message dissemination strategies.
- ▶ Apply the single person approach to understand a target audience.
- ▶ Discuss the three types of formative research in conducting a target audience analysis.

Tamra works for a successful event-planning agency in Washington, DC. She has a wide variety of clients and plans everything from private parties to large corporate events. Depending on the day and event, Tamra might be working with a bride and groom to finalize their wedding dinner selections or contacting hotel venues to arrange the logistics of a welcome reception for an international business conference. Tamra loves her job, but it is challenging: event-planning agencies survive on positive reviews and word-of-mouth advertising from former clients, good relationships with local vendors and venues, and by ensuring that every event exceeds client expectations. In each interaction, Tamra has to think carefully about the unique needs of her client and tailor her communication with them accordingly.

Scott is running for school board in the county he grew up in—Knox County, Tennessee. He has assembled a campaign team of close friends and colleagues and is in the process of developing his platform and campaign messages. Per the suggestion of one of his team members, Scott has created a large chart for their upcoming planner's meeting, with a column for every section of the county. That way, Scott can collect and record demographic information for each segment as well as try to understand what is important to voters in each area to help develop a comprehensive but authentic platform. Having grown up in Knox County, Scott knows that he might have to hone his messages and channels for constituents in each segment of the county—while staying true to his campaign promises and mission. Ultimately, Scott's success will rely on an in-depth understanding of the unique needs of the voters in each of these county segments.

Kriti has been a counselor in the Career Development Center for a large public university for ten years. In this time, she has helped hundreds of students figure out their career paths, apply for internships, edit résumés, and find their first "real" jobs. She has noticed, though, that some of the most popular and successful students on campus—the student-athletes—struggle the most in these areas. Rigorous and time-consuming practice, workout, and game schedules make finding time for internships and other career development activities nearly impossible. Kriti knows that some great student-athletes are slipping by, all because they need specialized help and need someone who understands their unique situation. To help do just that, Kriti has developed a program for the Career Development Center—the Better Shot Program—which will work with student-athletes to find internships and postgraduation positions that fit their unique needs. Their success—and hers—will depend on Kriti's ability to uncover the unique talents and aspirations of each student-athlete.

Although each of the individuals above is working on strategic communication initiatives in very different environments, and for very different purposes, at the heart of their work (and likelihood for success) is the people they serve. As we discussed in chapter 5, the planning process of a strategic communication campaign is intensive, iterative, and of incredible importance to the success of any organizational efforts to communicate with both internal and external audiences. We have now discussed the first four steps of this planning process, including (1) conducting background research, (2) identifying long-term goals, (3) selecting short-term objectives, and (4) conducting a SWOT analysis of your organization's ability to meet its goals and objectives. As you now know, this in-depth analysis of the internal and external factors that affect the organization is a good place for any necessary reassessment or adjustments to the strategic plan. However, the next step in the planning process, and the subject of this chapter, is the driving force of the strategic communication campaign: selecting and understanding your target audience. In this chapter, we discuss why a target audience is important to consider in the planning process. We discuss how to segment and select target audiences for a campaign, using the "single person method" for incorporating your target audience into your planning process, and how to conduct rigorous and appropriate research to achieve an in-depth understanding of your target audience. First, we will carefully define the term "target audience" and what this might mean to various organizations.

6.1 WHAT IS A TARGET AUDIENCE?

Although we have used the term a few times throughout our textbook already, before we begin this chapter we should revisit the term **target audience.** As you discovered in chapter 1, your target audience is the people who you intend to influence with your strategic communication campaign. These people might be internal or external to your organization. For example, an organization working to improve its organizational identity (see chapter 3) might focus on its current and incoming employees in its messaging. A for-profit organization, on the other hand, would normally consider its target audience to be potential buyers or consumers of a product. It is important in this step of strategic planning to decide who exactly your target audience is and to clearly define that group. Who is it that you want to influence? At this stage in planning, the answer to that question might be very broad—"Men over fifty" "Individuals with a driver's license in Alabama" "Cat owners"—and that is okay. In answering this question, you are defining the **target population,** or the larger group from which an eventual target audience will be selected.

To conduct a maximally effective strategic communication campaign, however, you should narrow this broader understanding of your intended message receivers to a more specific target audience. Why? To put it simply, the more carefully you define your target audience, the more you can understand them. Understanding your target audience is essential to any campaign, regardless of its type, scope, or purpose. Consider the following broad objectives a campaign might have:

- Design a user-friendly website to meet customer's needs
- Improve smartphone application functionality
- Rebrand company to reflect consumer's values
- Increase awareness of new product

At the center of each of these objectives is the target audience. Understanding your target audience and their needs, preferences, and habits will ensure that your messages say what they need to, when they need to, and where they need to, in order to be effective.

6.1.1 Three Overall Steps to Selecting Your Target Audience

A thorough understanding of your target audience—whether it be internal or external to your organization—will help ensure that the content, tone, and delivery of your messages will have the intended effect (i.e., successful communication). Helpful questions that can guide your decision-making in this area include:

- Who are these people?
- Why are they receiving this message?
- What needs or challenges are they experiencing that this message could help address?
- How can I formulate this message in such a way that it will appeal to this audience and its needs?

In this chapter we will discuss three overall steps to selecting your target audience:

1. **Define your target.** The first step is to broadly define your target population and determine which of the four groups of people you want to include based on your goals and objectives.
2. **Segment your target.** Second, you should understand the characteristics of your audience and segment your target audience according to them. Which subgroups exist in your target audience, and how might they be important to your cause?
3. **Select a message dissemination strategy.** Third, you should select a message dissemination strategy. Will you address particular segments, or send a broad, "one size fits all" message? Which strategy fits best with your brand and resources?

Each of these steps will be discussed in more detail in this chapter. Let's begin with the first step: considering the various groups that might be in your target audience.

6.1.2 The Four Types of People in Your Target Audience

The target population might be very broad in your initial stages of planning. However, if you closely examine your campaign objectives, you will likely notice that there are different audiences that could be addressed to achieve the same outcome. For instance, an objective such as "increasing the number of children twelve and under who receive vaccinations for the flu virus by 20 percent in the next six months" could involve attitudinal and behavioral changes among parents, physicians, and even children. It might involve increasing the amount of information that is disseminated in schools about the flu virus or increasing advertisements on television or the radio from local pharmacies. There are multiple audiences that can be included to address this one objective, and it is the job of the organization to determine who they want to target to achieve it. The wide variety of target audiences that might be included can be streamlined into the following four categories:

- **The people you want to think, feel, or act differently.** In chapter 5, we discussed three types of objectives that organizations might have in their strategic communication campaigns: informational, attitudinal, or behavioral. Each of these types of objectives can address individual behavior. What do you want individuals to be aware of? How do you want them to feel differently about your cause? What do you want them to do as a result of your messages? The group of individuals you envision thinking, feeling, or behaving differently is your **primary target audience.** Suppose that you are a nonprofit organization with the objective of increasing positive body image perceptions among adolescent girls in the United States. Adolescent girls ages thirteen to seventeen living in the United States would be your primary target audience. These are the primary audience members whose beliefs and perceptions you wish to change. However, changing their perceptions often involves communicating with more than just the adolescent girls, right? There are a wide variety of influences on how young girls perceive their bodies, from parents, to their peers, to what they see on television. As an organization planning a communication campaign, therefore, you might decide to focus on one or all of the next three types of target audience.
- **The people who communicate with your primary audience.** Sometimes your target audience doesn't just consist of the people whose behavior and perceptions you would like to change but also the people they talk to, seek advice from, and interact with on a daily basis. Young adults, for instance, are highly influenced by what their peers think and say regarding substance abuse, such that increases in peer acceptance and engagement of these behaviors predicts their own likelihood to use tobacco, alcohol, or cigarettes (Kreager, Haynie, and Hopfer 2012; Steele, Peralta, and Elman 2011). Communication researchers and intervention designers have begun to use this influence proactively by providing young adults with messages that

Figure 23 Your target audience is likely influenced by a wide variety of sources. from the people around them to the images they come across online and on social media.

discourage their peers from engaging in substance abuse while remaining supportive and nonjudgmental (Kam and Wang 2015; MacArthur et al. 2015). In addressing those who communicate with your target audience—in this example, peers—message designers are able to more effectively achieve their behavioral objectives.

- In the example of body image campaigns and adolescent girls, these communicative influencers might be parents, teachers, physicians, or coaches. Providing these audiences with positive and supportive messages may very well have a stronger impact on young girls than direct messages promoting a positive body image, or at the very least can bolster direct messages to your primary audience. In analyzing your target audience, then, an important consideration is *who* they listen to.

- **The media.** Scholars in media and communication have established a very strong link between what people see in the media (including television, radio, and social media) and their perception of reality. Such is the premise of one of the best-known theories in media effects research, cultivation theory (Gerbner and Gross 1976). Largely focused on the influence of television, cultivation theory posits that heavy viewers of television are more likely to see the world as a violent place. More recently, researchers have established that viewing images of sexualized athletes in popular media affects college students' own self-objectification and even the discussions that they have with their peers about appearance and body standards (Linder and Daniels 2018). In fact, media representations have been found to provide a social context in which eating disorders are more likely to develop and be maintained (Spettigue and Henderson 2004). This clear link between what we see in the media and how we think, talk, and act about ourselves suggests that individuals who create, deliver, and monitor mediated messages are an important group to consider in any communication campaign.

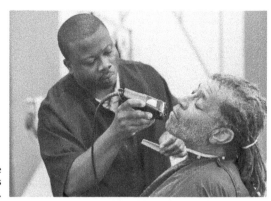

Figure 24 Think about who your target audience trusts and listens to—these midstream audiences might prove more effective in delivering your message.

- As an example of how the media might be addressed as a target audience in the body image context, take, for instance, the efforts of the nonprofit organization About Face. About Face is a nonprofit organization that aims to improve girls' self-esteem and body image by providing them with tools to understand and resist harmful media messages. Although they certainly do a lot to reach out to their primary audience—thirteen- to eighteen-year-old girls—they also act to change the mediated perceptions that are being produced. About Face actively writes emails and letters to any companies that produce messages that insult or degrade women or promote unhealthy body images, informing this company that they will not support or purchase their products until the advertising is changed. In this way, the media is being asked to change its behavior in order to support the goals and objectives of the organization. For more information, visit https://about-face.org.

- **Policy makers.** In developing a strategic communication campaign, your intended audience might be those in charge of setting regulations, new laws, or operating procedures. As the National Cancer Institute (2004) writes, "understanding what health communication can and cannot do is critical to communicating successfully" (14). Although strategic communication efforts are much broader in scope than traditional health communication, we echo this sentiment. It is important to realize when individual behavior is not enough to solve a problem; sometimes changes in the environment, such as new regulations or laws, are needed to advance an organization's goals. Hopefully the process of conducting a SWOT analysis (discussed in chapter 5) helps bring to the surface any potential target audiences in this category. By lobbying for a law that requires advertising companies to meet an ethical standard in editing their photos, for instance, you can aim for a much more effective change than simply asking young girls to be more aware and critical of the messages they see in the media.

Strategic Communication Mentor: Expanding Your Target Audience

As we discuss in this chapter, the target audience of a campaign does not necessarily need to be the people who we want to change—in fact, it is sometimes more effective to target those who *influence* our "primary" target audience. In the marketing literature, this is sometimes described, using a river metaphor, as targeting *midstream audiences*. Targeting the media, as we discuss in this chapter, would be targeting *upstream* audiences. And who is affected by upstream and midstream changes? Your primary target audience, or *downstream* audience. In the health communication literature, scholars have had much success with the midstream audience approach. Finding those who influence your target audience and/or social leaders in the community can be an incredibly effective means of delivering informative and persuasive messages.

As evidence of this success, a recent study has found that barbers can play a significant role in the blood pressure preventative behaviors of African American men. In working with seventeen barber shops in Dallas County, Texas, over a ten-month period, a research team led by Drs. Ronald G. Victor (Cedars-Sinai Heart Institute) and Robert Haley (University of Texas Southwestern Medical Center) found that barbers who offered blood pressure checks to their clients and encouraged physician follow-ups were able to achieve significant changes in blood pressure for their clients, as opposed to barber shop patrons who simply received pamphlets on high blood pressure.

Read the following account of this research, funded by the National Institutes of Health, below:

www.nih.gov/news-events/nih-research-matters/barbers-help-black-men-beat-high-blood-pressure

Why do you think that barbers were more successful sources of prevention messages than pamphlets?

How are the barbers a part of the "target audience" in this example? Using the river analogy, who would be the up-, down-, and midstream audiences in this example?

What are the benefits of using this approach to target audience analysis? What makes this approach more complicated than directly communicating with the primary target audience?

You may decide to focus on one of these groups, a combination of groups, or all four. In the above ways, communication campaigns can affect individuals, communities, and even have a society-wide impact. The groups that you ultimately select should align with your organizational mission as well as the goals and objectives you outlined previously. If your organization has no relationship or intended relationship with the media, for instance, then this group should not be considered a part of your broad target audience. Referencing your SWOT analysis and organization mission statement at this stage might be a helpful way to prioritize or eliminate target audiences from these four potential groups.

Once you have considered which of the four above groups is most appropriate to pursue in your campaign efforts, the second step in selecting your target audience is to identify segments that may be of importance to your communication efforts. **Segmentation,** or defining subgroups of your population according to common characteristics (National Cancer Institute 2004), allows you to develop messages and materials that are relevant to a particular group's current behaviors, needs, beliefs, preferences, knowledge, or attitudes. Segmentation as discussed by business, marketing, and communication professionals alike involves a complex set of such factors.

6.2 THE PROCESS OF SEGMENTATION: KEY CHARACTERISTICS AND THEORETICAL APPROACHES

The segmentation process breaks down your target audience into a series of relevant and specific factors. Consider Scott's challenge at the beginning of this chapter: in order to understand each section of the county he was campaigning in, there were a number of characteristics to consider that set voters apart, including where they lived in the county as well as what they prioritized for their children's education. In any campaign, whether it is political, for a nonprofit organization, or for a for-profit business, a few common characteristics tend to set members of your target audience apart from one another. These potential segmentation characteristics might include:

- **Demographics.** Demographics include age, gender expression, income, education level, marital status, race, religion, nationality, and occupation. If you have ever taken part in the US Census, then you are familiar with a wide variety of demographic questions. These demographic characteristics are popular for segmentation because they are typically readily available and tend to relate strongly with individuals' needs, preferences, behaviors, and attitudes (Lee and Kotler 2016). For-profit companies regularly develop pricing strategies based on the varied income levels of their target markets. For instance, high-end designers who develop lines of clothing for retailers such as Target or Kohl's are purposely creating and marketing their product for one particular economic segment of their target audience; the same is true when they develop clothing to be debuted at New York Fashion Week or sold exclusively in boutique stores in Paris. Demographics are an easy way to segment and differentiate your message.
- **Generation.** As an extension of demographics, one method of segmenting your target audience is to group individuals of the same generation. Although typically defined by birth year, generational differences are more culturally defined than simply using "age" as a segmentation characteristic. According to the Pew Research Center, the Millennial generation is anyone born between 1981 and 1996—the first generation to come of age in the new millennium. The Pew Research Center describes the Millennial generation as relatively unattached to religious institutions, burdened by debt, avoidant

of marriage, and linked heavily to their social media (2014). These characteristics could be very important to advertising or marketing efforts of organizations; for instance, this is not a group for which espousing traditional "family values" will work to move product. Similarly, an image depicting an age-similar individual researching an issue on his or her smartphone would be more relevant and accurate to a Millennial than an image of someone discussing the same issue with family members. It is likely worthwhile to do research on what is known about the generation your target audience falls in—particularly if you are not a part of it.

- **Location.** You may choose to segment your target audience based on where they live. This might include continents, countries, regions, states, counties, cities, or neighborhoods. The extent to which you narrow your scope will be dependent on your needs and resources. For instance, creating subgroups might include breaking up your target audience into regions of the United States (e.g., the Midwest, the Northeast), or it might be as specific as a particular neighborhood in your city. As an example of this type of segmentation, national retail or grocery stores will often create unique products for a particular geographic region—this might include t-shirts for the dominant collegiate sports team in the area or mugs with a local landmark. Similarly, national nonprofit organizations adapt marketing materials according to which events and resources are available in a particular community.

- **Culture.** Culture consists of all of the structures, symbols, and processes that communicate meaning for the target audience (Cobley 2008). These elements include religion, ethnicity, primary language, family structure, and typical foods and celebrations. For many communication campaigns, cultural elements have a significant impact on how messages will be perceived and interpreted. For instance, researchers have found religious beliefs to be a major reason that individuals will not sign organ donor cards in the past (see Morgan et al. 2008). An organ donation campaign should deliver different messages to religious segments based on their unique beliefs about the afterlife and the consequences (or lack thereof) of donating organs. This process might even lead to removing segments from your target audience—for whom your messages might not be culturally or religiously appropriate.

- **Behavior.** The way that you segment your target audience might also be based on what they have done, are currently doing, or want to do. Just as behavioral objectives are crucial to most strategic communication campaigns, behavioral differentiators are often the most important segmentation variable to consider. For a for-profit organization, the distinction between buyers and nonbuyers of the product is perhaps the most important characteristic to separate the target audience initially. You can also segment based on the frequency, timing, and duration of behaviors. In other words, communication with committed buyers, undecided consumers, and individuals who overtly and actively reject or disagree with your organization's message, must be distinct and reflect the segment's present position.

- **Psychographics.** The use of **psychographics** in marketing refers to dividing your target audience into subgroups based on their lifestyles and attitudes (Common Language Marketing Dictionary 2018). To do so, you will need to examine the different beliefs, values, interests, hobbies, personality characteristics, or lifestyles among members of your target audience. Notably, this segmentation technique focuses on the particular viewpoint of your target audience. If you are the producer of outdoor clothing with a mission statement centered on sustainability and environmental protection, for instance, you might find that targeting the subgroup of your population concerned with these issues is more fruitful than targeting a particular age or location. Perhaps the same company might consider targeting ambitious, outgoing, and high achieving personality types to support and promote their brand.

You will notice that each of the groups of characteristics vary in the extent to which they are visible or easily applied. For some, such as location, the information is assumed. For others, such as beliefs and attitudes, research will need to be conducted on your target population to determine subgroups. We will discuss this research process in more detail later in this chapter. Keep in mind that the segmentation process should consider characteristics that are relevant to your campaign goals and objectives. For some organizations, considering culture will be of utmost importance; for others, it will be irrelevant.

Alternatively or in tandem with the above approaches, you may select segments based on theory. In **theory-based segmentation,** the target audience is segmented according to a theory being used by the organization. Theories are often used to inform the goals and objectives of campaigns and can specifically be referenced in terms of selecting and understanding your target audience. A popular theory used for this purpose is the Transtheoretical Model.

6.2.1 The Transtheoretical Model as a Target Audience Segmentation Tool

The Transtheoretical Model (TTM) was originally developed as a means of understanding and promoting behavior change in the context of therapy for smoking addiction (Prochaska and DiClemente 1983), although it has been used to examine behavior change in a wide variety of contexts, from juvenile delinquency to weight management. Often referred to simply as Stages of Change, the TTM accounts for and describes how individuals stop negative behaviors or adopt positive behaviors by progressing through a series of five stages: precontemplation, contemplation, preparation, action, and maintenance. These stages can be used not only to diagnose individuals and groups in terms of their readiness and likelihood to change behavior (which is helpful for

Strategic Communication Mentor: Sample Segmentation Categories from the Survey of the American Consumer

The Survey of the American Consumer is an annual survey conducted by the advertising and marketing research company GFK MRI (Mediamark Research and Intelligence) on consumer behaviors. This survey queries over 25,000 respondents on their media choices, consumption of over 6,500 products and services, and a battery of demographic and psychographic questions. Below, we offer a series of example segmentation categories included in the survey. For more information on the Survey of the American Consumer, including the complete survey questionnaire, visit

https://mri.gfk.com/solutions/the-survey-of-the-american-consumerr/.

DEMOGRAPHICS

- Male/Female
- Age
- Employment (Yes/No)
- Parent (Yes/No)
- Marital Status (Married/Single/Engaged)

GENERATION

- Millennials (born 1977–1996)
- GenXers (born 1965–1976)
- Boomers (born 1946–1964)
- Early Boomers (born 1946–1955)
- Late Boomers (born 1956–1964)
- Pre-Boomers (born before 1946)

BEHAVIORS

- Voting in national, statewide, and local elections
- Purchasing behaviors
- International and national travel
- Intent to purchase real estate, clothing, or electronics in the next six months
- Investing and financial activities

PSYCHOGRAPHICS

- Political affiliation
- Diet control and eating habits
- Attitudes toward energy conservation and sustainability
- Interest in sports and sporting events
- Interest in seeking entertainment from online sources

---

clinicians and therapists) but also to adapt messaging strategies to encourage progress through each stage. In fact, most attempts to use the TTM in campaign development have used the stage model to develop materials and persuasive arguments applicable to the current stage of the target audience (Slater 1999). Let's examine the five stages of change in more detail:

- The first stage is *precontemplation*. In this stage, individuals have no intention to change in the near future (for categorizing purposes, the "near future" is typically considered to be the next six months). Further, individuals in the precontemplation stage may have no awareness that they *need* to change their behavior. Let's take the American Heart Association's recommendation to engage in moderate exercise for at least 150 minutes per week—or thirty minutes a day for at least five days—to improve and maintain cardiovascular health (heart.org). Adults who are in the *precontemplation* stage for this recommended behavior are not aware of these recommendations or even thinking that they need to start getting regular exercise. If your target audience is in this stage, your messages likely need to focus on education and awareness of the issue. The American Heart Association's "Why Walking?" page is a great example of this sort of messaging, with evidence-based reasons for moderate exercise as a means of achieving heart health.

- In the second stage, *contemplation,* individuals have recognized that a problem exists and are considering acting in the near future (i.e., within the next six months), but have not made any actual attempts to do so. People might stay in this stage for a very long time, particularly if they are unsure how to act or do not have the physical or emotional resources to do so (Prochaska, Norcross, and DiClemente 2013). Individuals in this stage might need help weighing the pros and cons of engaging in the behavior and need help with the "hows" of achieving change. In the exercise example from above, providing information on where to exercise, what clothing and shoes to wear, and ways to prevent injury would all be helpful to individuals in this stage.

- In the *preparation* stage, individuals are in a transition in which they have begun to experiment with or attempt to enact the behavior but have not fully modified their behavior accordingly. Temporally, the preparation stage is thought to involve individuals' consideration of modifying their behavior within the next month. Key messaging for individuals in this stage is support and commitment to their intended change—for individuals preparing to begin a walking or moderate exercise routine, finding a local community of walkers might help to make a commitment and verbalize that changes will be made.

- In the *action* stage, individuals have made specific, overt changes to their behavior within the past six months. Individuals in this stage should receive support or rewarding messages for their hard work and will need assistance in dealing with any challenges or barriers that arise as a result of their behavior change. Individuals who have just begun a moderate exercise plan, for instance, might consider posting their successes to social media to receive support. Alternatively, individuals might be encouraged to keep track of their miles in a log book and reward themselves when they reach a milestone.

- In the *maintenance* stage, the individuals attempt to continue the modifications to their behavior and avoid relapse (Prochaska and DiClemente 1983; Slater 1999). If your target audience is in this stage of exercise, messages on how to keep routines interesting and challenging might be helpful here.

You will notice in figure 25 that the visual representation of these five stages is often circular or spiral—this is because progress through the five stages is

---

Strategic Communication Mentor: Measuring Stages of Change

How do you classify individuals in your target audience according to their stage of change? Fortunately, research on the transtheoretical model has made this assessment relatively simple (see Sarkin et al. 2001; Vallis et al. 2003). A staging algorithm is used that asks individuals in your target audience one question—their response dictates which stage they are in regarding a particular behavior.

Let's take, for example, the behavior of healthy eating. Note that if you were to assess this in your target audience to see what stage of change they are in, you would want to be very clear by what you mean by "healthy eating." Below, we offer an assessment of how this might be done, based on a study by LaBelle (2014).

Instructions: The following questions concern your current behaviors related to healthy eating. For this study, healthy eating refers to a diet consisting of low fat and low calorie foods.

Please select ONE of the five options below to best describe your intentions toward *healthy eating.* Circle your response.

(1) No, I do not eat a diet of low fat and low calorie foods, and I do not intend to in the next six months
(2) No, I do not eat a diet of low fat and low calorie foods, but I intend to in the next six months
(3) No, I do not eat a diet of low fat and low calorie foods, but I intend to in the next thirty days
(4) Yes, I do eat a diet of low fat and low calorie foods, but I have been doing so for less than six months
(5) Yes, I do eat a diet of low fat and low calorie foods, and I have been for more than six months

Depending on an individual's response, they were classified into one of the five stages of change: (1) Precontemplation, (2) Contemplation, (3) Preparation, (4) Action, or (5) Maintenance.

Are there ways in which this staging algorithm might fall short for campaign designers? How so? What are the benefits of using this algorithm?
Are there other ways to assess what stage your target audience is in, other than asking these questions?

---

rarely linear. Individuals, particularly in the case of addiction, might skip certain stages or relapse to previous stages. In fact, research by Prochaska and colleagues indicates that about 85 percent of individuals who relapse from maintenance fall back into the contemplation stage; the remaining 15 percent regress to precontemplation (Prochaska, Norcross, and DiClemente 2013). For these reasons, it is important to provide individuals with encouraging and supportive messages, even in the later stages of action and maintenance. Positive thinking and support are often required to keep individuals from regressing to behaviors such as unhealthy eating, smoking, or drug use.

The benefits of using TTM to segment your audience is that it offers a fairly straightforward path for messaging depending on which of the five stages your target audience is in. Consider Kriti's work at the beginning of this chapter—by assessing which stage of looking for internships or postgraduation positions

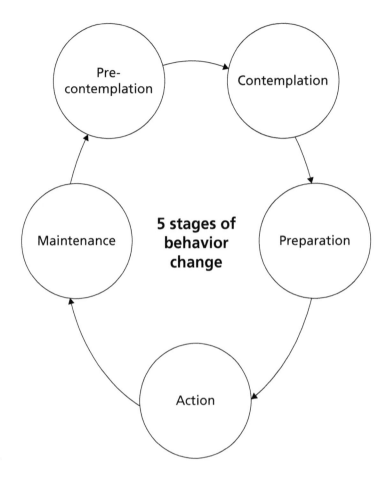

Figure 25 Stages of Change Model.

student-athletes are in, she can adjust her message accordingly. Some students might need basic information on how to apply for an internship because they have been thinking about finding an internship but don't know how (i.e., the contemplation stage), while yet others might have been diligently job searching but need the support and resources to keep looking even when they aren't getting interviews (i.e., the maintenance stage). Alternatively, you might need to reevaluate your campaign objectives as a result of this segmentation process. If your audience is in the precontemplation stage, expecting significant changes in behavior might be unrealistic. Fortunately, Slater (1999) offers a series of reasonable objectives that can be formulated based on which stage your target audience is in (see table 6.1). This might be a good reflection point in your strategic communication campaign planning process if you are using TTM.

In general, for people to progress through these stages (the goal of TTM), they need:

- An awareness of the advantages of changing, and how these advantages outweigh any disadvantages. This is referred to in the TTM literature as the *decisional balance.* In Kriti's work, it is important for her to stress that the benefits of spending time at an internship outweigh the costs; this might be challenging for students who think that 120 hours a semester at an internship is detracting from valuable time spent on homework, a job, or hanging out with friends on campus.
- Confidence that they can make and maintain change, referred to as *self-efficacy.* For Kriti, part of moving students toward the action stage likely involves fostering the belief that an internship and a good résumé will actually result in the desired outcome: a good postgraduation job.
- Strategies that can help them to make and maintain the recommended change, referred to as *processes of change.* This might include receiving information or education, creating a new self-image, making a commitment, receiving emotional support, or managing your environment such that it promotes positive change. What processes of change can you think of for Kriti? What strategies would she need to enact to move a student from contemplation to preparation?

Of course, TTM is just one of many theories that can be used to segment your target audience. In chapter 7, you will explore a few persuasion communication theories used in message development—as you read through these, think of how their principles might be applied to the segmentation process.

6.2.2 The Benefits of Segmentation

What are the benefits of segmenting your target audience for your strategic communication campaign? Perhaps the primary reason that an organization would use a segmented approach is to reserve resources. In segmenting, a particular section of your target audience is being targeted—thus eliminating the time, money, and effort in reaching all segments (i.e., a mass approach, discussed below). For some smaller organizations, saving resources in this way might be the difference between effectively reaching your goals or falling short. Another reason to segment is segmentation's direct impact on message effectiveness. For particular subgroups, some messages will be more or less effective in changing behavior. The more specific you can be to the needs, wants, and preferences of your subgroup, the more effective you will likely be. This also includes which channels you choose to deliver your message, which we will discuss more in chapter 7. Each subgroup likely has different channels through which they access and trust information; adapting your message delivery for each subgroup will ensure it actually reaches your intended audience.

Table 6.1 Appropriate Outcomes for Audiences at Each Stage of Change for Use in Designing Campaign Objectives

Stage	Outcomes
Precontemplation	Awareness or recall of basic message points, problem recognition, development of salience or availability in memory, knowledge gain (first key concepts), beginning of interpersonal discussion, increase number meeting criteria for contemplation stage.
Contemplation	Knowledge gain associated with relevant beliefs, increased attention to information or involvement, change in relevant beliefs and attitudes, increased salience or availability in memory, more extensive interpersonal discussion, increase number meeting criteria for preparation stage.
Preparation	Changes in behavioral intention, information seeking regarding skills or resources needed for enacting behavior, increased self-efficacy, increased accessibility of relevant or supportive attitudes, initiation of behavioral trials, increase number meeting criteria for action stage.
Action	Increases in number of behavioral trials, duration of behavioral trials, or both; increases number meeting criteria for maintenance stage.
Maintenance	Reinforcement of intentions, beliefs, and normative perceptions associated with behavior (e.g., increased confidence or certainty); increased incidence of sustained behavior.

SOURCE: Slater, M. D. 1999. "Integrating Application of Media Effects, Persuasion, and Behavior Change Theories to Communication Campaigns: A Stages-of-Change Framework." *Health Communication* 11, no. 4: 335–54. doi: 10.1207/S15327027HC1104_2.

Once you have your target audience segmented, you will have to decide whether to target individuals in all segments, a few select segments, or just one segment. For instance, if you are using TTM to segment your audience, will you develop different messages for individuals in each stage? Will you just target precontemplators and contemplators? Or focus exclusively on those in the maintenance stage to provide support? These considerations are a part of the third and final step of selecting your target audience—choosing a message dissemination approach.

6.3 MESSAGE DISSEMINATION APPROACHES

There are three general approaches to disseminating communication messages to your target audience. Next, we turn to defining each of these approaches as well as to discussing how they might be used in a strategic communication campaign.

6.3.1 The Mass Communication Approach

In a **mass communication** approach, one consistent message is sent to the entire target audience. This one-to-many style of communicating may also be referred to as *undifferentiated marketing, full marketing,* or *mass marketing.* In some cases, it might be most beneficial or profitable for an organization to target every audience that it can with its messaging. Consider companies like Pepsi or Coca-Cola—their commercials are rarely targeted at any one particular group but rather appear on television commercials for mass consumption. If you create a product or service that can be used by anyone or apply to anyone (e.g., food products, recycling behaviors, abiding by traffic laws), mass communication attempts are likely the best way to proceed in your messaging plan. However, a limitation to using a mass communication approach is that this "one size fits all" approach is not able to be adapted for audiences with unique preferences, experiences, or situations. Perhaps a segment of your target audience lives in a rural area and is not as exposed to typically used channels in mass media, such as television and radio—but instead would be much more likely to listen to and trust community leaders. In a case such as this, the second approach to message dissemination may be more useful.

6.3.2 The Targeted Communication Approach

In **targeted communication,** segments of the target audience are selected, and messages are adapted for each segment. Have you ever heard of the phrase "different strokes for different folks"? If that is your approach to campaign development, you are using a targeted communication approach. Referred to in marketing as *differentiated marketing,* this might include attempts to create "male" and "female" commercials for the same product or creating different advertisements for unique regions. If you live in an area with a National Football League team, you have likely seen products at your local grocery store that are regionally "targeted." Cereal boxes, beer labels, and apparel will be advertised that are specific to one geographic location and its associated team. This is one strategic communication campaign with one common goal—to sell product—but with unique messages developed for each geographical segment of the target audience.

In targeted communication, you may choose to focus on all segments at different points in time using a phased approach. For instance, a campaign to promote children's responsible use of technology might target children in the first six months of the campaign, teachers in the next six months, and parents in the last six months. Using this message dissemination strategy, organizations can address multiple segments even with limited resources or funding to carry out campaign messages.

You can also choose to just focus on one or two prioritized segments, known as *concentrated marketing.* In this approach, campaign designers focus on developing highly specific and unique strategies for one (or two) segment(s), and essentially eliminate the others. You might also hear of this as niche marketing, in which a company fills a particular "niche" by addressing a certain type of consumer. If our event planner Tamra from the beginning of this chapter chose to promote her services exclusively to nonprofits in need of fundraising events, she would be concentrating on a particular niche in her work. An example of niche or concentrated marketing in the profit world is the business Lefty's "The Left Hand Store" in San Francisco. Lefty's is the first store in the United States to focus exclusively on products made for left-handed people, selling tools for the home and garden, kitchen accessories, and office materials (among many other novelty items). Lefty's knows that not everyone is interested in an eleven-piece left-handed kitchen set, but left-handed people certainly are, so developing messaging for this "niche" is a more efficient use of their resources.

So, how do you select which segments (and how many) to focus on? As you are now likely realizing, there are a lot of decisions to be made at this stage in selecting your target audience. However, this decision does not need to be overwhelming—by considering the criteria below, organizations can make selections that are most appropriate and promising for their strategic communication campaign. Here are a few considerations that are common to for-profit, nonprofit, and government organizations:

> **Segment Size.** Particularly with for-profit organizations, it is more fruitful to select larger segments (that will therefore buy more of your goods and services). The number of people in a particular segment is also important in nonprofit and government work. It might be unrealistic to address a particularly large or diverse segment, particularly if budget restrictions or limited staff is an issue.
>
> **Segment Need.** The segment(s) that you select may be those that are most in need of your products, services, or messages. In a campaign designed to address railroad safety, the National Railroad Passenger Corporation (known as Amtrak) might decide to target segments of its national railways with higher incidents of accidents.
>
> **Segment Readiness.** To what degree is the segment willing to listen to your message? What likelihood is it that they will heed your messages? To what extent does a particular segment have the time, money, or ability to engage in the behavior you are promoting? This might be a particularly important consideration for nonprofit organizations with limited funding. You might hear the phrase "low hanging fruit" used by individuals in business and communication campaign fields—this refers to those people who are persuaded with little effort, either given their preexisting beliefs or motivations.

Overall Benefit. Much of selecting a particular segment has to do with the cost-to-benefit ratio. Will this segment be profitable for a for-profit company? Will targeting this segment be mutually beneficial for nonprofit companies? If a particular segment will require a lot of money and effort to reach, it might not be worth your efforts as an organization to develop your campaign around trying to influence them.

As you can see, the decision of which segments to target, and how many segments to target, is largely the result of the resources that your particular organization has. It is also largely a function of your mission as an organization: if your mission is to help ALL counties in the state clean up their parks, then your campaign strategy must account for this promise in its message dissemination approach.

6.3.3 The Tailored Communication Approach

The third and final message dissemination approach is **tailored communication,** in which unique messages are adapted based on the unique needs and characteristics of individuals in the target audience. Whereas targeted communication can be understood to be group-specific messaging, tailoring involves individual-specific assessment and personalized feedback based on those assessments (Campbell 2008). Tailoring most often involves computer-based programs and algorithms that can produce relevant, interesting, and appropriate messages for each individual member of the target audience. For instance, the degree to which information provided on wearable technologies, such as smart watches and fitness trackers, can be tailored and customized to a particular individual's preferences has an influence on attitudes toward health messages (Kim, Shin, and Yoon 2017). In the for-profit sector, this tailoring helps to increase brand loyalty and ensure return customers—think of Tamra's work as an event planner in the beginning of this chapter. Without a keen consideration of each client, Tamra would have limited success in her work.

Tailored communication is undoubtedly the most complex of the three message dissemination strategies; however, it is not necessarily the most expensive. As Campbell (2008) writes:

> In tailoring, appropriate messages for an individual are drawn from a "library" of pre-created messages, which can include text, graphics, photographs, audio or video information, or other types of message files. Each message is developed to address the demographic, health, behavioral, psychosocial, and/or cultural characteristics and determinants considered important for promoting change in a specific behavior or combination of behaviors. The messages are then turned into a single coherent communication by use of computer software that searches, selects, and assembles the messages on the basis of matching rules (algorithms). The development of tailored messages can be resource intensive; however, once developed, the production and delivery are usually of relatively low cost and the messages can be widely disseminated on a population basis. (1)

Figure 26 Tailored communication allows you to adapt and customize your message to individuals in your target audience—with the help of modern technologies that bring your message directly to your target audience's attention.

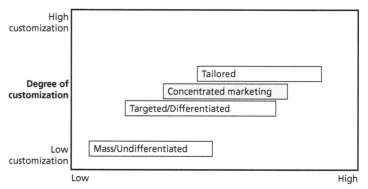

Figure 27 Customization-Segmentation Continuum.

As you can see in figure 27, these three approaches to message dissemination can be understood in terms of their degree of customization and segmentation of the target audience (Hawkins et al. 2008). As the figure illustrates, both segmentation and customization exist on a continuum from high to low. Segmentation is dividing the target audience into smaller, similar groups; customization is the process of individualizing each message in terms of content, style, and channel. Thus, the three messaging strategies above are not necessarily separate categories, but rather occur in degrees. Mass communication strategies are low in both segmentation and customization, whereas tailored messages are highly segmented and customized to a particular individual. However, your message dissemination campaign might have elements of more than one approach—concentrated marketing, for instance, is further along the segmentation and customization continuum than differentiated marketing.

The message dissemination strategy that you select will be dependent on your organization, its mission, and its long-term goals. There are advantages and disadvantages to each type. Whereas mass communication requires less research and often fewer resources to conduct, it can feel impersonal to receivers and therefore less effective. If you recall our discussion of brands in chapter 3, it might be harder to establish brand equity and loyalty among consumers when using mass, undifferentiated messaging. Regardless of which message dissemination strategy you choose, once you have your target audience selected, it is important to develop an in-depth understanding of the segment(s) you will seek to influence in your campaign. In the next section, we will discuss one way to think about your target audience to help achieve this level of understanding—the single person method.

6.4 THE SINGLE PERSON METHOD

For a communication campaign to be successful, it must be acutely aware of the needs, perceptions, and behaviors of its target audience. Although understanding your target audience appears to be a simple concept in theory, it becomes increasingly complex in practice. It also becomes increasingly more difficult as your target audience grows in number and diversity. One strategy that organizations can take to understand and focus on their target audience or audiences as they plan their strategic communication campaign is the "single person method." A term coined by communication scholar Athena du Pré (2014), the **single person method** is a mental exercise wherein the key demographics of the target audience are embodied into a fictional person or persons. Then, campaign messages can be thought of as affecting this *person* instead of the tens or hundreds of thousands of people who might be in an organization's target audience. You should name this person, give her/him an occupation, think about where he/she lives, works, and plays. What are this person's concerns? What is important to her/him? By thinking of your target audience as one person, you can come to understand her/him in more detail and more intimately—this will reflect in the messages that you develop. Note, this is not the same as the tailored messaging approach mentioned above; it is not that each message sent is individualized. Rather, the target audience either as a whole (mass) or in segments is thought of as one person.

As an example, the second author of your book worked on a message design project aimed specifically at Latino truckers who operate in the state of California. The California Air Resources Board was concerned about cultural and language barriers to truckers' ability and willingness to internalize principles and practices related to environmentally sound activities such as oil recycling. After performing background research on this very specific audience and interviewing a number of Latino truck drivers, the message design team had a fairly easy time creating a "single person" method that captured the thematic attitudes toward the campaign's target behaviors.

The single person method might be referred to or described differently depending on who you are talking to and what their primary strategic

Background:

*President of Founder Accounting, which he founded 32 years ago

*Graduated from the University of Wisconsin in 1974 and received his CPA designation in 1978

*Married for 40 years with 3 children (ages 28, 26 and 22)

Frank Founder

Challenges:

*Keeping existing customers from switching to cloud accounting providers (vs full-service model)

*Staying up-to-date with new technology

*Recruiting new talent to keep the business growing

Demographics:

*Male

*Age 62

*Annual HH income: $256,000

*Lives in a suburban, single family home

Hobbies & interests:

*Reading The Wall Street Journal

*Spending time at his family's lake house

*Hearing updates from his children

*Using email to keep in touch with family and friends

*Bowling

Common objections:

*I paid for a website five years ago, why should I pay for another one now?

*I just don't see how a website is going to help me grow my business in any meaningful way?

Goals:

*Keep business up-to-date in changing world

*Keep employees happy and turnover low

*Transition out of the business successfully on retirement

Biggest fears:

*Business falling apart after retirement

*Becoming irrelevant in the face of growing technology

*Not leaving a legacy he can be proud of through his firm

Figure 28 Example of a Buyer Persona.

communication field is. In business, the single person method will likely be referred to as a **customer profile.** A customer profile is a description of the customer that includes relevant characteristics such as demographics, location, culture, behavior, and psychographics. In advertising and marketing, the single person method is sometimes referred to as creating a target or **buyer persona.** A buyer persona is also a fictional person that carries the characteristics of your target audience. For example, see figure 28 for the buyer persona of digital marketing consulting company Single Grain. In this buyer persona, Single Grain has identified the background, demographics, hobbies, and challenges faced by their "typical" customer, Frank Founder. By having a profile for Frank, Single Grain can give its employees a clear sense of whom they are serving, as well as what needs, thoughts, and perspectives their clients might have. This buyer persona can then be used to make decisions regarding product development, advertising, and communication with stakeholders. Organizations can use buyer personas to reallocate spending on media channels (print, radio, television, internet) that their personas are more likely to use, use language that their persona uses, and even create unique content that appeals to different personas that have been identified (Devaney 2014). Regardless of whether you are referring to it as a single person method, customer profile, or buyer persona, all of these strategies focus on narrowing down not who your target audience is but how you think of them from this point forward in the planning process.

How do you create a persona as detailed as that provided by Single Grain? Where can you start? Marketing and sales software company Hubspot (2018) offers a few categories of questions to consider when developing this persona or "single person." These include:

> **Personal Background.** Personal background concerns demographic, education, and career-related factors for your target. What is their age? What is their annual income? Are they married? Do they have children? Where do they live? What level of education do they have? What is their career? How long have they been working in their industry (if applicable)? What does their typical day look like?

> **Goals and Challenges.** What challenges face your target persona? What are they concerned about? What worries them? What are their priorities? What does happiness look like to them? What goals do they have?

> **Watering Holes.** Who does your target talk to? Where do they obtain information? Who do they trust? What do they read? What association or networks are they a part of?

> **Interaction with Organization.** In what contexts does your target interact with you? Are they seeing your company online or in person? When and where will they encounter your messaging? When would they be considering your product versus a competitor's?

Once you have these questions answered, Hubspot suggests going through stock photos and finding an image that resonates with these responses. This process of selecting an image to accompany your target personifies your target audience or audiences and is a useful tool for internal organization. A target persona profile, such as the one provided in figure 28, can be distributed among all members of an organization to create a consistent voice and approach moving forward.

Although organizations do not often share these personas publicly (but rather use them as internal guideposts), there are a few famous examples of advertisements that use the "persona" method to connecting with target audiences. Consider Apple's use of Justin Long to embody the "typical Apple user" (see www.youtube.com/watch?v=ZwQpPqPKbAw); the ad depicts PCs side by side with Apple by using an older, less attractive, and less "hip" actor prone to getting viruses. The use of Justin Long in the "Get a Mac" campaign is a good example of what a single person approach or persona might look like; the casually dressed, young, and carefree "Mac" character is an embodiment of the customer Apple was attempting to connect with. There are of course risks to choosing to have one person embody your organization—particularly in the above example, some audiences found Justin Long's character to be smug, less funny, less relatable, and overall less likable than John Hodgman's portrayal of a PC as a middle-aged, overweight, and sarcastic PC (Stevenson 2006). The negative reactions to this character could potentially have been avoided by pre-testing these messages among target audiences first.

Note that you can create multiple personas for your target audience if you have multiple segments. Suppose you are using the Transtheoretical Model to segment your target audience into individuals in the precontemplation, contemplation, preparation, action, and maintenance stages—you should create a persona for each stage. What are these individuals like? What is important to them? What do they need to hear to act, or continue acting?

As this "single person method" implies, it is necessary to develop an in-depth understanding of your target audience at this stage in strategic planning. Once you have your target audience, relevant subgroups, and dissemination strategy selected, it is your duty to understand as much as you possibly can about this group or groups of people. How does an organization develop this in-depth understanding of its target audience? In the final section of this chapter, we will discuss a concept introduced in chapter 5—primary research. As you recall, primary research is the collection of original data. In understanding your target audience, you should gather as much information as you can from secondary data sources, which might include government databases, academic articles, or information found from reputable online sources. Using these methods, you might be able to find out quite a bit about your target audience. In certain circumstances, though, either the secondary data available doesn't address your topic, your specific target audience, or simply doesn't provide the information you need to know. In this case, conducting primary research will be necessary. Next, we are going to discuss a few ways to conduct primary research on your target audience.

6.5 UNDERSTANDING YOUR TARGET AUDIENCE: THE ROLE OF FORMATIVE RESEARCH

We have closely considered the term *target audience* and the three-step process for selecting an appropriate target audience or audiences for your strategic communication campaign. In the remainder of this chapter, we will discuss three ways to conduct research to understand your target audience: surveys, focus groups, and social network analysis. Keep in mind that this is just a brief introduction to a few key concepts, intended to get you thinking about how research should play a role in this stage of strategic communication campaigns. There are likely research methods courses offered in your major or at your institution that will teach you how to conduct research according to standard, accepted practices in the social sciences—if these courses are not already required, you should absolutely seek them out. Having the skill set of conducting effective research will be one of your biggest assets in entering the strategic communication workforce.

The process of conducting research to understand your target audience is referred to as **formative research** in campaign development. Formative research involves both qualitative and quantitative research methods used to help campaign designers develop their programs prior to implementation. At this point in strategic campaign development, you have already conducted research in understanding your company (i.e., the SWOT analysis discussed in chapter 5) and addressing your problem to create reasonable and meaningful campaign objectives. You may need to conduct research early on in selecting your target audience as part of the segmentation process. Now, the research you conduct is focused on your target audience and how you can develop messages that the target audience will respond to.

At this point, there are likely a wide variety of factors that you need to uncover to truly understand about your target audience. Commonly examined topics in formative research include:

> **Knowledge.** As we discussed in chapter 5, one of the types of objectives you might develop for your campaign are *informational* objectives. If you need your target audience to know something or learn something, it is important to establish a baseline of knowledge first (later, this will help you assess your campaign's effectiveness). You wouldn't want to develop messages that are considered condescending or "beneath" your target audience's level of awareness or understanding. Consider a hospital distributing materials on the benefits of vaccination to its physicians—after attending medical school for nearly a decade, this particular target audience might find that message to be a waste of their time and your effort.
>
> In the previously mentioned campaign designed to encourage Latino truck drivers' oil recycling habits, the message design team designed a questionnaire to assess the target audience's current levels of awareness about California law regarding oil disposal. In addition, the questionnaire helped the team determine the target audience's understanding of what oil recycling is, why it is important to the environment, and how to do it.
>
> **Attitudes and Beliefs.** Understanding your target audience's current viewpoint or stance on a product, event, or issue is a key starting point for developing persuasive messages. Whether your audience is supportive, ambivalent, or firmly against your product or organization is critical for how you will develop your messages. In some cases, audiences that are highly opposed to your organization or product might be eliminated from your target audience. This might seem like "giving up," but there is no sense on wasting your time and resources on an audience that considers your mes-

sage to be outside of their realm of acceptance. Asking questions about your organization or anticipated messages will help you make an informed decision about who to pursue influencing in your strategic message campaign.

Notably, these attitudes and beliefs might encompass audience perceptions of the **benefits** and **barriers** of a particular product, event, or idea. Benefits are the intangible or tangible things that your target audience gets out of listening to you. It might include saving money, having more self-confidence, or owning a shiny new sports car. The barriers are the tangible or intangible costs that your target audience gets out of listening to you. Sometimes referred to as the "pain point" in the traditional marketing literature, barriers are challenges or struggles faced by your target audience. Typical barriers include limited funds, time, energy, or enjoyment. For instance, a campaign promoting recycling typically asks people to go out of their way to recycle products from their home, with no immediate reward. The barrier of having to organize recycled materials and drive them to a recycling center keeps a lot of people from engaging in the behavior. These will be important to the messages you later develop, in which you will want to increase perceptions of benefits (and introduce any, if none currently exist) and minimize barriers.

In the consulting example we have offered regarding oil recycling habits, the messaging team conducted focus groups in which they explored truckers' perceived barriers to responsible oil disposal and the factors that contributed to their negative attitudes about oil recycling.

Behaviors. You might ask your target audience about their past, current, or intended future behaviors. If you have a *behavioral* objective, this might be to establish a baseline. For instance, you need to know how many people currently take the stairs at work in order to evaluate how successful your *Take the Stairs* campaign really was, right?

Preferred Communication Channels. Selecting the channel through which you deliver your message is a crucially important decision in the strategic communication campaign process. A well-designed message will not have an effect if it is never received. Who does your audience listen to? Who do they trust and admire? Where do they go for news or entertainment? Understanding this about your target audience, at this stage in planning, will help you to make evidence-driven decisions about where to place your messages.

Reactions to Your Message. Although this will likely come later in your planning, research with your target audience can also be useful in **pretesting** any preliminary message concepts that you have. Pretesting is the process of showing your messages or message concepts to a sample of your target audience and asking for feedback. Strategic communicators rarely go into a campaign without any idea of how they will create and disseminate messages. Why not ask your audience what they think first?

One of your textbook authors, Sara LaBelle, did this early on in developing a campaign aimed to reduce prescription stimulant misuse among college students. In her initial discussions with students, her target audience, she presented a series of potential messages that might be used in a campaign to address this topic. To her surprise, this process revealed that one of the most heavily favored messages among the campaign team was unclear (and completely misinterpreted) by these students. Specifically, a poster that read, "Only 1 in 10 college students misuse prescription stimulants as a study enhancer," was interpreted by students in the focus groups as implying that the campaign was encouraging *higher* misuse. The poster was of course intended to promote the opposite—by way of informing students of a **false consensus,** or the tendency to overestimate a certain behavior or belief as more normal and typical of others. The final poster, which read, "Not everyone is doing it: 9 out of 10 college students are NOT misusing prescription stimulants as a study enhancer," made this message and its intention much clearer. Other reasons to conduct formative research include ensuring that campaign materials will be culturally and geographically appropriate (Gittelsohn et al. 2006), or that stakeholders will react to "bad" news from organizations in a proactive and constructive way (see Lewis, Laster, and Kulkarni 2013). Now, in these early stages of planning, is a better time to learn that your messages are not resonating with your target audience in the way that you hoped they would.

This is not a comprehensive list of what you might be looking for in your formative research. You might have specific ideas in mind based on the segmentation characteristics we discussed earlier, such as demographics or psychographic questions. You might want to ask specific questions about lifestyles or personality traits. What you focus on in this assessment will also likely be influenced by the theory that you use to form your messages. In the final section of this chapter, we will discuss a few common ways to conduct formative research in strategic communication campaign development: surveys, focus groups, and social network analysis.

In conducting formative research, you will select a sample of people from your target audience to survey, speak with in a focus group, or examine on social networks. A **sample** is the term for the group of people included in your research—these are the research participants that answer your questions. This sample is selected to be representative of the larger population from which it was drawn (in this case, your target audience), so that the responses in the sample can be used to understand the population better. This means that the people in the sample should be pretty similar to the overall target audience or population. Why not just ask everyone in the population? Time and resources will

Interview with a Professional:
Kim Hackbarth, Boy with a Ball

The following interview is with Kim Hackbarth, president of the board of directors for Boy with a Ball Costa Rica. As you read, think about how Boy with a Ball relates to the content you have read so far in this chapter regarding analyzing and understanding your target audience. Does anything about this organization's approach surprise you? Do you think that their mission and approach could translate to organizations in the for-profit or government sectors?

Can you tell us about Boy with a Ball? What is the mission of this organization, and how was it founded?

Founded in 2001, Boy with a Ball is an international membership organization made up of local teams fighting to help young people thrive within their own communities. There is a tremendous need here: young people in developing countries and low-income communities face increased levels of violence, illiteracy, and poor health outcomes (see World Economic Forum 2014; World Health Organization, Fact Sheet on Adolescent Health 2015). To help youth in these communities, this volunteer-driven organization provides services at selected sites including outreaches, school suppliers, tutoring centers, mentoring groups, small groups, and equipping centers so that communities can be developed. Boy with a Ball is a youth leadership development, team-based organization that works to draw young leaders into volunteer situations in which they learn to serve others relationally in order to accomplish change in their lives and, as a result, in their communities. Currently, Boy with a Ball has locations in the United States, Kenya, Nigeria, Nicaragua, and Costa Rica.

As our mission states, "Boy with a Ball betters cities by reaching young people and equipping them to be leaders capable of turning and trans-forming their communities." Our long-term vision is a world where the young people in our hands, in our families, in our communities are growing, joyful, thriving. We see cities filled with vibrant, young leaders, rising to build neighborhoods, companies, and countries. We see cities filled with vibrant, young leaders, rising to build neighborhoods, companies, and countries. We are committed to doing whatever it takes to make this vision a reality.

In this chapter, we discuss the target audience as the people an organization intends to influence. Who is BWAB's target audience? Are there multiple target audiences?

Boy with a Ball in each city builds a deeply connected, highly skilled *team* that then works to attract sincere, passionate *volunteers* so that the team members and volunteers can go together to reach people and draw them into mentoring relationships and small groups from which they can be equipped to turn and reach others. Our teams are never just about the young person being reached. While we are reaching them, we are also developing the volunteer who is reaching that young person and developing the team member who is learning how to equip and lead that volunteer. Development is happening within Boy with a Ball at all times in three different ways.

What this means is that Boy with a Ball is constantly making a difference on three levels: team, volunteers, and those who we are working to reach. While this may not seem so different from the other organizations working in our community, it is in actuality both the secret to our success and dramatically different from those around us. As a Boy with a Ball team, every team member needs to not only understand this dimension of our organization but also to be able to help build it. Additionally, individuals within the organization need to know whether they are a team member, a volunteer, or part of a Boy with a Ball program and to understand what that means.

How does BWAB communicate with its target audience? In other words, how do you understand the people you are serving?

Boy with a Ball team members and volunteers go weekly out into communities and meet people through outreaches like walk-throughs, helping with urgent needs in ways that don't encourage dependence (dental clinics, job skills training, ESL classes, school supplies, tutoring). As we do these things, our team members and volunteers are trained to use these moments of interacting with people in order to build relationships with people in the community.

Once these relationships are built, outreach continues to provide us with the opportunity to go deeper and deeper. At one point, these relationships may be ready to be drawn into a mentoring relationships or perhaps to invite the person and several others we know into starting a small group where one team member or volunteer could come together with several community members to allow them to share their hearts, grow, and develop. Examples of these small groups include men's groups, women's groups, young men's groups, young women's groups, soccer groups, children's groups, community leader's groups, youth groups, home groups, etc.

What is exciting is when the relationships we are building and keep deepening result in lives beginning to change. Before too long, individuals in the community begin to feel a connection with the team that results in them asking to join the team.

What are the advantages and disadvantages of this approach?

It is a profound, lasting way to work and positively develop a community, starting with each individual. It is not fast or program-oriented, which can be a struggle for funding and "numbers" at times.

Do you have any advice for students reading this book about understanding target audiences?

There is no replacement for the power of relationships to propel the work you want to achieve. This cannot be created overnight or perfectly calculated, but must be cultivated by honesty, care, hope, and sacrificial love.

After reading Kim Hackbarth's interview, take some time and review the Boy with a Ball website (http://boywithaball.com)—specifically their About Us, Growing Heroes, and Why You(th) pages. Then, watch the following video on the Boy with a Ball manifesto,

www.youtube.com/watch?v=SomUzMV6RcY.

Then, discuss the following questions with a classmate:

1. Boy with a Ball refers to their approach as "Transformative Community Building" (see http://boywithaball.com/our-approach/). What are some of the strengths they see in this approach? Do they mention challenges or weaknesses to it? If not, what are some that you can think of?
2. In Kim's interview, she mentions that the three target audiences BWAB serves are its team, its individual volunteers, and they people they serve. How is this similar or different from how most organizations define their target audience? How is it helpful for a nonprofit organization to include its volunteer members as part of its target audience?
4. As Kim indicates above, BWAB comes to understand its target audience by "walking through" the community regularly, and adapts its daily and long-term activities based on the needs that emerge in these discussions. In what ways does this exemplify the ideas discussed in this chapter? Is this realistic for all organizations? Why or why not?

likely limit an organization's ability to do this—and even if they do have the time and resources to survey the whole population, known as a **census,** it usually isn't necessary. A good, representative sample is all you need to understand your target audience.

To demonstrate this, think about the following question: How difficult is parking at your school? Suppose you want to understand how students, faculty, and staff at your school feel about parking. Would you need to ask *every* student, staff member, and faculty member at your school to get an idea of how good or bad the parking options are? This might include asking one question of several thousand people. Most researchers would say no, this isn't necessary. Instead, you can select a representative sample of commuter and residential students, staff, and faculty to find a set of responses that covers the variety of thoughts and opinions on the issue. These **participants,** or individuals who participate in your research, will be used to understand the broader population. Next, we will discuss a few options that you have for this research as well as their benefits and limitations. We will start with the most common method of conducting formative research: surveys.

6.5.1 Survey Research

If you need to collect formative research, the most common and likely most appropriate methodology is to conduct survey research. You have likely heard of the term survey, and even participated in one—so what does it mean to you? If your definition has anything to do with questions and responses, you are pretty close to how a researcher defines them. In this textbook, we define **survey research** as the administration of a questionnaire to a sample.

In conducting a survey, you have a few options to choose from, including:

1. **Face-to-Face Surveys.** In a face-to-face survey, you read the questions to participants and record their responses. This might involve **intercept** surveys, where you stop people in a public place and ask them to participate in your research. If you have ever been to Disneyland, you may have been approached by a cast member and asked to respond to a few questions about your satisfaction with the park—this is an intercept survey method.
2. **Telephone Surveys.** Similar to the face-to-face survey, a telephone survey involves you as the researcher reading questions to participants and recording their responses. Recently, one of the authors of your textbook was selected by a major league baseball team to answer a few questions about attending a recent game—the team had obtained her cell phone number from the ticketing agency (with her agreement to be contacted later) and used it to conduct marketing research.
3. **Self-Administered Paper and Pencil Surveys.** In this survey method, participants are provided a survey and read the questions and indicate

responses on their own. You might choose to give these surveys in person or perhaps to mail them to participants. If you use this method, be sure to write clear questions and response categories that will make sense to you when you examine your data. For mailed surveys, you will also need to provide a self-addressed envelope and postage to help increase the chances your survey will be returned (typical response rates for mailed surveys hover around 20 percent)—this might be funding that your organization does not have. In person self-administered paper and pencil surveys are very common in communication studies research.

4. **Self-Administered Online Surveys.** Growing in popularity because they are easy to share and data is already entered for analysis, self-administered online surveys involve participants receiving a link to an online survey platform (e.g., AmazonTurk, Google Forms, Qualtrics, and SurveyMonkey are all popular and easy-to-use options) and completing the survey at their own convenience. If you are an online shopper, you may occasionally be provided with a link after you complete your purchase to review your shopping experience. This is a very convenient and easy way for for-profit organizations to improve their website and checkout process.

Each of these survey methods has its own advantages and disadvantages, so which one you select will likely be a function of your own preferences and resources as an organization. Work with existing communication channels or structures in your organization to conduct survey research whenever possible. If your organization has a monthly email newsletter, for instance, asking to include a link to your online survey would be a nice way to connect with an existing channel. Particularly when you can access your target audience easily, surveys are a popular method for formative research because they are relatively quick, easy, and inexpensive ways to collect a lot of information.

There are limitations to only using surveys to understand your target audience. For example, participants might suspect that there is a socially desirable answer and respond to your questions in a way that reflects on them positively. Suppose you ask the following question: "Do you know the proposed education reform Candidate Jones plans to enact if elected governor of your county?" A participant might respond "yes" just so that they don't look ignorant or uninformed, thus affecting the accuracy of your responses. This **social desirability effect** can be lessened by ensuring that participant responses are anonymous (and making participants aware of this), and by letting participants know that any responses are welcomed and acceptable.

When used correctly, surveys are an excellent source of information from your target audience. As we said in the beginning of this section, this is intended to be a brief introduction to formative research. If you would like to conduct surveys for your organization, more training is likely required. Writing survey questions so that participants are motivated and able to give accurate responses is a skill that takes time and practice. Alternatively, a social scientist or statistician might be helpful as a consultant in these stages of the campaign planning process. Keep in mind that survey data are more quantitative or numbers-driven in nature—your results will likely be expressed in terms of percentages or other numerical values. If you are looking for more qualitative data, the next methodology we discuss might be more appropriate.

6.5.2 Focus Group Research

If you feel that you need a more in-depth conversation with your participants, you might consider conducting a focus group instead of or in addition to using a survey methodology. Focus groups are generally defined as "small groups of people with particular characteristics convened for a focused discussion of a particular topic" (Hollander 2004, 606). Let's break down this definition a bit. First, focus groups should remain relatively *small.* The ideal size for a focus group discussion is anywhere from six to twelve participants; a group of fewer than six might not have a wide diversity of opinions (a huge benefit of this methodology is hearing diverse thoughts!), and in a larger group, everyone might not have the opportunity to speak in-depth about their perspective (Lindlof and Taylor 2011). Further, focus groups typically rely on **purposive sampling** techniques—meaning that participants are purposely selected based on some relevant, *particular characteristic* to the research interest (Noonan and Charles 2009). If you are leading a political campaign, for instance, you might convene a group of supporters to understand what it is about your candidate that they appreciate and would vote for again. A focus group is a *focused discussion* in that there should be a guide or purpose for the questions being asked. Typically a **moderator** is used to orient the group, stimulate discussion, and answer key questions. Moderating a focus group is a tough balancing act and requires practice to be efficient at doing it well. Similar to surveys, there are ways of framing and introducing the questions in a focus group that we do not have room to fully explore here—a carefully constructed interview guide will promote a logical progression of topics, establish rapport among participants, and will allow for a collaborative and useful discussion (Lindlof and Taylor 2011).

Although focus groups can be helpful in generating a number of ideas fairly quickly (typically lasting thirty to ninety minutes), these discussions can be affected by a number of relational elements that typically do not need to be considered in survey research. For instance, participants might not feel comfortable with the moderator or may feel pressured to give positive reviews of the organization. Quieter participants may be more hesitant to speak up in the group setting, particularly when there are dominant participants or if their position seems to be unpopular. Examining the results of a focus group might also take much more time than quantitative surveys; in fact, focus group discussions are often audio recorded (with participant consent) so that researchers can listen and even transcribe what was said to create a report. You likely need to conduct multiple focus groups to reach **theoretical saturation,** or a point where no new themes are emerging. Assuming that you have to pay a moderator and incentivize participants (and possible even rent a room to hold your focus group in), this can quickly become more expensive than a survey. Despite these limitations, focus groups remain one of the most popular and widely used market research tools for organizations. If you have a trained moderator who can establish the comfort of participants, and the resources to conduct multiple focus groups, then the result of having in-depth, in-person conversations with your target audience is likely worth it. When conducted well, focus groups give critical insight into the world of your target audience that is hard to obtain using other methods.

6.5.3 Social Network Analytic and Content Analytic Research

A very popular (and affordable) means of communicating with your target audience is social media. This communication channel can also be used, however, in the beginning phases of planning your strategic communication campaign. Chances are, your target audience is already talking about the topic you are interested in on these channels (Hawlk 2017). An inexpensive and easy way to see what they are thinking and saying is to explore social media pages and search for keywords. Look into Facebook groups, comments or posts on LinkedIn, Reddit forums, and Quora posts to "listen" to your target audience (Hawlk 2017). Below, we have a few tips for conducting this research on the most popular platforms.

FACEBOOK   The Facebook Insights feature is available to anyone who manages a Facebook page. This automatic feature easily breaks down audience interaction and reactions to your page and provides data on audience demographics, the length of time spent reading posts, audience retention over time, and even identifies top customers based on who engages the most with your posts and spends the most on your product (see analytics.facebook.com). As this implies that you already have a Facebook following, it might not be appropriate for creating a campaign for a new organization—older, more established organizations might use this information to understand how existing customers feel about product or brand and adjust objectives and messages accordingly.

TWITTER   Using the Audience Insights Dashboard on Twitter, you can access an online profile of your typical audience member. The information you receive includes their occupation, interests, gender, education, marital status, and even information on what they buy and where they buy it. This information can also help you assess if you need to grow or develop your Twitter followers in any way—if you are a for-profit running-shoe company, and very few of your followers are interested in running, you may need to create a campaign objective to increase followers with this interest.

These early insights into your target audience can be crucial to developing appropriate and promising messages for your strategic communication campaign. It is important to note these social media analytics require you to have followers to analyze—this becomes the group whose behavior and characteristics are reported to you—so this might not be the best option if you are in the earliest stages of determining who your target audience should be. Instead, these analytics might be best for the continual and ongoing process of understanding your target audience—an equally important endeavor.

6.6 TYING IT ALL TOGETHER: SELECTING AND UNDERSTANDING YOUR TARGET AUDIENCE

We began this chapter with a peek into the lives of three individuals working in very unique strategic communication contexts: the successes of Tamra, Scott, and Kriti are completely dependent on their ability to select, understand, and reach their target audience. Accordingly, in this chapter, we have discussed three steps for selecting your target audience. First, you must define which groups you would like to include in your target audience; this might include just your primary target audience, or it may involve those who influence or affect the lives of your primary audience through daily communication, mediated messages, or the laws and policies that regulate their lives. Second, you should segment your target audience into using criteria meaningful to your campaign's goals and objectives. Third, you should select a message dissemination strategy, ranging from the "one size fits all" mass communication approach to the highly individualized tailored communication style. Once you have made these decisions, you can use the single person approach to concentrate your efforts and organize your campaign team. In order to understand your target audience at this level of detail, we have provided a brief overview and some options for conducting formative research. Whether you decide to conduct surveys, focus groups, or social media analytics will depend on your needs and resources as an organization.

Although this chapter might make it seem as though selecting your target audience and understanding them in detail is a linear process with a finite end, it is in fact a continual and ongoing process for organizations. Consider if Scott is successfully elected to the school board—to do his job well, he will need to be able to adapt to the changing needs and concerns of residents in his county. Target audiences are, after all, made up of people—and people change frequently.

What is important to your target audience, how they react to a certain message, and what they pay attention to could fluctuate on a daily basis. Therefore, having systems in place to continually assess and stay in communication with your target audience is just as important as these initial steps of defining and understanding them. In the coming chapters, we will continue to cover the steps of planning a strategic communication campaign, including developing messages in accordance with principles and theories of persuasive communication and selecting effective channels to deliver these messages—but the importance of the target audience will continue to be a theme that guides your actions as an organization. Just as effective communication involves an ongoing awareness of your receiver, so too must organizations always keep their intended audiences at the forefront of their decision-making in communication.

CHAPTER 6 REVIEW

Questions for Critical Thinking and Discussion

1. Apply the segmentation process to Tamra's story at the beginning of the chapter. What segments exist for an event planning agency? How would being aware of these segments help the organization to perform?

2. How can the TTM be used to promote change in for-profit organizations? What might each stage look like for a potential or current customer?

3. What ethical issues do you think might arise from using a targeted or concentrated approach to campaigns on health or social awareness issues? How can these ethical issues be avoided or overcome?

4. What are potential problems with using a "single person method" to developing your messages? Are there situations in which this type of thinking would not work? Explain.

5. After reading this chapter, can you think of any examples of organizations not understanding and analyzing their target audience? This might be an organization that you have had personal experience with, or something that you heard about online or on the news. What effect did that have on their message? How do you think this failure could have been avoided using information from this chapter?

Key Terms

barriers: the tangible or intangible costs that your target audience gets out of listening to you.

benefits: the intangible or tangible things that your target audience gets out of listening to you.

buyer persona: a fictional person that carries the characteristics of your target audience.

census: a survey of an entire population.

culture: all of the structures, symbols, and processes that communicate meaning for the target audience.

customer profile: a description of the customer that includes relevant characteristics such as demographics, location, culture, behavior, and psychographics.

false consensus: the tendency to overestimate a certain behavior or belief as more normal and typical of others.

formative research: qualitative and quantitative research methods used to help campaign designers develop their programs prior to implementation.

intercept: a type of survey in which researchers approach people in a public place and ask them to participate in research.

mass communication: a dissemination approach in which one consistent message is sent to the entire target audience.

moderator: in focus group research, the person who orients the group, leads discussions, and answers key questions.

participants: individuals who participate in your research.

pretesting: the process of showing your messages or message concepts to a sample of your target audience and asking for feedback.

primary target audience: the group of individuals you envision thinking, feeling, or behaving differently following exposure to your campaign efforts.

psychographics: lifestyles and attitudes of your target audience that can be used for segmentation purposes.

purposive sampling: a sampling technique in which participants are purposely selected based on some particular characteristic of interest to the researchers.

sample: the group of people included in your research.

segmentation: defining subgroups of your population according to common characteristics.

single person method: a mental exercise wherein the key demographics of the target audience are embodied in a fictional person or persons.

social desirability effect: the tendency to provide more positive responses to questions posed in research.

survey research: the administration of a questionnaire to a sample.

tailored communication: an approach in which unique messages are adapted based on the unique needs and characteristics of individuals in the target audience.

target audience: the people you intend to influence with your strategic communication campaign.

target population: the larger group from which an eventual target audience will be selected.

targeted communication: an approach in which segments of the target audience are selected and messages are adapted for each segment.

theoretical saturation: a point in qualitative data collection where no new themes are emerging.

theory-based segmentation: an approach in which the target audience is segmented according to a theory being used by the organization.

Further Readings and Resources

Baxter, L A., and E. Babbie. 2004. *The Basics of Communication Research.* Belmont, CA: Wadsworth.

Krueger, R. A. 1988. *Focus Groups: A Practical Guide for Applied Research.* Los Angeles: Sage.

Skinner, C. S., M. K. Campbell, B. K. Rimer, S. Curry, and J. O. Prochaska. 1999. "How Effective Is Tailored Print Communication?" *Annals of Behavioral Medicine* 21, no. 4: 290–98.

WikiHow. "How to Write a Target Market Analysis." www.wikihow.com/Write-a-Target-Market-Analysis.

References

Campbell, M. K. 2008. "Communication and Tailoring." In *The International Encyclopedia of Communication,* edited by W. Donsbach. Oxford: Blackwell. doi: 10.1111/b.9781405131995.2008.x.

Cobley, P. 2008. "Culture: Definitions and Concepts." In *The International Encyclopedia of Communication,* edited by W. Donsbach. doi: 10.1002/9781405186407.wbiecc173.

Common Language Marketing Dictionary. 2018. https://marketing-dictionary.org.

Devaney, E. 2014. "14 Ways to Get More Use out of Your Buyer Personas." https://blog.hubspot.com/marketing/ways-to-use-buyer-personas.

Du Pré, A. 2014. *Communicating about Health: Current Issues and Perspectives.* 4th ed. New York: Oxford University Press.

Gerbner, G., and L. Gross. 1976. "Living with Television: The Violence Profile." *Journal of Communication* 26, no. 2: 173–99.

Gittelsohn, J., A. Steckler, C. C. Johnson, C. Pratt, M. Grieser, J. Pickrel, . . . and L. K. Staten. 2006. "Formative Research in School and Community-Based Health Programs and Studies: 'State of the Art' and the TAAG Approach." *Health Education and Behavior* 33, no. 1: 25–39.

Hawkins, R. P., M. Kreuter, K. Resnicow, M. Fishbein, and A. Dijkstra. 2008. "Understanding Tailoring in Communicating about Health." *Health Education Research* 23, no. 3: 454–66.

Hawlk, K. 2017. "Need Marketing Ideas? Ask Your Target Audience." *Journal of Financial Planning* 11: 28–29.

Hollander, J. A. 2004. "The Social Contexts of focus Groups." *Journal of Contemporary Ethnography* 33, no. 5: 602–37.

Hubspot. 2018. "20 Questions to Ask When Creating Buyer Personas." https://blog.hubspot.com/marketing/buyer-persona-questions.

Kam, J. A., and N. Wang,. 2015. "Longitudinal Effects of Best-Friend Communication against Substance Use for Latino and Non-Latino White Early Adolescents." *Journal of Research on Adolescence* 25, no. 3: 534–50. doi: 10.1111/jora.12147.

Kim, K. J., D. H Shin, and H. Yoon. 2017. "Information Tailoring and Framing in Wearable Health Communication." *Information Processing and Management* 53, no. 2: 351–58. doi: 10.1016/j.ipm.2016.11.005.

Kreager, D. A., D. L. Haynie, and S. Hopfer. 2012. "Dating and Substance Use in Adolescent Peer Networks: A Replication and Extension." *Addiction* 108, no. 3: 638–47. doi: 10.1111/j.1360–0443.2012.04095.x.

LaBelle, S. 2014. "Addressing The Role of Health Literacy in Social Science: The Revision and Validation of the Perceived Oral Health Literacy Scale." PhD diss. West Virginia University.

Lee, N. R., and P. Kotler. 2016. *Social Marketing: Changing Behaviors of Good.* 5th ed. Los Angeles: Sage.

Lewis, L. K., N. Laster, and V. Kulkarni. 2013. "Telling 'em How It Will Be: Previewing Pain of Risky Change in Initial Announcements." *Journal of Business Communication* 50, no. 3: 278–308. doi: 10.1177/0021943613487072.

Linder, J. R., and E. A. Daniels. 2018. "Sexy vs. Sporty: The Effects of Viewing Media Images of Athletes on Self-Objectification in College Students." *Sex Roles* 78, no. 1: 27–39. doi: 10.1007/s11199-017-0774-7.

Lindlof, T. R., and B. C. Taylor. 2011. *Qualitative Research Methods*. 3rd ed. Los Angeles: Sage.

MacArthur, G. J., S. Harrison, D. M. Caldwell, M. Hickman, and R. Campbell. 2015. "Peer-Led Interventions to Prevent Tobacco, Alcohol and/or Drug Use among Young People Aged 11–21 Years: A Systematic Review and Meta-Analysis." *Addiction* 111, no. 3: 391–407. doi: 10.1111/add.13224.

Morgan, S. E., T. R. Harrison, W. A. Afifi, S. D. Long, and M. T. Stephenson. 2008. "In Their Own Words: The Reasons Why People Will (Not) Sign an Organ Donor Card." *Health Communication* 23, no. 1: 23–33.

National Cancer Institute (US). 2004. *Making Health Communication Programs Work: A Planner's Guide, Pink Book*. www.cancer.gov/cancertopics/cancerlibrary/pinkbook/Pink_Book.pdf.

Noonan, R. K., and D. Charles. 2009. "Developing Teen Dating Violence Prevention Strategies: Formative Research with Middle School Youth." *Violence against Women* 15, no. 9: 1087–105.

Pew Research Center. 2014, March. "Millennials in Adulthood: Detached from Institutions, Networked with Friends."

Prochaska, J., and C. DiClemente. 1983. "Stages and Processes of Self-Change in Smoking: Toward an Integrative Model of Change." *Journal of Consulting and Clinical Psychology* 5: 390–95.

Prochaska, J., J. C. Norcross, and C. DiClemente. 2013. "Applying the Stages of Change." *Psychotherapy in Australia* 19, no. 2: 10–15.

Sarkin, J. A., S. S. Johnson, J. O. Prochaska, and J. M. Prochaska. 2001. "Applying the Transtheoretical Model to Regular Moderate Exercise in an Overweight Population: Validation of a Stages of Change Measure." *Preventive Medicine* 33, no. 5: 462–69.

Slater, M. D. 1999. "Integrating Application of Media Effects, Persuasion, and Behavior Change Theories to Communication Campaigns: A Stages-of-Change Framework." *Health Communication* 11, no. 4: 335–54. doi: 10.1207/S15327027HC1104_2.

Spettigue, W., and K. A. Henderson. 2004. "Eating Disorders and the Role of the Media." *Canadian Child and Adolescent Psychiatry Review* 13, no. 1: 16–19.

Steele, J. L., R. L. Peralta, and C. Elman. 2011. "The Co-Ingestion of Nonmedical Prescription Drugs and Alcohol: A Partial Test of Social Learning Theory." *Journal of Drug Issues* 41, no. 4: 561–85.

Stevenson, S. 2006. "Mac Attack: Apple's Mean-Spirited New Ad Campaign." www.slate.com/articles/business/ad_report_card/2006/06/mac_attack.html.

Vallis, M., L. Ruggiero, G. Greene, H. Jones, B. Zinman, S. Rossi, . . . and J. O. Prochaska. 2003. "Stages of Change for Healthy Eating in Diabetes: Relation to Demographic, Eating-Related, Health Care Utilization, and Psychosocial Factors." *Diabetes Care* 26, no. 5: 1468–74. doi: 10.2337/diacare.26.5.1468.

Developing and Designing Messages: Using Persuasion Theory and Evidence-Based Principles

CHAPTER CONTENTS

7.1 What Is Theory and Why Is It So Useful for Strategic Communication Practitioners? 192
    7.1.1 Defining Theory as Everyday Ways of Knowing 193
    7.1.2 Defining Theory as Scholarly Frameworks and the Process of Inquiry 195
7.2 Persuasion as a Key Element of Strategic Communication 197
    7.2.1 Goals of Persuasion 198
    7.2.2 The Human Tendency to Resist Change 200
    7.2.3 Evaluating a Persuasive Message Audience 202
    7.2.4 Credibility and Persuasion 204
    7.2.5 Appeals Used in Persuasion 208
7.3 What Are Some Prominent Theories of Persuasion for Strategic Communication? 213
    7.3.1 Extended Parallel Process Model 213
    7.3.2 Elaboration Likelihood Model 217
    7.3.3 Social Judgment Theory 219
7.4 Tying It All Together: Persuasion and Strategic Communication 220

LEARNING OBJECTIVES

After reading this chapter, you should be able to do the following:

▶ Define theory and explain its critical importance in the design, execution, and evaluation of strategic communication.

▶ Identify persuasive goals for strategic communication.

▶ Explain the types of appeals employed in persuasion.

▶ Apply three theories of persuasion relevant to strategic communication.

James is four years out of college with a degree in communication and his master's in corporate communication. He was recently hired by a small biomedical start-up to launch, manage, and evaluate a marketing campaign for its latest product. When she was recruiting James, the CEO was very clear and to the point: The company had experienced a number of setbacks and was running out of funding. She had great confidence in James and his ability to bring this innovation to market—and the company's future was riding on this campaign.

James thought long and hard about leaving his current, stable position, but reasoned that if he could succeed with this younger company, he'd have more opportunities for advancement, career growth, and creativity than if he stayed with the larger, established company he currently worked for.

He was confident and excited about the challenges that lay ahead. But he knew that he needed a sound framework around which to build his marketing strategy, and that neither he nor the company could afford for him to simply make guesses about what might work. To get support and ultimately succeed, James needed a solid, evidence-based theoretical framework to guide his strategy and quick access to the research suggesting that his plan was likely to succeed.

Although James was under a dramatic degree of pressure to succeed in his new job, his mandate was similar to that of anyone tasked with message design in a professional setting: to generate a persuasive and compelling narrative informed by valid, reliable research and theory. As college professors who frequently conduct research and provide communication consulting activities within organizations, your authors learned very quickly how useful a strong grasp of science, theory, and research is. Most organizations, whether they use the terminology of science or not, work from a scientific perspective. They rely on science to design products, assess market needs and trends, identify and understand target audiences, determine performance standards, defend product quality, promote products and services, test messages, influence others with innovative ideas, and so on. It is virtually impossible for an organization to thrive without the benefits of science. James's boss appreciated the scientific method as it relates to persuading people. She and James knew that relying on theory and research—the knowledge others had already produced—was the pathway to a defensible, objective, and well-documented marketing campaign that would help this struggling company attain its goals.

In this chapter, you will learn the relevance of theory, and *persuasion theory* in particular, in the practice of strategic communication. As a backdrop for learning several of the most prominent theories of persuasion that are used in strategic messaging, we will define persuasion as a specific type of communication and examine the processes and characteristics of persuasion. The iconic social scientist Kurt Lewin once famously wrote, "there's nothing so practical as a good theory" (1945, 129). This statement might seem counterintuitive if your experience with theory is that of dry, boring ideas appreciated only by scholars. After reading this chapter, you hopefully will have developed an appreciation for the practical role that theory can play in an organization's communication strategy.

7.1 WHAT IS THEORY AND WHY IS IT SO USEFUL FOR STRATEGIC COMMUNICATION PRACTITIONERS?

Several years ago, one of the authors of this book, Jennifer Waldeck, was asked to give a talk to a group of managers and executives about the role that social science theory and research can play in building effective teams. One skeptical participant interrupted early on in the discussion: "Theory?! This isn't a university! I just want less conflict, easier decisions, more productive meetings, more satisfied employees, greater competitive advantage, and a better bottom line." Jennifer responded by discussing Kurt Lewin's reflection on the practicality of theory and talked briefly about how theory held many of the solutions to these common workplace challenges. Although Lewin developed theories during his career and published many research studies, he was not sitting in a dusty academic office generating irrelevant, boring ideas. In fact, his life's work illustrates how theory and research can help address real-world problems.

For example, one major project Lewin worked on in the 1940s involved research commissioned by the United States government intended to learn more about how to combat prejudice in society. Tests of Lewin's theories of attitude change and group behavior suggested that people who learn by experience are more likely to change their attitudes and behaviors about people who are different from them than people who learn primarily through lecture and reading. This conclusion led to a methodology known as *T-groups*, in which people experiencing difference and conflict in their working relationships sat down with a trained facilitator and listened to one another share thoughts, feelings, and reactions. T-groups remain the foundation for the kinds of programs used in organizations today to foster learning and discussion about diversity, cultural awareness, and group communication. Lewin, and the countless people who have used his work and other social science developments, took theory and research into **applied settings,** or practical "real-world" environments (e.g., workplaces), to positively influence and transform human behavior and workplace functioning.

By the end of the session, Jennifer had convinced the skeptical executive that many solutions to the concerns he voiced about his day-to-day responsibilities could be found in theory and the research done to test it. Similarly, strategic communication professionals can find useful guiding frameworks for their tasks in theories that explain the complex process of influencing audiences. As you continue to read this chapter, you will see that communication theories, and particularly those focused on persuasion, are extremely useful in the design of strategic messages and campaigns.

7.1.1 Defining Theory as Everyday Ways of Knowing

In the simplest terms, a **theory** is a systematic explanation or description of some phenomenon (we build on this definition throughout this chapter). To some extent, we are all theorists because we have a near-constant need to describe or explain what happens in our lives. For instance:

- Consider the unfriendly classmate who never smiles or talks to you. You have probably engaged in some effort to determine why this is the case and evaluated whether you did anything to offend this particular person.
- Recall the last time you asked someone at work for a favor and received an unpleasant response. You undoubtedly tried to determine why the person didn't want to help you.
- Think about the last time you got an exam grade back from an instructor. You probably evaluated the factors that may have contributed to your performance—such as how much reading and preparation you did leading up to the test, the note-taking methods you used, and whether or not you met with the instructor to discuss the material.

In each of these situations, as you construct your theory of why something is the way that it is, you have specific objectives:

- to recreate situations that you find desirable (e.g., earn an A on the final exam);
- to alter or fix situations that you dislike (e.g., create a friendly rapport with your classmate);
- to create conditions that enable positive outcomes to emerge (e.g., develop supportive alliances with your coworkers so that you can count on one another for help).

See how useful theory can be? Our everyday efforts to theorize about events that occur establish some sense of order, knowing, and predictability.

How do we develop that sense of knowing? In building our descriptions and explanations of everyday events, we rely on many sources to inform our thinking that we refer to as *everyday ways of knowing.* Personal past experience (our own or someone else's), mental shortcuts or "rules of thumb" for common situations, customs and traditions, religious beliefs, popular culture, observations of other people, the advice of experts, our intuition, and even social media and internet content serve as frameworks for educated guesses about day-to-day phenomena. These mental shortcuts are known as **heuristics** (Tversky and Kahneman 1974).

Overreliance on heuristics can lead to subjective, biased thinking that represents a limited and limiting view of the world. In terms of a more rigorous understanding of theory, more specifically, everyday ways of knowing and heuristics may be inconsistent or unreliable. They are not likely to provide adequate insights that apply time and time again in the same or similar situations. For example, a simple but important rule of thumb for nonverbal business communication in the United States is to make eye contact and extend a firm handshake to an associate. This is a great rule to keep in mind when you do business in the United States but would be a disastrous practice in some other countries. In other words, this "rule" lacks global reliability. Similarly, your family of origin may have taught you never to boast about accomplishments or be assertive in your interaction with others. This lesson may have resulted in you being perceived as a kind and humble young person on the playground, but at work, where you must establish credibility and be appropriately assertive to advance a message, this advice might limit your effectiveness.

Recall James from the opening scenario to this chapter. His CEO has promised James the necessary resources to develop a marketing plan. Yet the boss wants to know that James's plan has a high likelihood of working. If James were to rely strictly on past experience or the advice of books and even mentors, he would probably fail. Experiences in random situations with random people don't typically generalize to other situations and people.

Further, everyday ways of knowing may not apply in the situation you are dealing with because they lack accuracy—or are just plain wrong. For example, Shiva is responsible for developing a wellness program at work. She follows a number of blogs and social media accounts that advance the argument that foods containing genetically modified organisms (GMOs) may be the source of significant health, energy, and stamina problems for people who consume them. Thus, Shiva decided to launch a campaign to raise awareness about the dangers of dietary GMOs and to influence employees to eliminate them from their diets. After implementing the campaign, her staff was making the recommended behavior changes, but she noticed that absenteeism was still high, people still seemed to lack energy, and illness was still a major problem. Although Shiva may have assigned credibility to the bloggers and experts whose work she read, she ignored or was unaware of more than 130 research projects summarized in *Scientific American* conducted over twenty-five years involving more than five hundred independent research groups. These studies concluded that GMOs are not riskier in terms of health outcomes than non-GMO food (Shermer 2015). The bloggers she read were expressing *opinions* and potentially biased or distorted arguments. Thus, her theory about why employees were suffering in the areas of energy and wellness (and her solution) had accuracy problems. She over-relied on everyday ways of knowing (i.e., social media and unvetted "experts"). As a result, she did not accomplish the objectives she'd hoped for with her employee wellness campaign. Communication theory specialists Griffin, Ledbetter, and Sparks would say that Shiva had a "hunch," but that it was not an "informed hunch" (2015, 4) because it didn't go beyond the speculation of a biased group of bloggers.

Everyday ways of knowing (e.g., asking an expert or reading books or internet content) and mental scripts and schema (e.g., rules of thumb and what we believe to be true based on past experience) can help us make sense out of everyday events. We use them all the time without much conscious thought. However, these frameworks are often flawed for application in strategic communication work—where we typically can't afford a trial-and-error approach to action. Next, we turn to an alternative approach: formal, tested, scholarly theory.

7.1.2 Defining Theory as Scholarly Frameworks and the Process of Inquiry

An alternative to everyday theory and ways of knowing is *scholarly theory*. Scholarly theories are the result of a much more rigorous process of development, inquiry, and testing than everyday ways of knowing. They represent systematic, rather than arbitrary, frameworks for approaching situations. These approaches represent a more solid basis for strategic communication because they are evidence-based, the result of rigorous inquiry and research. The evidence comes in the form of existing research findings and observations scholars make of human behavior when they test their theories. If James, for example, were to use evidence-based approaches to design his company's marketing plan, he would be much more likely to deliver a workable solution than if he made guesses based on what he'd observed at a past job. Specifically, scholarly theories are the result of a five-step process of inquiry:

- *Asking* questions about phenomena (e.g., why are messages designed to arouse fear in receivers sometimes effective at getting them to act in particular ways, and sometimes not?);
- *Hypothesizing* the relationships among variables of interest based on what prior research has already revealed about the concepts involved (e.g., fear can motivate people to simply reduce or discount their feelings of fear [e.g., think "that can't happen to me"], rather than eliminate the action that the message is telling them to be fearful of [e.g., quit texting and driving]; people with high self-efficacy are more likely to change their actions and believe that they will realize positive results than people with low self-efficacy);
- Systematically *observing* the phenomenon of interest using valid research methods (e.g., interviewing or surveying people who have been exposed to fear appeals; setting up an experiment in which half of the subjects are exposed to a fear appeal and half the subjects are exposed to a different type of persuasive message and then looking at how people responded to the messages based on their self-efficacy levels);

- *Testing* (e.g., analyzing the results of observation and, say, concluding that fear appeals are effective at encouraging people with high levels of self-efficacy to change their behaviors); and
- *Revising,* or altering the original theory based on the results of the test (e.g., if the researcher determined that both high and low self-efficacy individuals resisted fear appeals, he or she would have to begin the process of theory building again).

Communication scholars Rich West and Lynn Turner provide a refined definition of **formal, scholarly theory:** "a system of concepts with indications of the relationships among these concepts that help us to understand a phenomenon" (2014, 47). Additionally, as we will explain shortly, formal theories allow us to make predictions and to control or regulate phenomena. By control, we do not mean manipulation. Instead, in the context of theory, control represents an evidence-based means for promoting desired outcomes and avoiding undesirable ones. For example, theoretical perspectives on fear appeals in persuasive communication (which we will study in greater detail later in this chapter) give us the evidence we need to use fear effectively as strategic communicators. For example, we know that fear will only work when we offer a recommended action that the audience thinks will work and that they are personally capable of carrying out. When an audience might perceive the recommended action as burdensome or difficult, the message should emphasize how easy it is to implement. For instance, recall Shiva's employee wellness campaign. Encouraging this workaholic, sedentary crowd to walk ten thousand steps a day was bound to be difficult. Her audience wasn't particularly frightened by her messages about diabetes—and the existing literature suggested that this was most likely because they perceived her recommended behavior as far too difficult and unrealistic. Thus, Shiva needed to find a way to enhance their sense of self-efficacy for engaging in the suggested exercise. This is an illustration of what we mean by control.

In the language that theoreticians use, theories enable their users to *describe, explain, predict,* and *control* the concepts under consideration (e.g., in our previous example, fear appeals). An understanding of the theories related to fear and persuasion helps both scholars and strategic communication practitioners:

1. *Understand* what fear appeals are (i.e., describe them);
2. *Explain* why fear appeals work and don't work based on the concepts within the theory and how they relate to one another in scientific observations;
3. *Predict* the conditions under which fear appeals will successfully change message receivers' behavior; and
4. Know how to design messages that will maximize the likelihood of desired behavior change among the audience (i.e., *control*).

In addition, using a theoretical framework to guide message design provides strategic communicators with a sound method for evaluating the message's effectiveness in relation to its objective(s). A tested theory offers measurement techniques for determining outcomes of interest, such as audience resistance, attitude or behavior change, or perceptions of the message's credibility. You will see further examples of how theories help guide the development, dissemination, and evaluation of strategic messages throughout this chapter and as we explore specific theories.

By now, you should have a solid understanding of why and how theory can be useful to people in strategic communication contexts. Theories provide a useful road map or guide for approaching both routine and unusual circumstances. Particularly relevant to strategic communication are a genre of theories classified as theories of persuasion. In the remaining sections of this chapter, we will discuss the concept of persuasive communication and examine some of the more prominent theories of persuasion.

7.2 PERSUASION AS A KEY ELEMENT OF STRATEGIC COMMUNICATION

Central to the practice of strategic communication is the ability to use messages in ways that influence an organization's internal and external stakeholders and that consequently advance a particular mission or goal. Taken together, these approaches refer to persuasion. For instance, recall Shiva's wellness campaign from earlier in the chapter. It represented an effort to strategically influence the behaviors of an organization's employees. In addition, James was tasked with creating a marketing strategy that would successfully influence prospective customers to learn about, buy, and otherwise support the brand. In another instance, one of your textbook authors, Dr. Sara LaBelle, has directed a successful multiyear campaign at Chapman University designed to change students' attitudes and behaviors relevant to prescription stimulant misuse. All of these examples of strategic communication require expertise in persuasion. **Persuasion** is an activity that "involves symbolic communication between two or more persons with the intent to change . . . attitudes, beliefs, and/or behaviors of the receiver[s]" (Frymier and Nadler 2017, 6). Although how to influence other people to think or act in particular ways may seem like an impossible task, social scientists have studied the process of persuasion extensively and have identified an impressive array of variables that contribute to effective persuasion. Our modern understanding of influence and communication began with an influential series of studies conducted by Yale psychologist Carl Hovland and his colleagues, who sought to understand World War II propaganda messages and their effects on troop morale (Hovland, Janis, and Kelley 1953). Since that time, social psychologists and communication researchers have thoroughly investigated message, source, and receiver factors that contribute to a communicator's ability to influence or achieve some desired change among receivers of a message. Additionally, we know a great deal about why audiences **resist,** or display unwillingness to change in response to a persuasive message. To better understand the process of persuasion and its related components, let's examine the goals of persuasive communication.

7.2.1 Goals of Persuasion

Although the primary goal of any persuasive message is to advocate some type of change among the audience, strategic communicators operate with one or more specific goals in mind: to change how listeners feel or act. Although we will examine these one at a time, it's important to understand that these three goals are, to some extent, interrelated and often based on what audience members believe (the information or facts they have about a subject). Recall that organizations often have strategic *informational* goals. Information influences audience members' **beliefs** or perceptions of the truth or existence, or falsity, of something (e.g., "college students who misuse prescription stimulants typically have lower GPAs than those who don't" or "vaccines prevent the spread of certain diseases"). For the purposes of strategic communication, we differentiate informational goals from persuasive goals even though the two are linked.

People often act in certain ways because of feelings they have. For example, Janet avoids unprotected sun exposure (behavior) because she believes that sun exposure can result in undesirable health outcomes (belief or information that she has), and because she doesn't like the feeling of a sunburn (attitude). Sometimes, we feel a particular way because of a behavior we've engaged in. For example, every day in stores like Costco, shoppers develop positive attitudes toward certain brands of flavored water, pita chips, egg rolls, cookies, cheese, and other products after sampling them. After their purchase and subsequent enjoyment of the product (behavior), these consumers may form an overall positive attitude toward them because they like their taste and can purchase them for a good price at a store they regularly visit. Let's explore in greater depth the goals of persuasion.

The first involves influencing attitudes. **Attitudes** refer to our consistent feelings of like or dislike toward a particular object, person, concept, or idea. Attitudes are not genetic; people learn them. Thus, the good news in terms of persuasion is that people can un-learn their attitudes when they are effectively influenced. When we aim to alter someone's attitude, we hope to create either more positive or more negative feelings or emotions among the audience toward something. For example, consider the following simple persuasive messages that are aimed at influencing audience members' attitudes:

- Cooking healthy food can be fun.
- Volunteer work can make you feel optimistic about life's challenges.
- Risky behavior like binge drinking can create anxiety for those who engage in it.

Notice that all of these messages are geared toward changing receivers' feelings about the issue under consideration. Influencing attitudes is an important persuasive goal, because research indicates that they are often related to people's behavior (Ajzen and Fishbein 2005). Therefore, for example, if a university hopes to persuade an audience of high school seniors to live in a residence hall rather than at home, the university's messages must also address the audience's attitudes toward this concept.

Alternatively, some persuasive messages are aimed at altering audience **behavior,** or overt physical action. Messages or campaigns with the goal of influencing behavior encourage specific, explicit behavioral activities, in contrast to messages that emphasize attitude or belief change. If an organization has a strategic behavioral goal, it wants to motivate its audience to take some kind of action. For example, consider how organizations employ strategic persuasions to influence their target audiences to:

- Register to vote
- Use sunscreen
- Become and remain a loyal shopper
- Eat a plant-based diet
- Switch cell phone service providers
- Register to be an organ donor

In each of these examples, the organization's objective is to influence members of the audience to *do* something differently than they did prior to the message or campaign. However, as we've previously discussed, in order to alter behavior, a message may need to influence the audience's beliefs and attitudes first.

Sometimes, when our persuasive goal is behavioral change, the best we can hope for is that audience members will *commit* to acting or behaving in a particular way. This commitment is known as **behavioral intention,** or an individual's expectation or plan that he or she will behave in some particular way. For example, when a media campaign makes health-related recommendations to an audience about breast or testicular self-examinations, specific exercise or diet regimens, or smoking cessation, researchers can only immediately know the effects of these influence messages on behavioral intention—not actual behavior (Paek, Oh, and Hove 2012). In many cases, you will need to ask for behavioral intention and be satisfied with commitments to change rather than evidence of actual change as a result of your persuasive messages.

Once you determine whether you should aim to influence attitudes or behaviors with your message, your next task is to determine the level of resistance or potential agreement that already exists among your target audience.

7.2.2 The Human Tendency to Resist Change

Think about the last time someone tried to convince you to do something that you didn't want to do. Perhaps it was going to cost too much, be too time consuming or difficult, or maybe it was just an activity that you thought would be unpleasant. When someone tries to convince you to do something other than what you want to do, or attempts to influence you to do something differently than the way that you're currently doing it, how do you react?

According to **psychological reactance theory** (Brehm 1966; Brehm and Brehm 1981), persuasive messages threaten an audience's feeling of freedom to think, believe, and act as they wish. This threat is one of the primary explanations for why people resist influence messages. As a result of the fear that they are being talked into doing something they don't want to do, people will reassert their freedom by putting down the source of the persuasion and/or rebelling against the recommended attitude, belief, or behavior. In other words, psychological reactance is a negative response to persuasion that motivates resistance.

For example, when workplace changes are announced, many people react negatively and resist accepting the new policy or procedure. Recall from that strategic external communication—branding, image, and identity, for example—are all inextricably linked to internal culture. Thus, psychological reactance can create widespread problems for organizations when cultural change is necessary. When Jack made a presentation about a new sick leave policy at work, his employees were not only resistant but also openly hostile about the change reduced number of sick days available to them.

An additional scholarly tradition relevant to audience resistance to persuasion suggests that a growing number of people are rejecting consumerism and embracing simplicity and minimalism in their lives (Rumbo 2002). According to this **postmodern perspective** (a complex ideology characterized by skepticism about and, often, rejection of scientific claims, traditional power structures, and common or traditional beliefs or behaviors), consumers are increasingly concerned about:

- potentially unethical corporate control and manipulation over their purchase decisions; the belief that "our lived experiences are increasingly shaped and monitored by marketers" (Rumbo 2002, 134);
- the overwhelming onslaught of persuasive messages across media platforms (e.g., television, social media, product placement in programming, outdoor advertising) (Jhally 1990);

Strategic Communication Mentor: Why Do People Resist Change?

In this article, Harvard Business School professor Rosabeth Moss Kantner explores ten reasons related to psychological reactance why people resist change:

http://blogs.hbr.org/2012/09/ten-reasons-people-resist-chang/

As you read the article, generate two real or hypothetical examples to illustrate each reason for reactance Kantner provides. Be prepared to discuss, as directed by your instructor, communication strategies for minimizing reactance in the scenarios you generated.

- commodification and "overavailability" of information and material goods (Leys and Harriss-White 2012); and
- a culture in which mass-produced goods sold at "big box" corporate retailers or by massive online shopping sites is pushing local business and artisans out of the marketplace (Lasn 1999).

As a result, a growing number of consumers may be "tuning out" and avoiding advertising messages to the extent that they can. They are deactivating their social media accounts, throwing away their junk mail, blocking telemarketers' phone numbers, and fast forwarding through commercials (if they watch traditional television at all). They are embracing small local businesses and farmers' markets and doing less big box and online shopping. This perspective on consumer resistance poses unique challenges to strategic communicators and emphasizes the importance of knowing your audience as well as societal/cultural beliefs and trends about your message (and the subject/object of your message).

Research on the persuasion process provides some insight into how organizations can design messages strategically to avoid psychological reactance. For example, when organizations give their members the opportunity to voice their input about a proposed change, employee resistance to the change is minimized (Olison and Roloff 2012). All of the research on psychological reactance points to the importance of using proactive techniques for preventing it rather than waiting for it to occur and dealing with the problems later. In order to implement these techniques, strategic communication professionals must understand and adapt to their audience. Chapter 6 provided insights on the importance of audience analysis and specific strategies for engaging in systematic assessment of a target audience. Recall that part of what you might ask your target audience in this analysis includes their knowledge, attitudes, and behaviors regarding your organization, product, or idea. Here, we delineate

Figure 30 Many consumers are rejecting corporate appeals in favor of "shopping small" at farmers' markets and at locally owned businesses.

some of the audience analysis concepts that are most pertinent to persuasive communication.

7.2.3 Evaluating a Persuasive Message Audience

The most important thing that you can do for any type of audience is offer a strong rationale for the change you are recommending. To be strategic, you have to give your listeners sufficient, credible reasons to do things differently. To determine what a particular type of listener will consider "sufficient" and "credible," you will need to know which of the following three audiences you are about to address.

AN AUDIENCE THAT AGREES WITH YOUR POSITION   Persuasive messages that *reinforce* a receiver's present position on an issue are the easiest type to develop. Agreeable audiences are the friendliest; they have already made the decision to support you and your message, so your job is to reinforce and perhaps strengthen that support. For example, a minister's sermon to her congregation is designed to reinforce the religious beliefs and lifestyle that audience members have already adopted. A university president's presentation to a group of donors is intended to intensify their desire to give, and to give even more than they already do. What strategies will aid you in your efforts to intensify the support of an already supportive audience through strategic messages?

1. *Establish common ground.* Remind the audience that you share their attitudes and beliefs toward the topic and are already on the same page.
2. *Provide your audience with some motivation and encouragement to strengthen their agreement.* Narratives, direct or indirect personal examples, and emotional appeals work well. We will explore the various types of persuasive appeals available later in this chapter.
3. *Be straightforward.* Tell this audience exactly what you want or need. Because they are already supportive, they will appreciate this approach and often comply.

AN AUDIENCE THAT DISAGREES WITH YOUR POSITION   Because of psychological reactance, these are the most challenging audiences to influence. When we attempt to *change* someone's position on an issue, we design a message that encourages them to shift their current attitudes, beliefs, or behaviors. Change is very difficult to achieve among audience members who have already formed an opinion on an issue, believe something very strongly, or are accustomed to behaving in a certain way. For example, Tanya, a medical educator at a large hospital, is developing a series of health education materials for a group of cardiac patients who have self-reported sedentary lifestyles and diets high in sodium and fat. Her message, then, is targeted toward changing her audience's attitudes and behaviors about diet and exercise—ones that are already deeply formed and that they have practiced for a long period of time. Tanya has a very difficult job ahead of her and must avoid rejection of her message. Here are some suggestions for Tanya and for any communicator preparing messages for a difficult, disagreeable audience:

1. Research suggests that *messages should advocate for just small amounts of change when the audience's position is far from the one they are advocating* (see "Social Judgment Theory" later in this chapter). Do not expect a radical change all at once. For instance, Tanya should encourage her audience to start out taking a ten-minute walk five days a week rather than insisting that they work out on an elliptical machine intensely for an hour a day. She should propose incremental, realistic goals for her audience.

2. *Establish some common ground.* Acknowledge places where you agree and communicate respect for the audience's perspective. For example, when Jack had the unpleasant task of convincing his coworkers that they should feel positively about the company's new policy of fewer sick days, he worked hard to let the audience know that he understood that they were unhappy, and why. He acknowledged that he was not too happy, either, but he went on to argue the reasons why this change could ultimately provide employees with other benefits. However, he didn't overdo the list of reasons and evidence; instead, he took a softer approach to prevent reactance and resistance.

3. *Give resistant audiences plenty of credible evidence that there are problems with the status quo (the way things are currently).* Sometimes the audience isn't even aware that the way they currently do something is problematic. If you can arouse among your audience a sense that there is a clear need for change, you will grab their attention and direct it to your proposal. Tanya, our medical educator, was somewhat surprised to learn that her target audience had little idea which of their own behaviors were contributing to their health problems. However, this information helped her create a strong and urgent need for behavioral change among the cardiac patients.

AN AUDIENCE THAT'S NEUTRAL OR AMBIVALENT   When your audience is uninformed about the issue, is confused about it, or doesn't see how acting either way will benefit them, your task is to *shape* their attitudes and behaviors. To do so, your message needs to be informative to some extent. In addition, it should advocate a position on a particular issue when audience members have no previous stance. For example, Pat was tasked with creating a marketing plan that included giving out samples of a new cleaning product his company had formulated, along with discount coupons, in supermarkets. In other words, his goal involved shaping consumer response to the cleaning product because it was a new product that the target market had no direct experience with. Although the "blank slate" audience is pretty rare, it should be easy to influence. With neutral or undecided audiences, be sure to:

1. *Establish why they should decide.* Make the issue relevant to them.
2. *Explain your position and why you have adopted it.* Provide evidence that your position is a credible, useful, effective one (facts, testimonials, stories, and so on). But avoid overwhelming this audience with too much data.
3. *Establish common ground and similarity with your audience.* Suggest to the audience that what works for you might work for them, too, and encourage them to adopt what it is that you're advocating. For instance, Kreps (2016) reported on a project in which peer facilitators spread advocacy messages regarding AIDS and HIV prevention among community groups that had expressed distrust in mainstream medical professionals. By relying on similar sources with an audience that was neutral about the issue, but known to be resistant to messages about the same issue from medical professionals, the project was able to realize significant behavioral change among its target audience.

In all situations where your success rests on your ability to influence your audience to adapt how they feel, think, or act about something, one of the most important things you can do is to learn where the audience stands on the issue prior to your presentation. You can then build a case that meets their needs, overcomes their objections, and prevents psychological reactance and resistance. In considering your audience as well as the focus of your strategic message you will next want to select one or more persuasive appeals to use.

7.2.4 Credibility and Persuasion

Recall that source credibility refers to an audience's perception that a message source has expertise, is believable, and cares about the audience's best interests. Researchers have documented the kinds of behaviors sources can engage in to heighten audience perceptions of their expertise, trustworthiness, and goodwill. However, strategic communicators must consider all facets of message design and delivery that could affect receivers' impressions of their credibility and not rely on source credibility alone. Even if the source and audience have a preexisting relationship in which the audience perceives the source as credible, in order to be persuasive, strategic messages must incorporate cues that invoke the message source's credibility. The message itself might intensify or diminish any initial credibility the receiver assigns to the source of a message. In fact, a long history of research suggests that the credibility of a particular *message* is likely to have more long-term influence on an audience than any positive feelings the audience might have had about the *source* prior to the message. The **sleeper effect,** or idea that receivers exposed to low credibility sources develop more positive attitudes over time and those exposed to high credibility sources will weaken in their feelings of positivity toward that source over time, was documented by Kelman and Hovland in 1953. Later, communication researchers Allen and Stiff (1998) developed the **discounting model** as a probable explanation for why the sleeper effect occurs: Source credibility effects on message recipients are typically temporary. In other words, early attitude or behavior shifts may be explained by audience perceptions of the source, but over time, message content and characteristics have the greatest influence on audience behavior.

Let's consider a few examples of this. Suppose you select a new product based on brand recognition. You have purchased other products marketed by this particular company in the past and have been highly satisfied. However, when you try this new product, you discover it is not consistent with the quality of the others. The positive impact of the company's initial source credibility wears off quickly as you deal with a laundry detergent that doesn't make your clothes bright and spot free, a vacuum cleaner that doesn't remove your dog's hair from the carpet, or a candy bar that doesn't taste good. You bought the product based on source credibility, but over time, the source's credibility wore off and you discovered that the product was inferior or did not meet your needs. You either returned it or never purchased it again. Realize that the sleeper effect works in the opposite direction, too. Thus, if your brand is new or suffers from initial credibility problems, you can neutralize audience perceptions of poor initial credibility with a strategic message and have positive influence on their behavior.

How can strategic communicators cultivate audience perceptions of source credibility while delivering an equally credible message, so that the audience is compelled to act and stick with the behavior? Consider these strategies for building source credibility:

1. *Emphasize source credibility early and prominently in the message and/or campaign* (e.g., experience, previous positive results, training, education, or any other relevant indicators). The audience needs this information early in its efforts to determine what to do or how to think or act.

2. Over the course of a campaign and/or your relationship with the audience, *find ways to remind the audience of who the message source is and why they should believe that source to be expert, trustworthy, and caring.* Doing so will help you avoid the discounting effect.

3. *Encourage transparent, positive online reviews of your brand.* Xie and colleagues (2011) found that online reviews accompanied by reviewers' actual names were viewed as more credible "introductions" to hotel brands by consumers than reviews from anonymous sources and led to stronger behavioral intentions among the target audience about patronizing the brand being reviewed.

4. *Arrange for supportive introductions from sources that your audience will find highly credible when interacting with the audience face-to-face.* This is especially important when the audience has little information about you, your organization, or your brand.

5. *Ensure that all visual and written materials are consistent with your organization's style guide, or the style guide for this particular brand or project.* Use fonts, logos, and colors consistently to tell a cohesive, credible, and persuasive story.

6. *Communicate ethically: objectively, accurately, and transparently.* In chapter 4, we considered the critical importance of approaching strategic communication from an ethical framework. Relevant to persuasion, you should never conceal your intent to influence. Be thorough and exact in presenting facts and understand that social science research tells us that audiences find messages and sources that acknowledge multiple perspectives of a problem or situation more credible. Rely on **two-sided messages with refutation** wherever possible to maintain your credibility and the integrity of your message. A two-sided message involves articulating your position or making your request and acknowledging why the audience might not agree or might not want to comply. The refutation, then, involves giving your audience reasons why they should be interested in agreeing or trying out what your message advocates. Audiences tend to be suspicious of sources and messages that hammer them with a one-sided argument and fail to notice the reasons why the audience might be skeptical or even find the recommendation objectionable (McGuire 1962; Pfau 1992).

7. *Present messages strategically by using language that is relevant and will be understood by your audience.* Boster (2016) recommends paying careful attention to the readability of written messages by incorporating summaries in longer messages and using bullet point lists, images, and examples. Avoid technical jargon and instead favor simple declarative sentences that will "stick" with your audience. Tables, graphs, and pictures can help audiences digest complex or lengthy information. In summary, learn to speak your audience's language. Convey your message

using symbols they will understand. If your message is technical or complex, Boster recommends studying the communication style (e.g., books and online talks) of people who are good at translating difficult information for general audiences. He mentions Malcolm Gladwell (*The Tipping Point, Blink,* and columns in the *New Yorker),* Robert Cialdini (*Influence*), and Chip and Dan Heath (*Made to Stick*) as exemplars. These individuals are very capable of writing and speaking about technical issues for intelligent audiences who may lack knowledge and understanding specific to the niche topic of their expertise.

8. *Pay special attention to message organization.* Organized messages are positively associated with audience perceptions of source credibility (McCroskey and Mehrley 1969; Sharp and McClung 1966). Depending on the nature and context of your message, there are many ways to organize what you want to communicate. For example, research suggests that providing an audience some visual structure for oral messages (e.g., PowerPoint) can help organize and streamline their understanding of the content (Hynes and Stretcher 2008). Further, different audiences might have different preferences for the format and organization of a message. However, research shows that regardless of their preferences for specific format and structure, audiences prefer organized messages to disorganized ones (Smith 1951); so select a framework and stick with it. Although that same research suggests that audiences tolerate a small degree of message disorganization (e.g., a salesperson who needs to backtrack during a presentation or forego a point when time runs out), the more disorganized your message is, the more difficulty your audience will have understanding and remembering it (Darnell 1963; Thompson 1967). That is bad news for source and message credibility and your efforts to influence the audience to make attitude or behavior changes.

9. *Be sure that the content of your message is highly receiver-centered in order to maintain credibility.* Whether you are blogging, creating a social media post, developing a presentation, writing a report, creating a poster, or developing a website, be aware that your message needs to target its intended audience in a meaningful way if it is going to have any influence. Your audience will be scrutinizing all of your communication for an answer to the question, "What's in it for me?" Make sure you give them one (Volk 2013). Be respectful of their time and attention span. In these ways, you will demonstrate credibility.

10. *When working on social media platforms, balance self-promoting messages with ones your readers will find useful or entertaining, and never resort to clickbait.* **Clickbait** is a pejorative term that refers to sensational, provocative online content (e.g., provocative headlines that leave the reader wanting more or attention-grabbing photos) shared with the intent of arousing reader interest and drawing them to your website in

---

Strategies for Ensuring Message Source Credibility

1. Emphasize credibility early and prominently.
2. Find ways over time to remind the audience of the message source's credibility.
3. Encourage transparent, positive online reviews of your brand.
4. Arrange for supportive introductions when communicating face-to-face.
5. Ensure that visual and written materials adhere to a consistent style.
6. Communicate ethically: objectively, accurately, and transparently.
7. Use language that your audience will understand and perceive as relevant.
8. Pay special attention to message organization.
9. Keep your content audience-centered.
10. Balance self-promotion with useful content on social media; never use clickbait.
11. Proofread and edit all written communication.

---

order to generate traffic or online advertising revenue. Unlike valuable content, clickbait is typically inaccurate, hyperbolic, or inconsistent with what the headline promised (Gardiner 2015). For example, shared content on Facebook that reads something like "You'll never believe . . ." or "and you won't want to miss what happens next" baits you to click through to a website that generates revenue for the site owner based on the number of clicks. You may have noticed that when you fall victim to clickbait, what you find on that website after clicking is rarely relevant or satisfying. You do not want your target audience to lose trust in your messages, which will almost certainly happen if you use these tactics.

11. *Proofread and edit all written communication carefully.* Consider employing a professional proofreader or copyeditor if appropriate. A typo, grammatical error, misplaced comma, or other mistake can damage your credibility and that of your message significantly.

7.2.5 Appeals Used in Persuasion

Appeals refer to the evidence-based strategies that a strategic communicator uses within a single message or larger campaign to ethically compel and influence the target audience. Although there are many persuasive appeals available to communicators, they fall into two primary categories: logical and emotional.

LOGICAL APPEALS   Appeals rooted in reason and logic rely heavily on facts, data, statistical evidence, or the conclusions of known, high-status experts. These types of "hard" evidence are useful because they allow the message source to make powerful claims that something is true a certain percentage of the time, or under certain conditions, for example. Elena, a program director for a non-profit agency focused on promoting childhood literacy, relied on reason when preparing an annual report for her organization's donors. She integrated user data from the agency's website to illustrate the impact of their educational programs—indicators such as number of unique visitors, what features they interacted with, and so on. In addition, she was able to provide pre- and post-test quiz completion scores for the educational modules on the website to illustrate knowledge gains among site users. Evidence such as the data Elena offered her audience can be extremely effective—especially for people from certain professions or disciplines such as the sciences or engineering.

Research suggests some basic demographic and cultural data that you can use to make decisions about the types of appeals you should use in your messages. Some groups may value logical appeals more than others. For example, male audience members may prefer logic over emotional appeals, which we will discuss next. In addition, some cultural groups are more inclined to be persuaded by "hard evidence." Social psychologist Geert Hofstede's decades-long research program (2017) on cultural features that influence communication (including receiving and decoding messages) indicates that some cultures tend to avoid uncertainty more than others—and thus appreciate facts, figures, statistics, and precise background information that helps them interpret the data. Some of these countries include Greece, Belgium, Poland, Japan, France, Spain, South Korea, Mexico, and Israel. People from these countries or with cultural backgrounds emanating from them demonstrate great dependence on high-status experts and verifiable evidence. Some cultures (such as those in Scandinavian nations, the United Kingdom, and the Netherlands) are much more tolerant of uncertainty and will be more interested in personal stories and experiences than statistics or physical data when making decisions about how to think or act. Without facts and data, however, some audience members, because of their education, training, profession, or cultural background, may perceive your narratives or anecdotes as representing just unique or unusual cases. The United States is fairly moderate on uncertainty tolerance and will appreciate both types of appeals.

Research offers additional guidance on the use of logical appeals and evidence. One study, for instance, indicated that the context for communication influences how effective a logical versus emotional appeal will be. Wilson (2003) found that audiences preferred logical appeals in face-to-face communication, but that emotional message strategies were more effective in written and email transactions. In 1997, Allen and Preiss conducted a meta-analysis (a technique designed to summarize the effects of multiple research studies with conflicting results) that suggested that statistical evidence is a slightly more effective persuasive tool than emotional appeals. However, Allen and Preiss noted a key limitation associated with this conclusion: the samples studied were not culturally diverse. Thus, they did not represent the range of cultural preferences for persuasive appeals we have discussed. All data were collected in the United States from well-educated people, and there are wide cultural and educational differences in terms of what kinds of persuasive appeals will be successful.

EMOTIONAL APPEALS   A second type of appeal involves the use of strategies that arouse the target audience's emotions. Fear, guilt, excitement, happiness, anxiety, or regret all represent examples of the kinds of emotional reactions people have to experiences, words, phrases, and messages. Not all appeals need to be grounded in hard, objective facts. Some appeals provide a more personal feel for audiences and elicit particular emotional reactions that may lead to attitudinal and/or behavioral shifts. What kinds of persuasive strategies speak to receivers' emotions? Importantly, many emotional appeals are made in the form of a **narrative.** Simply put, narratives are stories. Stories help audiences connect with your brand and your message. When audiences connect, they identify and are motivated to act in particular ways. For example, in her work on effective communication for trial attorneys, one communication researcher found that defense lawyers are most successful when they learn to tell the defendant's story. Juries respond positively to a defendant's story when it is told in a way that allows the jury to connect with that person (SunWolf 2004). Further, good stories are entertaining, make sense, and arouse our attention. Often, a good story leaves us wanting to hear more and thinking about its topic even after the story has ended. Good stories are sometimes dramatic, sometimes suspenseful, sometimes funny, and sometimes tragic. But regardless of the tone or the topic, a good story grabs our attention and holds it.

Three of the most common forms of emotional appeals used in persuasion include humor, guilt, and fear. We will explore fear in greater detail in the last section of this chapter when we discuss Extended Parallel Process Model, a theory that defines the conditions in which fear appeals may be most effective. Here, briefly, we will discuss humor and guilt.

Humor involves a range of strategies designed to amuse an audience and can be a highly influential emotional appeal. Research suggests that appealing to an audience's sense of humor can get their attention (a prerequisite to persuasion) (Cline and Kellaris 1999), help shape favorable attitudes toward your message, and reduce the incidence of psychological reactance and resistance (Skalski et al. 2009). When used wisely and based on a reliable audience analysis, humor can help you establish rapport with your target audience and open them to your influence message(s). For example, the first author of this book, Sara LaBelle, was involved in a campaign designed to strategically influence male college students to perform testicular self-exams as a preventative screening measure for testicular cancer. In the research team's early efforts to learn about its target audience, they discovered that males are very uncomfortable

---

Strategic Communication Mentor: Hockey Fights Cancer

The National Hockey League (NHL)'s popular Hockey Fights Cancer campaign (www.nhl.com/community/hockey-fights-cancer) relies heavily on narrative to elicit audience support. NHL broadcasts, the campaign website, and social media platforms tell compelling stories about cancer survivors in varied ways. The following links present the stories of New Jersey Devils player Brian Boyle, who was diagnosed with leukemia (www.nhl.com/news/brian-boyles-mother-is-inspired-by-her-son-who-is-a-cancer-survivor/c-295867152?tid=282796264); Tampa Bay Lightning team efforts to honor the story of a six-year-old lymphoma patient (www.nhl.com/news/tampa-bay-lightning-wear-pin-to-support-child-with-cancer/c-295351026?tid=282796264); and Penguins player Phil Kessel, a testicular cancer survivor (www.cbssports.com/nhl/news/we-will-be-right-there-again-penguins-phil-kessel-on-life-cancer-and-the-stanley-cup/). The links integrate video, social media, and text-based narratives created by the NHL as part of a larger campaign that focuses on raising awareness about cancer, motivating behavioral change (i.e., to obtain regular checkups and screenings), and raising money for cancer research. What role do you believe these kinds of narratives play in accomplishing the overall objectives of the Hockey Fights Cancer campaign? Why can stories such as the three examples above be more effective in contexts such as Hockey Fights Cancer than logic, reason, statistics, and other objective evidence?

---

talking about testicular cancer and resistant to messages encouraging them to think about it or perform specific behaviors (like self-exams). This resistance effect seemed to soften when humor was used to discuss this serious topic. Rather than launch a sterile, "medical" sounding campaign, the team created one called Check Yo Nutz and adopted a squirrel mascot named Sammy. Not only did this campaign make its target audience more comfortable, it also led to significant changes in men's knowledge of testicular cancer symptoms and intent to perform monthly self-exams (Wanzer et al. 2014). This play on words and the visual image of the squirrel aroused humor among the target audience for the message with positive results.

Humor is a difficult emotional appeal to use effectively, however. Without careful and often direct audience analysis (e.g., testing messages in focus groups such as the Check Yo Nutz team did), humor is a risky strategy. It can just as easily offend as entertain. Some strategies for ensuring that humor will support your strategic persuasive goals include:

- Use sound audience analysis techniques that will help you determine what your particular audience might find humorous.

Strategic Communication Mentor: The Neuroscience of Guilt

http://healthland.time.com/2013/10/23/the-selfish-reasons-behind-why-we-give/

Take a look at this article that discusses research published in the *Journal of Neuroscience* that reports an alternative perspective on guilt. What did you learn about strategic communication from this article? Can you identify any examples of messages or campaigns that arouse guilt but then offer the audience a pathway (i.e., recommended behavior) to feeling better?

- Test your messages whenever possible with a sample from your target audience (referred to as *pretesting* in chapter 6).
- Use humor that is relevant to your message.
- Never use inappropriate or offensive humor such as sexual, racist, or sexist humor.

While humor creates positive emotional reactions among audiences when it is used effectively, guilt is a negative reaction that persuaders often shaped through message strategies to strategically motivate action within a target audience. We experience guilt when we believe that our behavior does not meet some standard. That standard might be our own or one established by someone else. Arousing a negative emotion such as guilt can be a risky strategy for a strategic communicator. Research by Robin Higie Coulter and Mary Beth Pinto (1995) involved exposing three audiences to three different guilt appeals: one designed to arouse high amounts of guilt, one aimed at moderate guilt, and one very little guilt. They found that low guilt appeals did little to alter the audience's behavior, and that the strongest guilt appeals made the audience angry and resistant. They concluded that moderate guilt appeals are most effective for influencing receiver behavior. Further, persuasive sources should aim to arouse moderate amounts of guilt using as implicit of an appeal as possible. The more explicit a source is in attempting to make a receiver feel guilty, the more resistant the receiver is likely to be.

The findings on **guilt** as a persuasive strategy are further moderated by the nature of the relationship between source and audience. Working with several research teams in the 1990s, communication scholar Frank Boster (Boster et al. 1995; Boster et al. 1999) studied the use of guilt as a compliance-gaining strategy in situations where the communicators had a preexisting relationship and in those involving strangers. Overall, they found that guilt can be an effective strategy among friends and those involved in existing relationships. They reasoned that guilt works in relationships because receivers want to restore positive feelings in relation to a friend when feeling guilty—and thus would comply with a request. Although Boster and his colleagues were interested in persuasion that takes place in personal relationships such as friendships, this work has important implications for strategic communication in organizations. Specifically, when organizations and their internal stakeholders cultivate relationships with external stakeholders, guilt might be an effective persuasion strategy.

7.3 WHAT ARE SOME PROMINENT THEORIES OF PERSUASION FOR STRATEGIC COMMUNICATION?

We should note here that more than one theory can explain the same phenomenon. When dealing with human behavior, there are no unchanging laws as there are in the physical sciences. If you drop a book one hundred times, gravity will pull it to the ground one hundred times. However, people vary too much—even a single person will behave differently at different times and under different conditions—for there to be a single explanation of how to influence people to buy a particular brand of peanut butter or recruit them to work for your organization. Theories are based on a complex range of assumptions, and the support that scholars generate for them are dependent on the research paradigms and methods they use. Although a thorough discussion of those ideas is beyond the scope of this chapter, you should know that there are numerous, and often competing, theories of persuasive communication. Our purpose here is neither to provide an exhaustive list of persuasion theories nor to provide a comprehensive treatment of the theories we have selected for discussion. Rather, we have selected three theories of particular utility for strategic communication.

7.3.1 Extended Parallel Process Model

Earlier, we stated that in addition to humor and guilt, fear is a common emotional persuasive appeal. Fear is probably the most widely researched of all emotional appeals. Early research on this topic explored the characteristics of fear and messages that can arouse fear, but failed to distinguish the kinds of strategies that characterize effective fear appeals—that is, those that actually persuade audiences do something differently (e.g., avoid risky drinking behaviors, practice health and safety guidelines in the workplace, get routine physical exams). Arousing fear simply for fear's sake is an ineffective strategy for promoting long-term or permanent behavior change. Thus, communication researcher Kim Witte developed and tested the Extended Parallel Process Model (EPPM) to provide a more comprehensive understanding of fear and when and how it works as a persuasive tool.

Our early understanding of fear as it related to persuasion focused narrowly on the emotion itself: arousing fear through the use of a message. But

Figure 31 Ineffective fear appeals might keep people awake at night but do not help them change their thinking or behavior to eliminate the threat.

researchers noticed that while a message might effectively create fearful feelings in receivers, that fear didn't necessarily lead the audience to engage in the behavior the source was advocating. Witte (1992, 1994) theorized that in order to create behavioral change, a fear appeal must also include a recommendation for how to deter the threat implied in the fear appeal. To further understand this idea, take a few seconds to view a widely televised antidrug message from the 1980s that used a fear appeal (www.youtube.com/watch?v=o5wwECXTJbg). Notice that although the message was designed to arouse fear, it did not tell the audience what to do to deter the threat. The message makes no explicit recommendations and fails to help its audience determine what strategies will help them avoid drugs.

Another perplexing aspect of early fear research involved the observation that when a message successfully aroused fear within an audience, receivers sometimes altered their behavior, but not in such a way that they deterred the actual threat. Instead, they modified their actions to deter their feelings of fear—while continuing to do the thing that was creating the threat. For example, you are undoubtedly aware that texting while driving can be dangerous and deadly and is illegal in most states. You have probably seen messages like this one (www.youtube.com/watch?v=jtQ9H1MrrPo), part of AT&T's "It Can Wait" campaign, designed to arouse fear surrounding texting and driving. But many of you have probably still persisted in texting while driving, at least occasionally. Perhaps you reason that you can safely text when there isn't much traffic, while sitting at a red light, or if you don't take your eyes off the road "very long." These negotiations that we have with ourselves represent what Leventhal (1970) referred to as a **fear control response.** In other words, sometimes fear appeals motivate people to merely change their behavior in ways that help them feel less fearful but that do not actually lessen the threat of the behavior. More desirable is the **danger control response.** This response occurs when a fear appeal successfully results in receivers assessing the threat and taking steps to eliminate it. Keeping your phone in your purse or bag or otherwise out of reach would be an example of a danger control response to the "It Can Wait" campaign. In developing EPPM, Witte was concerned with determining what led audiences to danger control responses rather than the less desirable fear control response. The result of her work, the Extended Parallel Process Model, illustrates four components of an effective fear appeal (see figure 33):

1. *Severity:* When exposed to a fear message, receivers evaluate just how severe the threat is. Perhaps a receiver perceives the threat to be a minor inconvenience rather than a life-altering consequence of some undesirable behavior. If the threat is not severe for the receiver, the fear appeal will fail at this point. If the receiver does evaluate the threat as severe, he or she engages in second assessment of the threat, how susceptible he or she is to it. Thus, the message must provide a clear statement about the severity of the threat that is appropriate for the target audience.

2. *Susceptibility:* If a receiver does not believe that the threat could realistically happen to him or her, he or she will not feel fear and is unlikely to take any of the recommended actions. Consequently, the fear appeal will fail. For instance, many people remain unconcerned about certain kinds of cancer, believing that if they don't have a family history, that they are highly unlikely to get it. However, if the receiver perceives a severe threat that he or she is susceptible to, then fear is aroused and the receiver then engages in two further assessments that lead to either fear or danger control. Thus, fear appeals must be explicit and direct in showing audience members evidence that "it could happen to them."

3. *Response efficacy:* We established earlier that an effective fear appeal must make some recommendation of what the receiver can do to eliminate the threat creating the fear. Otherwise, the receiver will simply feel afraid (as long as he or she perceived a sufficiently severe and possible threat) but not know what behavior(s) will alleviate the threat. If a physician, for instance, creates fear in a patient about the possibility of diabetes with evidence of elevated blood sugar, he or she must also recommend some behaviors that will help deter the threat of diabetes. These might include a modified diet and exercise. Key to this part of the EPPM

is the receiver's belief and understanding that the recommended behaviors *will actually be effective in curbing the danger associated with the threat.* If the message is not designed and delivered in a way that helps the receiver understand how and why the recommendations will be effective, or if the receiver has contrary evidence that the source does not refute, EPPM contends that he or she will favor fear control over danger control. Thus, strategic communication must be designed accordingly with attention paid to message factors that will heighten the receiver's confidence in response efficacy. Some of these include message repetition and redundancy, simplicity, concreteness, and providing sufficient evidence of the solution's effectiveness.

4. *Self-efficacy:* Perhaps the physician in the example we just provided recommended six hours of high intensity exercise at a health club a week as a recommendation for reducing the receiver's blood sugar. If the receiver has never engaged in formal exercise, has limited financial resources for a gym membership, or works extended hours that prevent a great deal of physical activity, these recommendations will likely seem overwhelming and unrealistic. Even when a solution is likely to work (that is, the receiver perceives high response efficacy), if that receiver believes that he or she isn't capable of using the solution (that is, the receiver perceives low self-efficacy), then fear control is likely to occur. Some common reasons why people might perceive low self-efficacy include lack of resources (time, money) to engage in the behavior, or lack of confidence, training, or experience on carrying out the recommendation. Thus, sources must assess audiences and determine what kinds of recommendations receivers would feel capable of trying. Strategic fear messages must offer palatable solutions that audiences can actually visualize themselves using.

EPPM and its associated research gives strategic communicators a clear map for using fear in a way that will lead to lasting behavior change rather than superficial receiver efforts to manage their fears. First, communicators need to remember that fear is a negative emotion and consider whether other appeals might be more appropriate given the message topic and intended audience. Second, to arouse fear, the message must heighten receivers' awareness of a threat that is both severe and reasonably likely to occur. Consider advertisements for auto insurance that depict accidents resulting from common, everyday driving situations, for example. Third, the message must recommend one or more behaviors that will deter the threat associated with the fear. For example, security systems are advertised as an easy and cost effective way to protect the audience's family, home, and belongings. Fourth, the message must present the recommendations in such a way that the audience will recognize their benefits and believe that they will actually work to minimize the threat. And

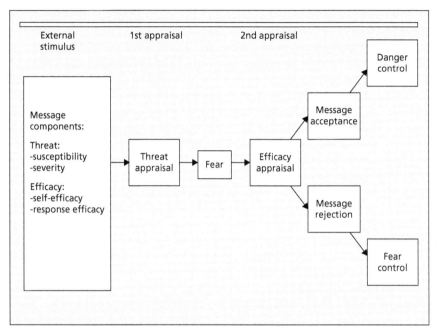

Figure 33 Extended Parallel Process Model.

finally, the audience must feel capable of engaging in the recommended behavior(s).

7.3.2 Elaboration Likelihood Model

Simply put, some messages make us think. They require what theoretician/ researcher Petty (1981, 1986) refers to as **elaboration,** or the amount of conscious thought or scrutiny that a receiver applies to a message. However, some messages elicit an immediate and unconscious response. We don't think or elaborate much on what we read, see, or hear and rely on easily sensed cues to decide what to do and how to act on the message. For instance, we are often compelled to buy beauty products, athletic shoes, or even food on the basis of an attractive celebrity endorsement alone, without giving much thought to the characteristics of the actual product. Elaboration Likelihood Model (ELM) is a powerful theory because it provides insight on why people elaborate on messages or do not. This, then, allows us to control the persuasive process and design effective strategic messages.

ELM indicates that when receivers elaborate on a message, they are relying on **central route processing.** When they engage in little or no elaboration, they are using the **peripheral route** to persuasion. The processing route a receiver uses is largely dependent on his or her **motivation** (i.e., how much the receiver wants to elaborate on the message) and **ability** (i.e., how capable the receiver is of elaborating on the message). When motivation and ability are high, a receiver is likely to engage in central route processing. Tests of ELM suggest several predictors of motivation. One of the strongest is personal involvement with the issue. Your audience analysis should reveal how personally relevant your topic is to members of the target audience. The more involved they are and the more relevant they find your message, the more motivated they will be to think carefully about it. In addition, when receivers feel personally responsible for the action required, they will be more motivated to engage in it. Messages that suggest "we're depending on you" (and you alone) are likely to boost this feeling. Third, if your message content is contrary, or incongruent, to what your audience already believes, they may be motivated to carefully process the new information in order to resolve the discrepancy. And finally, some receivers have a predisposition to effortful cognitive activities, such as elaboration. This personality characteristic is referred to as **need for cognition (NFC).** In simple terms, high NFC individuals are thinkers. They analyze, critique, fact-check, and attempt to reconcile new information with what they already know or believe. Thus, you shouldn't be surprised that high NFC receivers are likely to centrally process most messages, regardless of their personal involvement or the message's content. Those with lower NFC are generally more likely to rely on peripheral route processing.

Ability, the second predictor of central route processing, is dependent on a receiver's prior knowledge about the issue and message characteristics that influence how easy it will be for your audience to comprehend it. The message must be organized and use language that is familiar to members of your audience to heighten their comprehension of it. When a message is clear and incorporates language and visual images that are appropriate for the members of the audience, they will understand it and think about it. Tests of ELM have indicated that written messages may be easier for audiences to comprehend than oral ones. Regardless of message channel, repetition and purposeful redundancy can enhance message clarity and receiver comprehension, regardless of message channel.

So what predicts peripheral route processing? Highly credible sources, attractive sources, and the promise of rewards or punishments can be powerful cues that trigger audiences to make snap judgments without a great deal of thought. In addition, research indicates that receivers in positive moods will be more likely to engage in peripheral route processing than those in bad moods or who are uncomfortable. Consider the range of phrases used to help people feel the "therapeutic" effects of shopping: FTD sells "pick-me-up" bouquets, luxury department store Bergdorf Goodman encourages website visitors to "reward yourself," the home shopping platform QVC promises "the joy of discovery," and curated online food marketplace Goldbely helps shoppers "indulge." All of these words and phrases create a sense of comfort. Atalay and

Meloy (2011) found that such strategies elevated shoppers' moods and lowered feelings of guilt or regret associated with purchases.

Another predictor of peripheral route processing involves the number of arguments (e.g., reasons to alter your perceptions or behaviors) included in a message. Petty and Cacioppo (1984) found that six to nine arguments were more persuasive than a smaller number (three). This effect was strongest for audience members who perceived the message to have low personal relevance. In other words, a moderately long list of arguments or reasons seems to lead to peripheral route processing for people with low involvement in the issue. They are not typically motivated to process those arguments in any deep or meaningful way. In addition, low involvement people tend to look to others for cues about how they should react to a message. Thus, others' reactions can be a peripheral cue (Axsom, Yates, and Chaiken 1987).

Why does the processing route that an audience uses matter? Simply put, attitudes formed through peripheral route processing tend to be temporary and less stable over time than those formed using peripheral route processing. Thus, when a persuader wants quick, one-time compliance (e.g., where to go to lunch), peripheral route source and message cues should help produce this outcome. But when the goal is long-term, permanent change (e.g., where to go to college), a persuasive source should aim to trigger central route processing. In addition, attitudes formed through central route processing tend to be better predictors of a receiver's behavior than those formed through peripheral route processing. Thus, this theory can be helpful in guiding the design of strategic, persuasive messages once you have identified the overall objective for your communication.

7.3.3 Social Judgment Theory

Social Judgment Theory (SJT) is the work of Sherif and Hovland (1961) and examines the cognitions that persuasive message receivers experience. The central contention of SJT is that relative to any issue (e.g., the value of a college education, willingness to rescue a pet, attitudes toward saving and investing money), people have a position. This position is referred to as their **attitudinal anchor** and it represents the perspective that the individual finds *most acceptable* on the issue (e.g., college is important to a successful life, people should rescue pets rather than buy them from breeders, I can't afford to save or invest money). However, Sherif and Hovland theorized that people typically have a range of attitudes rather than a single, fixed point (e.g., "college is important, but there are plenty of examples of people who have succeeded without a college education"; "rescuing is a good idea, but if you have your heart set on a particular breed, you might want to work with a breeder"; "I have a hard time setting aside money to save, but can manage a few dollars a week"). Thus, according to this perspective, attitudes are not "black and white." Using the language of SJT, this range of positions that a receiver finds acceptable is known

Figure 32 Social Judgment Theory teaches us not to ask for too much change at once. For example, for best results, ask a friend who doesn't exercise to take a nature walk or a bike ride rather than join an expensive gym and commit to lifting heavy weights five days a week.

as the **latitude of acceptance.** Using the anchor metaphor, consider that a boat still drifts a bit when it is anchored—we can think of the latitude of acceptance as that motion. The **latitude of rejection** lies outside of the latitude of acceptance and includes all of the positions that a receiver finds unacceptable. SJT also describes a **latitude of noncommitment,** which represents the positions toward which a receiver is neutral or has no opinion.

A persuader's task, then, is to determine just how much change to ask for without pushing the receiver outside of his or her latitude acceptance. Just how broad is the latitude of acceptance? The answer to this question helps an influencer determine how far the receiver is likely to budge from that "most preferred" anchor position. If a receiver perceives a message to be within the latitude of acceptance, he or she might accept it. If a receiver perceives a message to be in contrast or conflict with his or her range of acceptable positions, resistance will ensue. Sometimes, when a persuader pushes too hard and for too much change, the resulting effect will be what SJT refers to as the **boomerang effect.** An extreme form of resistance, the boomerang effect involves the receiver actually moving his or her attitudinal anchor *away* from the persuader's advocacy message. As with all of the theories we have summarized here, your ability to appropriate SJT for designing persuasive, strategic messages rests in the quality of your audience analysis. Your ability to create a message that appeals to the audience's latitude of acceptance requires your understanding of who these people are: their beliefs, attitudes, values, and involvement in the issue you hope to influence them regarding.

7.4 TYING IT ALL TOGETHER: PERSUASION AND STRATEGIC COMMUNICATION

In this chapter, you have learned about two types of theory: everyday theory and formal, scholarly theory. Like James, whom we met in the opening scenario of this chapter, we can rarely afford the risks associated with making decisions in organizations using everyday ways of know as our guide. We discussed how we all engage in everyday theorizing on a routine basis, but that our common explanations for why things happen the way that they do lack credibility for professional, high-stakes situations such as strategic communication. Formal, scholarly theoretical frameworks offer a better alternative for sound decision-making in strategic communication situations. As a foundation for learning about several key theories of persuasion, we explored the concept of persuasion as a key communication behavior in strategic organizational settings. To advance its mission, organizations must operate according to what research suggests will be influential with stakeholders. Toward that end, you have learned about source and message credibility and the types of logical and emotional appeals that contribute to effective persuasion under certain conditions. Finally, we gave a very brief overview of three important theories of persuasion and how these offer road maps for communicators in applied settings. Taken together with what you learned in chapter 6 about audience analysis, you should have a solid understanding of how to use these theories to create messages that will influence target audiences to change their attitudes and behaviors relative to your established objectives.

CHAPTER 7 REVIEW

Questions for Critical Thinking and Discussion

1. After reading this chapter, has your perspective about the meaning of theory changed? Explain your understanding of how theory can be useful to strategic communication practitioners.
2. How does scholarly theory improve on the utility of everyday theory and everyday ways of knowing?
3. Why is audience analysis so important to successful persuasion?
4. What is the difference between attitudes and behaviors? List three to five examples of each. Why does a strategic communicator need to identify which of these he or she wants to modify through messaging?
5. What are the elements of an effective fear appeal, according to Extended Parallel Process Model? Identify a fear appeal on television, the internet, or in print. Evaluate that message using the components of EPPM.
6. Select three advertisements from any medium (e.g., a magazine ad, social media post, television commercial). Identify the cues within the ad that are likely to trigger central and peripheral route processing. How would an Elaboration Likelihood Model expert evaluate this ad in terms of its ability to generate lasting, stable audience change?
7. How would you summarize Social Judgment Theory for a communication professional unfamiliar with the theory? What takeaway lessons does a strategic communication practitioner need to learn from this theory in order to design persuasive messages?

Key Terms

ability: within Elaboration Likelihood Model, a predictor of central route processing that focuses on how capable the receiver is of elaborating on a particular persuasive message.

appeals: evidence-based strategies that a strategic communicator uses within a single message or larger campaign to ethically compel and influence the target audience. Appeals may be emotional or logical.

applied settings: practical "real-world" environments (e.g., workplaces).

attitudes: humans' consistent feelings of like or dislike toward a particular object, person, concept, or idea.

attitudinal anchor: within Social Judgment Theory, the position that a receiver individual finds most acceptable relative to a particular issue.

behavior: observable physical action.

beliefs: perceptions of the truth or existence, or falsity of something.

boomerang effect: an extreme form of resistance, the boomerang effect involves the receiver actually moving his or her attitudinal anchor *away* from the persuader's advocacy message.

central route processing: a type of cognitive response to a persuasive message proposed by Elaboration Likelihood Model that occurs when receivers elaborate on a message.

clickbait: a pejorative term that refers to sensational, provocative online content shared with the intent of arousing reader interest and drawing them to a website in order to generate traffic or online advertising revenue.

danger control: a response to a fear appeal proposed in the Extended Parallel Process Model that involves receivers assessing the threat and taking steps to eliminate it.

discounting model: as a probable explanation of the sleeper effect that demonstrates how early receiver change may be explained by their perceptions of the source, but over time, message content and characteristics have the greatest influence on the audience.

emotional appeals: refer to the use of persuasive strategies that arouse the target audience's emotions, such as fear, guilt, excitement, happiness, anxiety, or regret.

fear control: a response to a fear appeal proposed in the Extended Parallel Process Model in which receivers merely change their behavior in ways that help them feel less fearful but that do not actually lessen the threat of the behavior.

formal (scholarly) theory: a set of concepts with explanations of the relationships among these concepts that help users understand a phenomenon.

heuristics: cognitive frameworks that people apply to make decisions and solve problems quickly and efficiently.

humor: a type of emotional appeal designed to amuse an audience.

latitude of acceptance: within Social Judgment Theory, the range of positions that a receiver finds acceptable relative to a particular issue.

latitude of noncommitment: within Social Judgment Theory, the positions toward which a receiver is neutral or has no opinion at all relative to a particular issue.

latitude of rejection: within Social Judgement Theory, all of the positions that a receiver finds unacceptable relative to a particular issue.

motivation: within Elaboration Likelihood Model, a predictor of central route processing that involves how much the receiver wants to elaborate on a persuasive message.

narrative: a type of message that involves one or more stories.

need for cognition (NFC): a personality characteristic that indicates the extent to which an individual is inclined toward effortful cognitive activities.

peripheral route processing: a response to persuasion suggested in Elaboration Likelihood that involves little or no audience elaboration on persuasive messages.

persuasion: an activity that involves communication between two or more persons with the intent to change the receiver(s)' attitudes, beliefs, and/or behaviors.

postmodern perspective: a complex ideology characterized by skepticism about and, often, rejection of scientific claims, traditional power structures, and common or traditional beliefs or behaviors.

psychological reactance theory: an explanation of why receivers resist persuasion that examines how persuasive messages threaten an audience's feeling of freedom to think, believe, and act as they wish.

sleeper effect: a condition in which receivers exposed to low credibility sources develop more positive attitudes over time, and those exposed to high credibility sources will weaken in their feelings of positivity toward that source over time.

theory: a systematic explanation or description of some phenomenon.

two-sided message with refutation: involves exposing the audience to the opposing argument in small amounts, followed by a return to the source's own argument with an explanation of why it is superior to the opposition's.

Further Readings and Resources

Cialdini, R. B. 2006. *Influence: The Psychology of Persuasion.* 2nd ed. New York: HarperCollins.

———. 2016. *Pre-suasion: A Revolutionary Way to Influence and Persuade.* New York: Simon and Schuster.

Larson, C. U. 2013. *Persuasion: Reception and Responsibility.* 13th ed. Boston: Cengage.

Perloff, R. M. 2017. *The Dynamics of Persuasion: Communication and Attitudes in the Twenty-First Century.* 6th ed. New York: Routledge.

References

Ajzen, I., M. Fishbein. 2005. "The Influence of Attitudes on Behavior." In *The Handbook of Attitudes,* edited by D. Albarracín, B. T. Johnson, and M. P. Zanna, 173–221. Mahwah, NJ: Lawrence Erlbaum.

Allen, M. and R. W. Preiss. 1997. "Comparing the Persuasiveness of Narrative and Statistical Evidence Using Meta-Analysis." *Communication Research Reports* 14, no. 2: 125–31.

Allen, M. and J. B. Stiff. 1998. "An Analysis of the Sleeper Effect." In *Persuasion: Advances through Meta-Analysis,* edited by M. Allen and R. W. Preiss, 175–88. Cresskill, NJ: Hampton Press.

Atalay, A. S., and M. M. Meloy. 2011. "Retail Therapy: A Strategic Effort to Improve Mood." *Psychology and Marketing* 28, no. 6: 638–60.

Axsom, D., S. Yates, and S. Chaiken. 1987. "Audience Response as a Heuristic Cue in Persuasion." *Journal of Personality and Social Psychology* 53, no. 1: 30–40.

Boster, F. J. 2016. "Providing Research Services for Clients." In *Consulting That Matters: A Handbook for Scholars and Practitioners,* edited by J. H. Waldeck and D. R. Seibold, 259–76. New York: Peter Lang.

Boster, F. J., M. M. Mitchell, M. K. Lapinski, H. Cooper, V. O. Orrego, and R. Reinke. 1999. "The Impact of Guilt and Type of Compliance-Gaining Message on Compliance." *Communication Monographs* 66, no. 2: 168–77.

Boster, F. J., J. I. Rodriguez, M. G. Cruz, and L. Marshall. 1995. "The Relative Effectiveness of a Direct Request Message and a Pregiving Message on Friends and Strangers." *Communication Research* 22, no. 4: 474–84.

Brehm, J. W. 1966. *A Theory of Psychological Reactance.* New York: Academic Press.

Brehm, S. S., and J. W. Brehm. 1981. *Psychological Reactance: A Theory of Freedom and Control.* New York: Academic Press.

Cline, T. W., and J. J. Kellaris. 1999. "The Joint Impact of Humor and Argument Strength in a Print Advertising Context: A Case for Weaker Arguments." *Psychology and Marketing* 16, no. 1: 69–86.

Coulter, R. H., and M. B. Pinto. 1995. "Guilt Appeals in Advertising: What Are Their Effects?" *Journal of Applied Psychology* 80, no. 6: 697–705.

Darnell, D. K. 1963. "The Relation between Sentence Order and Comprehension." *Speech Monographs* 30, no. 2: 97–100.

Frymier, A. B., and M. K. Nadler. 2017. *Persuasion: Integrating Theory, Research, and Practice.* 4th ed. Dubuque, IA: Kendall Hunt.

Gardiner, B. 2015, December 18. "You'll Be Outraged at How Easy It Was to Get You to Click on This Headline." *Wired.* www.wired.com/2015/12/psychology-of-clickbait/.

Griffin, E., A. Ledbetter, and G. Sparks. 2015. *A First Look at Communication Theory.* 9th ed. New York: McGraw-Hill.

Hofstede, G. 2017. *National Culture: The 6 Dimensions of National Culture.* www.hofstede-insights.com/models /national-culture/.

Hovland, C. I., I. L. Janis, and H. H. Kelley. 1953. *Communication and Persuasion: Psychological Studies of Opinion Change.* New Haven, CT: Yale University Press.

Hynes, G. E., and R. Stretcher. 2008. "A Missing Link in Business Schools." *Business Communication Quarterly* 71, no. 2: 207–11.

Jhally, S. 1990. *The Codes of Advertising.* New York: Routledge.

Kelman, H. C., and C. I. Hovland. 1953. "'Reinstatement' of the Communicator in Delayed Measurement of Opinion Change." *Journal of Abnormal Psychology* 48, no. 3: 327–35.

Kreps, G. L. 2016. "Consulting in the Healthcare Context: A Case Study of the Community Liaison Project." In *Consulting That Matters: A Handbook for Scholars and Practitioners,* edited by J. H. Waldeck and D. R. Seibold, 279–86. New York: Peter Lang.

Lasn, K. 1999. *Culture Jam: The Uncooling of America.* New York: Eagle Brook.

Leventhal, H. 1970. "Findings and Theory in the Study of Fear Communications." In *Advances in Experimental Social Psychology,* edited by L. Berkowitz, 5:120–86. New York: Academic Press.

Lewin, K. 1945. "The Research Center for Group Dynamics at Massachusetts Institute of Technology." *Sociometry* 8, no. 2: 126–36.

Leys, C., and B. Harriss-White. 2012, April 2. "Commodification: The Essence of Our Time." www.opendemocracy.net/en /opendemocracyuk/commodification-essence-of-our-time/.

McCroskey, J. C., and R. S. Mehrley. 1969. "The Effects of Disorganization and Nonfluency on Attitude Change and Source Credibility." *Speech Monographs* 36, no. 1: 13–21.

McGuire, W. J. 1962. "Persistence of the Resistance to Persuasion Induced by Various Types of Prior Belief Defenses." *Journal of Abnormal and Social Psychology* 64, no. 4: 241–48.

Olison, W. O., and M. E. Roloff. 2012. "Responses to Organizational Mandates: How Voice Attenuates Psychological Reactance and Dissent." *Communication Research Reports* 29, no. 3: 204–16.

Paek, H. J., H. J. Oh, and T. Hove. 2012. "How Media Campaigns Influence Children's Physical Activity: Expanding the Normative Mechanisms of the Theory of Planned Behavior." *Journal of Health Communication* 17, no. 8: 869–85.

Petty, R. E. 1981. *Attitudes and Persuasion: Classic and Contemporary Approaches.* Dubuque, IA: William C. Brown.

———. 1986. *Communication and Persuasion: Central and Peripheral Routes to Attitude Change.* New York: Springer Verlag.

Petty, R. E., and J. T. Cacioppo. 1984. "The Effects of Involvement on Responses to Argument Quantity and Quality: Central and Peripheral Routes to Persuasion." *Journal of Personality and Social Psychology* 46, no. 1: 69–81.

Pfau, M. 1992. "The Potential of Inoculation in Promoting Resistance to the Effectiveness of Comparative Advertising Messages." *Communication Quarterly* 40, no. 1: 26–44.

Rumbo, J. D. 2002. "Consumerism Resistance in a World of Advertising Clutter: The Case of *Adbusters.*" *Psychology and Marketing* 19, no. 2: 127–48.

Sharp, H., Jr., and T. McClung. 1966. "Effects of Organizations on the Speaker's Ethos." *Speech Monographs* 33, no. 2: 182–83.

Sherif, C. W., and C. I. Hovland. 1961. *Social Judgment: Assimilation and Contrast Effects in Communication and Attitude Change.* New Haven, CT: Yale University Press.

Shermer, M. 2015, April 1. "Are Paleo Diets More Natural Than GMOs?" *Scientific American.* www.scientificamerican.com /article/are-paleo-diets-more-natural-than-gmos/.

Skalski, P., R. Tamborini, M. Limon, and S. Smith. 2009. "Effects of Humor on Presence and Recall of Persuasive Messages." *Communication Quarterly* 57, no. 2: 136–53.

Smith, G. R. 1951. "Effects of Speech Organization upon Attitudes of College Students." *Speech Monographs* 18, no. 4: 292–301.

SunWolf. 2004. *Practical Jury Dynamics: From One Juror's Trial Perceptions to the Group's Decision-Making Process.* New York: LexisNexis.

Thompson, E. 1967. "Some Effects of Message Structure on Listening Comprehension." *Speech Monographs* 34: 51–57.

Tversky, A., and D. Kahneman. 1974. "Judgment under Uncertainty: Heuristics and Biases." *Science* 185, no. 4157: 1124–31.

Volk, A. 2016, May 3. "How to Write Something They Actually Care About." *Huffpost Arts and Culture.* www.huffingtonpost .com/allison-volk/how-to-write-something-th_b_9820158 .html.

Wanzer, M. B., S. C. Foster, T. Servoss, and S. LaBelle. 2014. "Educating Young Men about Testicular Cancer: Support for a Comprehensive Testicular Cancer Campaign." *Journal of Health Communication* 19, no. 3: 303–20. doi: 10.1080 /10810730.2013.811320.

West, R., and L. H. Turner. 2014. *Introducing Communication Theory: Analysis and Application.* New York: McGraw-Hill.

Wilson, E. V. 2003. "Perceived Effectiveness of Interpersonal Persuasion Strategies in Computer-Mediated Communication." *Computers in Human Behavior* 19, no. 5: 537–53.

Witte, K. 1992. "Putting the Fear Back into Fear Appeals: The Extended Parallel Process Model." *Communication Monographs* 59, no. 4: 329–49.

———. 1994. "Fear Control and Danger Control: A Test of the Extended Parallel Process Model (EPPM)." *Communication Monographs* 61, no. 2: 113–34.

Xie, H., L. Miao, P. J. Kuo, and B. Y. Lee. 2011. "Consumers' Response to Ambivalent Online Hotel Reviews: The Role of Perceived Source Credibility and Pre-decisional Disposition." *International Journal of Hospitality Management* 30: 178–83.

Selecting Channels

8

CHAPTER CONTENTS

8.1 The Importance of Channel Selection in Planning a Strategic Communication Campaign   228

    8.1.1 Traditional and New Media Channels   229

    8.1.2 Common Channels in Strategic Communication Campaigns   235

8.2 Selecting the Right Channel: Six Important Considerations   243

    8.2.1 Media Richness Theory   248

    8.2.2 Two-Step Flow Model of Communication   252

8.3 Tying It All Together: Developing an Integrated Media Mix   255

LEARNING OBJECTIVES

After reading this chapter, you should be able to do the following:

► Discuss the importance of channel selection in planning a strategic communication campaign.

► Identify and describe common channels used in strategic communication campaigns.

► Identify six important considerations in channel selection.

► Evaluate channels according to Media Richness Theory.

► Explain how two-step flow theory contributes to a campaign channel strategy.

► Apply communication principles to developing an integrated media mix.

Dai has recently been hired as a campaign manager for the reelection of her state's senator. This is a huge opportunity for Dai—she has successfully managed several local government campaigns and has established herself as someone who understands how to reach and connect with younger voters. The incumbent senator hired her for this purpose—with an upcoming election, the senator is concerned that voters who have come of voting age during his term are unaware of his accomplishments and mission as a senator. Among her many responsibilities, Dai must maintain a strong base of support from the incumbent's current supporters as well as reaching out to new, younger audiences. To be successful, Dai has to keep all members of the campaign team on the same page, handle any communication with constituents with grace, and maintain relationships with donors large and small. After her first meeting with her campaign team, Dai starts strategizing where she will connect with these younger voters. Dai starts by going through her day as a twenty-five-year-old—where does she spend her time, and who does she listen to? Within a few days, Dai has developed a strategy to reach existing and potential supporters—she will not only have radio advertisements and a social media presence but also plans to meet voters where they are by going to local coffee shops, gyms, and community centers. She has teams of volunteers assembled to make phone calls, go door-to-door to talk with members of the community, and connect with online communities. Dai's goal is to get the most amount of people talking that she can, in the most ways that she can. If she succeeds, this will be a huge victory for not only the senator but also her own career.

Quinn is the vice president of corporate communication for a for-profit education company based out of Singapore, Pintar. Her job responsibilities include overseeing internal communication, media and public relations, crisis communication, and implementing internal and external communication strategies to advance Pintar's mission. In her everyday work, Quinn serves as a communication advisor to Pintar's lead executive team, an ambassador for the organization, and works to build and maintain strong relationships with local and international media.

Recently, Quinn had to fire a social media intern who wasn't coming in to work, was not following Quinn's formatting and language protocol for social media content, and who generally had a bad attitude about the work. To Quinn's horror, this disgruntled former intern tweeted a couple dozen crass and foul-mouthed tweets from Pintar's account before Quinn could change the passwords. The former intern accused the company of unethical practices in their recruitment processes, of sexist practices in their hiring, and of mistreating both students and employees. In a manner of minutes, Quinn was receiving emails and tweets from employees, students, and administrators that were a mixture of alarmed, irritated, and shocked reactions. Quinn went from a somewhat routine Wednesday morning to a full-blown crisis management situation in a man-

ner of minutes—fortunately, she had a detailed plan in place to delete and address the rogue tweets, to assure executive leaders of the security of these accounts, to contact the media to correct these false accusations, and to provide current students, faculty, and administrators with an account of what happened and reassurance that Pintar had their best interests at heart. To do this, Quinn had carefully constructed not only her messages but also how they would be delivered to each of these audiences. The CEO, for instance, would require a face-to-face explanation of what had occurred. Students, faculty, and staff were sent personalized emails. Phone calls were made to local media to control the story that would follow. As Quinn is well aware, this was not a "tweet once to fix it all" scenario. Ultimately, though, Quinn know that the extent to which this affects Pintar's public image is unfortunately in the hands of the 175,000 followers of Pintar's twitter account.

Think about the last time you had to communicate a request from someone in your personal life. You may have been asking your manager for a day off from work, or asking your teacher for an extension on an assignment deadline. You may have been asking your parent for a ride to class, or asking your friend for a rain check on dinner because you weren't up to it. In each of these situations, you likely spent some time thinking about *how* you would ask. Depending on the size of the request and the degree to which it would inconvenience the recipient of your message, you may have spent anywhere from a few seconds to a few hours contemplating your message. Asking your relationship partner to "take a break," for instance, is likely something that takes a good deal of time to plan and consider. If you are a competent communicator, as we discussed in chapter 1, you will have spent just as much if not more time deliberating the most appropriate and effective means of delivering your message. While texting might be an appropriate means of asking your parent to pick you up from school, it is certainly not appropriate to text your manager to request a week off from work during the busy season. The urgency of the message will also affect how it is delivered—sending a handwritten letter to your grandmother is an effective way to let her know you are thinking about her, but calling her is more appropriate if you are concerned about her safety as a dangerous storm approaches her neighborhood. Just as we carefully consider the advantages and disadvantages of our message channels before we engage in these interpersonal communication processes, so too must organizations take the time in planning their strategic communication campaigns to ensure that their messages are being delivered through the most appropriate and effective channels possible. As you can see in both Dai's and Quinn's work, the channels organizations use to communicate can have vast and lasting consequences for strategic communication efforts.

As you recall from chapter 1, the channel is the means through which a message is delivered from a source to a receiver. As we have provided examples of above, this might include face-to-face or **mediated communication,** in which technology is used to deliver information between senders and receivers. In the case of mediated communication, the **medium** is the specific mode or device that moves information over time or distance so that people who are not face-to-face can communicate—this includes telephones, "snail" mail, or the internet. In this chapter, we discuss the seventh step in planning a strategic communication campaign—selecting your channels of communication. We examine several channels available to organizations in this process, being sure to make distinctions between traditional and new types of media. We will discuss six important considerations in channel selection, including characteristics of the organization, its target audience, the message, and the channel. In discussing these characteristics and the process of choosing appropriate channels, principles of communication theories such as Media Richness Theory and the Two-Step Flow Model will be used to inform evidence-based decision-making. Finally, we will complete this chapter by discussing the importance of creating an integrated channel strategy—the goal of any successful strategic communication campaign. To begin, we turn to why channel selection is so critical in the strategic communication campaign planning process.

8.1 THE IMPORTANCE OF CHANNEL SELECTION IN PLANNING A STRATEGIC COMMUNICATION CAMPAIGN

As Dai's challenge in the beginning of this chapter indicates, the selection of a channel to deliver your message is a critically important aspect of planning a strategic communication campaign. From a practical standpoint, not spending time carefully considering and selecting an appropriate channel is a waste of an organization's resources. Imagine you are planning a surprise birthday party for a friend. You spend time carefully choosing decorations, venue, and a menu. As part of your plans, you also make sure that you contact guests who your friend would be happy to see on the special day. Depending on the guests and your relationship with them, you might call, text, email, or use social media to notify them of the party's details and when to arrive. Given how much time you spend planning this party, you would also want to make sure that the invitees actually received the message—perhaps you would ask folks to RSVP by a certain date so that you can make sure you are prepared. In much the same way, organizations need to ensure that their carefully researched and planned strategic messages actually reach their intended audience using appropriate channels—otherwise, what is the point of working so hard to create a theoretically sound, brand consistent, persuasive message?

Reaching your target audience is a necessary but not sufficient criterion for the success of a strategic communication campaign. As communication scholar Contanze Rossman (2011) argues, "no matter how well a campaign message is prepared it will only have an effect on individuals' cognitions and behaviors if it reaches them" (418). A major principle of effective campaign design is to place your messages in channels that are widely used by your target audience. The notion that channels affect how messages are perceived is far from new, particularly to scholars who study mass communication. As early as 1964, Marshall McLuhan declared that "the medium is the message." What does this mean? McLuhan was arguing that the means by which we deliver messages (i.e., the medium) inextricably become a part of how the message is perceived. Information that we receive via written word will be different from information received face-to-face, regardless of how similar the content is. The medium is a part of how the message is received. For organizations designing strategic communication campaigns, the selection of appropriate media to deliver their messages therefore becomes as integral a part of the planning process as any other planning decision.

In chapter 1, we discussed the definition of campaigns provided by communication scholars Rice and Atkin (2013). To refresh your memory, these scholars argue that a campaign is a purposive attempt "to inform, persuade, or motivate behavior changes in a relatively well-defined and large audience . . . by means of organized communication activities involving mass and online/interactive media, and often complemented by interpersonal support" (526–27). Therefore, by their very nature campaigns necessitate varied organized communication activities and the use of communication channels such as print, radio, television, social media, and even face-to-face communication. In the sections that follow, we provide a brief overview of these types of channels and the research that supports their use (or lack thereof) for various types of strategic communication efforts. First, we begin with an overview of two broad choices organizations have in selecting communication campaign channels—traditional or new media.

8.1.1 Traditional and New Media Channels

Adults in the United States report spending nearly half of their day—over eleven hours—interacting with media (Nielsen 2018). Further, time spent listening to, watching, reading, or otherwise using media continues to increase each year (Nielsen 2018). In selecting a channel for your strategic communication efforts, it will be helpful to categorize different types of media. In this section, we will discuss the important distinctions between traditional and new media channels.

Traditional media channels have an established record in communication campaigns—heavily relied on channels include television, radio, and printed materials such as pamphlets and press releases (Noar 2006; Silk, Atkin, and Salmon 2011). If you have a television, radio, or have walked down a busy city street you have almost certainly been on the receiving end of messages encouraging you not to smoke, to recycle, to exercise, to use a particular cellular company, or to drink a certain type of caffeinated beverage. Traditional media are used in advertising, public health, social marketing, and countless other forms of communication on behalf of organizations. Traditional media capitalize on the oldest forms of communication—the spoken and written word. These channels, television in particular, also have a prominent place in the history of political campaigns in the United States. The first televised campaign messages were launched by Republican candidate Dwight D. Eisenhower (and running mate Richard Nixon) in the 1952 presidential race (Green 2016). The campaign advertisements smartly capitalized on the rapid rise of the television as a staple in American households and featured a relatively simple script of an "average" citizen asking Eisenhower a question, to which he responded by looking directly into the camera. The campaign followed up on this message with a now iconic "I Like Ike" animation (www.youtube.com /watch?time_continue=1&v=Y9RAxAgksSE), a seemingly simple ad that is often attributed to Eisenhower's ultimate landslide victory and end to a twenty-year presidential run by the Democratic Party (Green 2016). The success of this traditional media political campaign had a lasting impact—nearly seventy years later, television and radio are expected, if not overused, channels for local and national political campaigns.

However, the emergence of new media channels has caused new evolutions and developments to occur in strategic campaigns of all contexts and purposes. **New media** includes any communication using digital technologies; this includes the internet, email, text messaging, mobile phone and smartphone technology, video, or computer games. As analyzed by public health and communication scholars Abroms and LeFebvre (2009), the use of new media in Barack Obama's 2008 presidential campaign is a dramatic illustration of the power of new media in the political context specifically, but with implications for communication campaigns more broadly.

Obama's 2008 "Change We Can Believe In" campaign gained supporters and created a movement previously unprecedented in political campaigns (Abroms and LeFebvre 2009). Through the use of a campaign website, YouTube site, social network sites, and mobile phones, the Obama campaign built a political movement following a major tenet of strategic communication campaigns that we have been repeating in this text: focus on your target audience. For example, the campaign website housed a special section called "MyBO" (i.e., My Barack Obama); in this section, users could register to be a part of a private community of supporters, communicating with one another to coordinate fund-raising events, fund-raise, and blog about the campaign. The YouTube site featured not only videos on the presidential candidate but also a series of videos highlighting campaign volunteers, supporters, and future voters. Social networking sites included not only Facebook and MySpace but also

Figure 35 Social media can be a powerful tool for building community and organizing action.

profiles on targeted sites such as MiGente.com and BlackPlanet.com. For mobile phones, an app was developed that used geodemographic marketing to send tailored messages to users based on their zip code; this included updates on the campaign, requests for involvement and ways to get involved, and persuasive messages based on whether a user lived in a swing state versus a state likely to vote Democrat.

At every turn, Obama's presidential campaign focused on building community and engaging with the audience. By the end of the campaign, MyBO had 1.5 million registered supporters and led to the organization of over 100,000 events. The YouTube site had more than five times the number of videos uploaded compared to Obama's opposition, John McCain, in the 2008 election. MyBO also had about nine times the number of views on those videos. On Facebook alone, Obama had nearly 2.38 million followers to McCain's 620,359. The mobile app had 2.9 million subscribers. Perhaps most notable, however, was the way in which new media were used to support user-generated content. Blogs, emails, songs, essays, and videos generated by supporters received millions of views and shares, extending the reach of the campaign far beyond the capabilities of the campaign team (Abroms and LeFebvre 2009). Thus, the use of new media in the 2008 presidential campaign marked a changing point not only in political campaigns but also of the nature of strategic communication campaigns in general. New media was not only used to spread awareness and persuade but also to build a community of support for campaign goals—a lesson for any type of strategic communication campaign. Specifically, Abroms and LeFebvre (2009) draw a series of implications for those responsible for channel selection in campaigns based on Obama's successes:

- *Consider new media as part of a comprehensive media mix.* In the business world, the combination of channels an organization selected to meet its objectives is called its **media mix.** Ultimately, organizations should select a media mix of channels that are appropriate for the organization, the message, and the target audience. As we will discuss later in this chapter, it is not

enough to rely on one channel exclusively—even if that channel is particularly "catchy" or attractive in terms of new media. Rather, build new media
into a comprehensive campaign strategy. We will discuss several common
channels used in strategic communication campaigns in this chapter, with
the intention that multiple channels be employed depending on your campaign goals, objectives, message, resources, and audience.

- *Encourage horizontal communication of campaign messages.* Whereas
  much of traditional media follows the mass media paradigm of **vertical**
  communication, meaning information comes from the "top" (i.e, one mass
  media source) and flows down to the receivers of the message, new media is
  most effective when horizontal communication is occurring. **Horizontal**
  communication is when information is being created and shared by sources
  and receivers equally. This allows your target audience to not only interact
  with the message but also to engage in self-expression—something that
  cannot be done using traditional media channels. Campaigns should
  embrace and encourage user-generated content, a unique characteristic of
  new media, that can lead to even greater levels of social influence and behavior change.
- *Use new media to encourage small acts of engagement.* Perhaps the most
  successful aspect of using new media in the Obama campaign was that it
  was able to engage and involve audiences that were previously ambivalent or
  only marginally politically inclined. To indicate support, audiences did not
  have to engage in time-consuming or committed behaviors—clicking "like"
  on a social media post, forwarding an email message, or adding an Obama
  badge to their Facebook page all constituted a public demonstration of support (Abroms and LeFebvre 2009). This is critical to persuasion in two ways.
  First, by encouraging a small commitment (e.g., liking a tweet from the
  Obama campaign), campaign designers could later ask for a larger, more significant commitment (e.g., voting for Barack Obama in the presidential
  election). Referred to as a **foot-in-the-door** persuasion strategy (Freedman
  and Fraser 1966), this sequential method works because we have an innate
  need to act consistently with our past behavior (cognitive dissonance theory; see Festinger 1957). This is a technique used very frequently by modern
  organizations of all types and for all purposes. If we, the consumer, provide
  our email to a newsletter, follow an Instagram page, or take a laptop sticker,
  we are making a small commitment to the organization. Later, when the
  organization asks us for support, money, or a purchase, we will be more
  inclined to do so out of an innate drive to be consistent in our beliefs and
  behaviors. New media provides an incredibly efficient channel to make
  these requests.
- *Use new media to facilitate in-person activities, not to replace them.* As we
  will discuss more throughout this chapter, the success of new media in the
  Obama campaign and elsewhere should not indicate that new media is the

only communication channel necessary for campaign success. Rather, the advantages of new media should be used to complement and extend the reach of messages delivered via other channels and for other purposes.

Relatedly, it is important to consider the characteristics of new media that make it unique from traditional channels. As discussed by Waldeck, Kearney, and Plax (2016), the term *new media* has a few important connotations that distinguish it from other media types. Namely, new media are:

- ✔ **Digital.** New media are electronic and operate on digital codes. This means that a large amount of information can be stored in very small spaces—think of the amount of text, images, and video stored on your smartphone. New media allow for the creation, storing, and access of very large amounts of information with relative ease. This allows for organizations to not only store a vast amount of content about their consumers with relative ease but also to provide a much wider array of information than traditional media allows. In fact, many organizations use traditional media to drive traffic to their new media for this purpose. If an interesting commercial can encourage potential customers to visit the organization's website, this is an "in" to provide more information and a more interactive experience.
- ✔ **Used for networking. Networking** is the interconnectivity of digital devices and the people who use them. Perhaps the greatest example of this in new media are **social networking sites,** or web-based platforms that allow individuals to construct personal profiles, build social networks with other users, and view content produced by other users of the system (Boyd and Ellison 2007).
- ✔ **Built for information exchange and communication.** Unlike traditional media, which follows the "one-to-many" approach of mass communication, new media allow for users to produce and exchange their own content. In addition to this being an obvious characteristic of the social networking sites mentioned above, there are various other types of new media that allow for this type of exchange. Bloggers, shopping websites, and user-content-centric sites such as Reddit and Tumblr fall into this category.

Understanding what makes new media "new" is necessary to using it effectively in your strategic communication campaign. These three characteristics are a fundamental part of new media, and may be the reason an organization should (or should not) use them in campaign efforts. New media are digital, used for networking, and built for information exchange and communication.

Think of how often you use these new media in your own life. At this moment, you likely have a smartphone nearby. On this device, you have access to an entire world of communication—social media applications like Twitter and Instagram, video and content sharing apps like YouTube and Reddit, and countless other applications that make getting through your day easier. You can order a ride-sharing service to take you to a restaurant that you found on your Yelp app and text message your friends what time to meet you. Our phones and our connection to new media are a ubiquitous and inextricable part of our lives. In fact, recent research by the PEW Research Center indicates that roughly one in four Americans say that they are "almost constantly" online (Pew Research Center 2018). As a result, new media has undeniably changed the way that organizations communicate with their stakeholders, and as communication scholar Ledford (2012) notes, has also changed the way that communication campaigns are conducted—"we now engage our audiences directly at an unprecedented level, stimulated by and resulting in increased audience expectations of engagement" (175).

Indeed, new media are unique from traditional media channels in that they allow for information exchange and interaction among users. As health communication scholars Cassell, Jackson, and Cheuvront (1998) noted in the early emergence of the internet as a channel for health promotion, the internet is unique in that it has both the mass media ability to reach large and geographically diverse audiences and the feedback ability of interpersonal communication. The ability of a website or app to adapt to a user's preferences, knowledge, and needs is much higher than any mass communication channel (Atkin 2001). In this way, newer media are more easily used for the tailored communication efforts discussed in chapter 6. Information provided online is generally cheaper and independent of issues with time or place—which makes it preferable to many traditional media platforms (Rossman 2011). The combination of mass media's reach with the effects of discussion and mediated interpersonal communication make new media channels an attractive option for organizations (Neuhauser and Kreps 2003). In sum, new media offer an opportunity for organizations to broaden their bases of support, extend their reach, and actively engage their target audiences (Abroms and LeFebvre 2009), but they are not and should not be treated as the only communication channel worth pursuing. In the sections that follow, we will discuss the various types of channels available for use in strategic communication campaigns as well as the considerations that must be made regarding which channels are likely to be most effective and appropriate for an organization's mission, campaign purpose, and target audience.

Undoubtedly, in deciding which of these two categories of channels to proceed with—or whether to include both as complements of each other, as we will discuss later in this chapter—you should always come back to your target audience. Hopefully, you have incorporated a few questions regarding channels into your formative research. Important questions you can ask your target audience related to channel selection include:

- Where does your target audience obtain information related to your topic?
- Who does your target audience listen to about this topic? Whose opinion is important to them? Who do they find credible?

- Where does your target audience spend their time? Where can you reach them when they are willing to consider your message?
- Where can you place your message so that it will stand out?

Among other considerations discussed later in this chapter, the answers to these questions should be a key component of which channels you select. In sum, the nature of new media as digital, networking, and connection-based technologies offer a number of benefits for strategic communication campaigns of all organizational types. However, there are a number of evidence-based "best practices" that should be followed, and above all else the target audience's familiarity and comfort with these new media should be prioritized in selecting communication channels. Even in campaigns using new media, campaign designers should seek to develop a comprehensive media mix that reaches the target audience in multiple places and builds a connected community surrounding campaign goals. To help achieve this, in the next section we will discuss with more specificity a number of channels commonly used in strategic communication efforts.

8.1.2 Common Channels in Strategic Communication Campaigns

We have discussed two broad categories of channels available to organizations—traditional and new media. However, these two broad categories do not fully cover the wide variety of options organizations can choose from to communicate with their target audience in strategic communication efforts. Below, we will cover in more detail the number of specific channels available to campaign designers, along with evidence of their effectiveness in existing strategic communication campaigns.

- **Television.** In the 2017–18 TV season, the Nielsen Company estimated that there were 119.6 million homes in the United States with at least one television (Nielsen 2018). As a result of its prevalence in the household not only in the United States but also worldwide, television in particular has been heavily relied on as a channel in communication campaigns (Noar 2006). The types of messages conveyed through this channel might include standard advertisements, short films, press coverage on local and national news, and public service announcements (PSAs). There are countless examples of campaigns that have used television as a channel to communicate messages about health, the environment, politics, to sell products, and to spread awareness. In August 2018, all NBC- and Telemundo-owned stations teamed up with hundreds of shelters across the country to host a "Clear the Shelters" day; this campaign consists of repeated appearances on local TV stations such as this one, in which a local TV anchor couldn't resist adopting a rescue puppy (see www .cleartheshelters.com/Telemundo-39-Anchor-Norma-Garcia-Adopts-a-New-Family-Member_Dallas-Fort-Worth-491182611.html). This campaign led to the adoption of nearly 100,000 shelter pets in one day—strong support for the power of TV as a source of not only informational but also persuasive messages.

- **Radio.** You might be inclined to think of radio as a "dated" or "old school" channel, and it certainly is one of the longest standing traditional media channels available to organizations. However, it has remained a prominent and often-used channel for a reason: radio continues to reach the highest proportion of the population. Specifically, the 2018 Nielsen report found that 92 percent of US adults listen to the radio each week; this number is even higher (96 percent) for those identifying as Hispanic. The challenge with using radio as a channel is that you must use your thirty- or sixty-second spot to grab your audiences' attention without the help of visual aids that can be used in television or other channels. To succeed given these challenges, a good radio ad gets listener's attention, is simple, and has a clear call to action. Consider the 2018 Radio Mercury Award winner for the "PSA Spot or Campaign" category (see www.radiomercuryawards.com/2018Winners.cfm) produced by advertising company BBDO New York for the nonprofit Sandy Hook Promise. This thirty-second PSA, titled "Thoughts and Prayers," has the following script:

[Musical intro simulating Breaking News alert]

Female Reporter: I am here on the scene of tomorrow's shooting. It's just a typical day at school. But tomorrow, we expect a drastically different scene.
Young boy: When the shooter finally gets in to the classroom, I am going to pretend to be dead so that he doesn't think that I am the target.
Female Reporter: The mayor is expected to hold a press conference, and offer his thoughts and prayers. We will provide live updates as soon as that begins tomorrow.

[Musical outro]

Male Voiceover: Help prevent tomorrow's shootings by knowing the signs today, at SandyHookPromise.org.

In thirty seconds, this PSA grabs the attention of the listener (using the musical intro we come to associate with breaking news as well as the content of the message being delivered), is simple in both concept and delivery and directs listeners to the nonprofit's website. As this award-winning commercial demonstrates, radio can be an incredibly effective channel to disseminate campaign messages.

- **Print media and other forms of traditional advertising.** Print media includes newspapers, magazines, posters, billboards, brochures, leaflets, and even direct mail to your target audience. A key benefit of using this type of channel is the ability to directly target a subgroup of the population, saving the organization both effort and funds. Take for instance a wedding catering business in need of outlets for advertising—print media offers a series of smart, strategic options for disseminating information on the organization:

flyers at bridal shops, brochures at wedding expos, and for a broader geographical audience, advertisements in bridal magazines. When it comes to print media, it is essential to envision where your target audience will be throughout the day—where can you meet them with your message? In the part of the country where your textbook authors live—Southern California—billboards along major highways are an incredibly effective channel for advertising local events, businesses, and laws (such as those against drunk and distracted driving). When your target audience is sitting on the highway much of their morning and evening, meet them there with a message!

- Another key element to successful print messaging is to develop strategies that will not only ensure your target audience will encounter your message, but will also place your messages where they are engaging in the target behavior (i.e., "place"; Lee and Kotler 2011, 291). Let's take for example a campaign conducted by communication researcher Thomas Meade (2015) to promote the disinfecting of gym equipment at the University of Alabama fitness center. As Meade (2015) notes in his work, by simply wiping down equipment such as bikes, treadmills, and weights before and after use, fitness center users can prevent a wide variety of bacterial and viral infections, the least of which is the potentially life-threatening MRSA bacterial infection. By developing a series of theory-based posters, strategically placed around the "decision points" in the cardio and weight-lifting rooms of a university fitness center, Meade was able to successfully alter individuals' perceptions of their responsibility to disinfect their equipment. Specifically, posters reading "75% of University of Alabama students disinfect their gym equipment. Shouldn't you?" led to relatively large changes in behavior—Meade observed just 5 percent of gym users disinfecting their equipment prior to his poster campaign, whereas 31 percent of gym users were continuing to disinfect their equipment one week following the posters being removed. This suggests that posters alone can have long-term effects on behavior—good news for organizations seeking low-cost channels to promote their messages.

- **Promotional items.** You might not think of a promotional item as a channel, but when emblazoned with company logos, websites, or event information, products such as t-shirts, stickers, mugs, and pens are a relatively low-cost and enduring way to keep your message visible among your target audience. The next time you are at your doctor's office, take a look around at the writing pads, pens, and office supplies that the staff is using. You are likely going to see quite a few logos for pharmaceutical companies or specific drug treatments. Pharmaceutical sales representatives visit on behalf of these organizations to strategically place their product where they want it—in the offices where these drugs will be prescribed. As a patient, if you see a brand name drug logo printed on your doctor's mug, it might increase your familiarity with it and cause you to ask your doctor about the drug. When this happens, that promotional item has done its job.

To achieve maximum effectiveness, choose promotional items that correspond with the behavior you are promoting. In selecting channels for a campaign involving students' study habits, the first author of this textbook chose to print campaign messages and branding materials on laptop stickers, pens, and water bottles—handing them out at the school's library—all materials that students might place around them while studying for their midterms and finals.

For nonprofit organizations, one potential channel might be the production of goods and services that can be sold for fund-raising and awareness purposes. Following the "place" suggestion mentioned above, the partnership of for-profit and nonprofit organizations often meets customers where they are to simplify the donation process. Take for instance the partnership between the World Wide Fund for Nature (formerly World Wildlife Fund) (WWF), an international nonprofit organization dedicated to environmental and wildlife conservation, and Build-A-Bear Workshop, a toy retailer that allows children to design and create their own personalized stuffed animal. For nearly twenty years, Build-A-Bear Workshop has partnered with the WWF through their Collectifriend plush animal series by donating $1 to the WWF for each plush animal purchased. Throughout this partnership, Build-A-Bear Workshop has featured several endangered and threatened species including the zebra, gray wolf, lion, cheetah, giraffe, and polar bear. Each Collectifriend wears a medallion featuring the WWF logo and a hangtag that provides information on the species. In the use of this promotional item, Build-A-Bear has raised $1.8 million for the WWF.

- **Websites.** Websites are a collection of web pages, images, video, text, and other digital material used by organizations to communicate information, interact with potential consumers or clients, and help promote their brand. From a strategic communication campaign perspective, the organization's website is an important part of your messaging that should not be overlooked. If your target audience is interested in a message they have seen on any one of the channels we have mentioned thus far—be it television, radio, or print media—in the modern age they will likely perform a quick search to find out more about your organization. You want to provide a means for them to find out about your organization's mission, product, services, and any other key information easily. There are two key reasons that websites offer a compelling channel for strategic communication efforts:
  - **The website is often your target audience's first impression of your organization.** Although having a poorly designed website is arguably worse than not having a website at all, your target audience will expect that you have an organizational platform. If they search for you and cannot find anything, they will move on to spend or donate their money and time elsewhere. As Leinbach-Reyhle (2014) notes, your website should

Figure 36 Consider partnerships and promotional items that will not only help you achieve your campaign objectives, but that your target audience will also enjoy.

give the appearance that it is maintained regularly—even if it isn't updated weekly or even monthly. There are plenty of templates available that make this achievable for organizations ranging from a small business with three employees to a nonprofit organization with hundreds of volunteers. If your website is not well designed, interesting, or professional, it is all too easy for your target audience to move on to the next organization that shows up in their internet search.

- **Websites offer continual access to your target audience.** A professional website that functions easily, contains quality content, and offers an engaging experience will be an expectation of your target audience. Your website can also be used to sell products or provide information at any time—an invaluable resource to organizations of any size or type. Consider government websites such as usa.gov—with this resource, you can find an answer to virtually any question about government services without having to depend on the nine to five workweek schedule. Your website is a 24/7 employee of your organization—and should be a very valued one.

An organization's website offers low-cost advertising and visibility; when done well this can be of great assistance to your strategic campaign efforts.

- **Mobile phones.** If you feel like everyone you know is on his or her phone all the time, you may be right. Recent national research indicates that the average US adult spends close to four hours a day using digital media, 62 percent of that time exclusively on smartphones (Nielsen 2018). In fact, 95 percent of Americans own a mobile phone, with 77 percent of these being "smart" phones with internet capabilities (Pew Research Center 2018). Mobile phones in particular have the ability to offer a continual, tailored, and interactive source of messaging to target audiences (Silk, Atkin, and Salmon 2011). Mobile applications and text messages give organizations the ability to reach target audiences anywhere and anytime. This can be a useful channel for organizations of all types, including long-standing for-profit organizations looking to revitalize their product and engage their consumers in new ways. Consider for example new initiatives by the Coca-Cola Company, in which the company placed 200,000 vending machines in Japan to allow customers to purchase beverages with a mobile app (Coca-Cola Company 2018). There are limitations to communicating with your target audience using mobile apps, however. In an analysis of health-related mobile app users, Chae (2018) found younger non-Hispanic individuals with higher incomes are more likely to use these technologies. Considering their limitations in reach, if you choose to use mobile phones in your media mix, be sure to also provide channels that do not require smartphone technologies.

- **Social media.** The ubiquitous nature of social network sites (SNS) has led scholars to examine the effects of being "permanently online" and "permanently connected" (Vorderer, Krömer, and Schneider 2016, 695). Combining the reach of traditional mass media with the interactivity of interpersonal communication, social media provide the opportunity for the target audience to become an active part of the strategic communication campaign. In the course of doing so, their involvement increases, which has two key effects. First, their involvement amplifies the target audience's positive perceptions of and behaviors toward the organization. Second, social media provides an easy opportunity to express support for an issue and forward information to friends; with one "Like" or "Share," your target audience can not only demonstrate support but also inform others in their network of your campaign message. In this way, not only do messages reach a greater audience but they are also spread by people the originators of the messages know and trust and who are therefore more likely to be influential (Heaney and Israel 2008).

    However, as Quinn's crisis at the beginning of this chapter illustrates, new media offers an increasing number of challenges for the same reasons it brings new opportunities. Social media presents somewhat of a double-edged sword for organizations, in that its potential for quickly (and cheaply) spreading information is much stronger than other channels, but this information can run contrary to the goals of the organization or the image it seeks. In the age of Twitter, YouTube, and Facebook, a mistake made by an organization can quickly become a trending topic.

- **Face-to-face communication.** In addition to the various traditional and new media channels mentioned above, an organization should implement interpersonal or community-based means of communicating with their target audience (US Department of Health and Human Services 2002). The use of interpersonal communication might include family and friends of your target audience, or individuals that might interact with your target audience at work or in their personal life. As we discussed in chapter 6, these midstream audiences can be incredibly effective at achieving attitude and behavior change. Community channels might include community workshops or events, health and fitness expos, gaming conventions, events at schools or places of work, farmer's markets, county fairs, music festivals, and even messages distributed at cultural and faith-based centers. As Dukes (2016) writes, large in-person community events can serve as cost-effective channels with which to reach thousands of members of your target audience in a place where they are comfortable and having fun. However, given that these might be crowded and with a lot of distractions, Dukes (2016) shares four tips for making sure you are using these platforms successfully:

✓ **Choose the event carefully.** Be sure that the event is actually a good fit for your organization. Do some research on who typically attends, as well as your topic. If it doesn't seem like a natural fit, it might do more harm than good for your organization to message at this event. If you are a fitness apparel company focused on using natural and sustainable resources, becoming a vendor at a yoga festival is a natural fit, where your product is likely to attract interest.

✓ **Keep it simple.** Your audience is a moving target and will not want to spend a lot of time listening to a complicated message. Depending on the size of the event, you likely have very little time and a lot of competition for your audience's attention. Focus on one or two key messages delivered in multiple ways (e.g., promotional items and a flyer).

✓ **Pay attention to timing.** The first few hours of an event are critical—your audience will grow wearier and more tired as the day goes on. Be sure to adjust your approach to energy levels.

✓ **Be interactive.** People come to community events to talk and have new experiences—so offer what they are looking for in the way of a compelling exhibit, professionals on hand to answer questions, or games that will engage your audience in your product.

These tips of course will vary in their utility based on the event and context, but in general you want community-based channels to serve as a carefully thought out, purposeful, and positive means of engaging with your target audience.

Of course most communication campaigns do not use one type of channel, but rather employ a variety of strategies to convey their message to their target audience (Noar 2006). Take for instance the partnership we discussed between the WWF and Build-A-Bear; included in this partnership are messages on television, radio, direct mail, press releases, website, in-store events, and signage (and this is just the promotion for ONE of each organization's many partnership initiatives!). At the end of this chapter, we will discuss a few tips for

Figure 37 Do not underestimate the potential of interacting with your target audience where they already live, shop, eat, and play—just be careful to follow the tips mentioned in this chapter to approach this channel with the highest likelihood for success.

Strategic Communication Mentor: Internal Communication Channels

In addition to having to select channels to use to communicate with external audiences, which is the focus of much of this chapter, organizations must also decide on the means by which they will communicate with members internal to the organization during the strategic communication campaign. The implementation of a strategic communication campaign is a complex and important part of ensuring that messages are delivered correctly and consistently with organizational goals and objectives. This implementation involves coordinating members of the organizational team to work effectively, which will likely require different channels from those used to reach external audiences. A few of these channels include:

- **Email.** Email continues to be one of the most common new media channels to use to network and connect with others, for both business and personal applications.
- **Video conferencing.** Video conferencing is a cost-effective means of conducting meetings, particularly with organizational teams in different locations.

- **Web conferencing.** In a web conference, each participant sits at his/her own computer and connects to other participants. Popular options for this include VoIP (Voice over Internet Protocol), which allows communicators to use the internet to make telephone audio and video calls. Skype is an example of a very popular VoIP software.
- **E-learning.** Depending on the needs of the organization, organizational members might be encouraged to complete e-learning seminars via the internet. In this, the organizational members would interact with a training website to click on links and complete assessments.
- **Text messaging.** Organizational members might exchange images and text using mobile devices—texts can also be used with voting or polling apps to make organizational decisions.
- **Internet or cloud-based workspaces.** Internet and cloud-based platforms such as GoogleDocs and Dropbox allow for organizational members to work from separate locations, which allows for organizations to become more diverse and global in their work teams. A nonprofit organization in Idaho can develop content that can instantly be

reviewed by colleagues in the United Kingdom.

- **Face-to-face communication.** Finally, you might choose to *not* use all of the mediated communication channels available to you and instead meet with employees in person. This option is more difficult to schedule and poses a challenge to work groups from diverse locations, but face-to-face meetings might be more appropriate for certain tasks or needs.

Just as you will carefully consider which channels to communicate with your target audience, so too should you carefully consider how organizational members will communicate with one another. Important questions to consider in deciding on the above channels include:

- ✔ What is the goal of this communication? Do you need collaboration or to simply provide information? Do you need your message to be visual or supplemented with images? The answers to these questions will affect which channel you choose.

- ✔ How quickly do you need the message to be received, and do you need feedback? Each of the above channels varies in whether it allows for synchronous communication, or the ability for the receiver to provide an instantaneous response. If you need a quick response, text messaging might be more appropriate than email.

- ✔ What is your relationship to the receiver? Will they be comfortable with this channel? If you are a manager asking your employees for a personal cell phone number to text, you may be crossing a line with their privacy.

- ✔ Does the channel ensure that you can check for accuracy? It will be important that you ensure that your organizational members understood your message correctly. Given the lack of non-verbal cues in email or text messaging, meaning might be lost or misinterpreted from sender to receiver. In selecting your media channel, ensure that you can check for accuracy and misunderstanding among your team.

developing messages across these channels that are consistent with one another and the goals of your campaign. For now, we turn to the important studies organizations must undergo when selecting which of these above channels they will employ in their strategic communication campaign.

8.2 SELECTING THE RIGHT CHANNEL: SIX IMPORTANT CONSIDERATIONS

As should now be evident, channel selection in the strategic communication campaign is of critical importance in the planning process. We have discussed types of channels, both in broad categorical terms and specific applications. In this next section, we will discuss some of the considerations an organization might have in selecting appropriate and effective channels for communicating their message. The relative weight or importance of each of these considerations will depend on the organization and its members—there is unfortunately no set way to decide or strategize on channel selection. Rather, what follows is a list of what organizational members should keep in mind as they make this important decision in the planning process.

- **Organizational identity and image.** In chapter 3, we discussed organizational identity and image as a key part of the strategic planning process. As you recall, organizational identity refers to how its members perceive, think, and feel about the organization; related but distinct is organizational image, which is how others view the organization. In this step in planning a strategic communication campaign, an organization should be careful to use messages that will be consistent with how those both internal and external to the organization perceive it; if the channel is inconsistent, it should be a favorable violation of those expectations. The use of the social media platform Snapchat by a general health practitioner, for instance, is likely a negative violation of what is expected and appropriate.

On a related note, an organization's brand should also be a part of channel selection. An organization's brand should be clear and consistent, and this should be reflected in the channels it uses to communicate with its target audiences. Before adopting a new channel, digital marketing specialist Stacy Jackson (2017) recommends organizations ask the following three questions:
- ✔ Would you expect an organization like yours to use this channel?
- ✔ Would you trust an organization like yours on this channel?
- ✔ Does your target audience use this channel?

If the answer to any of these questions is "no," then perhaps the channel in mind is not the best means of conveying your campaign messages.
- **Campaign goals and objectives.** As we discussed in chapter 5, the long-term goals and short-term objectives of your strategic communication campaign give your efforts purpose and meaning. As you are selecting communication channels, come back to these important pieces of information and ask: "Does this channel help our organization achieve our goals? Will it help us to achieve our objectives?" If the answer is yes, then proceed. If the channel does not help, then it isn't worth the effort.
- **Target audience.** As you recall from chapter 6, every decision made in a strategic communication campaign should keep the target audience in mind. Based on your formative research, what channels does your target audience use? Where do they get information, and who do they trust? Where does your target audience live, play, or work? The answers to these questions are likely the most important consideration in selecting a communication channel for your strategic communication efforts. The best channels to use are those that are close, familiar, and regularly accessed by your target audience (Kreps 2008).

For instance, in deciding whether to use traditional or emerging media channels, an important consideration will be the comfort and familiarity your target audience has with various types of media. In the best-case scenario, you are able to conduct formative research on the preferences and channel usage behaviors of your target audience. However, sometimes organizations do not have the resources—time, money, or otherwise—to answer these questions. Use your background research wisely to find any available information on how your target audience uses and perceives various communication channels.

The use of relevant media channels is particularly important when addressing issues in vulnerable populations, such as those groups that do not have high levels of education or income (Kreps 2008). In particular, Kreps (2008) recommends using a variety of channels (such as television, radio, print, online, and interpersonal) that are attractive, familiar, and easy to understand. However, the extent to which the channel is novel may also garner additional attention from the target audience (Snyder 2007). Therefore, there is a fine balance between "familiar" and "new" in channel selection that campaign designers must understand. See also the Strategic Communication Mentor in this chapter regarding message fatigue; you should not overwhelm your audience, but rather put yourself in their shoes: when do they want information from you? When will it be most convenient and useful to receive your messages?

- **Message content.** The content of the message itself should be considered in the channel selection process. The theory being used in your communication campaign should have a central role in channel selection, and it informs the content and purpose of your messages (Ledford 2012). As we discuss more below, more complex messages may require that channels capable of conveying their complexity are used (see Media Richness Theory). If your message requires a visual aid, such as demonstrating how to use a child's car seat effectively, a video or in-person event will likely work more effectively than a flyer.

- **Channel characteristics.** There are many communicative dimensions of these channels that ultimately influence their effectiveness. Channel reach, as we have defined previously in this chapter, is the proportion of the target audience exposed to the message. As Snyder (2007) writes, "channels should be selected and used in a way to reach a high percentage of the target population multiple times in a given period of time" (S36), as greater exposure to campaign messages is associated with greater campaign effectiveness. The use of traditional media channels might not seem "exciting" to new strategic communication campaign designers, who may prefer to use new media technologies, but the reach of channels such as television and radio continues to dominate other channels (Nielsen, 2018). In addition to reach, you might consider channel **frequency,** or the number of times a specific person is reached by a campaign. Using a variety of channels might therefore increase not only the reach but also the frequency of your communication messages (Snyder 2007). Achieving high reach and frequency is harder than it may sound—with an increasingly "cluttered" media environment, campaigns struggle to have their message seen by their target audience (Wakefield, Loken, and Hornik 2010).

Keep in mind that just because a particular channel has high reach does not mean it is the right choice for your message. Often, channels with high reach lack the next important channel characteristic, specialization. Channel **specialization** is the degree to which a channel can be adapted for a specific subgroup, or segment, of the target audience. You may also hear of this as specificity, as it refers to the degree to which a message can be specified for a particular age group, gender, education level, or interest. To illustrate the difference between reach and specificity, think of broadcast television—television has a very high reach, with an estimated nearly 119 million televisions in homes across the United States (Nielsen 2018). An advertisement played on a national network's nightly news broadcast is likely to be seen by many people—however, the message has very little ability to be adapted to particular subgroups or segments of TV viewers. A trade magazine, on the other hand, has a high degree of specialization. Individuals interested in *Better Homes & Gardens* magazine can be assumed to share a number of characteristics and interests that can be helpful for advertising purposes.

- **Budget.** Budget plays a pragmatic and pivotal role in campaign channel selection (Silk, Atkin, and Salmon 2011). Unlike commercial advertisers who can place numerous messages in mass media, and rely on repetition and mere exposure to influence their target audience, smaller organizations and nonprofit organizations may need to rely on more efficient channels to convey their message using less resources. If you are developing a campaign aimed at training organizational employees to engage in interpersonal communication and tailored messages, this is likely more costly than using traditional mass media approaches—whether the potential impact is worth the cost is a decision the organization has to consider.

Together, these six considerations should weigh in to which channels are selected to convey strategic organizational messages. The organization, the message, and the channel characteristics are the three pillars to which each channel should be measured against; ideally, a channel serves all three well. You will mostly likely find yourself having to weigh the advantages and disadvantages of each channel—no medium or mix of channels will be perfect, just as no campaign is perfect. These considerations are a good starting place from which to point your campaign in the right direction and are common to organizational campaigns of all types. In the next section, we will discuss how communication scholars suggest channels and messages be considered prior to implementation—according to the richness of the medium and the clarity of the message.

Strategic Communication Mentor: The Risk of Message Fatigue

In selecting your channels, you should be aware of the amount of exposure and frequency you are having with your campaign messages—and realize that there is such a thing as "too much." Although the assumption is that greater levels of exposure to campaign messages leads to greater campaign success (Snyder and Hamilton 2002), there is also evidence to suggest that audiences exposed *too much* to campaign messages might have a negative (or unintended) reaction to the campaign (Jeong, Tran, and Zhao, 2012). Communication scholars So, Kim, and Cohen (2017) refer to this as *message fatigue*, or the process by which people grow tired of being repeatedly exposed to identical or similar messages. The researchers argue that when individuals experience message fatigue, it is due to some combination of the following four dimensions:

- Perceived overexposure: the perception that they have been exposed to the message or messages beyond their desired frequency.
- Perceived redundancy: the perception that messages overlap and/or are repetitive.
- Exhaustion: a feeling of being burned out or tired of hearing messages.
- Tedium: a feeling that messages are boring, tedious, or dull.

These four dimensions often appear together and can be from exposure to both mediated and interpersonal channels (So, Kim, and Cohen 2017). So and colleagues (2017) examined message fatigue in the context of obesity prevention. As the authors note, the public health domain is one in which target audiences are often overexposed to messages about safe sex, quitting smoking, exercise, and other behaviors they *already know* are important. Their predictions regarding message fatigue and their obesity prevention messages were supported in their study—participants who indicated fatigue across the above four dimensions were less likely to pay attention to messages or seek more information on obesity and were more likely to report being annoyed or argue against the messages.

These findings translate to traditional advertising as well—studies show that individuals exposed to the same advertisement four or more times on Facebook show a much higher likelihood of "clicking through" and essentially avoiding the message (Karlson 2016). So, how can you avoid this fatigue and its negative consequences?

✓ **Limit the frequency of your messages to just three or four times per person.** This might sound hard to do, but social media analytics for sites like Facebook allow you to control things like ad frequency. If you are using traditional media, or face-to-face communication, what are ways that you can work to put an upper limit on your message frequency?

✓ **Rotate the messages that you use on each channel.** If you vary your messages, your target audience will continue to be intrigued and interested in them. On most social media, you can create schedules of when your messages are released to your target audience—vary which messages are displayed when, to keep things interesting and different.

✓ **Make slight, low-cost alterations to the content and appearance of your messages.** Changing things like background color, or even just reversing images, make the ad appear "different" enough. If it sounds silly, consider this: AdExpresso found that their cost-per-click lowered by 10 percent by simply reversing their message images. (Cost-per-click refers to how much an organization pays for each time someone "clicks" on their internet advertisement.)

Although the examination of message fatigue is a relatively new area of study for communication scholars, the evidence that exists thus far suggests that organizations should pay careful attention to their message exposure and frequency to not exhaust target audiences. For more tips on how to avoid message fatigue, particularly for social media advertisements, see https://adespresso.com/blog/overcome-ad-fatigue-keep-cpa-down/.

8.2.1 Media Richness Theory

For communication scholars, there are important theoretical considerations that should also be made of channels prior to their being selected for use in campaigns. The extent to which the channel can fully and accurately convey the message, for instance, falls under the purview of Media Richness Theory (MRT). Originally proposed by communication scholars Daft and Lengel (1986) to understand how information is processed and shared in organizations, MRT argues that every medium through which messages are sent has a certain capacity to convey messages and cues. Specifically, the researchers argue that every medium varies in its **richness,** or its ability to provide and clarify complex information in a timely manner. In short, a media's richness lies in its ability to create a shared understanding (Daft, Lengel, and Trevino 1987). Media that are more rich are subsequently more able to handle more complex and potentially confusing messages.

The richness of a medium is determined by four questions (Daft and Lengel 1986; Daft, Lengel, and Trevino 1987):

1. **Does the medium offer the ability to send feedback and how quickly?** A rich medium allows for the receiver to ask questions to increase understanding, and for the sender to make corrections.
2. **Can the medium communicate multiple cues?** As we discussed in chapter 1, there are both verbal and nonverbal components to the

messages that senders embed and send to receivers. These include the content of the message as well as the tone, body gestures, and any other number of symbols. A rich medium, according to MRT, will be able to include more of these cues.

3. **Does the medium offer language variety and the opportunity for natural language?** According to Daft, Lengel, and Trevino (1987) language variety is the range of meaning that can be conveyed with language symbols—whereas numbers convey greater prevision of meaning, natural language can be used to convey broader concepts and ideas.

4. **Does the medium have a personal focus?** A message is conveyed more fully when it includes personal feelings and emotions in the communication. Further, messages that are richer can be tailored to the frame of reference of the recipient.

Richer media allow for communicators to exchange information more efficiently and to better understand potentially ambiguous messages. In order from most to least rich, communication media discussed by Daft and Lengel (1986) included face-to-face communication, telephone, personal documents such as letters or memos, formal written documents, and numeric documents. Face-to-face communication is the most rich medium according to the above criteria because it allows for immediate feedback, allows for multiple cues such as tone of voice and body language, and message content is expressed in natural language. In a face-to-face interaction, messages are delivered, interpreted, and able to be adjusted and clarified instantly. Comparing this to an audio telephone call, the exchange of messages is also rapid, but any nonverbal cues such as tone of voice are filtered. Thus, telephone calls are a relatively rich medium, but slightly less so than face-to-face communication. For an illustration of how several major channels fall along this continuum, see table 8.1.

These four questions are also important in terms of how customers feel about a particular channel. Research by Tseng and colleagues (2017) examined the impact of the above four dimensions of media richness on consumers' perceptions of and loyalty to mobile instant messaging (MIM) platforms, such as WhatsApp or Facebook Messenger. The researchers presented MIM consumers with a series of questions related to the feedback, cues, language variety, and personal focus of their favorite MIM. Specifically, the researchers asked consumers to indicate whether they agreed to the following set of questions:

Multiple cues

While using this MIM, I can send/receive information through text.

While using this MIM, I can communicate with others through icons /stickers.

While using this MIM, I can communicate with others through verbal or video phones.

Immediate feedback

While using this MIM, I can send/receive information quickly.

It does not take long to express my reactions to others while using this MIM.

I do not wait long to receive the responses I requested from others while using this MIM.

Personal focus

This MIM allows the infusion of personal feelings and emotions.

While using this MIM, I can tailor text messages/stickers/ emoticons to the needs of the receiver.

While using this MIM, I can customize messages to meet the current situation of the receiver.

Language variety

While using this MIM, I can use a large pool of symbols to communicate rich meanings.

While using this MIM, I can express my ideas by choosing from a large pool of emoticons.

While using this MIM, I can express my ideas by choosing from a large pool of stickers.

Tseng and colleagues (2017) found that consumers' responses to these questions were related to their overall assessment of the MIM—which in turn was related to their **consumer loyalty,** or their intention to repeatedly use a product, service, or good. Interestingly, language variety was the most important of these four considerations in terms of its impact on both overall assessments and intentions to continue to use the MIM. From a strategic communication perspective, this is an important finding: if the richness of a channel affects how likely a consumer is to use it in the future, then organizations should certainly consider the feedback, cues, personal focus, and language variety of the channels they use to communicate with both internal and external audiences.

However, the essential benefit of using an MRT approach in strategic communication campaign design is its emphasis on the message itself—as we discussed previously, the content of your message should be a major consideration in selecting your channel. The key principles of MRT echo this assertion, as a central proposition of the theory is that the nature of the message should dictate the richness of the channel selected. Specifically, in determining which medium to send a message, Daft and Lengel (1986) argue that a sender should determine the **equivocality** of the message, or how many ways the message can be interpreted and misinterpreted. The sender should then fit the equivocality of the message to the medium—with "richer" mediums being selected for messages that may have multiple interpretations. Precise information, such as numerical data, can be communicated via a medium relatively low in richness; however, highly equivocal (and therefore more easily misinterpreted) messages should be conveyed with richer media. This isn't to say that "leaner" media should never be used—in fact, it is preferable in situations where the message to be delivered is relatively straightforward. To illustrate this, let's consider a situation that is relatively common in organizational life: the merging of two or more organizations. Suppose you are a regional manager of a family-owned national grocery store, and you have just received word that your company is going to be bought by a much larger "big-box" chain at the beginning of the next fiscal year. As a regional manager, you are responsible for communicating this information to your eighty-five employees. This announcement has the potential to be very unnerving for your employees, and you know they will have a lot of questions, the most important of which likely concern job security. Will employees maintain their benefits, or be transferred to a new system? Will new training be required? When will the change officially take place? In this situation, the message itself is highly equivocal and can be interpreted many ways. As a regional manager, you should therefore select a richer medium to deliver this message—preferably a large conference with all employees, or even a series of smaller group meetings to discuss the anticipated changes with each department of the store. This way, as the source of information, you are able to answer questions and provide immediate feedback as well as to offer tailored information that might be useful. You can imagine how inappropriate (and potentially disastrous) a lean medium such as flyers would be in this situation! However, a lean channel such as a memo or email to all employees would be perfectly appropriate for the much more straightforward information regarding when and where these face-to-face sessions will be held. The date and time of a meeting is not subject to multiple interpretations. Messages are effectively communicated when the equivocality of the message matches the richness of the channel selected.

You likely have made such decisions in your own life in the ways that you communicate with family and friends. Have you ever started to send a text message, and then stopped to call your message recipient instead "because it's too complicated"? On the other hand, we don't need "richer" media for a lot of messages. A quick text message to your roommate to let her know that you will be home late is probably more efficient than a video call. Similarly, when organizations choose rich messages to deliver clear information, they may be wasting resources and time and even leading to information overload as we discuss in the Strategic Communication Mentor in this chapter. Thus, channel selection in MRT focuses on making better use of time and establishing understanding among communicators—which is why this theory is so helpful to think of at this stage in planning a strategic communication campaign.

Table 8.1   The Media Richness Continuum

Richer Media	Face-to-Face
↑	Video conferencing, social networking, interactive websites
	Telephone
	Email
	Texting, instant messaging, microblogs
	Video or audio recordings
↓	Memos, letters
Leaner Media	Bulk mail, brochures, pamphlets, flyers

Table adapted from Dainton, M., and E. D. Zelley. 2015. *Applying Communication Theory for Professional Life: A Practical Introduction.* 3rd ed. Los Angeles: Sage.

8.2.2 Two-Step Flow Model of Communication

Although it may sound like organizations need to choose one channel, or one type of channel, to be effective, this is not the case. In fact, most successful campaigns employ a strategic mix of channels and messages to best reach their target audience. To understand how the various channels we have discussed in this chapter might work together, we turn to a classic concept in mass communication research: the two-step flow model of communication. Developed by Katz and Lazarsfeld (1955), the two-step flow model argues that messages from the mass media reach opinion leaders first, who in turn pass on that information to those in their personal and social networks. Thus, the influence of mass media occurs in two stages: First, the opinion leaders (who pay more attention to the media) receive information. Second, the general public receives that information from opinion leaders (see figure 38 for a visual representation of this process). These **opinion leaders** are so termed because they continually influence individuals in their social networks. This was a revolutionary concept at the time, as most mass media research assumed that messages from the media had a direct impact on individual's attitudes and beliefs in the context of persuasion (Davis 2009). What the two-step model instead proposes is that information from the mass media is filtered, or indirectly provided to the masses, by opinion leaders.

The original research that led to this hypothesis was a study by a group of sociologists (Lazarsfeld, Berelson, and Gaudet 1944) on voting behaviors in a presidential election. What the researchers expected to find was a direct effect of messages in the media on voter preferences and behavior; what they instead found was that interpersonal discussions about candidates were more predictive of individuals' attitudes and voting behaviors. These findings led to decades

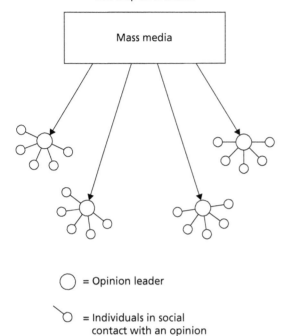

Two-step flow model

Mass media

○ = Opinion leader

○ = Individuals in social
contact with an opinion
leader

Figure 38 The Two-Step Flow Model of Communication.

of research that attempted to test, support, and sometimes falsify the theory. As summarized by communication scholar Maurer (2008), there are five general assumptions that emerged from early studies testing the two-step flow of communication:

1. Most people are not directly exposed to mass media; rather, they are informed through interpersonal communication with opinion leaders.
2. Opinion leaders are more exposed to mass media, and are much more engaged than the general public.
3. Opinion leaders not only inform followers but also transmit mass media content to them. In other words, followers receive both mass and interpersonal media based information.
4. The general public is not only informed but also influenced by opinion leaders. Opinion leaders are capable of changing attitudes and behaviors of their followers.
5. Opinion leaders are not passive gatekeepers of information—their opinions affect how they transmit information.

What is important from a strategic campaign perspective about this body of research and its resulting conclusions, however, is that it has largely supported the role of interpersonal communication in achieving campaign outcomes. As we discussed earlier in this chapter, horizontal communication can lead to greater levels of influence and behavior change not only in the political context but also in strategic communication efforts more broadly. We know from communication research that target audiences are much more influenced by people they know and trust (Heaney and Israel 2008). As such, this research reiterates that interpersonal channels should be used to reinforce and deliver key messages (Kreps 2008).

Note that there are some situations where mass communication is more appropriate than interpersonal communication. Namely, in creating awareness in emergency or crisis situations such as the one Quinn deals with at the beginning of this chapter, mass media are preferable in their ability to spread a message quickly to a target audience (Crawford and Okigbo 2014). Interpersonal channels, however, are more effective in situations requiring persuasion, attitude change, and behavioral modifications (Crawford and Okigbo 2014). Ideally, mass media and interpersonal communication should be used not in contrast to each other, but in coordination with one another (Crawford and Okigbo 2014). In analyzing the impact of the Truth campaign, for instance, Yoori Hwang (2012) found that both a person's exposure to campaign messages and engagement in campaign-related conversations with others had an impact on beliefs and intentions related to smoking. Further, campaign messages influenced the occurrence of conversations among peers about smoking, which had a direct impact on outcomes associated with the campaign. Thus, by ensuring that target audiences are BOTH exposed directly to campaign messages and engaging in interpersonal discussions about the campaign topic, strategic communication designers can achieve success in affecting attitudes and behavior (Hwang 2012). As Hwang notes, the implication of this research is that campaign designers must find ways to encourage and generate conversation regarding their campaign message. New media and opinion leaders offer two means through which strategic communication campaign designers can do this.

Given the availability and accessibility of new media, and the familiarity of traditional media, campaigns are certainly moving toward integrated communication strategies, but that doesn't mean you should "kitchen sink" it and include as many channels as you can afford. As health communication scholar Seth Noar (2006) warns, there is little evidence to support that "more is better" when it comes to campaign channel selection (35). In using MRT and the two-step flow model as communication guides for how to select messages, organizations should remain aware that three aspects of the strategic communication process guide channel selection above all else: your organization, your campaign goals and objectives, and your target audience.

8.3 TYING IT ALL TOGETHER: DEVELOPING AN INTEGRATED MEDIA MIX

An often-quoted adage by health communication scholars is that we must reach our target audience multiple times, from multiple sources, and in multiple settings to be effective (McGuire 1984). As we have discussed throughout this chapter, there are many options available to organizations to communicate their messages to their target audience. From traditional media such as television and radio, to emerging social media networks, and even community and interpersonal communication, there are a tremendous amount of choices organizations must make at this stage in their planning process. For example, the crisis faced by Quinn at the beginning of this chapter requires an understanding of the intricacies of various channels and each of the target audiences she must communicate with to restore faith and trust in Pintar. The balance of traditional and new media requires organizations to understand the benefits and best practices of using each, and each of the common channels we included in this chapter would be evaluated differently according to the six considerations for selecting your channel. Further, your choices should be driven by principles of communication theory, such as media richness and two-step flow. The outcome of employing these theories successfully will be messages that are appropriately matched to their channel and mediated messages that encourage persuasive interpersonal discussion surrounding your campaign.

In selecting your media mix, it will be important to develop an **integrated narrative** among all of your campaign channels, or a complementary set of messages that make sense with one another. You do not want your social media presence to be markedly different from your print media; radio advertisements should be similar to target audiences that have been to your community events, and so on. Think carefully about the tone your organization will have, and keep it consistent across channels. You can think of this as a messaging "personality" that should stay consistent—even if you need to make small adjustments for each platform, it should still sound like the same "person" talking (Jackson 2017). All campaign messages, regardless of channel, should also have the same appearance, brand, and tone. Ultimately, organizations should strive for **synergy** across their campaign channels, wherein a message delivered in one channel increases the effectiveness of messages delivered in other channels. Synergy among the channels used in a campaign can not only increase exposure and the likelihood that a message will be seen by a target audience but also the likelihood that the message will make an impact (Rossman 2011). Consider Dai's challenge at the beginning of this chapter—she needs to reach multiple target audiences using multiple channels, but to be successful she will need to make sure that the senator's reelection campaign has one consistent, strong voice across these efforts.

Achieving an integrated and synergistic media mix should come naturally if you have been following the suggestions throughout this text, such as basing your messages in communication theory (chapter 7). In the next chapter, we will discuss the last major consideration in the campaign planning process: the stakeholders involved in your organization, and how you should incorporate them into the strategic communication campaign process.

CHAPTER 8 REVIEW

Questions for Critical Thinking and Discussion

1. In this chapter we discuss six central considerations for selecting a channel for a strategic communication campaign. The first is organizational identity, or how members think of and perceive the organization. How do you think the various types of traditional and new media might challenge organizations in this way? Should an organization ever change its identity to accommodate new types of channels? Why or why not?

2. Take a closer look at the various types of channels included in table 8.1, the Media Richness Continuum. Are there other channels mentioned in this chapter that are not included? Can you think of additional channels that you have either used or been exposed to? Where would you place these channels in the continuum? Explain your choices using the four media richness criteria.

3. What is an example of a strategic communication channel that you have found to be particularly effective in your life experiences? Perhaps you used this channel in your own strategic communication efforts, or were the target audience of an organization's campaign. What about the use of this particular channel was influential, and how would you use this experience to guide your own strategic communication efforts in the future?

4. At the end of this chapter, we discuss five key assumptions of the two-step flow model of communication. Take a closer look at each of these assumptions. Based on your experience, indicate whether you would agree or disagree with each assumption. Can you find evidence to support your assumptions here?

5. How do the characteristics of new media (i.e., digital, used for networking, built for information exchange and networking) present a challenge to developing an integrated media mix? Do you think new media help or hurt organizations' ability to achieve synergy among channels? Explain your response.

Key Terms

consumer loyalty: consumer intention to repeatedly use a product, service, or good.

equivocality: how many ways a message can be interpreted and misinterpreted.

foot-in-the-door: a persuasion strategy in which a small commitment is secured followed by a request for a larger, more significant request.

frequency: the number of times a specific person is reached by a campaign message.

horizontal: when information is being created and shared by sources and receivers equally.

integrated narrative: a complementary set of messages that make sense with one another.

media mix: the combination of channels an organization selected to meet its objectives.

mediated communication: communication in which technology is used to deliver information between senders and receivers.

medium: the specific mode or device that moves information over time or distance so that people who are not face-to-face can communicate.

networking: the interconnectivity of digital devices and the people who use them.

new media: any communication using digital technologies, including the internet, email, text messaging, mobile phone, smartphone technology, video, or computer games.

opinion leaders: individuals who influence others in their social networks.

richness: a channel's ability to provide and clarify complex information in a timely manner.

social networking sites: web-based platforms that allow individuals to construct personal profiles, build social networks with other users, and view content produced by other users of the system.

specialization: the degree to which a channel can be adapted for a specific subgroup, or segment, of the target audience.

synergy: when a message delivered in one channel increases the effectiveness of messages delivered in other channels.

vertical: information comes from one mass media source and flows down to the receivers of the message.

Further Readings and Resources

Booth-Butterfield, S. n.d. "Sequential Messages." http://healthyinfluence.com/wordpress/steves-primer-of-practical-persuasion-3-0/var/sequential-messages/.

Dennis, A. R. 2009. "Media Richness Theory." In *Encyclopedia of Communication Theory*, by S. W. Littlejohn and K. A. Foss, 642–43. Thousand Oaks, CA: Sage.

Lewis, B. K, and C. Nichols. 2011. "Social Media and Strategic Communication." In *The Routledge Handbook of Strategic Communication*, edited by D. Holtzhausen and A. Zerfass, 545–60. New York: Routledge.

McDonald, D. G. 2008. "Media Content in Interpersonal Communication." In *The International Encyclopedia of Communication*, edited by W. Donsbach. doi: 10.1002/9781405186407.wbiecm021.

Plowman, K. D., and C. Wilson. 2018. "Strategy and Tactics in Strategic Communication: Examining Their Intersection with Social Media Use." *International Journal of Strategic Communication* 12, no. 2: 125–44. doi: 10.1080/1553118X.2018.1428979.

Shi, J., T. Poorisat, and C. T. Salmon. 2018. "The Use of Social Networking Sites (SNSs) in Health Communication Campaigns: Review and Recommendations." *Health Communication* 33, no. 1: 49–56. doi: 10.1080/10410236.2016.1242035.

References

Abroms, L. C., and R. C. LeFebvre. 2009. "Obama's Wired Campaign: Lessons from Public Health Communication." *Journal of Health Communication* 14, no. 5: 415–43. doi: 10.1080/10810730903033000.

Atkin, C. K. 2001. "Theories and Principles of Media Health Campaigns." In *Public Communication Campaigns*, 3rd ed., edited by R. E. Rice and C. K. Atkin, 49–68. Thousand Oaks, CA: Sage.

Boyd, D. M., and N. B. Ellison. 2007. "Social Network Sites: Definition, History, and Scholarship." *Journal of Computer Mediated Communication* 13, no. 1: 210–30.

Cassell, M. M., C. Jackson, and B. Cheuvront. 1998. "Health Communication on the Internet: An Effective Channel for Health Behavior Change?" *Journal of Health Communication* 3, no. 1: 71–79.

Chae, J. 2018. "A Comprehensive Profile of Those Who Have Health-Related Apps." *Health Education and Behavior* 45, no. 4: 591–98. doi: 10.1177/1090198117752784.

Coca-Cola Company. 2018, April 25. "Digitizing the Enterprise—Increasing Creative Engagements and Modernizations in a Click and Swipe World. www.coca-colacompany.com/stories/digitizing-the-enterprise-becoming-a-seamless-part-of-peoples-lives?utm_source=annual-review-2017.com&utm_medium=referral&utm_campaign=Annual_Report.

Crawford, E. C., and C. C. Okigbo. 2014. "Strategic Communication Campaigns." In *Strategic Urban Health Communication*, edited by C. C. Okigbo, 11–23. New York: Springer.

Daft, R. L., and R. H. Lengel. 1986. "Organizational Information Requirements, Media Richness, and Structural Design." *Management Science* 32, no. 5: 554–71.

Daft, R. L., R. H. Lengel, and L. K. Trevino. 1987. "Message Equivocality, Media Selection, and Manager Performance: Implications for Information Systems." *MIS Quarterly* 11, no. 3: 355–66. doi: 10.2307/248682.

Davis, D. K. 2009. "Two-Step and Multi-Step Flow." In *Encyclopedia of Communication Theory*, edited by S. W. Littlejohn and K. A. Foss, 970–71. Thousand Oaks, CA: Sage. doi: 10.4135/9781412959384.n384.

Dukes, S. 2016, January 14. "Come One, Come All: Leveraging Community-Based Events." www.vancomm.com/2016/01/14/leveraging-community-based-events/.

Festinger, L. 1957. *A Theory of Cognitive Dissonance*. Stanford, CA: Stanford University Press.

Freedman, J. L., and S. C. Fraser. 1966. "Compliance without Pressure: The Foot-in-the-Door Technique." *Journal of Personality and Social Psychology* 4, no. 2: 195–202.

Green, M. 2016, August 29. "Ten of the Most Successful Presidential Campaign Ads Ever Made." www.kqed.org/lowdown/3955/ten-of-the-best-presidential-campaign-commercials-of-all-time.

Heaney, C. A., and B. A. Israel. 2008. "Social Networks and Social Support." In *Health Behavior and Health Education: Theory, Research, and Practice*, 4th ed., edited by K. Glanz, B. K. Rimer, and K. Viswanath, 189–210. San Francisco: Jossey-Bass.

Hwang, Y. 2012. "Social Diffusion of Campaign Effects: Campaign-Generated Interpersonal Communication as a Mediator of Antitobacco Campaign Effects." *Communication Research* 39, no. 1: 120–41. doi: 1 0.1177/0093650210389029.

Jackson, S. 2017. "Importance of Brand Consistency: 7 Key Approaches for Keeping Aligned." www.clearvoice.com/blog/brand-consistency-why-its-so-important-how-to-achieve-it/.

Jeong, Y., H. Tran, and X. Zhao. 2012. "How Much Is Too Much?" *Journal of Advertising Research* 52, no. 1: 87–101.

Karlson, K. 2016, July. "12 Speedy Ways to Overcome Ad Fatigue (and Keep Down Your Cost-per-Action)." https://adespresso.com/blog/overcome-ad-fatigue-keep-cpa-down/.

Katz, E., and P. Lazarsfeld. 1955. *Personal Influence*. New York: Free Press.

Kreps, G. 2008. "Strategic Use of Communication to Market Cancer Prevention and Control to Vulnerable Populations." *Health Marketing Quarterly* 25, no. 1–2: 204–16. doi: 10.1080/07359680802126327.

Lazarsfeld, P. F., B. Berelson, and H. Gaudet. 1944. *The People's Choice: How the Voter Makes Up His Mind in a Presidential Campaign.* New York: Columbia University Press.

Ledford, C. J. W. 2012. "Changing Channels: A Theory-Based Guide to Selecting Traditional, New, and Social Media in Strategic Social Marketing." *Social Marketing Quarterly* 18, no. 3: 175–86. doi: 10.1177/15245004124606671.

Lee, N. R., and P. Kotler. 2011. *Social Marketing: Influencing Behaviors for Good.* 4th ed. Los Angeles: Sage.

Leinbach-Reyhle, N. 2014. "3 Reasons Websites Are Vital for Small Businesses." www.forbes.com/sites/nicoleleinbachreyhle /2014/09/29/websites-for-small-businesses/#2b72e31c2026.

Maurer, M. 2008. "Two-Step Flow of Communication." In *The International Encyclopedia of Communication,* edited by W. Donsbach. doi: 10.1002/9781405186407.wbiect063.

McGuire, W. J. 1984. "Public Communication as a Strategy for Inducing Health-Promoting Behavioral Change." *Preventative Medicine* 13, no. 3: 299–319.

McLuhan, M. 1964. *Understanding Media: The Extensions of Man.* New York: McGraw-Hill.

Meade, T. 2015. "Disinfect the Rec: Creating and Implementing a Disinfection Campaign at Gyms Using the Theory of Planned Behavior." *Recreational Sports Journal* 39, no. 2: 157–69. doi: 10.1123/rsj.2015–0037.

Neuhauser, L., and G. L. Kreps. 2003. "The Advent of E-Health: How Interactive Media Are Transforming Health Communication." *Medien and Kommunikationswissenschaft* 51: 541–56.

Nielsen Company. 2017, August 25. "Nielsen Estimates 119.6 Million TV Homes in the U.S. for the 2017–18 TV Season." www.nielsen.com/us/en/insights/news/2017/nielsen-estimates-119–6-million-us-tv-homes-2017–2018-tv-season .html.

———. 2018. "The Nielsen Total Audience Report." www.nielsen .com/us/en/insights/reports/2018/q1–2018-total-audience-report.html.

Noar, S. M. 2006. "A 10-Year Retrospective of Research in Health Mass Media Campaigns: Where Do We Go from Here?" *Journal of Health Communication* 11, no. 1: 21–42. doi: 10.1080/10810730500461059.

Pew Research Center. 2018, March 14. "About a Quarter of U.S. Adults Say They Are 'Almost Constantly' Online." www .pewresearch.org/fact-tank/2018/03/14/about-a-quarter-of-americans-report-going-online-almost-constantly/.

Rice, R. E., and C. K. Atkin, eds. 2013. *Public Communication Campaigns.* 4th ed. Los Angeles: Sage.

Rossman, C. 2011. "Strategic Health Communication: Theory- and Evidence-Based Campaign Development." In *The Routledge Handbook of Strategic Communication,* edited by D. Holtzhausen and A. Zerfass, 409–23. New York: Routledge.

Silk, K. J., C. K. Atkin, and C. T. Salmon. 2011. "Developing Effective Media Campaigns for Health Promotion." In *The Routledge Handbook of Health Communication,* 2nd ed., edited by T. L. Thompson, R. Parrott, and J. F. Nussbaum, 203–19. New York: Routledge.

Snyder, L. B. 2007. "Health Communication Campaigns and Their Impact on Behavior." *Journal of Nutrition Education and Behavior* 39, supplement 2: S32–S40. doi: 10.1016/j.jneb .2006.09.004.

Snyder, L. B., and M. A. Hamilton. 2002. "A Meta-Analysis of U.S. Health Campaign Effects on Behavior: Emphasize Enforcement, Exposure, and New Information, and Beware The Secular Trend." In *Public Health Communication: Evidence for Behavior Change,* edited by Robert Hornik, 357–83. Hillsdale, NJ: Lawrence Earlbaum Associates.

So, J., S. Kim, and H. Cohen. 2017. "Message Fatigue: Conceptual Definition, Operationalization, and Correlates." *Communication Monographs* 84, no. 1: 5–29. doi: 10.1080/03637751 .2016.1250429.

Tseng, F. C., T. C. E. Cheng, K. Li, and C. I. Teng. 2017. "How Does Media Richness Contribute to Customer Loyalty to Mobile Instant Messaging?" *Internet Research* 27, no. 3: 520–37. doi: 10.1108/IntR-06–2016–0181.

US Department of Health and Human Services. 2002. *Making Health Communication Programs Work: A Planner's Guide.* Bethesda, MD: National Cancer Institute.

Vorderer, P., N. Krömer, and F. M. Schneider. 2016. "Permanently Online—Permanently Connected: Explorations into University Students' Use of Social Media and Mobile Smart Devices." *Computers in Human Behavior* 63: 694–703. doi: 10.1016/j.chb.2016.05.085.

Wakefield, M. A., B. Loken, and R. C. Hornik. 2010. "Use of Mass Media Campaigns to Change Health Behaviour." *The Lancet* 376, no. 9748: 1261–71.

Waldeck, J. H., P. Kearney, and T. G. Plax. 2016. *Strategic Communication at Work: Contemporary Perspectives on Business and Professional Communication.* 2nd ed. Dubuque, IA: Kendall Hunt.

9

Cultural Diversity and Stakeholder Awareness

CHAPTER CONTENTS

9.1 The Deep Significance of Knowing Your Audience and Other Stakeholders   261

9.2 Communicating Strategically in a Diverse Society   266

    9.2.1 What Is Culture?   266

    9.2.2 Cultural Inclusion: A Contemporary Approach to Message Design   268

    9.2.3 Cultural and Co-Cultural Features That Influence Communication   270

9.3 Strategies for Strengthening Stakeholder Relationships and Enhancing Message Effectiveness   281

    9.3.1 Use Appropriate Theory and Research as Your Guide   281

    9.3.2 Communication Skills Can Make a Difference   282

9.4 Tying It All Together: Building and Sustaining Stakeholder Relationships That Contribute to Message Effectiveness   287

LEARNING OBJECTIVES

After reading this chapter, you should be able to do the following:

▶ Explain the importance of vigilant awareness of a campaign's stakeholders throughout the process of design, implementation, and evaluation.

▶ Apply principles of cultural communication competence to address the needs and concerns of a wide range of diverse campaign stakeholders.

▶ Practice heightened cultural awareness to anticipate receiver objections, manage responses, and adapt message strategies.

▶ Use tested strategies for building and maintaining relationships with diverse stakeholders.

Dr. Gary Kreps is a professor at George Mason University, where he also serves as director of the Center for Health and Risk Communication. In addition to conducting his own research, for much of his career Dr. Kreps has developed evidence-based health message programs aimed at a diverse group of receiver stakeholders—including health care providers, health educators, public health officials, and health care consumers. He delivers his educational programs through a variety of channels and technologies and relies heavily on sophisticated, strategically designed communication campaigns. In one particular project, Dr. Kreps was asked to design, implement, and evaluate a health education project to promote participation among people of color in HIV/AIDS vaccine clinical trials (Kreps 2016).

The problem driving Dr. Kreps's project was the disproportionate harm done by HIV/AIDS inflicted on minority populations in the United States, particularly African Americans, and the low rates of participation among those populations in promising clinical research. The Centers for Disease Control (2016) estimated that although African Americans/blacks represent about 14 percent of the population in the United States, they account for almost half of new HIV cases nationally. One of the most promising solutions to this epidemic is HIV/AIDS vaccines; however, minority participation in clinical trials of these vaccines historically has been very low (Frew et al. 2010). Dr. Kreps's formative research indicated a compelling explanation for this. Minority communities were rejecting traditional approaches to HIV/AIDS information dissemination by "official" sources and authority figures, citing a lack of trust.

Although this challenge would be a difficult one to face, Dr. Kreps and his team had a research-based framework for proceeding. Specifically, some of his earlier work (Kreps and Sparks 2008) suggested that health messages shared within social networks, especially among those with similar racial and/or ethnic backgrounds, are generally accepted and potentially more influential on some groups than information from health care professionals, government agencies, or research clinics. This assumption, then, served as the foundation for the design and dissemination of "culturally sensitive messages about HIV/AIDS vaccine research" (Kreps 2016, 281). Although changes in health outcomes can take years to recognize, early evaluations of this campaign reveal beneficial results. These include positive evaluations of the campaign messages' clarity, believability, usefulness, and trustworthiness; a significant increase in self-reported HIV awareness among target audiences; and willingness among those exposed to the campaign to share the messages in their social networks of at-risk people.

Like all of the strategic communication programs discussed and illustrated in this book, Dr. Kreps's Community Liaison Project exemplifies the importance of understanding a campaign's target audience and using research-based frameworks for designing the appropriate approach for a strategic messaging program. In particular, his project highlights the importance of understanding unique characteristics that might affect how stakeholders relate to your message—receive it, think it through, accept or reject it, talk about it with their friends and family, and so on. This chapter underscores the inherent diversity among people associated with a strategic communication campaign (e.g., developers, audiences, and other stakeholders) as well as features an audience might have in common that provide guidance relative to design and dissemination. In this chapter, we explore some of the more advanced and challenging stakeholder characteristics you will want to understand before designing messages; characteristics that go beyond age, gender, profession, or zip code. We will introduce you to some of the research and thinking on how cultural identification can influence how audiences receive messages. We will define culture broadly as the groups and interests that stakeholders identify with and that influence how they send, receive, and interpret messages. Further, we will consider additional stakeholder characteristics you will want to maintain awareness of throughout the strategic communication process. And, this chapter will provide you with strategies for strengthening your relationships with the diverse body of stakeholders associated with any strategic communication program as a means for enhancing the program's eventual effectiveness. Throughout the chapter, we will explore aspects of Dr. Kreps's project, along with a number of other examples, to strengthen your understanding of these important concepts.

9.1 THE DEEP SIGNIFICANCE OF KNOWING YOUR AUDIENCE AND OTHER STAKEHOLDERS

Kreps's project, the Community Liaison Project, offers us some important insight into the critical importance of truly understanding your audience. HIV is considered the most significant pathogen to emerge in the twentieth century, and HIV/AIDS has caused a worldwide epidemic. In other words, it is a very serious public health concern. Anytime public health is at risk, we must consider who is vulnerable or at heightened risk and why. In our example, African Americans and other ethnic minorities are affected disproportionately, suggesting heightened risk or vulnerability. Scientists ruled out any medical explanation (i.e., African Americans do not have a genetic predisposition to AIDS/ HIV) and, thus, experts began to examine how prevention messages were being disseminated in high-risk communities and populations. Several studies have explored this phenomenon that has historically affected African American communities since high-profile cases of unethical and disparate treatment of blacks within the health care system came to light (e.g., for two of the most egregious cases, investigate the Tuskegee Syphilis studies and HeLa cancer cell research). Jacobs et al. (2006) in particular examined African Americans' perceptions of trust in physicians through a focus group study and identified a range of reasons why blacks tend to reject information from health care professionals such as physicians. These reasons included:

1. physicians' lack of interpersonal skills and inability to "translate" highly technical medical information for lay people,
2. their perception that physicians' primary goal is financial gain,
3. an assumption of racism among providers, and
4. concerns about experimentation during provision of health care.

The researchers noted, importantly, that when health care consumers distrust professionals, they avoid the medical system and fail to comply with prevention and treatment guidance offered by their providers and public health officials. When people trust the source of health-related information, they are more likely to adhere to recommendations made and engage with professional health care providers. Kreps and his team were focused, then, on a message design program that would overcome African Americans' lack of trust in the message source and the message itself.

You may be thinking at this point, "but *all* African Americans don't distrust medical professionals and reject their recommendations!" Perhaps you are black and thinking, "I trust my doctor and almost always comply with what professionals recommend for my health care." Or, "I know plenty of white people who don't trust 'the system.'" And of course, all of these statements would be true. That's why simply knowing a demographic characteristic that binds an audience together is necessary, but insufficient, for building effective relationships with the communities you are interested in reaching, and designing effective strategic communication programs.

To illustrate this point, in a study published in the *American Journal of Public Health,* University of Pennsylvania researchers Armstrong, Ravenell, McMurphy, and Putt (2007) found that, indeed, blacks and Hispanics reported higher levels of distrust in physicians than whites. But when they examined the statistical interaction effects present in their study, they found that ethnicity alone didn't have the most powerful effect on trust. The effect of ethnicity was stronger when the individual also had lower socioeconomic status (i.e., lower income, less education, and lack of health insurance). In some cases, whites with lower socioeconomic status reported higher levels of distrust than blacks with higher socioeconomic status. The researchers also found that geographic region or city made a difference. There is a long history of research on neighborhood and area effects on health and perceptions of health care (Diez-Roux 2001) suggesting a complex set of historical, economic, political, and social factors that lead to differential health outcomes in neighborhoods, cities, and geographic regions. Finally, gender appeared to mediate the relationship between race and trust as well, with men perceiving physicians as less trustworthy than females. Studies like these reveal critical "pathways" to distrust in health care professionals that help practitioners anticipate objections to their messages and design strategies for overcoming barriers to reaching intended communities. Later in this chapter, we will see exactly how Kreps and his colleagues did this in the Community Liaison Project.

Although we have selected a public health example to frame this chapter, the importance of knowing and relating to your targeted communities in deep and appropriate ways is critical in all phases of strategic message design, regardless of your project's goals. For example, a group of university researchers worked on a campaign for a state agency aimed at increasing awareness among Latino truckers about the importance of oil recycling, and ultimately influenced this population to engage in more environmentally friendly practices relative to oil disposal. The team conducted focus groups to learn more about the truckers' awareness of state regulations relative to oil disposal, level of motivation to comply with them, and pilot test reactions to outreach educational materials. One member of the team recalls the difficulty of getting the groups talking and wondering what he could do to get the truckers to speak openly. He empathized with their reluctance, discomfort, and potential distrust talking with this white, male university professor who seemed so different from them and who was working on behalf of a state agency with the power to fine them. He worked hard in ways we will explore later in this chapter to build affinity and develop a communication relationship with the trucker participants.

Awareness of **salient audience characteristics** (those that emerge as most influential) is essential for guiding the design and implementation of any program or campaign and how you interact with stakeholders. As the Community Liaison Project example illustrates, what defines a "salient" characteristic is sometimes a complex question and is rarely something as simple as a single demographic category. Kreps and Sparks (2008) wrote, "Messages should be designed to appeal to key beliefs, attitudes, and values of targeted audience members, using familiar and accepted language, images, and examples to illustrate key points" (329).

The importance of understanding and relating to your constituents extends beyond the target audience and applies to other stakeholders as well. At all times, you must be vigilant about who your stakeholders are and what they value, how they think and make decisions, and how you can illustrate the benefits of your program in ways they will relate to and agree with. When working with various stakeholders, you will often need to make subjective decisions about whose needs and requests are most worthy of project resources at any given time. In a project documented by Waldeck (2008), she worked as a consultant on a project with three organizations that sought to provide professional training and development for employees of one of the partner organizations. The other two partners provided content and resource materials for the courses, funding, and advertising. In return for their investment of cash and other resources, the two outside partners expected to see results—increased

Figure 40 As a strategic communication professional, you may find yourself developing and testing messages with professional groups you have little or no experience with. You will need to be highly sensitive to all of your audiences' requirements.

enrollment in the professional development training opportunities (as a metric of program success), enthusiasm and motivation from the target audience, and focused professionalism from the communication and instructional design professionals working on the program. They presented a variety of requests and requirements over the course of the project. Some of their needs were reasonable and relevant to the project; others were not. Some represented "power plays" designed to assert the particular partner's importance to the overall project, but would have meant little to the program's goals or even weakened the program.

As the lead consultant working on the project, Waldeck recognized firsthand how important understanding all of her stakeholders' needs were and how to attend to them in sensitive, tactful ways. No one wants to feel that their requirements for, say, routine project updates, information, or recognition are unimportant. Stakeholder personalities, needs, and roles were critical for the communication team to learn and respect throughout the process of designing and implementing the training program. Initiating, maintaining, and nurturing relationships with stakeholders and maintaining the integrity, focus, and direction of your program can be a balancing act! As a communication professional working on strategic messaging programs, you must learn to make decisions and communicate in ways that avoid or manage "potential conflict stemming from divergent interests of stakeholders" (Frooman 1999, 193).

The balancing act suggested in the last paragraph is no easy task. Idiosyncratic personalities, communication style differences, power, and organizational politics all make the challenge of keeping stakeholders satisfied a daunting one. To guide you, we offer the three defining characteristics that communication professionals should keep in mind as they evaluate stakeholder needs, anticipate their objections and requirements, and prioritize responses (Mitchell, Agle, and Wood 1997). They are:

• **Stakeholder power:** Stakeholders that provide funding have a great deal of power to impose their will. In the project Waldeck worked on detailed in earlier paragraphs, the team prioritized communication with this partner for this reason and carefully evaluated messages to and from this particular stakeholder.

- **Legitimacy:** Legitimacy refers to the appropriateness or desirability of a stakeholder's position or actions. Even though a stakeholder might have a lot of power, the campaign or program team is responsible for evaluating what the stakeholder is requesting and determining whether it is in the best interest of the campaign. Campaign partners or stakeholders might present suggestions or requests that simply aren't good ideas for the overall goals of the project. They will inevitably assert personal agendas or those they perceive to be in the best interest of the organization they represent. Although these ideas and agendas should be assessed carefully rather than dismissed outright (after all, they might actually benefit the project), those that appear to work against project goals will ultimately waste time. They must be tactfully eliminated from consideration and given no further resources.
- **Urgency:** Urgency refers to the degree to which a stakeholder's claim is sensitive, pressing, and critical to the overall project. This particular characteristic of a stakeholder request or requirement is common to all project management tasks. All stakeholders will want something at one time or another, and these requests need to be evaluated in terms of their urgency. For example, in the context of organizational change, Lewis (2007) points out that as stakeholders cope with the request to change their work processes and patterns, they will all consider their needs for information or to have their voices and concerns recognized as "urgent." You might see things differently. However, alienating stakeholders can have disastrous implications when asking them to cooperate with a strategic organizational change or attempting to influence them in any way. Using some of the communication strategies we discuss later in this chapter, communication professionals must find ways to assess the urgency of stakeholder concerns and reduce stakeholder uncertainty in authentic ways that leave the stakeholder feeling valued.

Stakeholders with all three of these characteristics at any given time are referred to as "definitive" stakeholders. Project managers, communication professionals, and program leaders should focus their resources on definitive stakeholders' requests while still assessing them for their relationship to overall program goals. This is not to say that stakeholders not meeting the criteria for "definitive" should be ignored. However, the reality of strategic communication is that in any organizational environment, some stakeholders do matter more than others and require special attention and resources.

In the next section, we examine the concept of diversity as it applies to stakeholders and target audiences in strategic communication programs. We will define and discuss how cultural and co-cultural identification influences how people communicate and respond to strategic communication and advocate for an inclusive approach to message design.

9.2 COMMUNICATING STRATEGICALLY IN A DIVERSE SOCIETY

Key to understanding strategic communication is understanding the diversity inherent in the communities where message design programs are disseminated. Cultural identity is a much-discussed topic because it relates to many aspects of living, but unfortunately, what we know about its specific influences on message design and processing via rigorous research is limited. One thing that is very clear, however, is that the nature of group membership—cultural identification—and communication are inseparable. Anthropologist Edward T. Hall argued that culture is communication, and communication is culture (1959). He explained that how we communicate, what we believe, what we say, what language system we use and respond to, and even the types of media we enjoy are all functions of the cultural groups we are a part of. How we speak, how we listen, how we respond to nonverbal and written messages, how we use time, what foods and smells we enjoy, and how we relate to people in positions of power and authority, are all guided, to some extent, by the culture of our particular society or predominant **in-groups** (smaller groups within society with which people psychologically identify as a result of shared characteristics or interests). Although it can be difficult to apply general tendencies of groups to all people who belong to those groups, these patterns can serve as starting points for our own formative research and informal activities designed to become better acquainted with a campaign's stakeholders and, eventually, build relationships with them.

The United States is a culturally diverse society that values and appreciates differences among people as the basis for a rich and interesting place to live and work. That diversity can make the design and successful dissemination of strategic messages difficult, however. Communicators need to consider the impact of diversity in their choice of language, in their use of evidence, in their selection of organizational structure, logical or emotional appeals, media, and as Dr. Kreps's health research indicates, message sources. In our interpersonal interactions with stakeholders, we need to consider the impact of diversity in how we use eye contact, words and phrases, and rhetorical devices that affect how others perceive us. In every step of a campaign, we need to be sensitive to audience expectations and responses to the message and source that may be related to identity. To ignore or only pay lip service to the impact of difference on how communicators design, package, and disseminate strategic messages is to remain ineffective as a communicator. In this section, we define culture, discuss the vast meanings of culture, and advance an inclusive approach to message design and stakeholder relationships.

9.2.1 What Is Culture?

Culture is a term first introduced by anthropologist Edward B. Tylor in 1871 when he wrote "Culture . . . is that complex whole which includes knowledge, belief, art, law, morals, custom, and any other habits acquired by man [and woman] as a member of society" (1: 1). This broad definition of culture is still applicable today. Key to understanding this concept as it relates to strategic message design and dissemination for particular audiences is the fact that culture and society are two different things. Society is simply a number of people carrying on a common life, the primary features of which might be shared, but that is additionally characterized by great differences. Culture is what people collectively produce and do—the things they value or prefer, the beliefs they share, and the patterns of behavior they tend to follow.

Culture is an inclusive concept that covers different types of groups. **Mainstream culture** in the United States brings a degree of uniformity to the lives of people living in an incredibly diverse society. This basic set of characteristics allows you to predict very basic things about how to best relate to stakeholders in your program. Most people living in the United States, for example, purchase items in supermarkets and retail stores with US currency, watch some form of television, value children, condemn crime, and rely on employment for income. Mainstream culture allows individuals to communicate superficially with one another in relatively predictable ways regardless of birthplace, ancestry, race, or the first or second language spoken.

Co-culture is the second and equally powerful category of culture we must consider. **Co-culture** illustrates the unique, specialized ways of thinking, behaving, and interacting that characterize people in particular racial and ethnic groups, religious organizations, social classes, regions of the country, occupations, and so on. Just a few examples include Latinos, African Americans, the very wealthy, vegetarians, college students involved in Greek life, athletes, gays and lesbians, men, first-year college students, organizational newcomers, members of the military, engineers, scientists, and artists. Distinctive patterns of beliefs, attitudes, and normative behavior set each co-culture apart from others in society.

People typically identify with a number of co-cultures, all of which affect how they think, feel, and behave and consequently respond to strategic messaging. The primacy of the various groups with which people identify is important to keep in mind as you interact with them in the context of a strategic communication program or campaign. For example, an individual might identify himself as an Asian American, a male, a physician, a Catholic, a Democrat interested in social justice issues, a tennis player, and a New Orleans Saints football fan. The amount of influence an individual's affiliation with the mainstream culture or any of these co-cultural groups has on him or her depends on a number of factors. For example, one's gender might not be his or her dominant identity for most interactions, but it may become incredibly important, say, when discussing issues related to workplace family leave policies, economic parity, or equal pay. On the other hand, consider Anne, a Catholic immigration attorney with strong ties to social justice advocacy groups in her community.

Her religious, professional, political and social identities are tightly linked to her passion for social justice for all members of society. This particular co-cultural identification overshadows most of her other group memberships.

Co-cultural diversity in the United States is greater than that of any other nation in history. The opportunities to explore interests, connect with our in-groups, and develop unique identities are rich and numerous. As a result, communication can be challenging. The inherent differences that distinguish people based on their in-group identifications creates the potential for misunderstanding and, often, rejection, of influence messages.

9.2.2 Cultural Inclusion: A Contemporary Approach to Message Design

A traditional approach to public and strategic communication assumes that mainstream cultural values will outweigh those that emanate from the various co-cultures that people identify with. However, this is simply not always the case. For example, the problem that Dr. Kreps's team was confronted with was rooted in this assumption. Previous efforts to reach the African American community were based on the messaging strategies that had worked with other target audiences and segments. The fact that minorities remained underrepresented in vaccine clinical trials suggested that what worked with other groups would not work for all groups. The traditional approach represented one of cultural exclusion or **ethnocentrism** (the tendency to perceive that there is one dominant, best way to go about something). Sullivan (1993) argued that too many communicators—even those in positions of authority and credibility—are uninformed when analyzing the communication patterns and preferences of groups other than their own, and as a result, practice cultural exclusion. Cultural exclusion takes many forms in strategic communication. For instance, producing message materials exclusively in the English language or relying only on social media instead of a media mix that includes traditional channels are examples of cultural exclusiveness. Further, consider the traditional approach to developing educational video or audio messages that involves selecting a "well-spoken," formal authority figure. Although standard white English speakers may evaluate message sources with dialects, accents, or alternative speech patterns as unintelligent, unsuccessful, or lacking in credibility, some groups might find message sources with those characteristics to be more credible, relatable, and influential. Recall the white male university researcher tasked with conducting focus groups of Latino truck drivers. The characteristics that lent the researcher credibility and prestige in many settings were barriers to effectively building a trusting relationship with his focus group participants.

Another example of cultural exclusion in messaging involves the traditional emphasis on using statistics and other forms of objective, or hard, evidence to support a recommended attitude or behavior change. Although this approach is consistent with the decision-making patterns of some co-cultural groups (e.g., males, scientists, European Americans), the use of statistical evidence is less meaningful to some other groups. For instance, many Latinos and African Americans find personal testimony, personal examples, and stories with emotional appeal more compelling. Disregarding these kinds of preferences is ethnocentric and ignores the powerful advantages of adapting messages to their intended audiences.

On the other hand, we advocate a more contemporary approach to strategic message design that reflects cultural inclusion. To be an effective strategic communicator, in designing and implementing programs and relating to stakeholders, be inclusive rather than exclusive. Being aware of the demographic characteristics of your target audience is important, but not enough. You should make every effort to understand the complexity of your target audience's identities, much like Dr. Kreps delved into the research indicating complex interactions of race, gender, and socioeconomic status to learn about his intended audience's preferred message source regarding medical information. Strategic communication professionals must recognize, respect, and try to adapt to how others prefer to send and receive messages. In the Community Liaison Project, researchers recognized that the intended audience would prefer to receive information about HIV/AIDS vaccine research and trials from peers rather than medical professionals. Thus, the team designed a message campaign that relied on trained community members as information sources.

As a final illustration of cultural exclusion and inclusion, consider a consulting experience that the second author of this book had many years ago. Dr. Waldeck had been contracted to assist an organization during a period of downsizing. The client hired her to coach executives on their messaging strategies and to design an "outplacement" program that would support laid-off employees by helping them create or update their résumés and interview skills. When she began her consulting engagement, she realized that part of her job involved doing some "clean-up work" to fix some preexisting problems with the company's messaging strategy. One top-level executive had already met with a group of department managers to break the news of impending layoffs, and his efforts to communicate strategically had not gone well. Negativity was spreading rapidly throughout the company, and top management was losing control of the narrative they had hoped to create.

As she investigated the root cause of the contagious anger and ill-will, Jennifer discovered that the "strategic" message the executive had prepared and delivered had reflected cultural exclusion. You see, the executive was Asian American. He was very uncomfortable, as anyone would be, to have to deliver bad news to a group of loyal employees and friends. But his cultural background amplified the extremely unpleasant nature of this task for him and influenced his message in unfortunate ways. He had spent a lot of time praising them, telling them how valuable they were to the organization, and expressing

Figure 41 Organizational communicators are heavily influence by their cultural affiliations. Strategic organizational communicators are aware of their own, and their audiences', cultural preferences for messaging.

his sorrow at seeing them all go. These predominantly white, American managers were confused and angry: If they were such great, valued employees, why were they the ones being let go? But anyone familiar with the norms of many Asian cultures might recognize that his approach, while kind, was actually ethnocentric and lacking in strategy. Many Asian cultures value sensitivity to others and face-saving (Ting-Toomey 1988). Rather than being honest and straightforward and telling the managers that their productivity had dropped or that they lacked updated essential skills, the executive had worked to assure them that they could leave the company with dignity, honor, and pride. What do you think would have been a more culturally inclusive approach to this downsizing message?. If you were the communication consultant hired by this organization, what advice would you have given the Asian American manager prior to his meeting?

9.2.3 Cultural and Co-Cultural Features That Influence Communication

As we have established in this chapter, the influence of differences (individual or those related to group membership) on how members of a target audience receive a message can be difficult to predict with precision. People are complex, and so are their identities and the ways in which they engage in communication. In the absence of specific research or theoretical frameworks (such as those that were available to the Community Liaison Project team), we have some general research that sheds light on the challenge of establishing communication relationships with campaign stakeholders. As a starting point for making less ethnocentric and more culturally inclusive decisions about strategic messaging, we turn to the research pioneered by social psychologist Geert Hofstede, whose research team has identified six cultural features that make a difference in how people form relationships and process messages. In this section of the chapter, we will explore them and their implications for strategic communication and relationships among stakeholders. Before we do so, though, we want to emphasize three critical points adapted from Waldeck, Kearney, and Plax (2017), who wrote about how culture influences various forms of communication.

1. **First, we must never assume that just because someone belongs to a given co-cultural group, he or she will necessarily exhibit all its characteristics.** The danger associated with the helpful knowledge of group patterns is the very human tendency to stereotype all individuals affiliated with that group. Just because many women, for example, are more likely to appreciate personal stories and other narrative evidence to support a campaign's recommended action does not mean that all women will share this preference. Because there is diversity within groups, we must be open to exceptions and individual variations at all times.

2. **The cultural characteristics researchers have identified are based on limited available data.** Much of the intercultural communication research, including Hofstede's, is designed to look for similarities within and differences between groups. Although this provides some important insights for understanding campaign stakeholders, it also fails to consider all the diversity that persists among members of groups. Further, although Hofstede's work is generally regarded as the most rigorous and credible in this area, it pertains primarily to nations and does not account for the numerous co-cultures within those nations that can influence how people communicate. As a result, the co-cultural characterizations made in this chapter and elsewhere should be viewed as guidelines, not rules, for the decisions we must make in designing strategic messaging programs.

3. **We need to keep in mind our almost inevitable tendency to be ethnocentric.** When examining the unique nature of our audiences and other stakeholders, we need to suspend judgment and instead rely on the principle of **cultural relativity:** We all do things differently. A group's preferred norms are important to understand and incorporate into our communication programs, even if they are different from our own preferred ways of making decisions.

Hofstede's cultural features exist along value continua. No group actually represents the extreme ends of these continua, but a group may prefer one value orientation over its opposite. Many will fall in the middle of the spectrum with no clear orientation to either end. In addition, research conducted over the past thirty-five years indicates that cultural tendencies relative to communication—message encoding and decoding—change over time.

INDIVIDUALISM AND COLLECTIVISM   The first cultural feature that Hofstede identified that affects how people encode and decode messages relates their

Table 9.1   Contrasts in Emphasis between Common Collectivistic and Individualistic Values

Continuum of Values

Collectivistic	Individualistic
Interdependence	Independence
Obligations to others	Individual rights
Rely on group	Self-sufficiency
Adhere to traditional values	True to own values and beliefs
Maintain traditional practices	Continuously improve practices (progress)
Fulfill roles within group	Pursue individual goals/interests
Group achievement	Individual achievement
Competition between groups	Competition between individuals
Group or hierarchical decision making	Self-determination and individual choice
Shame/guilt due to failing group	Shame/guilt due to individual failure
Living with kin	Independent living
Take care of own	Seek help if needed
Property shared within group	Strong individual property rights
Elders transmit knowledge (often oral)	Individuals seek knowledge (often textual)

SOURCE: Black, R.S., K.D. Mrasek, and R. Ballinger. 2003. "Individualistic and Collectivistic Values in Transition Planning for Culturally Diverse Students with Special Needs." *Journal for Vocational Special Needs Education* 25, no. 2/3: 20–29. https://files.eric.ed.gov/fulltext/EJ854903.pdf.

tendencies toward **individualism and collectivism** (2017). A cultural group with an orientation toward individualism places a high value on people who can speak or stand up for themselves and not have to depend on others beyond their immediate family. Hofstede identifies Canada, the United States, Italy, Australia, New Zealand, the United Kingdom, and Germany as the countries with the strongest inclinations to be individualistic. Individualistic people think of themselves as self-reliant and independent of social, organizational, or institutional affiliations. They prize individual drive and achievement, personal property, and the right to their own opinions.

Alternatively, collectivists are part of close-knit, family-like groups who define their identities based on their membership in the group. Collectivists tend to take care of other members of their in-groups, avoid competing with them, and express respect and willingness to cooperate and collaborate. Those countries highest in collectivism include China, Iraq, Greece, and most Latin American nations.

> **Strategic Communication Mentor: Hofstede in His Own Words**
>
> Take a look at this video featuring Geert Hofstede. In it, he discusses individualism and collectivism and helps us understand this continuum of values and how where someone falls may explain their behavior. In it, he gives plenty of examples that will help you identify a communicator's orientation and better understand how to interact with someone based on where they fall on the continuum.
>
> https://www.youtube.com/watch?time_continue=2&v=zQj1VPNPHll

UNCERTAINTY AVOIDANCE   A second cultural feature that can affect how people react to you (and other sources associated with your campaign) and your messages is **uncertainty avoidance** (Hofstede 2017). Uncertainty avoidance refers to how members of a particular group deal with the unknown and unfamiliar. People from groups with high uncertainty avoidance tendencies are typically uncomfortable with ambiguous, unknown situations and unfamiliar information. They like to use and will respond well to others' use of communication strategies that help them reduce their uncertainty and unfamiliarity with a situation or issue. Some countries that score high on Hofstede's uncertainty avoidance scale are Egypt, France, Greece, Israel, Mexico, Japan, and most Asian and Latin American countries.

When designing messages for high uncertainty avoidant stakeholders, you will want to be explicit, precise, and accurate. Rely on simple, clear language and use logical, step-by-step explanations. Provide sufficient facts, figures, and other background information that help the audience determine what to think and how to act based on your message. Avoid leaving anything to their imaginations or assuming they will use anything other than the information you provide when accepting, or not, your recommendations. With these types of stakeholders, be sure to use message sources they will view as highly credible experts or authority figures. Sources of lower status will have to work harder to compel high uncertainty avoidant stakeholders to attend to the message; they will instead experience uncertainty about the source's qualifications to deliver it! Similarly, seek information about the communication channels these audiences prefer, or use a strong media mix to ensure that your channel selection won't be a barrier to attention, comprehension, or retention of campaign messages.

Low uncertainty avoidant communicators are much more comfortable with the unknown and require less explicit, clear messaging. They are, in general, skilled at understanding a lot of a message's meaning by considering the setting or context in which it is delivered. They "read between the lines" to understand information and are willing to accept vague, versus highly specific, information. They like to have the freedom to think about recommendations rather

---

Strategic Communication Mentor: Hofstede in His Own Words

To learn more about uncertainty avoidance, watch this video featuring Geert Hofstede now.

   https://www.youtube.com/watch?v=fZF6LyGne7Q

   How might you go about using formative research techniques suggested in this book to determine the overall uncertainty avoidance tendencies of your audiences? Clearly, this knowledge will provide you with a great deal of insight regarding effective message design and delivery.

---

than being told what to do. They prefer taking risks and exploring options rather than following the advice of authority figures or technical evidence. Indeed, low uncertainty avoidant stakeholders may even take offense at an overly prescriptive message that advocates one particular course of action. They want the freedom to listen, interpret the message, and use it or apply it as they see fit. Recalling a concept from chapter 7, low uncertainty avoidant communicators may be more apt to exhibit psychological reactance tendencies than high uncertainty avoidant audiences when exposed to persuasive messages. In terms of nations, Denmark and most Scandinavian countries, India, the United Kingdom, and the Netherlands are among those documented as being lowest in uncertainty avoidance.

POWER DISTANCE   The third cultural feature identified in Hofstede's research is **power distance,** which refers to how groups distribute power, rank, and status among people. Some groups promote equal status, rank, and power among people; others emphasize status differences and hierarchies. The United States is a clear example of a low power distance culture (others include Austria, Canada, Costa Rica, Ireland, and the Netherlands). We generally value equality. Anyone can speak to virtually anyone about almost in any topic without having to consider a person's power, rank, or status. We can email our elected officials and interact with high-profile people via social media. As low power distance message receivers, we want and often have the opportunity to participate in discussions and want direct access to interact with message sources. Low power distance stakeholders are likely to:

- Appreciate accessible, approachable, and humble message sources.
- Assert themselves by questioning message sources and critically analyzing sources and messages.
- Enjoy the opportunities for interaction provided by social media channels and conversely rate traditional "one-way" message dissemination channels and strategies as less compelling.

Strategic Communication Mentor: Hofstede in His Own Words

Take a look at this video in which Hofstede discusses power distance and how peoples' cultural values about it affect their behaviors and lifestyles.
   https://www.youtube.com/watch?v=DqAJclwfyCw
   Be prepared to discuss, as directed by your instructor, your views on how to address differences in uncertainty avoidance in a strategic message campaign.

However, even within the United States, organizations exist that have very clear "pecking orders." In some businesses, communication is hierarchical and those lower on the ladder have little access to those with the most power. Others are much more egalitarian. Cultural groups differ in terms of what topics are appropriate and which are taboo when speaking with elders or authority figures.

Groups that place a high value on social status, birth order, and occupational or political rankings are referred to as high power distance cultures (e.g., Mexico and most Latin American countries, China and most Asian countries, Iran, Iraq, Kenya, Morocco, and Russia) (Hofstede 2017). In these groups, members have less access to and direct communication with people of high status. People tend to accept the recommendations and decisions of those with high rank without much question or evidence. Can you think of any groups besides nations that exhibit tendencies toward high power distance?

What else does high power distance imply for strategic communication? High power distance receivers are likely to:

- Appreciate message and message source formality.
- Avoid questioning messages and message source.
- Be uncomfortable with the open and egalitarian dialogue of social media channels.

MASCULINE AND FEMININE CULTURES   The fourth cultural feature is the extent to which groups are traditionally more masculine or more feminine in their orientation. ***This continuum does not refer to biological sex***. Both males and females can behave in masculine and feminine ways as they are defined here. **Masculinity** refers to the degree to which a group values and encourages assertiveness—sometimes illustrated as achievement, heroism, success, ambition, and competitiveness. **Femininity,** on the other hand, has to do with a group's preference for nurturance—often defined as friendliness, modesty, affection, compassion, and general social support (Hofstede 2017). You can expect a great deal of variability within any co-cultural group on this dimension. Later in this chapter, we will provide you with some general communication strategies designed to emphasize similarities and closeness (rather than differences and distance) that you can use to build relationships with campaign stakeholders when some of their features are unknown to you.

Note that for many of the cultural dimensions, we can make some generalizations about "most Asian countries" or "most Latin American countries," yet Hofstede's research reveals distinct differences on masculinity and femininity across nation cultures on the same continent or within the same ethnic group. For example, although they are both Middle Eastern countries, Iran is a typically feminine culture, and Iraqis tend to be more masculine in their orientation. Hofstede identified a number of cultures scoring high on masculinity (e.g., Mexico, Austria, China, Japan, Hong Kong, Italy, Iraq, Venezuela, the United States, South Africa, and Kenya). Personal achievement and competitiveness are highly valued in masculine cultures; relational concerns are secondary. Winning is more important than how one plays the game. Ambition is a highly desirable personal quality, as is being a good provider for the family. Thus, in strategic communication situations, we can expect that masculine stakeholders might object to a message or source that they perceive as weak or unassertive. They will appreciate statistical data and expert testimony as credible forms of evidence.

For more masculine-oriented cultures, gender roles are clearly differentiated; males are supposed to be aggressive, and females passive. In masculine cultures, a "can-do" attitude is highly valuable; therefore, masculine audiences tend to react well to positive, encouraging, motivating, and high-energy messages and sources. More feminine audiences might find such an approach overwhelming or too pushy. Masculine speakers might be directive and prescriptive in the recommendations they make to audiences, and masculine audiences will likely appreciate a directive, straightforward, and prescriptive approach to strategic communication.

Feminine-oriented cultures (e.g., Chile, Denmark, the Netherlands, Norway, Costa Rica, and Portugal) de-emphasize strictly held role definitions. Gender roles are more flexible, and equality between the sexes is likely. In feminine cultures, social and personal relationships are highly valued. Feminine communicators seek consensus rather than take a win-lose approach. Thus, in strategic communication contexts, your framework should include opportunities for these stakeholders to provide input and perspective. Feminine audiences and other stakeholders are likely to be put off by a message source that seems insensitive to them or their thoughts and experiences about the issue. Being a good person and showing sympathy and concern for others are culturally valued qualities. We might predict, then, that feminine audiences will appreciate a friendly, gain-framed message and a message source that encourages approachability and arouses their perceptions of similarity and warmth. Feminine audiences prefer logic and evidence that appeals to their feelings and personal experiences, over objective data or statistics. Masculine audiences might find

---

Strategic Communication Mentor: Hofstede in His Own Words

In this video, Geert Hofstede describes the masculinity/femininity continuum and what it means for communicators and their identities. Watch it now and be prepared to discuss ways you might formally and informally assess a target community's preferences for masculine and feminine communication. Why do you think awareness of this characteristic of your audience matters?

https://www.youtube.com/watch?v=Pyr-XKQG2CM

---

this message design approach too informal or unprofessional, and even lacking in credibility.

LONG-TERM ORIENTATION (LTO) AND SHORT-TERM ORIENTATION (STO)   The next cultural feature that can affect strategic communication is **long- and short-term orientation.** This cultural feature helps us understand how people balance their need for a link to the past—tradition and "the way things have always been"—and living in the present while looking toward the future. Understanding this cultural feature can be extremely important in the context of strategic communication programs asking people to make changes that represent a major departure from the status quo.

People with moderate to strong LTO cultural backgrounds (e.g., countries such as China, Japan, and most continental European countries) are dynamic and forward-thinking, but pragmatic at the same time. They value perseverance, service to others, self-sufficiency, goal-setting, education, and financial planning for the future. They are slow, deliberate decision makers and know how to preserve and ration resources so that they last over time. LTO cultures believe the best results come slowly, over time, with sustained efforts; there are no "get rich quick" schemes or paths to overnight success.

In strategic message design situations, our recommendation is to embody the values we just discussed when directing messages toward known LTO stakeholders. In developing message content and style, prioritize those strategies that encourage audiences to think about and plan for the future. LTO stakeholders will exhibit a great deal of vision in their reactions to strategic messages asking for action or change; if they perceive the message as compelling enough, they will be willing and motivated to take risks and get on board even when they still perceive some uncertainty. Structure messages for LTO stakeholders in ways that help them recognize the need for careful preparation and action in pursuing whatever it is you are asking them to do.

Take, for example, Alex, who is representing her nonprofit addiction recovery clinic at the city council's public forum on drug-related crimes in the city.

Alex, taking an LTO approach, created and delivered a message that emphasized a long-term plan to combat drug-related crimes. Her plan included a timeline and a variety of options for encouraging people arrested for drug-related crimes to accept addiction treatment. She emphasized that there was no quick or easy solution and that fixing the drug problem in her city would require planning and investment on the part of city leaders. LTO stakeholders appreciated the kind of thinking Alex exhibited in her message delivered to the city council. If they find that a message is too focused on something that already occurred and not forward-oriented, they will either question it or stop listening. For instance, even though Alex was generally long-term oriented with her message, her introduction included a lengthy list of the negative ways the city had been affected by drugs. At that point, LTO listeners interrupted to say, "OK, we know all that—but what are we going to do about it?" She then realized she needed to stick to her forward-thinking plan.

Short-term orientation (STO) stakeholders, on the other hand, prefer to follow time-honored traditions and look to the past for solutions to present problems. They view change with a degree of skepticism. Some short-term orientation national cultures include the United States, Australia, Morocco (and most African countries), Israel, Mexico, Denmark (and most northern European countries), Jordan (and most Middle Eastern countries), Peru, and Venezuela (and most South American countries). These cultures emphasize stability, religious faith, family obligations, national pride, living up to others' expectations, and showing pride in one's family (especially of one's children). How should the short-term orientation cultural approach influence message design? Sources, messages, evidence, and organizational structures should emphasize the values of obligation and stability.

STO stakeholders will appreciate messages and sources that resonate with them through personal stories and emotional appeals. The human resources director of a small family-owned retail business, for instance, created a presentation and related materials to strategically inform the staff about the family medical leave act as it applied to their company with the goal of influencing employees to have positive feelings about the policy. The company pays staff their full salary and benefits for any amount of documented time they need to take to care for family. In her presentation, instead of focusing on the facts and procedures associated with the policy, the director gave dramatic examples of past employees with sick family members who needed care and explained how these narratives served as the genesis for the owners' decision to be fully supportive of employees with similar needs. She designed lunchroom posters and other documentation about the policy that repeated the emotional foundation for the company's policies in visual and written formats. Her overriding message was, "When you have a crisis, family comes first."

STO audiences will be alienated by messages that seem to disrespect the past or any of the values associated with the short-term orientation. Of course, in this example, STO employees responded very well to the campaign.

> **Strategic Communication Mentor: Hofstede in His Own Words**
>
> To learn more about the long-term/short-term orientation continuum, watch this video. In it, Geert Hofstede gives plenty of examples of each orientation and explains how to determine how people might fall on this continuum.
>   https://www.youtube.com/watch?v=H8ygYlGslQ4

Elsewhere, employers would afford them the time, as required by law, but not necessarily maintain their full salary and benefits. A presentation and visual messages about the policy in one of those companies might emphasize very different points than this particular campaign and be quite off-putting to the STO audience that is connected in deep ways to tradition and family values. Because an audience is likely to be diverse on this particular dimension, you will want to develop messages that appeal to both LTO and STO stakeholders. The human resources director in our example probably found her approach to be ineffective with a number of employees who found it overly emotional and lacking in logic, facts, or sound reasoning.

INDULGENCE AND RESTRAINT   The last documented cultural feature that makes a difference in terms of strategic communication and influencing stakeholders in positive ways has to do with how those people perceive relaxation, fun, enjoyment, and freely fulfilling their needs in these areas (Hofstede 2017). In an **indulgent** culture, people feel free to do what they want to do—to be impulsive, spend time with friends, spend money on themselves, and enjoy life. In indulgent cultures, the assumption is that "life is good and should be enjoyed." Hofstede has identified some of the more indulgent countries, and they include the United States, Canada, Mexico, Ireland and the United Kingdom, most of South America, South Africa, New Zealand, Sweden, and Denmark. Within the United States, can you think of any co-cultures you are familiar with that might exhibit more indulgent tendencies?

In designing strategic messaging programs aimed at more culturally indulgent audiences, you should emphasize the benefits of the message's recommendations for the stakeholders. More indulgent stakeholders are motivated to do something or accept new information based on the ability of the recommended courses of action to help them feel or look good and to facilitate their goal of having a good life. Indulgent audiences are typically willing to take risks and can be easily discouraged from thinking too much about the consequences of their actions. "Just do it!" messages resonate well with them. They appreciate positivity, enthusiasm, and messages with a "can-do" approach that says, "you can do this, and here's how." They can be bored with messages that emphasize restraint, careful planning, or duty.

Strategic Communication Mentor: Hofstede in His Own Words

To learn more about the indulgence/restraint continuum, watch this video featuring Geert Hofstede.

    https://www.youtube.com/watch?v=V0YgGdzmFtA

On the other end of this continuum, we have **restraint.** Restrained people emphasize duty to work, family, and society over self-gratification. They place little emphasis on leisure time, self-fulfillment, or personal development. Restrained cultures include Germany (and most of continental Europe, although some countries, such as France, score more moderately and lean toward indulgence), China (and most of Asia), India, Vietnam, and Lebanon (and most of the Middle East with some countries such as Saudi Arabia scoring more moderately) (Hofstede 2017). In these cultures, people feel shame associated with having too much fun or focusing too much on themselves. They believe in following the rules, working hard, and living cautiously as opposed to doing risky things.

Strategic messages and their sources should emphasize a message of moderation or modesty. Their messages and approach will emphasize their values of "self last" and "work before fun." Restrained stakeholders don't require as much approachability or enthusiasm from message sources as indulgent ones. The second author of this book has facilitated training sessions in organizations with highly restrained orientation (due to corporate culture, national origin, or a combination of both) and found participants to be highly uncomfortable with things like icebreakers, games, or forced participation. Restrained stakeholders are likely to reject, or at least be skeptical of, messages that encourage them to take risks, spend money or time on themselves, enjoy life or work more, or simply have fun.

Again, we want to emphasize that these research findings offer strategic communicators some general guidelines and some considerations that go beyond obvious stakeholder demographic characteristics. This research was designed to explain differences associated across nations but can be interpreted and applied to other kinds of group memberships with caution. Also remember, you will rarely, if ever, find yourself creating message programs for an audience made up of only, say, individualistic or masculine or restrained people. The mix of stakeholders associated with a campaign requires you to consider some of the more nuanced and complex values and preferences of a wide and diverse group of people. You will want to consider the full spectrum of each cultural dimension and rely on a variety of message strategies, sources, and media to appeal to a diverse set of stakeholders.

9.3 STRATEGIES FOR STRENGTHENING STAKEHOLDER RELATIONSHIPS AND ENHANCING MESSAGE EFFECTIVENESS

In our experience, although stakeholder assessment data and cultural awareness are critically important to a campaign's success, the communication competence of campaign staff is often the key factor in building successful partnerships and having lasting influence. In this section, we will overview the strategies communication research suggests will help you develop rapport and build relationships with your stakeholders, regardless of differences.

9.3.1 Use Appropriate Theory and Research as Your Guide

We opened this chapter with the story of the Community Liaison Project and have made references to it several times throughout the chapter. But have you noticed that we have left you hanging? We indicated that a number of research studies and theoretical frameworks led Kreps and his colleagues to conclude that African Americans and other minorities were reluctant to participate in the vaccine trials because they didn't trust traditional message sources, like doctors and other medical practitioners, but instead preferred to receive information from people with whom they felt greater similarity. So, how did the campaign team solve this problem? Guided by theory and research, they developed an innovative community participatory approach, where trusted members of minority communities were trained by the researchers and became actively involved in disseminating HIV/AIDS information within their personal social networks. The community liaisons then, in turn, encouraged members of those social networks to also disseminate the information to others, creating a snowball effect whereby accurate information encouraging message receivers to further explore HIV-vaccine trials was spread by trusted sources. Further, the original set of community liaisons collected feedback about the messages and information about preferred channels and media (e.g., interpersonal, print, social media) directly from the target audience. They also were able to obtain feedback about the cultural appropriateness of printed materials for revision and further circulation. Over the course of the project, the research team implemented various assessments of the effectiveness of their messaging strategies. They concluded that loss-framed messages would be most effective when used with the target audience on print messages, and that gain-framed messages would be most effective when disseminated through interpersonal communication. Further, the team found evidence of a significant increase in HIV awareness and community members' willingness to spread the positive HIV-vaccine message further into their social networks.

None of this would have been possible without the research- and theoretically based framework that the message design team employed. The positive outcomes of the message design used by the Community Liaison Project illustrate the reflexivity of theory and action, and how empirical research and theoretical frameworks can be applied to solve real-world problems through better communication. The true lesson here is that sometimes, research and theory offer strategic communication professionals sound answers to their most perplexing questions about how to build strong relationships with stakeholders that will result in desired program outcomes. With or without such a framework, interpersonal communication competence will be helpful. We now turn to an exploration of some fundamental skills you will want to be sure to exhibit in your interactions with campaign stakeholders.

9.3.2 Communication Skills Can Make a Difference

Interpersonal communication is a special form of transactional human communication that we use to influence and manage our relationships with others (Beebe, Beebe, and Redmond 2014). Being able to effectively relate to your stakeholders is vital to the success of any campaign or strategic communication program. The primary skills you will want to become proficient in are listening skills and rapport-building skills (Beebe 2016). These communication skills will enhance your ability to reach audience members and develop important, influential relationships with funding agencies, donors, contractors working on your project or providing goods and services, and other members of your organization and community.

   Listening skills. In terms of listening skills, you may be familiar with the communication literature that suggests you should *look* like a good, active listener. Nonverbal behaviors such as nodding, making eye contact, leaning forward, taking notes, and maintaining an open body position all contribute to others' perception that you value what they have to say. More recent research, however (Bodie et al. 2015), indicates that verbal listening behaviors may be even more important as you seek to build relationships with your campaign stakeholders. Specifically, Bodie and colleagues found that verbal behaviors such as asking questions and paraphrasing signal greater sensitivity to another than less active, silent behaviors. To illustrate, your authors have found that in facilitating focus groups for formative research purposes, verbal interjections and confirmation are highly effective in making participants feel comfortable and eliciting high quality data from them. Similarly, when meeting with campaign funders or consulting clients, we prioritize listening over speaking but view these interactions as interactive conversations that require verbal responsiveness.

   In communicating with audiences, clients, your boss, and other stakeholders, you will also want to develop an awareness of their **listening styles,** or patterned ways they process what they hear (Bodie and Worthington 2011). Learning a particular person's listening style takes time, but you can accomplish this by being observant of their own communication styles (both verbal and nonverbal) and attentive to the types of questions they ask. In terms of broad campaign audiences, you should remember that all of the listening styles are probably represented (but the demographics of your audience might suggest a predominant style). Being able to adapt to others' listening styles is critically helpful when you perceive differences that could pose barriers to relationship-building and influence.

Relational listeners focus on emotions and feelings. They are highly empathic and place an emphasis on relationships. You will be well served to adapt your own style and the messages associated with your campaign to reflect an interest in feelings, emotions, and relationships when dealing with these stakeholders. Communicating with relational listeners and designing campaign messages aimed at them can be very difficult for communicators who lean toward one of the other three listening styles. **Analytical listeners** tend to suspend judgment and listen to all sides of an issue. They like to gather all the information they can before they determine the validity of the message. Consider the needs of analytical listeners as you design and present messages, which will include details, a multidimensional message that represents all "sides" of the issue, and expert analysis of these dimensions. Analytical listeners object to one-sided advocacy messages.

Task-oriented listeners are preoccupied with action. They prefer brief, clear, and efficient messages. If they perceive the message and source as credible, they will want specific recommendations and action steps. Beebe (2016) recommends using precise verbs, task lists, and logical step-by-step illustrations of what you want critical listeners to do in response to your messages. For example, in a program designed to enhance the virtual teamwork skills of US government employees, a consulting team quickly learned that the target audience was largely made up of task-oriented listeners. They were overwhelmed with work responsibilities and ongoing training requirements and just wanted the "nitty gritty" without a lot of background. They responded well to bullet points and precise, "do this, not that" messages; they disregarded lengthy messages that provided rationale or what they perceived to be unnecessary background.

Finally, **critical listeners** share some similarities with analytical listeners. They appreciate a lot of evidence and data as support for campaign recommendations, but rather than wanting a multifaceted message that they evaluate themselves, they prefer that the message simply advocate a position and offer sufficient evidence for that position. Critical listeners are highly observant; they watch for inaccuracies or inconsistencies between information they are provided and what they already know or believe to be true and will use these as justification to reject campaign messages. In the same project on team communication that we just mentioned, the lead consultant was taken aback by critical email messages from a manager within the government agency who was responsible for reviewing message content. A quick internet search of this person's name revealed that he had obtained a degree in communication over twenty years ago. Therefore, some of the current research that the message design team had included in the program was "new news" for this obviously critical listener who questioned why some content (that the consulting team considered outdated) wasn't included in the program. Critical listeners can be difficult to work with because they require additional resources (and a highly sensitive and adept interpersonal approach) to convince them to consider alternative perspectives or updated information.

There is no single best listening style. What is important in terms of building stakeholder relationships is an awareness of your own and the ability to detect cues that reveal others' listening styles—and then being flexible in your orientation. This will enable you to address your stakeholders' needs, demonstrate their value to you and the project, build positive relationships with your audience, and build support and buy-in for the campaign's overall goals. In the example of the client with the critical listening style, the team worked hard to show him the evidence supporting some of the new approaches to team communication that had largely replaced some of the outdated frameworks he was familiar with (and insisted should be included in the program). Importantly, they adopted an approach that honored his expertise and emphasized collaboration rather than a "one-up/one-down" relationship that prioritized the consulting team's expertise. In other words, they avoided communicating with this person in ways what would make him (and his ego) feel threatened.

Rapport-building skills. Your technical ability to design messages or use media effectively is strengthened by your interpersonal skills, such as listening, and your ability to build rapport with all stakeholders involved in your campaign. Rapport is the "ability to develop a positive relationship between two or more people that results in liking and mutual positive feelings" (Beebe 2016, 132). The second author of your text, Jennifer Waldeck, has worked with a project team over the years headed by an experienced leadership development expert named Bob Ross. Bob's consulting firm is particularly known for its work with local and state policing agencies. Interestingly, Bob has never worked in policing or as a police officer, yet he has established strong credibility and developed positive relationships in this tight-knit culture that tends to mistrust outsiders. Working alongside Bob, Jennifer has learned many lessons about the importance of rapport-building in strategic messaging work. He has an outstanding ability to win friends and influence people with his expertise, caring nature, and affable, outgoing personality. Well known among police departments in several midwestern states, you would have difficulty finding anyone who didn't like Bob. Not only is his ability to develop good relationships important to his ability to get business and secure resources for his programs, it also makes him a highly effective communicator with the target audience for his training programs and leadership development programs.

Two communication strategies for building rapport include using verbal and nonverbal immediacy (Andersen and Andersen 1979; Gorham 1988) and affinity-seeking (Bell and Daly 1984; Frymier 1994; Frymier and Thompson 1992; McCroskey and McCroskey 1986). **Immediacy** is the perception of physical and psychological closeness between communicators. The documented effectiveness of immediacy behaviors is based on the simple premise that people are drawn toward what they like and that they avoid or move away from things they dislike. The question then becomes, how do we create conditions that promote liking and approach rather than dislike and avoidance? Communication researchers Janis and Peter Andersen (Andersen and Andersen 1979) theorized that immediacy communication may help explain why people approach or avoid other people and engage with or resist certain issues and topics. A great deal of subsequent research has shown that receiver perceptions of immediacy predict an array of positive outcomes including perceived source credibility and receiver compliance with requests and persuasive messages. The Andersens' early work yielded a number of nonverbal behaviors that enhance connection between communicators and encourage receivers to approach messages and message sources. The strategies most relevant to strategic message design include:

- Using vocal variety (nonmonotone speaking voice)
- Smiling
- Maintaining a relaxed body posture
- Making eye contact
- Gesturing while speaking
- Communicating using appropriate social distance with as few barriers as possible (e.g., desk, podium)
- Professional but not overly formal dress and attire, or dressing to enhance perceptions of approachability and similarity

Later, researcher Joan Gorham explored verbal behaviors aimed at the same objective of building closeness among message sources and receivers. Her findings yielded the following inventory of communication behaviors you should incorporate into your practices:

- Including brief and appropriate personal disclosures in verbal messages
- Using stakeholders' first names when possible
- Asking stakeholders for feedback and reactions to campaign goals, processes, and messages
- Using small talk when possible to build rapport

Of course, these verbal and nonverbal behaviors are germane to face-to-face communication, which may not always be the preferred channel for strategic communication. Waldeck, Kearney, and Plax (2001) identified mediated message strategies that stimulate receiver perceptions of immediacy and close-ness. We have adapted some of those for the strategic communication context:

- Maintaining frequent contact (e.g., mail, email, or social media posts)
- Personalizing mediated messages by incorporating the receiver name or other personal details
- Signing off with the source's first name
- Using humor as appropriate for the setting
- Being responsive to communication from target audience (e.g., answering direct messages and comments on social media platforms, returning phone calls, and responding to email in a timely fashion)
- Seek to contain and manage stakeholder concerns, complaints, and dissatis-faction as soon as you become aware of them through direct and personal-ized communication

Immediacy is an incredibly powerful communication behavior that results in a very long list of positive outcomes. When your goal is to build positive rela-tionships with communication campaign stakeholders—clients, partners, and audiences—you can only benefit from the competent use of these behaviors. You might not feel comfortable with all of them, but you are most likely already good at some. Use them whenever you can, and choose others from the list to try with friends and family in order to build your skills in this area.

A final set of interpersonal communication behaviors that facilitate positive relationships involves strategies that seek others' **affinity,** or liking, for you and your message. In interacting with our clients, focus group participants, volun-teers, and other stakeholders, we have found these strategies to be particularly helpful (Bell and Daly 1984; Frymier 1994; Frymier and Thompson 1992; McCroskey and McCroskey 1986):

- **Encourage enjoyment.** For example, when we facilitate focus groups to pilot test messages, we tell participants we want them to have fun and enjoy themselves while talking to us about issues that are important to them. You can encourage enjoyment in these and other settings involving stakeholders by telling appropriate stories, using humor that is appropriate for the set-ting, and generally establishing a comfortable and relaxed environment (Beebe 2016).
- **Practice dynamism.** In all of your stakeholder interactions, be active and enthusiastic. Remember, if you seem bored by the project or its initiatives, your client or manager and target audience will be, too.
- **Keep conversational rules.** Don't interrupt, change the topic abruptly, dominate conversation, or allow others to do so in settings where you have facilitation or leadership responsibilities.
- **Be comfortable.** Do everything you can to communicate to those around you that you are at ease and comfortable. Practice small talk so that you are

confident in easily engaging other professionals and project stakeholders in socially graceful ways. Avoid nonverbal behaviors that "leak" your discomfort, such as looking at or using your phone, leaning back when the other person is leaning forward, or crossing your arms.

- **Assume equality.** Present yourself as a credible equal rather than a superior expert. Be a good listener, be concerned and caring, and establish closeness through your communication rather than distance. Of course, be mindful not to detract from your credibility as you seek to build equality with your stakeholders.

9.4 TYING IT ALL TOGETHER: BUILDING AND SUSTAINING STAKEHOLDER RELATIONSHIPS THAT CONTRIBUTE TO MESSAGE EFFECTIVENESS

Your ability to communicate ethically with campaign stakeholders in both culturally and interpersonally sensitive ways will help you overcome challenges and inevitable conflicts and misunderstandings with finesse for the benefit of the project. For example, when researcher Gary Kreps, whom you met in the introduction to this chapter, achieved a true understanding of his audience, his messaging program ultimately achieved greater success from the perspective of all stakeholders, including his funding agency and other people and organizations interested in the problem of HIV in the African American community. Although we cannot provide you with empirical evidence, we can, as a result of our personal relationship with this particular researcher, tell you that he is also an extremely skilled interpersonal communicator who excels at rapport, immediacy, and affinity building—attributes that no doubt contribute to his strategic communication success. This chapter has introduced you to a wide range of skills and strategies (such as those Dr. Kreps employed in his project) for building and maintaining positive relationships what will enable you and your team to sustain a long-term program or campaign that has the buy-in and support of key stakeholders.

CHAPTER 9 REVIEW

Questions for Critical Thinking and Discussion

1. Summarize briefly three to five lessons learned from the Community Liaison Project summarized in this chapter that you could apply in other projects for building relationships that lead to project success.

2. What are three to five formal techniques you could use to measure and assess group identity among your target audience in designing a campaign?

3. If you don't have the resources or opportunity to formally measure some of the aspects of group

identity discussed in this chapter as potential impacts on how audiences receive campaign messages, what informal strategies could you use?

4. In the absence of any formative evaluation to help you, what interpersonal communication strategies will help you build culturally sensitive, productive relationships with your stakeholders?

5. Briefly discuss what you learned in this chapter about how to prioritize stakeholders and their needs. What strategies will you use to maintain the integrity of your campaign without alienating or offending stakeholders?

Key Terms

affinity-seeking: the purposeful use of communication strategies researchers have found to generate liking for message sources and their messages.

analytical listening style: a patterned way of hearing messages in which receivers tend to suspend judgment and listen to all sides of an issue.

co-culture: the unique, specialized ways of thinking, behaving, and interacting that characterize people in particular racial and ethnic groups, religious organizations, social classes, regions of the country, occupations, and so on.

cultural relativity: the view that people and groups all do things differently, and that there is no best or singular way to go about something; the opposite of the construct of ethnocentrism.

culture: what a group of people collectively produce and do—the things they value or prefer, the beliefs they share, and the patterns of behavior they tend to follow.

ethnocentrism: the tendency to perceive that there is one dominant, best way to go about something; the opposite of the construct of cultural relativity.

immediacy: the perception of physical and psychological closeness between communicators.

individualism-collectivism continuum: a range of cultural orientations theorized by Geert Hofstede that at the individualistic extreme illustrates people who value speaking or standing up for themselves and avoiding dependence on others beyond their immediate family. At the collectivistic end are people who define their identities based on their membership in a primary in-group and who tend to take care of other members of their in-groups, avoid competing with them, and express respect and willingness to cooperate and collaborate.

indulgence-restraint continuum: a range of cultural orientations theorized by Geert Hofstede that refers to the extent to which members of a cultural group value relaxation, fun, enjoyment, and freely fulfilling their needs in these areas.

interpersonal communication: a unique form of transactional human communication that people use to enact influence within and generally manage their personal one-on-one relationships with others.

listening styles: patterned ways that communicators process what they hear.

long-, short-term orientation continuum: a range of cultural orientations theorized by Geert Hofstede that refers to how members of a cultural group balance their need for a link to the past—tradition and "the way things have always been"—and living in the present while looking toward the future.

mainstream culture: an overarching set of norms for thinking, behaving, and interacting that brings a degree of uniformity to a diverse society.

masculinity-femininity continuum: a range of cultural orientations theorized by Geert Hofstede that refers to the extent to which a group values more stereotypically masculine behaviors (e.g., assertiveness) or stereotypically feminine behaviors (e.g., nurturance) regardless of individual members' biological sex.

power distance continuum: a range of cultural orientations theorized by Geert Hofstede that refers to how groups distribute power, rank, and status among people.

relational listening style: a patterned way of hearing messages in which receivers focus on relationships, emotions, and feelings and respond with empathy.

salient audience characteristics: distinguishing features of a message receiver (or group of receivers) that emerge as most influential on a source's communication behavior.

task-oriented listening style: a patterned way of hearing messages in which receivers are typically concerned with acting and show a preference for highly credible message sources; brief, clear, and efficient messages; specific recommendations; and action steps.

uncertainty avoidance continuum: a range of cultural orientations theorized by Geert Hofstede that refers to how members of a particular group deal with the unknown and unfamiliar.

Further Readings and Resources

Beebe, S. A., and J. T. Masterson. 2015. *Communicating in Small Groups: Principles and Practices.* Boston: Pearson.

Gibb, J. R. 1961. "Defensive Communication." *Journal of Communication* 11: 141–48.

Hawkins, K. W., and B. P. Fillion. 1999. "Perceived Communication Skill Needs for Work Groups." *Communication Research Reports* 14: 59–71.

Hofstede, G., G. J. Hofstede, and M. Minkov. 2010. *Cultures and Organizations: Software of the Mind.* New York: McGraw-Hill.

Samovar, L. A., R. E. Porter, E. R. McDaniel, and C. S. Roy. 2017. *Communication between Cultures.* 9th ed. Boston: Cengage.

Toogood, G. N. 2010. *The New Articulate Executive: Look, Act, and Sound Like a Leader.* New York: McGraw-Hill.

References

Andersen, J. F. and P. A. Andersen. 1979. "The Measurement of Nonverbal Immediacy." *Journal of Applied Communication Research* 7, no. 2: 153–80.

Armstrong, K., K. L. Ravenell, S. McMurphy, and M. Putt. 2007. "Racial/Ethnic Differences in Physician Distrust in the United States." *American Journal of Public Health* 97, no. 7: 1283–89.

Beebe, S. A. 2016. "Communication Skills for Consulting Excellence." In *Consulting That Matters: A Handbook for Scholars and Practitioners,* edited by J. H. Waldeck and D. R. Seibold, 127–46. New York: Peter Lang.

Beebe, S. A., S. J. Beebe, and M. V. Redmond. 2014. *Interpersonal Communication: Relating to Others.* Boston: Pearson.

Bell, R. A., and J. A. Daly. 1984. "The Affinity-Seeking Function of Communication." *Communication Monographs* 51, no. 2: 91–115.

Bodie, G. D., A. J. Vickery, K. Cannava, and S. M. Jones. 2015. "The Role of 'Active Listening' in Informal Helping Conversations: Impact on Perceptions of Listener Helpfulness, Sensitivity, Supportiveness, and Discloser Emotional Improvement." *Western Journal of Communication* 79, no. 2: 151–73.

Bodie, G. D., and D. L. Worthington. 2010. "Revisiting the Listening Styles Profile (LSR-16): A Confirmatory Factor Analytic Approach to Scale Validation and Reliability Estimation." *International Journal of Listening* 24, no. 2: 69–88.

Centers for Disease Control and Prevention. 2016. "HIV Surveillance Report." www.cdc.gov/hiv/statistics/overview/index.html.

Diez-Roux, A. V. 2001. "Investigating Neighborhood and Area Effects on Health." *American Journal of Public Health* 91, no. 11: 1783–89.

Frew, P. M., S. I. Hou, M. Davis, K. Chan, T. Horton, J. Shuster, B. Hixson, and C. del Rio. 2010. "The Likelihood of Participation in Clinical Trials Can Be Measured: The Clinical Research Involvement Scales." *Journal of Clinical Epidemiology* 63, no. 10: 1110–17.

Frooman, J. 1999. "Stakeholder Influence Strategies." *Academy of Management Review* 24, no. : 191–205.

Frymier, A. B. 1994. "The Use of Affinity-Seeking in Producing Liking and Learning in the Classroom." *Journal of Applied Communication Research* 22, no. 2: 87–105.

Frymier, A. B., and C. A. Thompson. 1992. "Perceived Teacher Affinity-Seeking in Relation to Perceived Teacher Credibility." *Communication Education* 41, no. 4: 388–99.

Gorham, J. 1988. "The Relationship between Verbal Teacher Immediacy Behaviors and Student Learning." *Communication Education* 37, no. 1: 40–53.

Hall, Edward T. 1959. *The Silent Language.* Garden City, NY: Doubleday.

Hofstede, G. 2017. "National Culture: Dimensions of National Culture." https://geert-hofstede.com/national-culture.

Jacobs, E. A., I. Rolle, C. E. Ferrans, E. E. Whitaker, and R. B. Warnecke. 2006. "Understanding African Americans' View of the Trustworthiness of Physicians." *Journal of General Internal Medicine* 21, no. 6: 642–47.

Kreps, G. L. 2016. "Consulting in the Healthcare Context: A Case Study of the Community Liaison Project." In *Consulting That Matters: A Handbook for Scholars and Practitioners,* edited by J. H. Waldeck and D. R. Seibold, 279–86. New York: Peter Lang.

Kreps, G. L., and L. Sparks. 2008. "Meeting the Health Literacy Needs of Vulnerable Populations." *Patient Education and Counseling* 71, no. 3: 328–32.

Lewis, L. K. 2007. "An Organizational Stakeholder Model of Change Implementation Communication." *Communication Theory* 17, no. 2: 176–204.

McCroskey, J. C., and L. L. McCroskey. 1986. "The Affinity-Seeking of Classroom Teachers." *Communication Research Reports* 3: 158–67.

Mitchell, R., B. Agle, and D. Wood. 1997. "Toward a Theory of Stakeholder Identification and Salience: Defining the Principle of Who and What Really Counts." *Academy of Management Review* 22, no. 4: 853–56.

Sullivan, P. A. 1993. "Signification and African American Rhetoric: A Case Study of Jesse Jackson's 'Common Ground and Common Sense' Speech." *Communication Quarterly* 41, no. 1: 1–15.

Ting-Toomey, S. 1988. "Intercultural Conflict Styles: A Face Negotiation Theory." In *Theories of Intercultural Communication,* edited by Y. Y. Kim and W. B. Gudykunst, 213–35. Newbury Park, CA: Sage.

Tylor, E. B. 1871. *Primitive Culture.* 2 vols. London: John Murray.

Waldeck, J. H. 2008. "The Development of an Industry-Specific Online Learning Center: Consulting Lessons Learned." *Communication Education* 57, no. 4: 452–63.

Waldeck, J. H., P. Kearney, and T. G. Plax. 2001. "Teacher Email Message Strategies and Students' Willingness to Communicate Online." *Journal of Applied Communication Research* 29, no. 1: 54–70.

———. 2017. *Public Speaking in a Diverse Society.* 5th ed. Dubuque, IA: Kendall Hunt.

Implementing Campaigns

CHAPTER CONTENTS

10.1 The Importance of a Detailed and Organized Plan for Implementation 292

10.2 How Should I Prepare, Enact, and Monitor an Implementation Plan? 295

    10.2.1 Principle 1: Clarify Purpose and Objectives 295

    10.2.2 Principle 2: Rely on the Strategic Plan to Translate Objectives into Action Steps 298

    10.2.3 Principle 3: Audit, Mobilize, and Manage Resources 300

    10.2.4 Principle 4: Assign Responsibility for Implementing Campaign Activities 303

    10.2.5 Principle 5: Be Prepared for Contingencies 305

    10.2.6 Principle 6: Pause, Reflect, Evaluate: Constantly Monitor Performance and Results and Revise Plan as Necessary 306

    10.2.7 Principle 7: Push for Commitment: Ensure Campaign Sustainability 308

    10.2.8 Principle 8: Demonstrate Team Communication Competence at All Times 309

10.3 Tying It All Together: Implementing Communication Campaigns and Programs 312

LEARNING OBJECTIVES

After reading this chapter, you should be able to do the following:

- ► Explain the importance of an effectively organized and managed program implementation plan.
- ► Create a team-oriented program management plan for internal and external strategic communication campaigns that reflects a list of important principles for campaign implementation.
- ► Apply message dissemination and related deliverables to strategic objectives.
- ► Analyze campaign strategy based on process evaluation results.
- ► Evaluate in-person and virtual team communication to ensure that key staff stay focused on assigned tasks.
- ► Analyze campaigns for sustainability, message strategy effectiveness, and their ability to attain objectives within the parameters of the project timeline and budget.

Maria is a program manager for a state-funded organization focused on enhancing health outcomes for children and families through nutrition literacy. More specifically, Maria's job is focused on training health professionals to educate and motivate their clients and patients to make healthy eating choices in their daily lives. She is preparing to implement a yearlong multimedia health communication campaign aimed at health practitioners that includes social media posts, a YouTube channel, an app, podcast, email blasts, and several print resources such as a grocery list "prescription pad" that professionals can use to help their patients plan shopping trips and meals. One aspect of the campaign that Maria is especially invested in is a quarterly newsletter designed to "translate" the most current nutrition research into actionable suggestions for talking to patients and clients about making sound dietary choices. She came up with the idea based on health professionals' responses to a needs assessment survey. Time and time again, health professionals reported that they don't have time to read all of the nutrition research journals, but that they value giving evidence-based advice. They want materials that summarize the research in an easy-to-read, quick manner, and that give them ideas for sharing that knowledge with clients. Maria's newsletter, called "Bites: Current Nutrition Trends for Health Professionals," was designed to meet these expressed needs. The first issue of her publication was scheduled to launch soon. Her boss told her she had four issues, or one year, to make the idea work. She couldn't afford to wait until after the fourth issue to determine whether the newsletter was effective; she needed a plan for monitoring how it was being used and evaluated by its target audience after each pilot issue or risk cancellation of the program. She had a small team of researchers, writers, and designers assigned to her campaign, and one of her first tasks was to make sure these valuable resources were given the tools they needed to help her pet project succeed. Although Maria and her organization had a lot of experience using social media for disseminating information, this type of newsletter was uncharted territory. Maria was under a lot of pressure but knew that with a sound and organized plan, her campaign would go well, and the newsletter would fit in with the other communication pieces she planned to use to help her achieve her information dissemination objectives.

Like many of the communication professionals we have met in previous chapters, Maria has a great deal of responsibility. Not only does she have a complex program to manage, she also has the weight of a very important intended outcome on her shoulders—helping children and families achieve better health through better eating. Strategic communication and communication campaigns are not designed and implemented simply to give program managers something to do; they are intended to help achieve important organizational objectives that often have substantial social, cultural, economic, and educational benefits within society. In addition, effective strategic communication requires a significant organizational investment of a wide range of resources.

Thus, a sound implementation plan is critical to ensuring that a campaign meets its objectives within the time frame and budget specified.

In this chapter, you will learn the vital importance of attention to detail and pristine organization as the foundation for accomplishing your objectives when implementing a strategic communication program or campaign. We will provide you with a series of principles central to implementing a strategic communication campaign and disseminating messages and assessing and revising programs as they occur. In addition, this chapter will offer you a brief primer on effective virtual and in-person team communication that supports desired campaign outcomes. Campaigns are rarely the work of one person, and the process of implementing, monitoring, evaluating, and fine tuning programmatic strategic messaging requires that groups of people function and communicate as unified teams. Finally, because strategic, persuasive communication most often occurs in stages and over a protracted period of time, you will need to be mindful of your program's overall sustainability. Thus, this chapter will expose you to important considerations relative to keeping your audience and key personnel motivated and ensuring resource availability over time.

To make this chapter consumable and relevant to you as a prospective communication professional, we have organized the material around a number of real-life examples. The projects and campaigns we describe are good illustrations of how campaigns are implemented in practice after careful conceptualization; they are case studies of what goes wrong and what goes right, and how an implementation plan can help a program succeed. We use these examples to demonstrate the basic principles for preparing, using, and evaluating an implementation plan.

10.1 THE IMPORTANCE OF A DETAILED AND ORGANIZED PLAN FOR IMPLEMENTATION

There are many factors to consider in the period between designing your strategic communication program and implementing the campaign. Once the campaign launches, you will need to reserve your time, energy, and other resources for monitoring outcomes, making alterations to the plan as needed, managing obstacles and challenges (or even crises), and providing team leadership. Before you activate a communication campaign, the action steps for doing so, along with a plan for dealing with any reasonably predictable challenges or obstacles, should be clearly spelled out in specific detail. By their very nature, strategic communication programs, such as the one Maria in the introduction to this chapter is involved in, require strategy—and cannot be executed randomly or arbitrarily. A sound implementation plan is specific and complete in the way it addresses the project's context timeline, financial and staffing requirements, additional required resources, assignments and responsibilities, people and task management, and possible **contingencies** (reasonably predictable, but uncertain, events or circumstances that could require alterations to your plan). Once your campaign launches, there will be no time for planning "on the fly." Unexpected events will quickly become crises without some forethought and strategy. The details of implementing your planned strategy must be carefully thought out and detailed in a written (and editable) plan that the entire team has contributed to and will have access to throughout the campaign.

Hopefully, you understand by now that every element of a strategic messaging program must have a carefully conceived rationale. The reasoning behind all elements of the message, including the language, visual elements, chosen medium/channel, and the type(s) of persuasive appeal used must be based on a rigorous analysis of your intended audience and an understanding of how specific messages, the audience, source, and channel(s) interact with one another to produce an intended outcome. In addition, the activities required to implement the strategic messaging program—who does what, when, where, and with what costs associated—must be equally thought out and detailed, at all times keeping in mind your objectives, audience, and available resources. A thoughtfully developed and well-written implementation plan will address needed resources, budget, and materials. The plan will give the team direction for quality performance, handling problems, perceiving important long- and short-term benefits to their work, and communicating those benefits to other campaign stakeholders. The implementation plan reminds its users of the scope, objectives, costs, and time frame of the campaign (Abbasi and Jaafari 2018). Moreover, the implementation plan accounts for the complexities of programs and campaigns that are executed in different locations, where requirements may vary. For instance, Harrison and colleagues (2011) studied workplace campaigns and determined that the norms of different organizations and work sites had important bearings on campaign effectiveness. In other words, implementation plans need to consider unique audiences and settings for campaign activities.

In this chapter, we discuss a number of factors that should be addressed by a well-crafted implementation plan. These factors, taken together, are like a map for getting from Point A to Point B or a recipe for making your favorite brownies. Even if you have packed all of the right clothes for the trip or purchased all of the necessary ingredients for making the treats, if you don't have a proper plan to execute (i.e., a map or a recipe), the vacation might be spoiled by detours and time wasted getting lost, or the brownies might lack flavor or that perfect texture. Similarly, a strategic communication campaign needs an implementation plan that specifies exactly how to make the planned strategies unfold in such a way that you accomplish your objectives.

For example, a great deal of research reveals the best times to post for specific audiences on various social media platforms. If your strategy includes social media posts, your implementation plan must carefully detail the days and times for these posts as determined by the best available research (more on this later in the chapter)—otherwise, the audience might not see them. You will also need

Table 10.1   Sample Implementation Grid

Campaign Activity	Responsible Team Member	Time Frame	Location	Necessary Resources
1.				
2.				
3.				

to identify and document in the plan the person best suited to creating compelling posts and making sure that the person understands the scope of his or her responsibility. In addition, if paid media such as television, radio, or internet advertising is part of your strategy, the implementation plan should address the frequency and timing of this advertising so that the program stays within budget (another topic we will discuss in more depth later in this chapter). And, many years of communication research (and probably your own experience working with groups and teams) suggests that in order to accomplish their goals in a coordinated, harmonious, and efficient manner, groups of people working together on high stakes tasks (such as a communication campaign) need leadership and a high degree of communication competence. If the team lacks organization, coordination, leadership, or accountability, or if individuals lack the ability to communicate competently with one another, members might not know who is supposed to be doing what. Often, when group communication is problematic, teams fall victim to conflict and other problems like **social loafing,** where members exert little or no effort toward shared goals because they assume another person or persons will pick up the slack (Forsyth 2009; Jackson and Harkins 1985; Latane, Williams, and Harkins 1979).

An implementation plan is the product of frequent team discussions, systematic strategic planning, and leadership. We cannot emphasize enough the importance of thinking through and discussing the process of implementing each aspect of your strategic communication plan with exacting detail so that every step of the campaign is coordinated, understood, approved, and ready to execute as smoothly as possible. Although the format and appearance of your written implementation plan may vary, its essential components—the what, when, who, where, and how much of each aspect of the campaign—must be included and documented (i.e., the plan should be written and not just in someone's head!). Each of these components should be linked directly back to one or more of your campaign's specified objectives. And, every phase of campaign implementation must be measurable and assessable so that you know during and after the campaign just how successful your messages were (and why). Table 10.1 offers a sample template for an implementation plan. However, there is no specified format for a written plan; you should format it in the way that makes the most sense for you and your team. You might use the grid format presented in the sample, a

Eight Principles of Campaign Implementation

1. Clarify purpose and objectives.
2. Rely on your strategic plan to translate objective into action steps.
3. Audit, mobilize, and manage resources.
4. Assign responsibility for campaign activity implementation.
5. Be prepared for contingencies.
6. Take time to pause, reflect, and evaluate how the implementation plan is working.
7. Push for team commitment.
8. Demonstrate leadership and communication competence.

spreadsheet, or a text outline. You may also choose to create a much more detailed plan. The sample includes the most basic essential information.

10.2 HOW SHOULD I PREPARE, ENACT, AND MONITOR AN IMPLEMENTATION PLAN?

Although there is no way to anticipate all factors that might pose challenges during a strategic messaging campaign, a well-designed implementation plan will ensure that the program stays on track. A sound plan will specify exactly what needs to happen to keep the project within budget and to increase the likelihood that the campaign will accomplish the organization's objectives. And, the implementation plan specifies who is accountable for what campaign tasks. There is no single template for an implementation plan. Nor are there systematic steps for creating one due to the unique nature of each campaign. Therefore, we have organized this section around a set of eight principles that implementation plans should be based on regardless of their content or format. These principles do not represent a set of sequential steps for implementing a strategic messaging program; rather, each principle should be thoughtfully considered at each phase of a campaign.

10.2.1 Principle 1: Clarify Purpose and Objectives

Critical to the campaign's effectiveness is clear insight of exactly what the disseminated messages are intended to accomplish—by each and every individual involved in the campaign. A clear overarching purpose and results-driven objectives provide the basis for the action key campaign personnel take at any given time. In addition, a clear statement of the campaign's objectives will help determine the resources, skills, and expertise required to implement the strategy.

Although you wrote campaign objectives well before the point of implementation, there are a number of reasons that discussion of campaign objectives must continue throughout the duration of a project. For one, staff may lose momentum and focus if the project is lengthy. A second reason is that the campaign team typically gets larger as the project nears implementation. Key personnel are added to perform specific tasks, and these individuals may not have been involved in early strategic planning discussions (see chapter 5) relative to the purpose and objectives of the messaging program. Third, stakeholders might lack clarity regarding exactly what they are supposed to be doing and/or why. Clearly, if someone does not know what he or she is responsible for, the campaign will suffer. Less obvious is the fact that when team members do not realize the full scope of the project, and instead only focus on their narrow specialization or responsibility, the project is likely to falter (Parisi-Carew 2015). Campaign staff must function as a cohesive unit with collective understanding of how all moving parts of the project work together to produce results and meet the project's objectives.

Importantly, when team members who are expected to contribute to team objectives are included in discussions about those objectives, they become increasingly invested in the campaign. They understand the big picture and become motivated to work toward the overall purpose of the project. In his classic book *The Five Dysfunctions of a Team*, Patrick Lencioni (2002) describes a team's lack of clarity and buy-in to program objectives as one of the most highly damaging things that can happen to a project.

Thus, the project team must have frequent check-in discussions before and during implementation of the campaign to be reminded of what they are doing and why. The project manager and others in leadership roles must communicate the campaign's objectives clearly to the rest of the team and seek support and commitment to those outcomes. Moreover, the team needs to frequently pause and refocus its attention on those objectives. The objectives established in the early stages of campaign planning, by definition, give clear direction for the team's work (no matter how large or small the team is). Without the opportunity to discuss and clarify those objectives at regular intervals, the team may perceive only vague direction on what to do or how to do it. Campaign personnel should frequently revisit the following questions (Waldeck, Kearney, and Plax 2017) in their formal interactions with one another, realizing that although the overall purpose and objectives for the campaign remain the same, the answers to these questions will change over time depending on what aspects of the campaign are being implemented:

- Why are we here?
- What do we need to accomplish?
- How will we know when we get there?
- How will we evaluate progress?

In practice, these conversations typically occur at the beginning of the project but are quickly forgotten. Failing to take the time to regularly review project objectives and refocus staff attention to them is a mistake that can be detrimental to successful accomplishment of your campaign's objectives.

It may be helpful to think of the necessary task of keeping campaign objectives front and center as a campaign itself. For example, the second author of your book worked with a consulting team on a campaign for a police department with the purpose of improving police/civilian relationships in a midwestern US community (see Ross and Waldeck 2016). The campaign involved internal strategic messaging within the police department designed to shape and change individual officers' beliefs about how police can most effectively demonstrate power and authority. In addition, the team created a series of externally focused messages aimed at shaping and reinforcing civilians' positive perceptions of police. The scope of the project was complex. The audience was multilayered (within the police department the team had different messages depending on officer rank and tenure on the police force, and for community-oriented messages, the team considered a range of demographics that resulted in numerous audience segments). And, as you might guess, the work on this campaign was lengthy—about five years. Thus, the consulting team as well as its partners within the police department needed frequent reminders of its purpose and objectives. The team created visual messages (e.g., signage, computer screen savers, and text messages) to focus internal stakeholders' attention on key objectives. For example, one poster in the department briefing room read, "Remember: We Are Here to Help." This simple visual reminded officers of the team's campaign objective to enhance citizens' positive perceptions of police and policing within the community. In addition, they held weekly briefings during most phases of the campaign that included key consulting staff as well as personnel from the police force, where meeting leaders reminded those present of the purpose and the key objectives of the current phase of the project.

The lack of direction that some campaign teams feel is not unlike what you have probably experienced working on semester-long group projects in school. Members each have their own perceptions and understandings of the purpose of the project and the teachers' expectations, personal interests and goals, and ideas about how to complete required tasks. Sometimes the instructor does not provide clear instructions or guidance. In the end, groups may struggle or even fail because they lack necessary direction. Their own processes or the ways they are managed preclude a clear focus on project objectives, and work becomes chaotic and uncoordinated.

How you keep the team focused on objectives should depend on a number of factors. For instance, long-term campaigns such as the policing project will require unique strategies (we will discuss more of the special concerns related to sustaining a campaign later in this chapter) such as the visual and mediated reminders we mentioned. Campaign teams that struggle with commitment or motivation will require even more frequent discussions about the campaign's overall purpose and objectives, and a less top-down approach favoring one that makes staff feel involved and invested in the work. (We will discuss strategies for building commitment later in this chapter, also.) The bottom line is that when people work together to implement a campaign strategy, the program's objectives should be a consistent rallying conversation for the team. The project manager, in collaboration with the team, must determine the best way to communicate about campaign objectives regularly. In summary, this principle of campaign implementation reminds communication professionals that program objectives must be the primary focus of the campaign; all decisions and activities should be tied to one or more objectives. Organizational members need to be informed of the campaign's purpose and objectives, and you need to determine the best ways to keep personnel clearly focused on those objectives through internal communication.

10.2.2 Principle 2: Rely on the Strategic Plan to Translate Objectives into Action Steps

Recall that chapter 5 introduced you to the strategic planning process. During that process, communication professionals solidify campaign purpose, goals, and objectives. We have just discussed the importance of keeping campaign objectives at the forefront of the project in order to keep the team focused and ensure that campaign activities will contribute to specific desired outcomes. But those objectives on their own are of limited use to the people responsible for implementing the campaign. They must be further operationalized as action steps: A list of concrete, clear, and detailed tasks that need to occur during the campaign, along with an explanation of their component parts (Raab and Rocha 2011). In addition to specifying the nature of the campaign's activities, the implementation plan includes time frames for each action step and provides a logical sequence for implementation.

Action steps flow from goals and objectives. They represent the activities that take the organization from a need or problem state to the attainment of its objectives and goals. Some questions to guide your thinking about action steps include:

• **What needs to be done first? What actions must be taken before others can successfully begin?** For instance, in the student-led Rethink campaign on the Chapman University campus that focused on the issue of prescription stimulant misuse, visual messaging played a large role in accomplishing overall objectives. Central to the creation of effective visual messages was the campaign's brand identity—including a mascot and logo. Those assets had to be created before work could proceed.

- **What is the logical sequence of tasks that need to be completed?** For example, a South African edutainment campaign designed to raise awareness about gender-based violence relied on multiple episodes of television and radio dramas. First, the team identified the issues to dramatize. Given the costs associated with producing television and radio programming, the campaign could not afford failure. Therefore, the next step in the implementation plan included producing pilot programming. Then, the team tested the pilot with a carefully sampled audience and evaluated their reactions before writing further scripts (Raab and Rocha 2011; Singhal et al. 2004).
- **Is there a particular location associated with task listed?** In the previously mentioned Rethink project, campaign staff sought to interact with students on campus about prescription stimulant abuse. The central gathering point for students on their particular campus, where student organizations often held tabling events, was the logical choice for doing so. In identifying the location, component parts of this action step were specified—such as obtaining the permit to table there.
- **What is the time frame for each task?** Be realistic and as accurate as possible, but be aware that in most program managers' experience, everything takes longer than anticipated and projects can grow in unexpected ways as contingencies arise (more on this topic later in the chapter). Again, be realistic, but your implementation plan should allow for sufficient extra time to deal with unexpected obstacles.
- **What resources are required to accomplish each necessary task?** Campaigns require a wide range of resources for each planned strategy. Some of them are already available within the organization, and others might need to be acquired. For instance, to hold a tabling event, campaign staff needs a table and chairs and materials such as the pamphlets and promotional items they plan to give away to people who visit the table, banner and signage, staff for the event, and other resources that contribute to successful tabling events (e.g., music, food, video). Resource needs are unique to each campaign strategy, but here is a list of common needs (US Department of Health and Human Services, National Institutes of Health 2002):
  - ✔ Staff
  - ✔ Time
  - ✔ Supplies and equipment
  - ✔ Mailing costs and printing
  - ✔ Existing services or materials available from other sources
  - ✔ Media kits
  - ✔ Contacts and allies outside the organization
  - ✔ Promotional items related to the campaign purpose ("swag") branded with your logo, slogan, and/or contact information
  - ✔ Funding

Figure 43 An effective implementation plan includes a realistic and detailed timeline.

Action steps represent the real work of any strategic communication program. They specify what needs to happen, when, and in what chronological order in order to execute the campaign strategy (which was, recall, designed to maximize the likelihood of successfully accomplishing the campaign's goals). As we just noted, action requires resources. The next principle of effective campaign implementation explores the process of identifying, mobilizing, and managing necessary resources, including funding, in greater depth.

10.2.3 Principle 3: Audit, Mobilize, and Manage Resources

In order to successfully implement a campaign, your team must determine the organization's ability and readiness to do so given available resources. In operationalizing precise action steps that are carefully aligned with campaign objectives, you will quickly realize the vast array of resources required to carry out a strategic communication program. Although unexpected resource demands may arise after the campaign is launched, a thorough implementation plan anticipates a comprehensive list of necessary funding, staffing, supplies, and so on (see the previous section and examples on action steps). Auditing available resources well in advance of campaign implementation gives you and your team time to assess the availability of those resources within the organization, procure those that are not available, and to seek funding.

This principle of campaign implementation requires that you determine the feasibility of your proposed communication strategies in light of available resources. It requires you to ask and answer these questions (adapted from Goodstein, Nolan, and Pfeiffer 1993):

- Are our objectives/strategies/action plans workable?
- Does this organization have the resource capability right now to implement the campaign's required action steps?
- Have we established partnerships that can provide necessary resources?

- If not, why not? What resources do we need to create or obtain? What partners can we network with to create necessary resource?

These questions represent the kinds of thinking behind **resource audits,** or the activities that help you determine what needed resources are already available to you and what you need to obtain in order to implement your strategy.

Central to the need for resources is the issue of funding. You will need to prepare a comprehensive budget, or financial plan, for all campaigns. **Budgets** are documents that indicate specific costs and expenses associated with the campaign (known as **line items**) and the sources and amounts of revenue coming in to the campaign.

To demonstrate the process of auditing available resources, consider the following example. The second author of your book, Jennifer Waldeck, was involved in a campaign designed to improve landscape workers' occupational health and safety. Her communication consulting team was hired by a national professional association of land-care business owners who were interested in influencing their employees' attitudes and behaviors about on-the-job safety. The association had a limited budget and staff for message dissemination and little experience with large-scale strategic message design and implementation. Thus, they sought the help of our consulting team. Like all of the other campaigns discussed in this book, this program was not destined to be a simple task. The campaign required message design in multiple languages targeted at a wide range of receivers (within the landscaping industry are dozens of skill specializations with different health and safety concerns). Further, the association's primary channel for communicating with its members and their employees was a website. Outdoor land-care workers are not sitting at computers or even using smartphones to access professional websites during their workday. In early strategic planning conversations with this client, we guided association leaders to identify industry partners that could provide necessary resources, including communication channels that were capable of reaching this massive and diverse audience. The association formed an alliance with the publisher of their industry's leading professional magazine and a variety of newsletters related to all aspects of land care. This strategic partnership provided the campaign with an infusion of cash from the new stakeholder, the ability to disseminate messages in the new partner's publications, three staff people committed by the publisher, and a vast library of print and online health and safety educational resources for campaign content. Further, because the success of this campaign required exposing thousands of land-care employees in North America to our messages, we had to promote and advertise the project. The publisher partner had extensive expertise in this area and could provide necessary resources and funding for message dissemination. This case, documented by Waldeck (2008), illustrates how organizations must audit what they have and what they are capable of doing relative to campaign goals and seek solutions (often in the form of partnerships, but sometimes through grants or loans) to fill resource gaps. In this case, we mobilized an array of internal resources as well as those committed by a partner.

Once you have created a budget and mobilized necessary resources (or obtained commitment for them), your implementation plan should address how you will manage and oversee them. A common problem that we have observed among communication practitioners over the years is their lack of "business sense." They focus on the creative aspects of message design and often have a sound understanding of the theoretical underpinnings of a well-crafted campaign and even a set of technical skills that serve programs well. But to ignore the financial and resource management requirements of a project is to set oneself up for failure. No organization has an unlimited budget, and very few campaigns have the luxury of "sky's the limit" thinking when it comes to resources. The financial bottom line is as important as the campaign's success or failure at achieving the intended attitude or behavior change. We have adapted the following strategies for maintaining control over a project budget from Alexander (2017):

- **Ensure that campaign goals are clear and that program objectives address all key stakeholder expectations.** We may sound like a broken record at this point, but if you don't understand the importance of clear goals and objectives yet, we are reminding you again. If your campaign activities do not address stakeholder goals and expectations, you will be asked to modify the program once it is in the implementation stage. This is a primary source for cost overruns. The first step to a well-managed campaign budget is making sure that campaign requirements are identified, documented, and cleared with all stakeholders and communicated to the campaign team. This enables the team to plan appropriate campaign activities that focus on needs related to objectives (rather than "wants") and set an accurate, realistic budget. One of your authors taught a class in which a student group planned an anniversary celebration campaign for a nonprofit organization. The group failed to identify concrete objectives other than celebrating the fact that this organization had existed for twenty-five years. Thus, many of the campaign activities they planned were fun and celebratory but arbitrary and without purpose relevant to the organization's mission and goals. When the instructor began to question the relevance of their campaign activities, the team realized they needed to clarify their objectives and plan more purposeful communication strategies. Their existing budget quickly became obsolete. In practice, we have seen actual professional communication campaign budgets suffer in similar ways.
- **Budget for unexpected needs.** Later in this chapter, we will discuss the importance of planning for contingencies. Your budget should be realistic and as accurate as possible but should also include some "wiggle room" for unexpected needs, pricing changes on assets for which you do not have a

---

Strategic Communication Mentor: The Importance of Competent Project Management

In this brief article

https://thinkaxiom.com/axiology/defining-project-management-project-over-sight-and-its-importance-to-your-company/

Axiom Technology Group discusses the importance of project management and oversight to organizations. After reading it, consider the following questions:

- What are the project management and oversight duties central to a campaign you have worked on in the past or are currently working on (including a class project)?
- What are some of the risks or threats inherent in failing to provide project management and oversight to a strategic communication campaign?
- Beyond this brief introduction, what are some steps you can take to learn more about the "business" side of campaign management? What resources can you identify that will help you as you create budgets and oversight plans for future projects?

---

contracted cost, and other kinds of challenges or crises. A key piece of Maria's health communication campaign was a printed newsletter mailed to health professionals. When the printer she had contracted with unexpectedly stopped operating due to illness, she could not negotiate the same pricing with another printer. Thus, without some allowance for contingencies, she would have had a cost overrun.

• **Revisit and monitor budget and resource usage constantly during the campaign.** Your budget should be monitored on a weekly basis for overruns and unexpected expenditures. A 10 percent overrun is much easier to correct (perhaps by cutting back in another area or securing additional funding) than a 40 or 50 percent overrun. In addition, the campaign's project manager should review current and future resource needs and audit supplies and other tangibles to make sure that current resources are being used properly and that you have the right resources mobilized for the duration of the campaign.

8.2.4 Principle 4: Assign Responsibility for Implementing Campaign Activities

You will need a general staff to perform many of the routine tasks associated with a strategic message campaign. But, complex goals require complex

Figure 44 This team member is canvassing neighborhoods to raise awareness about a candidate for the US Senate. Importantly, she has the communication skills and willingness to meet strangers and interact with them in friendly and nonthreatening ways.

solutions, and one individual is rarely able to provide all of the necessary expertise and specialized skills For example, Maria's campaign for health professionals included original video, disseminated via a YouTube channel, as an important strategy. Maria is a dietician by training and has no experience creating or publishing videos. Not just any team member could provide video production and editing services; Maria needed to identify either a current organizational employee or a contractor with these skills. Important to your campaign's success is your willingness to recognize and maximize your strengths and build a team that can help you do what you can't do well on your own (Plax 2006). Thus, the implementation plan should address the required **roles,** or specialized functions, that team members must provide. Thoughtful planning will help define your campaign's staffing needs and assist you in identifying roles and responsibilities up front to minimize ambiguities and role conflicts later.

Important to the campaign's success, you must consider your program's needs, assess the skills and personalities of your team, and assign roles and responsibilities systematically. In the implementation plan, designate an accountable team member for each campaign activity—but be sure to think strategically about who gets what assignments. Campaign staff should be selected and assigned their tasks selectively and strategically. Successful campaigns are staffed by people, both organizational members and volunteers from partner organizations and the community, with specific, needed skills. Once key personnel are recruited, you must delegate tasks to those people with specific talents and be sure that each member's roles are clear. Some roles are predefined and assigned, and others will emerge as the campaign plan develops, but clear communication should establish individual responsibilities. Members need to know why they have been chosen for the team and what is expected of their role on an ongoing basis.

Table 10.2   **Matrix for Campaign Contingency Planning**

Risk	Probability (0 = Highly unlikely— 10 = Highly likely)	Impact (0 = Insignificant— 10 = Highly serious)	Strategies for minimizing and mitigating risk
1.			1. 2. 3.
2.			1. 2. 3.

Table 10.2, adapted from Raab and Rocha (2011), provides a matrix for assessing risks that campaign teams should be prepared for.

In selecting team members, it's important to consider individual personalities. Certain people may not work well together, and some people don't work well with others at all, no matter how skilled they seem. In other words, just because an individual has sought-after skills does not mean that they are right for your team, or right for your campaign. You may not have a choice in who is assigned to your campaign team or you may not have the luxury of "screening" volunteers, but you can manage personnel effectively to maximize their usefulness to the work and minimize the amount of conflict or chaos they create. When team members do not function effectively in their roles or interact competently with other team members, constructive feedback may help. But if the organization is not prepared to do some counseling and rehabilitation of the offending member, he or she should be removed so that the team can continue to function effectively.

8.2.5 Principle 5: Be Prepared for Contingencies

Contingencies are low probability events, but if they occur, they bring a high probability of distress and change to the campaign strategy. Therefore, a good campaign implementation plan should address events or occurrences that might disrupt the campaign and its activities. Your SWOT analysis can help you identify risks to be aware of and answers to the question "what can go wrong?" For example, in their work on media campaigns surrounding the issue of violence against women, Raab and Rocha (2011) noted several contingencies that communication professionals working in this area should be aware of and create plans for:

- External changes within the target audience's environment that may affect their exposure or response to tested campaign messages (e.g., new laws, religious influences)

Strategic Communication Mentor: Contingency Planning

Read this brief blog from a marketing professional:

www.6pmarketing.com/articles/branding-science/72-marketing-strategy/345-contingency-planning

Based on your understanding of contingency planning, what are some sample contingency strategies you could plan in advance for the following scenarios? In other words, if any of the following situations were to occur, what could you do? Remember, contingency plans are not reactive; they are plans that are prepared in anticipation of general or specific disruptions to a campaign. Sometimes you cannot plan for highly specific contingencies but can adapt general strategies to particular circumstances.

1. You have planned a campaign designed to promote awareness about human trafficking on your campus. The day the campaign launched, a massive storm comes through your town. The campus loses power and high winds and rain damage much of your visual messaging.
2. As part of an ongoing campaign to raise awareness about hate crimes in society, you have invited a speaker to campus who directed a documentary film on this topic. The morning of the event, a high-profile hate crime occurs in your campus's community. Students and faculty are highly emotional and upset.
3. You have invited members of the community to participate in focus groups designed to collect information and test messages for a city council candidate you are working with. Only two people show up to the first focus group and no one to the second group. You are up against a deadline for publishing the messages across various platforms and do not have time to run additional focus groups.
4. A disgruntled customer is reviewing your brand unfairly and inaccurately across numerous social media platforms and seems to be recruiting friends to post similar fake reviews.

- Internal threats that impact the effective, efficient operation of the campaign (e.g., a partner might leave the campaign, key staff resignations)
- Lack of donor response to fundraising efforts

8.2.6 Principle 6: Pause, Reflect, Evaluate: Constantly Monitor Performance and Results and Revise Plan as Necessary

In a study funded by the National Science Foundation, Loughry, Ohland, and Moore (2007) explicated the characteristics of effective project teams that are relevant to campaign work. Effective teams do what it takes to stay on track. Effective campaign team members monitor and evaluate how one another perform, provide constructive feedback, motivate one another, and consistently ensure that resources are available to sustain the campaign. Campaign teams take the time to "hit the pause button" on their work and informally evaluate how the work is going. To ensure sustained focus, regularly check in and revisit the critical questions:

- Why are we here?
- What do we need to accomplish today, this week, this month, before this campaign closes?
- How are we doing?
- How do we know?

While taking the time to review objectives, revisit standards of performance as well. Members should collectively evaluate their current levels of performance and what compromises they may have made. Most importantly, use the time to reflect on how well the team is doing. Give recognition for both individual and team accomplishments along the way. Remember that sometimes the process is even more meaningful than the immediate outcome. Teams that work, spend time reflecting on their group identity and ensuring that everyone feels valued for his or her contributions.

In addition, campaign teams must engage in more formal assessment methods as they implement strategies. Specifically, effective campaign teams engage in **process evaluation.** Process evaluation provides feedback about the effectiveness of campaign strategies and the campaign's overall impact as it unfolds during implementation. Process evaluation is typically concerned with collecting feedback about the execution and dissemination of messages rather than the program's impact on the audience (Berkowitz et al. 2008). Communication professionals rely on frequent process evaluations to help them revise or refine campaign strategy as the campaign evolves. Some methods of process campaign evaluation include the following (Atkin and Freimuth 2012; Berkowitz et al. 2008):

- Monitoring channel usage patterns: Do usage metrics (e.g., number of clicks, unique first time visitors to website, campaign-related materials or products ordered) reveal sufficient target audience engagement with campaign messages?
- Surveying, testing (e.g., for recall or comprehension), or observing members of the intended audience during and after exposure to various campaign messages.
- Individual in-depth interviews and focus groups.
- Monitoring any media coverage of the communication campaign.

In a report by Berkowitz and colleagues (2008), the authors include a list of process evaluation techniques used for a campaign aimed at increasing physical activity levels among children ages nine to thirteen. This list will give you an idea of how the kinds of evaluation strategies listed above are used in practice, along with the kinds of data each method yields and what an actual campaign team did with those data. Access this table, published in the *American Journal of Preventive Medicine,* here: https://tinyurl.com/y3x97b5u.

10.2.7 Principle 7: Push for Commitment: Ensure Campaign Sustainability

Commitment to the campaign and to the team is crucial for team success. Members must feel some enthusiasm for the campaign's goals, the process established, and about working with one another. They must be galvanized to pursue the team's common goal, sublimating destructive or counterproductive personal agendas. Committed team members will do just about anything to assure that the team succeeds. They will shift and assume one another's responsibilities as the job requires. Moreover, members share an identity with the team and the campaign focus (Larson and LaFasto 1989; Lencioni 2002).

Even on the most committed teams, organizational members may be pulled in different directions and face competing demands on their time and resources. Horberg (2008, para. 3) noted that "a team meeting is burdened by as many agendas as there are participants, plus the official agenda." Although personal agendas are inevitable, to sustain beneficial commitment, the campaign team can never let them dominate without examining them. Individual agendas must be brought into balance with the team's purpose and objectives through communication to enhance commitment and ensure campaign effectiveness. How can campaign teams do this?

- **Learn to recognize personal agendas.** Be alert for extreme bias, gossip, and generalizations about people, programs, partners, or ideas. In addition, be sure to notice and probe silence. What is missing during a meeting is typically significant. Ask questions when campaign team members fail to provide facts or details to support their proposals with a logical rationale.
- **Ask questions to bring hidden agendas into alignment with campaign and organizational goals.** People with hidden agendas often push for quick decisions based on little discussion or information. Pressure is seldom in the team's best interest. Slow down and obtain necessary information to fill in the blanks of omission before implementation moves forward.
- **Acknowledge that personal agendas are sometimes valuable to the campaign.** As the team probes and asks questions, be mindful that what you learn might help you alter the predefined strategy in positive ways. The personal agenda might not be an attempt to sabotage the team or be disagreeable; perhaps the individual really has a valuable, or better, idea or plan.

You will also need to consider your volunteers and external stakeholders and strategies for keeping them motivated and committed to the campaign's purpose. What will inspire these stakeholders to stay motivated and continue their work with the campaign? Orientation and periodic meetings, resource materials such as a "frequently asked questions" document, and planned social events can create solidarity among campaign staff members and keep them committed. Don't forget to say "thank you." Acknowledge campaign volunteers' as well as organizational members' contributions in visible ways that you know (based on your relationship with them) they will value.

10.2.8 Principle 8: Demonstrate Team Communication Competence at All Times

The final critical principle on which campaign implementation plans must be based focuses on the importance of competent team communication and leadership. Consider the case of Ted, founder and president of a successful marketing and advertising organization in California. His firm specializes in social and political cause-related campaigns. Ted is an Emmy-award-winning director and producer of television documentaries targeting health care, education, and environmental issues. His core staff is small, but he knows how to put together successful teams of highly technical and specialized players to do research, design campaigns, produce videos, provide training and instruction, and much, much more. Not only is Ted well respected for his own talents and skills, but he's also well recognized for his ability to assemble the right resources, people, and subcontractors into a team to do just about anything.

The second author of your textbook has served as an external communication consultant and researcher on several of Ted's campaigns. One of the first was designed to encourage oil recycling behaviors that were friendly to the environment. What did a communication professor know about oil recycling? Not much. Nothing! Ted assured her that she was being brought into the team not as an expert on recycling or on marketing or advertising. Instead, he wanted to use her expertise in communication, survey research, and focus group interviewing to help develop, test, and evaluate campaign messages. He found others to join the team who knew quite a bit about recycling. Others were good at graphic design. He relied on the client to provide background on waste management. And Ted knew all about how to market a service or product.

The first thing he did was to get the team together at a retreat. There, members identified goals, delegated tasks, collaborated on strategy, produced a timeline, established ground rules for their work and their interactions with one another, and developed an identity as Ross Campbell's recycling project team. Everyone knew who was responsible for what. They learned to work together, to depend on one another, and to value one another's contributions.

Over the last twenty years or so, Jennifer and several of her colleagues have collaborated with Ted and other members of his team on numerous projects, including college student loans and financial literacy campaigns, alternative vehicle technologies (such as hydrogen, hybrid, and electric cars), re-refined oil, hazardous waste, and of all things, California truckers' oil and filter disposal. In considering why these campaigns have been so effective, and why the teams Ted has so capably assembled have worked together so well, Jennifer has been able to identify what makes Ted so successful. He has a keen understanding of the importance of group communication competence. He models it, he encourages it, and he insists on it. And the competencies reflected in how his organization's campaign teams work together reflect what many years of communication research and theory have demonstrated about group interaction. Following is a summary of this key work, adapted from Waldeck, Kearney, and Plax (2017) and Waldeck, Ross, and Ross (2017).

- **Campaign team members must communicate with intention.** Simply communicating with the team—talking, writing, reading, listening—is an insufficient condition for accomplishing program goals. You must communicate strategically and with intention with your teammates. Set goals for your interactions; know why you are communicating at any given time and what you hope will happen. Select verbal and nonverbal behaviors that are consistent with those goals. Although communication is important, merely communicating without an objective in mind and an appropriate strategy for accomplishing it can actually be harmful to your ability to work well with others. Remember, communication is neither a good thing nor a bad thing; it is a tool that can be used well or misused. In addition, keep in mind that listening is often more important than speaking when working as part of a team.
- **Campaign teams must create, agree on, and follow ground rules for individual accountability and norms for performance.** High-performing teams generate and agree to ground rules, which remind team members how they are supposed to behave in relation to one another in both general and specific situations. Here are some sample ground rules generated by an actual campaign team working on a program designed to educate college students about how to manage debt:
  - ✔ *Everything we do matters. Our work is important.* This ground rule helped sustain team engagement and commitment over an extended period of time.
  - ✔ *Keep expectations high at all times.* Ground rules like this one encourage accountability among team members and remind one another, "we are watching."
  - ✔ *We respond to messages within an hour.* In the implementation stage, team members need to be accessible and responsive in case of resource needs or contingencies.

✓ *We arrive for videoconferences on time, and we stay for the duration of the meeting. We don't text, IM, email, or work on other projects when this team is in virtual meetings.* The campaign team we are referring to in this example operated out of four cities and two states. Therefore, everyone needed to be available, engaged, and accountable during meetings.

✓ *Planning works. Our efforts are not wasted.* A well-constructed plan is a half-implemented one. Although we need contingency plans and must be able to change course when needed, we must also have confidence in our implementation plan and not stray off course too easily or quickly.

✓ *We listen at all times, whether we agree or not.* This particular project team was assembled to leverage and capitalize on a diverse array of member strengths, skills, and backgrounds. This diversity sometimes led to disagreements but almost always led to outcomes that enhanced the quality of our campaign. Thus, we put ground rules in place like this one that would promote open communication and the expression of different ideas.

✓ *If one of us will be late on a deadline or run into a problem with an assigned task, we will let the team know with an email, IM, or text message.* This ground rule reminded members of our team that we were, in fact, a team. Individuals were responsible for their tasks but knew that they could count on the rest of us for help and input.

✓ *Two people will edit and proofread every document our team produces.* This operating procedure helped ensure that our team would meet its stated standards of excellence.

As a general rule, high-performing team members commit to excellence and quality in their processes, results, internal communication, and external messaging.

• **Campaign teams must build and sustain trust and facilitate conflict and disagreement.** Working well together is fundamental to the success of any team. At first glance, you might suspect that working well together means always getting along, easily agreeing, achieving consensus most if not all of the time, and thinking and acting alike. But your suspicions would be wrong. Working well together is often messy, complicated, and tiring.

Effective team members trust one another. They show their trust in a number of important ways. First, they say what they think and they mean what they say. Second, they listen to what others in the team say and they fully respond. Third, they treat others with dignity and respect at all times. (It's okay to disagree, but it's not okay to be disagreeable.) Fourth, they come across as consistent, predictable, and dependable. They hold themselves and others in the group accountable. They also know that it's safe to voice minority views or controversial ideas. Finally, if individual members stumble momentarily, others will compensate by stepping in and ensuring the job gets done for the sake of the project.

Figure 45 Strategic communication teams must commit to excellence, quality, trust, and open communication.

How do campaign team members damage trust? By being unfair and disrespectful to others, not keeping their word, lying, behaving in moody and unpredictable ways, shirking accountability when things go wrong, stealing credit for things that go well, being closed-minded, and hoarding information or resources. Can you think of anything else?

Campaign teams need to be strategically planned, built, nurtured, and sustained. Perhaps most critical to team success (and failure) is you. Whether your role is to lead or to participate as a member of the team, what you say and do can make all the difference in how the team functions and what outcomes might result. Given the transactional nature of communication that occurs in campaign teamwork, both sources and receivers, both leaders and followers, are mutually responsible for the processes and results.

In the following "Interview with a Professional" feature, Chapman University graduate Athena Saxon discusses her teamwork experiences associated with the Rethink campaign.

10.3 TYING IT ALL TOGETHER: IMPLEMENTING COMMUNICATION CAMPAIGNS AND PROGRAMS

Maria's educational messaging program for health care professionals (that we first read about in the opening case study of this chapter) was ultimately evaluated, by a variety of measures, as highly successful. Central to her success was a sound implementation plan that enabled her to rely on channels and strategies that her organization had used for message dissemination in the past and incorporate a new strategy. Maria, like the other communication professionals,

Interview with a Professional: Athena Saxon Discusses Implementation of the Rethink Campaign

1. Athena, could you briefly tell us your impressions of how teamwork contributed to the overall effectiveness of the Rethink campaign?

ATHENA: The Rethink campaign was a collaborative project. We had about a month to put everything together before we ran the campaign, so we had to work fast and articulate our ideas early to get the ball rolling. By the second class I was already drawing sketches for a possible mascot. This time barrier forced the team to work quickly, present raw ideas, and brainstorm solutions. Many of the students were passionate about the project, and this resulted in a climate that enabled open and honest discussions. Our class would debate ideas and concerns very candidly. Without these face-to-face meetings, I do not believe we would have had as much positive and effective input as we did.

2. Can you provide any examples of how the principles of effective team communication discussed in this chapter (e.g., communicating with intention, setting ground rules, establishing trust, and managing conflicts and disagreements) helped the Rethink team achieve its objectives?

ATHENA:

Communicating with intention
- Having a purpose when going into class or team discussions is key. The most effective discussions came from students who were very intentional and invested in the topic.
- Classmates who consistently show up late without reading the research lead meaningless discussions. For example, one class period Dr. LaBelle spoke on the potential ineffectiveness of fear appeals, referencing the D.A.R.E. program. At the next class

a student, who was not present the class before, suggested messages focusing on the similarities of meth and Adderall. This led to a long and very heated argument that ended up wasting a lot of time.

Setting ground rules
- For the Rethink campaign, the class was divided into different teams: Research, Fundraising and Budget, Traditional and Print Media, Event Planning, Social Media, and External Messaging (PR/Promotion). Each team compiled its own list of ground rules.
- One of the first conversations that teams should have needs to focus on the preferred channels for communication. I was a part of the Research team. We determined that a group text would be the best means of communication for us.
- One expectation we had was that teammates would respond to a message, at the latest, by the end of the day. We understood that we all had unique and busy schedules and that quicker response times were probably unrealistic.

Establishing trust and managing conflicts and disagreements
- Prescription stimulant misuse is a sensitive topic. In our campaign, we touched on mental health, substance abuse, self-esteem, addiction, sexual performance, among other very personal topics.
- Remembering the goal of the campaign was integral in maintaining trust throughout the process. When disagreements arose, the conversation steered toward, "is this furthering our message?" not simply disagreeing with the person.
- Listening fully to each other and having intention behind the disagreements strengthened our trust and fostered this sense of safety within the class.

3. What would you say were the greatest team communication challenges the Rethink team faced? What factors contributed to these challenges, and how were they resolved?

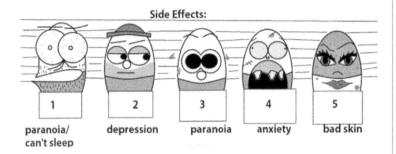

Side Effects:

| 1 | 2 | 3 | 4 | 5 |
| paranoia/ can't sleep | depression | paranoia | anxiety | bad skin |

Figure 46 The original Rethink team rejected this early visual representation of their message. The designer learned an important series of lessons about team communication in the process of developing an appropriate and effective set of images to depict the messages behind their prescription stimulant abuse campaign.

ATHENA: A major conflict we had was discussing how lighthearted we wanted the campaign to be. Some classmates thought the campaign should take a serious tone. Part of the class thought the mascot was too cartoonish and would miss the target audience. Others thought it could be even more lighthearted. Many discussions were begun with, "If I saw this on campus, I would . . ." Many perspectives were very personal and stemmed from individual biases. Some of the conversations became heated arguments that unintentionally made students uncomfortable. Revisiting our mission and goals helped redirect the conversation. Our mission was about "inspiring peer-driven conversations about the risks of misusing prescription stimulants to study." Our goal was not to lecture or scare students into not misusing medication, it was to further the conversation.

4. In terms of team communication effectiveness, what two to three primary lessons did you learn working on the Rethink campaign? Please discuss them briefly.

ATHENA: Everyone on a team is human and brings their own experiences and biases. Rethink taught me to think of every possible response to our messages. I might think that

a message or photo is funny, but someone else might find it offensive, or possibly not understand it.

For instance, I'd like to direct readers' attention to a drawing I created early on in the project. I thought a lineup would be a visually interesting way to represent the legal and psychological consequences of misusing prescription stimulants. When presenting it to the class, I received harsh criticism for my lineup drawings. Looking back, visually representing a mental illness with cartoonish drawings does not even remotely sound like a good idea. I was disappointed at the time, but I learned a lot from that experience. We do not want to offend people with our messages. That is very important.

Ultimately, a lot of people liked the overall idea of having a pill as a mascot. Most people, including me, gravitated toward the one labeled "3" in the lineup visual. We ended up basing our mascot on that drawing and named him Addy, short for Adderall. He plays a prominent role in the campaign logo.

This experience also taught me to speak up when I had ideas or responses. I didn't have to be a

Figure 47 An effective mascot can be a great ambassador for your campaign's message. However, the process of designing and agreeing on the "right" mascot can be challenging.

5. *If you had the opportunity to give advice about communication to another campaign team based on your experience, what would it be?*

ATHENA: Don't be afraid to speak up, even if you are not sure of the logistics or details. Small, even silly ideas can end up being such a pivotal part of a campaign. Take the Rethink mascot, Addy, for example, he was just a quick sketch in my notebook and he became the face of the campaign. Don't underestimate yourself.

hundred percent sure or confident with my ideas because a collaborative environment doesn't require that. Being on a team gives space to develop and refine ideas.

program managers, and consultants cited in the examples in this chapter, was adept at applying the principles of campaign implementation in an organized, precise fashion. In addition, she understood the sophisticated communication competencies required of effective teamwork. In this chapter, you explored the foundational concepts for moving a campaign strategy from its formative, conceptual stage to operation, launch, and implementation. Although implementation processes will vary based on the unique nature of each campaign, they are all based on the key idea that detailed planning is critical to success.

CHAPTER 10 REVIEW

Questions for Critical Thinking and Discussion

1. Complete a list of action steps for Maria's newsletter strategy. Be as detailed and comprehensive as you can in anticipating and organizing the steps that it will take for a campaign team to write, produce, and disseminate this newsletter based on the information you were given about the project in the introduction to this chapter.
2. Again considering the newsletter strategy from the introduction to this chapter, identify the task roles that need to be filled in order to disseminate this message four times a year. Be as detailed and comprehensive in identifying necessary roles and the specialized skills or expertise required to fill them.
3. Create an implementation grid for a hypothetical messaging campaign, or one that you are working on for class. Use the format provided in this chapter or one of your own design, but be sure to include the relevant information discussed in this chapter.

4. In thinking about her intended audience (health care professionals), and her purpose (providing her audience with evidence-based current trends in nutrition science), what contingencies might arise during the course of her campaign that would prevent her from reaching this audience successfully (and compelling them to pay attention to her messages)? Complete the contingency matrix in response to this question.

5. Briefly explicate your reactions to Athena Saxon's interview in which she shares her experience working in a team setting on a university campaign on the topic of prescription stimulant misuse. What are three to five things you learned from her experience that you could apply in your own teamwork with others? Why do you think Athena and her team were able to accomplish so much and be so successful based on what she shared about their group communication competence?

6. What are the primary task roles critical for a team you are currently participating on or had a recent experience with? In other words, what functions are people performing to get the work done? In your own experience, do the groups you've been a part of do a good job systematically assigning task roles based on clear criteria? Explain why or why not. Are the right people performing the right jobs? Or is role assignment arbitrary? How could roles be shifted to maximize what team members contribute—as well as their motivation and enjoyment?

Key Terms

budget: a financial plan that details a campaign's expenses and income for a specified period of time.

contingencies: reasonably predictable, but uncertain, events or circumstances that could require alterations to a plan.

line items: within a budget, these refer to the specific individual costs and revenues associated with a project.

process evaluation: a type of assessment that involves feedback about the effectiveness of campaign strategies and the campaign's overall impact as it unfolds during implementation.

resource audits: activities that help campaign teams determine what needed resources are available to them and what they still need to obtain in order to implement the strategy.

roles: specialized functions that team members must provide.

social loafing: a condition in which group members exert little or no effort toward shared goals because they assume another person or persons will pick up the slack.

Further Readings and Resources

Backer, T. E., and E. M. Rogers. 1993. *Organizational Aspects of Health Communication Campaigns: What Works?* Newbury Park, CA: Sage

Harrison, T. R. 2014. "Enhancing Communication Interventions and Evaluations through Communication Design." *Journal of Applied Communication Research* 42, no. 2: 135–49. doi: 10.1080/00909882.2013.825047.

Heath, R. L. 1990. "Effects of Internal Rhetoric on Management Response to External Issues: How Corporate Culture Failed the Asbestos Industry." *Journal of Applied Communication Research* 18, no. 2: 153–67.

Ulmer, R. R. 2001. "Effective Crisis Management through Established Stakeholder Relationships: Maiden Mills as a Case Study." *Management Communication Quarterly* 14, no. 4: 590–615.

———. 2012. "Increasing the Impact of Thought Leadership in Crisis Communication." *Management Communication Quarterly* 26, no. 4: 523–42. doi: 10.1177/0893318912461907.

References

Abbasi, A., and A. Jaafari. 2018. "Project Management Research and Industry Innovations." *Journal of Modern Project Management* 6 (May/August): 60–69.

Alexander, M. 2017, August 18. "Project Management: 5 Tips for Managing Your Project Budget." *CIO.* www.cio.com/article/2406862/project-management/project-management-project-management-4-ways-to-manage-your-budget.html.

Atkin, C. K, and V. Freimuth. 2012. "Guidelines for Formative Evaluation Research in Campaign Design." In *Public Communication Campaigns,* 4th ed., edited by R. E. Rice, and C. K. Atkin, 53–68. Thousand Oaks, CA: Sage.

Berkowitz, J. M., M. Huhman, C. D. Heitzler, L. D. Potter, M. J. Nolin, and S. W. Banspach. 2008. "Overview of Formative, Process, and Outcome Evaluation Methods Used in the VERB™ Campaign." *American Journal of Preventive Medicine* 34, no. 6: S222–S229.

Forsyth, D. R. 2009. *Group Dynamics.* New York: Wadsworth.

Goodstein, L. D., T. M. Nolan, and J. W. Pfeiffer. 1993. *Applied Strategic Planning: A Comprehensive Guide.* New York: McGraw-Hill.

Harrison, T. R., S. E. Morgan, L. V. Chewning, E. A. Williams, J. B. Barbour, M. J. Di Corcia, and L. A. Davis. 2011. "Revisiting the Worksite in Worksite Health Campaigns: Evidence from a Multisite Organ Donation Campaign." *Journal of Communication* 61, no. 3: 535–55.

Horberg, P. 2008. "Hidden Agendas." www.meetingsinternational.com/articles.php?id=27.

Jackson, J., and S. Harkins. 1985. "Equity in Effort: An Explanation of the Social Loafing Effect." *Journal of Personality and Social Psychology* 49, no. 5: 1199–206.

Larson, C. E., and F. M. J. LaFasto. 1989. *Teamwork: What Must Go Right/What Can Go Wrong.* Sage Series in Interpersonal Communication 10. Thousand Oaks, CA: Sage.

Latane, B., K. Williams, and S. Harkins. 1979. "Many Hands Make Light the Work: The Causes and Consequences of Social Loafing." *Journal of Personality and Social Psychology* 37, no. 6: 823–32.

Lencioni, P. 2002. *The Five Dysfunctions of a Team.* San Francisco: Jossey-Bass.

Loughry, M. L., M. W. Ohland, and D. D. Moore. 2007. "Development of a Theory-Based Assessment of Team Member Effectiveness." *Educational and Psychological Measurement* 67, no. 3: 505–24.

Parisi-Carew, E. 2015, September 23. "8 Reasons Why Teams Fail." https://leadchangegroup.com/8-reasons-why-teams-fail/.

Plax, T. G. 2006. "Raising the Question #2: How Much Are We Worth? Estimating Fees for Services." *Communication Education* 55: 242–46.

Raab, M., and J. Rocha. 2011. "Campaigns to End Violence against Women and Girls." UN Women. www.endvawnow.org/uploads/modules/pdf/1342724232.pdf.

Ross, S., and J. H. Waldeck. 2016. "White Shirts, Blue Shirts: A Case of Leadership Development Consulting for Law Enforcement." In *Consulting That Matters: A Handbook for Scholars and Practitioners,* edited by J. H. Waldeck and D. R. Seibold, 319–30. New York: Peter Lang.

Singhal, A., S. Usdin, E. Scheepers, S. Goldstein, and G. Japhet. 2004. "Entertainment-Education Strategy in Development Communication." In *Development and Communication in Africa,* edited by C. Okigbo and F. Eribo, 141–56. Lanham, MD: Rowman and Littlefield.

US Department of Health and Human Services, National Institutes of Health. 2002. *Making Health Communication Programs Work: A Planner's Guide.* Bethesda, MD: National Cancer Institute.

Waldeck, J. H. 2008. "The Development of an Industry-Specific Online Learning Center: Consulting Lessons Learned." *Communication Education* 57, no. 4: 452–63.

Waldeck, J. H., P. Kearney, and T. G. Plax. 2017. *Strategic Communication at Work: Contemporary Perspectives on Business and Professional Communication.* Dubuque, IA: Kendall Hunt.

Waldeck, J. H., R. Ross, and S. Ross. 2017. *Managing Virtual Teams: Closing the Distance Gap.* Washington, DC: US Department of Health and Human Services.

Evaluating Campaigns

CHAPTER CONTENTS

11.1 **The Importance of Evaluation** 320
    11.1.1 Reasons to Conduct an Evaluation 321
    11.1.2 Conducting Research Using the Scientific Method 323

11.2 **The Three Phases of Campaign Evaluation** 327
    11.2.1 Before the Campaign: Conducting Formative Research 328
    11.2.2 Four Types of Formative Research 329
    11.2.3 During the Campaign: Conducting Process Research 330
    11.2.4 After the Campaign: Conducting Summative Research 332
    Summative Research: Outcome Evaluation 332
    Summative Research: Impact Evaluation 333

11.3 **Five Considerations in Creating an Evaluation Plan** 334
    11.3.1 Consider Your Objectives 334
    11.3.2 Decide What to Measure 334
    Using a Logic Model 335
    Distinguishing between Effects, Effectiveness, and Efficiency 336
    11.3.3 Determine Your Research Design 337
    Qualitative and Quantitative Research 337
    When to Collect Data: Cross-Sectional and Longitudinal Research Designs 338
    11.3.4 Assign Measurement Responsibilities 339
    11.3.5 Consider the Cost of Measurement 339

11.4 **Considerations in Writing an Evaluation Report** 342

11.5 **Tying It All Together: The Structure and Timing of Strategic Communication Campaign Evaluation** 346

LEARNING OBJECTIVES

After reading this chapter you should be able to do the following:

▶ Discuss the reasons why campaign evaluation is important for organizations.

▶ Outline the five steps of the scientific method and describe how they might be applied to campaign evaluation.

▶ Distinguish between the three phases of campaign evaluation and explain their role in the campaign evaluation process.

▶ Compare and contrast campaign effects from campaign effectiveness.

▶ Apply knowledge of logic models and research design to the development of an evaluation plan.

▶ Design an appropriate outline for an evaluation report.

Mariana is the founder and CEO of Love the Earth Cosmetics, a cruelty-free and vegan cosmetic company based out of San Diego, California. Mariana founded this company ten years ago after becoming a makeup artist and conducting her own research on makeup development and testing. She has created a small empire in San Diego, with Love the Earth products selling very well in small boutiques and tourist shops. However, in the past ten years, competition has increased exponentially—the increasing popularity of living a vegan lifestyle has been great for business, but it also has led to an explosion of similar brands in Mariana's market. If Love the Earth is going to survive, Mariana needs to not only set herself apart but also reach larger, national distributors. To do this, Mariana has been reaching out to her loyal customers—the ones who consistently order from her Etsy shop and have signed up to be on her email list—to see how her product has made a positive impact on their life and why they continue to choose Love the Earth over its growing competitors. The results of her work will inform a sales pitch that could literally make or break Love the Earth cosmetics—and she needs help to make sure she does this right.

Harper is the business manager of a railroad museum in a small town in southern West Virginia. A nonprofit organization, the museum is home to a series of artifacts, photos, and records related to the late nineteenth-century railroad industry. The museum relies on entry fees, gift-shop profits, and donors to keep its doors open. Part of Harper's job is to provide evidence of the impact of this museum on the local economy and community. Recently, Harper found a call for grant funding from a national history and education foundation—if she can provide evidence of this small's museum's effects on the local community as well as the state, she is confident that she can keep the museum operating through the next fiscal year if she receives a grant. The only issue Harper faces is what evidence to collect—how can she show this foundation that this small museum and its collection of historical artifacts matter?

Malik works for the Office of Energy Efficiency and Renewable Energy in the US government. Over the past few months, Malik has been compiling a report on how the programs initiated by this office have addressed the objectives outlined in their strategic plan. This report, due every four years, will summarize the efforts of his office and how they are in line with its mission. In conducting the necessary research to complete this report, though, Malik is noticing deficiencies and wasted funds in the program—some message channels, for instance, are very expensive and are doing little to advance the overall goal of the program. Considering these are continuing programs, Malik asks his supervisor to call a meeting to go over the data. Just because the programs aren't working doesn't mean they cannot and should not be fixed.

At this point in our text, the amount of effort and careful planning that is required of a strategic communication campaign is likely very evident. As we have discussed over the past several chapters, the creation of a campaign requires a thorough analysis of not only your organization, but also the intended target audience you wish to influence. The final set of campaign messages and activities is the product of weeks (if not months or years) of hard work, creativity, and evidence-based decision-making. So how, after all of this effort, does an organization assess if a campaign "worked"? The evaluation of campaigns is an important part of the strategic communication process and is much more complicated than what the organization's members *liked* or *felt* about the campaign. As you recall from chapter 5, the ninth and final step of planning a strategic communication campaign is to conduct implementation and evaluation plans. You have learned how to develop an implementation plan in the previous chapter; in this chapter, we discuss the various types of evaluation and considerations you need to make in this final step.

Evaluation is the systematic research process used to understand the effectiveness of a campaign. The word "evaluation" might make you think of the end of the campaign process, but in reality the evaluation of a campaign is a critical part of the planning process and should be considered at the beginning and throughout the life of a campaign. Knowing the criteria you will use to measure the effectiveness of your campaign will help you design a better plan. The evaluation techniques discussed in this chapter will help you to objectively assess the success of your campaign efforts and to adjust certain aspects either during or after your campaign so that you avoid mistakes and pitfalls that lead to campaign failure. When it comes to campaign evaluation, the key questions you will have might include:

- How many people did we reach with our messages?
- Did we change the attitudes and behaviors of our target audience?
- What channels were most effective?

In order to answer these key questions, you need to plan ahead to collect integral pieces of data at multiple points in the campaign process.

In this chapter, we introduce several key concepts in campaign evaluation, including the various phases during which you may conduct these evaluations, the type of information that you might collect, and how and when you will collect this information. We discuss key considerations in developing not only your evaluation plans but also your ultimate report of campaign activities and outcomes. First, we turn to a more thorough discussion of the importance of evaluation in the strategic communication campaign process.

11.1 THE IMPORTANCE OF EVALUATION

From a communication researcher's perspective, there is very little reason to conduct a campaign without also conducting an evaluation of its outcomes.

This might seem odd to you. After all, what is the harm in conducting an after school reading program, or a community exercise program, or advertising a new brand of potato chips without assessing the levels of effectiveness of these messages? Aren't all messages helpful in that they are seen by some target audience and therefore increase awareness? The answer to these questions connects back to the purpose of campaigns as well as the resources available to conduct them. As we have reiterated throughout this text, an essential element of strategic communication campaigns is that they intend to generate *change* in an intended target audience in a specified time period. Therefore, the nature of campaigns dictates that they be evaluated. Second, whether they be conducted by for-profit, nonprofit, or government organizations, campaigns are always being conducted with a set number of resources. These resources might be in terms of financial means, volunteers, employees, or any other boundary that faces the organization. As such, a campaign should always be evaluated in terms of its ratio of inputs (resources used) to outputs (change generated). Next, we will review a few specific reasons for conducting an evaluation—all of which apply to the various organizational types and structures we discussed in chapter 2.

11.1.1 Reasons to Conduct an Evaluation

Campaign evaluations are important for many reasons, the most integral of which is that organizational resources should not be wasted on messages that are not affecting your target audience. Depending on the nature of the organization conducting this campaign (e.g., for-profit, nonprofit, or government), other reasons for conducting evaluations might include:

FUNDING   Particularly for nonprofit and government organizations, evaluations are a critical aspect of retaining funding. As you read in Harper's story at the beginning of this chapter, these evaluations can also be a critical piece of the argument to request additional funding. These funding considerations are also important to for-profit organizations; for example, a store branch manager needs to provide evidence that her particular location is bringing in money for the organization relative to the cost of keeping it open.

RESOURCES   Related to funding, evaluations allow organizations to justify their activities, costs, and use of resources. They might also justify requests for additional resources, such as staff, space, training, or whatever else is needed to achieve the objectives of the campaign. Suppose you are the manager of a local branch of a national bank and in need of an assistant manager to help with day-to-day functioning. To rationalize this additional expense, it will be necessary for you to document your need to leaders in the company.

MORALE   If you have ever worked on a team, which most of us have, you know the motivational power of success. Keeping track of sales, customers acquired, monies raised, houses built, or whatever outcome you seek allows your organization to recognize group and individual success. Consider Mariana's work at the opening of the chapter—this report will be a source of pride and encouragement for Love the Earth's employees, and it will also serve as inspiration and socialization for newly introduced employees. Without these indicators, your organizational members might lose interest, motivation, or hope that their efforts are achieving change.

STAKEHOLDER SUPPORT   Suppose you are an investor in an entrepreneurial company; it would be in your best interest to have updates on the success of this company, right? If you do not know how the company is performing or whether it is growing, you might be less inclined to continue to financially support it. The same applies to donors of nonprofit organizations; open lines of communication foster trust, support, and overall credibility. As an organization, keeping track of your efforts (and their outcomes) allows you to maintain a positive, open relationship with internal and external stakeholders.

NEW OPPORTUNITIES   For organizations of all types, having evidence of prior success will be crucial to seeking new opportunities and forging new partnerships and cooperative relationships. Think of your record of successes as a portfolio of what your organization can do—creating a streamlined, evidence-based argument for why your organization is the best will help you to earn new clients, donors, or partners.

TO IMPROVE   Last but certainly not least is likely the simplest of reasons to conduct an evaluation of your campaign: to improve your campaign! As we will discuss in this chapter, evaluations of your campaign might occur at the beginning, middle, or end of the campaign time period. At each point, an evaluation offers a chance to reflect on what is working and what is not. You might find, for instance, that a particular message you are sending is not being interpreted how you anticipated it to be by your target audience. Perhaps a particular media channel is costing more of your organization than it is worth in terms of reach and influence. In Malik's case at the beginning of this chapter, we see a program that is not effective. Without consistent evaluations, Malik would not be aware of these problems and wouldn't be able to pinpoint the source of the issue. By conducting assessments, your organization can make corrections to the campaign implementation that will help you achieve your goals. At the end of the campaign, these evaluations will help you form a plan for the future. This, ultimately, is perhaps the most valuable aspect of conducting evaluation assessments.

As health promotion and preventative medicine expert Thomas Valente (2001) summarizes, evaluation is conducted to know whether a campaign worked, why and in what ways it worked, and how it can work better next time. Given the importance of conducting research throughout the campaign, it is necessary for those in strategic communication to conduct research that is accurate, nonbiased, and capable of uncovering both failures and successes. To do this, an organization should ensure that its research is being conducted using standards and practices accepted in the scientific research community. This applies to any sector or type of organization—the situations that Mariana, Harper, and Malik face could all benefit from using the scientific method to evaluate their campaign activities. We will next learn about the scientific method and what steps researchers can take to follow it.

11.1.2 Conducting Research Using The Scientific Method

At this point in our textbook, we have mentioned research several times. We discussed secondary data analysis as part of background research, conducting research on your organization to complete a thorough an objective SWOT analysis, and the use of formative research such as surveys, focus groups, and social media analytics to understand your target audience in chapters 5and 6. As you now realize, research is an integral and continual part of the campaign development, implementation, and evaluation process. Regardless of which step in the campaign research is being conducted, it should ideally follow the scientific method to ensure that the information gathered is an accurate reflection of the target audience and campaign. The **scientific method** is a process of conducting research that is used to test research questions and hypotheses. In general, research follows procedures that have been accepted and validated by social scientists across disciplines and over time (Keyton 2011). The five steps of the scientific method outlined below are adapted from those forwarded by communication scholar Joann Keyton (2011) and can be used to conduct research at any stage or for any purpose in strategic communication campaign evaluation. See figure 49 for an illustration of this process.

1. **Start with a question that interests you.** At some point in your academic career, you might conduct a research study with a professor in which you can examine some phenomena of interest to you personally. This might be a research topic based on current events or an idea inspired by an article or something you read in a textbook. In general, all research starts in the same place—with a curious researcher. When it comes to campaign evaluation, the question is usually something relatively straightforward, such as, "Did our message have the intended effect?"

2. **Formulate a hypothesis.** The second step is to form a hypothesis based on your knowledge of the topic you are addressing. A **hypothesis** is an educated guess about the relationship between two or more variables. A hypothesis is generally a short statement, such as, "If there is an increase in y, there will also be an increase in x." The hypothesis is the driving force of the research study. In campaign research, hypotheses are often used to test the effectiveness of one type of message over another. For instance, communication scholars Megan Dillow and Keith Weber (2016) sought to examine if messages promoting organ donation would be more effective among West Virginians if they were targeted toward the needs in this particular state as opposed to more general messages about the need for organ donors. The authors reasoned that being a "West Virginian" is an important part of how their research participants view themselves in social situations, referred to as their social identity, and that this would be an important factor in deciding to be an organ donor. To test this, the researchers developed nearly identical messages, with one mentioning a particular need for donors in West Virginia (i.e., a social identity targeting message) and the other providing more general information on this topic. Residents of West Virginia viewed these messages and were then given the option of providing their information to be signed to the organ donor registry. One of the hypotheses Dillow and Weber included in their study was: "Individuals who receive a social identity targeting message will be more likely to register to become organ donors than will individuals who receive a generic information-based organ donation message" (241). This hypothesis makes a testable statement that assesses the relationship of one variable (type of message) to another (organ donation).

   However, sometimes there is not enough information available to make such a prediction. In this situation, a researcher will instead forward a **research question,** which asks about potential relationships or concepts in a particular context. For communication researchers Foster and colleagues (2014), their research on mother-son communication on testicular cancer forged a path that had been previously unexplored in the literature. In designing their study, the researchers found that there was very little scientific knowledge on how mothers communicate with their sons about the risks of testicular cancer (TC) or even about health issues in general. As such, the researchers addressed research questions in their work, such as, "What health issues do mothers discuss with their sons?" and "Would mothers be willing to discuss TC with their sons?" (68). You will see a noticeable difference between these types of questions, which are very exploratory, and the definitive statement set forth by Dillow and Weber mentioned above. In each case, the researchers selected the appropriate choice—hypothesis or research question—for the context and goals of their particular study. Research questions such as those set forth by

Foster and colleagues (2014) would likely be more appropriate in formative research, where researchers do not yet understand the perceptions, communication, and behaviors of the target audience.

3. **Design and conduct measurement.** The third step in the scientific method is to design and conduct your study. It is your job as the researcher to design a research study that can appropriately and validly assess your research questions or test your hypotheses. There are many guidelines and suggestions in the literature, so we recommend taking courses in research methods to learn what is expected in your academic area of study. If you are an individual working in an organization and do not have the opportunity to take such courses, you likely need to hire a methods consultant to help you with this work and the next step, analyzing your data.

4. **Analyze data.** Once you have your data collected, it is time to analyze the responses provided by your participants. If you are using quantitative research methods—such as surveys or experiment—you will be working with numbers, percentages, and (possibly) statistical analyses. If you have collected qualitative data—through methods such as observation, focus groups, or surveys—you will likely be searching for themes in the words your participants provided or in the observations that you have made. Together, all means of statistical and qualitative analysis require extensive training to do correctly.

5. **Develop conclusions and contribute to new knowledge.** The fifth and final step of the scientific method process is to reflect on the contribution of the data to the problem posed in step 1. How did your research contribute to answering this question? What do you now know as a result of this research process? What still remains to be known, or should be investigated in future research? This is perhaps the most important step—without reflecting on our findings critically, there is little point to conducting research.

As figure 49 illustrates and we discussed in step 5 above, the steps of the scientific method are not linear. Rather, one study builds on the next, resulting in a never-ending cycle of research on human communication behavior. In a similar way, a researcher might return to previous steps as they move through the process of conducting scientific research. You may realize, for instance, in designing your research study that your hypothesis is not clear enough, or cannot be objectively tested. You would then need to return to step 2, to more critically analyze and reflect on your hypothesis in order to design a clear and more valid study. The scientific method should also be used for each type and phase of research conducted during the life of a campaign, from the initial development stages to the final evaluation. Thinking of yourself as a researcher practicing the scientific method will be important for how you approach your research at each of these stages—you will produce nonbiased, informative, and

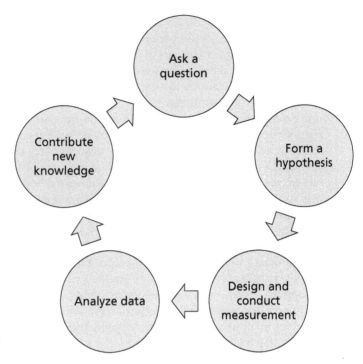

Figure 49 The Five Steps of the Scientific Method.

Strategic Communication Mentor: What Is "Big Data" and What Do I Need to Know about It?

You have likely heard of the term *big data* before, either on the news or in your classes. **Big data** refers to extremely large data sets that can be analyzed to reveal trends, patterns, and associations in human behavior and communication. These data sets, collected from a wide variety of sources including both traditional and social media outlets, is very difficult—if not impossible—to analyze in standard data analysis software programs. While the emergence of big data sets has occurred over several decades (and was used by researchers at NASA as early as 1991), the term came into more popular use as it was defined by industry leader Doug Laney in 2001 using the three V's: volume, velocity, and variety. In order for a data set to be considered "big data" it must be high in volume, acquired almost immediately (often in real time), and be highly varied in terms of content. Some examples of common "big data" sets include activity on Twitter feeds, clicks on mobile apps, and buying behaviors among online consumers.

Watch the following advertisement (embedded in the website) produced by Oracle, a global provider of cloud computing software, that provides an overview of big data and why it matters in the modern business world (according to their company):

www.oracle.com/big-data/guide/what-is-big-data.html

Once you have watched this video, read the Oracle page on Big Data and answer the following questions with a friend:

1. What are some of the benefits for organizations using big data?
2. What would be the hesitations or barriers associated with using these types of data? Does Oracle address these in their advertisement? If so, do they do so effectively? Why or why not?
3. Closely read the "Big Data Best Practices" section of this web page. Which of these best practices align with content in this chapter? In what ways could big data be incorporated into developing an evaluation plan for a communication campaign? Which stage of research do you think "big data" could be most effective in?

accurate knowledge about your campaign. Next, we will turn to the three main phases of research you might conduct throughout the development, implementation, and evaluation of a strategic communication campaign.

11.2 THE THREE PHASES OF CAMPAIGN EVALUATION

Over the course of a campaign there are three types of information that should be collected, each of which corresponds to the development, implementation, and evaluation phases of the campaign process (Rice and Atkin 2013). The information that is collected can be broadly defined as formative, process, and summative research; each of these cycles will provide critically important information before, during, and after your campaign's implementation. In the coming sections, we will define and discuss examples of each of these types of research and how they have been used in actual campaign assessment. Keep in mind as you read this chapter that not only should each of these types of research follow the scientific method, each type should also be related to and informed by research collected at previous stages. As a campaign designer, it is your responsibility to ensure that the research your organization conducts is systematic, helpful, and (perhaps most importantly) feasible given your organization's resources. You will learn how to make these judgments in later sections of this chapter.

11.2.1 Before the Campaign: Conducting Formative Research

Formative research is conducted to understand the issues facing your target audience, to understand how and when to best reach the members of the target audience, and to develop preliminary understandings of how they will react to campaign activities. As we discussed in chapter 6, the quantitative and qualitative research conducted *prior* to the development of your messages is central to understanding your target audience. Formative research therefore refers to any research conducted before your campaign is implemented, which may include research conducted before or after your messages are developed (Atkin and Freimuth 1989). Using surveys, focus groups, or social media platforms, this research might help you understand your target audience's preferences, behaviors, opinions, or values. This information is invaluable when selecting appropriate messages for your campaign, appropriate channels, and improving existing programs. In fact, in his review of ten years of international mass media campaigns, scholar Seth Noar (2006) found that the most effective campaigns were consistent in their use of formative research to understand their target audience.

An excellent example of this is research by the National Institute for Occupational Safety and Health (NIOSH) on coal miner exposure to hazardous silica dust. Researchers Haas, Willmer, and Cecala (2016) conducted formative research to not only understand miners' attitudes and behaviors related to dangerous silicon exposure but also to assess the potential for helmet cameras to be used as a preventive tool. The researchers worked with two target audiences—mine workers and mine management—to address formative research questions such as, "What are mine workers' current knowledge and attitudes toward respirable silica dust exposure?" and "What are worker and management perceptions of dust assessment technology?" (3). To answer these questions, the research team attended stakeholder meetings, observed coal miners at work at several industrial mine sites in the United States, conducted interviews with mine workers at these locations, and held focus groups with mine management. The researchers also met with mining engineers and technology experts to fully understand the hazards of silica dust exposure and how helmet camera technologies might be implemented as a preventive measure.

As the researchers note, health communication theories were used to develop their questions for all methods, which was a particular strength in organizing their research and understanding both of their target audiences in more depth. The results of this in-depth formative research revealed a wealth of information that helped the NIOSH researchers to develop a six-week intervention, including the need to increase and improve manager-miner communication, allow for managers to have one-on-one time with employees to review their helmet camera footage and work on safety practices (an excellent example of tailored communication, as discussed in chapter 6), and including stakeholders in the process to build trust and commitment to using new technologies to address this critical health issue.

Formative research can also be used after messages have been developed. Referred to by communication scholars Roberto, Murray-Johnson, and Witte (2011) as *postproduction* research, research that exposes target audiences to potential campaign messages and assesses their reaction is helpful for creating clear, appealing, and appropriate messages. This also allows you the opportunity to identify and correct potential problems before a campaign is enacted (Roberto, Murray-Johnson, and Witte 2011). Always keep in mind that you are not the "expert" in how your target audience feels, believes, or interacts with your organization; your target audience must be the first and continual source of that information. To achieve this level of understanding of your target audience and its members' reaction to your campaign messages, there are four types of formative research you might consider conducting.

11.2.2 Four Types of Formative Research

The following summarize the four most commonly discussed types of formative research, but keep in mind that formative research constitutes any information collected prior to the implementation of your campaign. An organization might use one, a combination, or all of the following types of formative research in developing a strategic communication campaign. In general, the more formative research you can conduct, the better your chances of achieving success.

- **Baseline assessments.** A key aspect of campaign evaluation starts at the beginning of your process—collecting baseline measures from your target audience. You likely have information on your target audience's current buying behaviors, attitudes, or levels of awareness already—these were helpful in developing your goals and objectives in chapter 5 and understanding your target audience in chapter 6. When it comes to evaluation, these same pieces of information will be helpful in knowing if your communication efforts actually made an impact.
- **Developmental research and concept testing. Concept testing** is when you present your target audience with initial concepts for the visual and verbal messages of your campaign and ask for feedback. This feedback is then incorporated into the development of complete messages, which are used in the pretesting stage discussed below.
- **Pretesting.** In chapter 6, we discussed pretesting your messages with your target audience. In this audience-centered process, your messages can be shaped and refined by representatives of the groups you seek to influence (Maibach and Parrott 1995). In pretesting you are seeking to assess critical questions in the development and refinement of your messages, including

questions about target audience reception of the message (i.e., was the message received), comprehension (i.e., was the message understood correctly), and response (i.e., what effect did the message have). Ultimately, including your audience in this way can also increase the audience's level of involvement and participation in your efforts (Minkler 2000).

- **Pilot testing.** A **pilot test** is a small-scale implementation of your larger campaign. You can think of a pilot test as a sort of "trial run" of the campaign, in which all campaign activities are implemented in order to catch any mistakes or issues prior to a full-scale launch. You might realize in a pilot test, perhaps, that your staff needs further training, that some activities take more time than anticipated, or that your messages are not achieving their intended effect. Pilot testing can also be used to assess the utility of the measurement instruments you intend to use in your evaluation plan.

You will find that these types of research are regularly discussed in various fields related to strategic communication, from marketing to advertising. Approaching formative research with a communication studies lens and using the scientific method, however, offers a distinct advantage. Communication scholars focus on effective message delivery and understanding both sources and receivers of communication—and as such are well equipped to design studies that understand target audience perceptions and reactions. Communication scholars are experts in audience analysis and message-testing research (Atkin and Freimuth 1989), and this perspective will serve you well in creating a plan for formative research in your campaign process.

11.2.3 During the Campaign: Conducting Process Research

The second phase of evaluation research is conducted while your campaign is being implemented. As you recall from chapter 10, process research refers to the assessment of ongoing campaign activities. You may also hear of this as monitoring research, as it provides a monitoring of campaign activities for both their cost-benefit ratio and overall impact. As we have discussed previously in this chapter, evaluation is not something that occurs solely at the end of a strategic communication campaign. It is also not a one-time activity. Rather, evaluation efforts are ongoing and continually implemented aspects of the campaign process.

Part of process evaluation includes keeping a record of campaign activities, including the number of people reached through various communication channels, target audience interaction with the product, and initial indicators of changes in attitudes or behavior. Feedback mechanisms such as comment cards, hotlines, help desks, consumer surveys, and focus groups are all common means of conducting monitoring research (Kreps 2008). In their inter-

Figure 50 Process research helps to track if your target audience is being exposed to your messages—this is increasingly important in the modern, competitive advertising environment.

views with eighteen key personnel in social media marketing firms, researchers Keegan and Rowley (2017) found that metrics such as the number of mentions, likes, and followers on social media are important (and easily obtained) metrics. However, as the participants in Keegan and Rowley's research noted, the statistics that can be obtained on social media sites or in external data collection mechanisms (e.g., Hootsuite) should be framed in the context of the larger objectives for the social media marketing campaign, lest the sometimes overwhelming amount of numbers become meaningless. In other words, knowing that you had three thousand likes on a particular post might be informative but not helpful if your campaign objectives did not include exposure to social media posts.

In advertising campaigns, this process research is sometimes referred to as "tracking" an ongoing campaign (Pai, Siddarth, and Divakar 2007, 233). Tracking examinations are meant to assess if ad campaigns are working, how they compare to messages being sent by competitors, and to provide diagnostics that can improve advertisement effectiveness (Pai, Siddarth, and Divakar 2007). Process research is also key to ensuring that organizational campaign activities stay consistent with the budget and timeline, as we discuss in chapter 10. As we saw with Malik in the beginning of the chapter, process research offers an opportunity for organizations to be reflective and flexible; this fluidity and adaptability differentiates successful and unsuccessful campaigns. In sum, conducting process research is an important aspect of developing your campaign evaluation and implementation plans, as it provides a means of if your campaign is headed on a path to achieving its objectives.

11.2.4 After the Campaign: Conducting Summative Research

The final phase of data collection relevant to your campaign is summative research. **Summative research** refers to any research conducted following the conclusion of your campaign or a campaign cycle. This will include assessments of the campaign's impact, what improvements can be made for future campaign iterations, and plans for the dissemination of findings related to these assessments (Valente 2001). This is likely the phase most people think of when referring to evaluating a campaign's effectiveness. Summative research requires careful planning; despite being the evaluation at the *end* of the campaign process, it should also be outlined in the beginning of your planning. That way, all campaign activities should be directed at achieving that end goal, whether it be increased sales, reduction in crime, or increased awareness of a public health hazard. In this way, you can think of summative research as being similar to final exams at the end of the semester. Your course is carefully designed to ensure that you gain the requisite knowledge to perform well on final assessments. Should you do well throughout the entire course and fail the exam, the instructor will reevaluate the course assignments, the exam, and the reasons why you did not learn the content as intended. In a similar way, campaigns and their accompanying summative evaluation are considered together in the planning process and are used to inform improvements of future iterations of the campaign. In strategic communication campaigns, summative research will include assessments of both *outcomes* and *impact.*

Summative Research: Outcome Evaluation

In **outcome evaluation,** the first and most obvious phase of summative research, data are collected to examine if the campaign met its intended objectives. Outcome evaluation concerns the effects that directly result from your campaign, and whether your campaign achieved what it intended to do. If you followed the SMART method for objective development discussed in chapter 5, then you have already carefully considered how to measure your objectives—your job here is to follow through on those measurement plans. If you have not developed your objectives following this method, you may not have collected the data along the way that are needed to know if you met your targeted effects (and those effects will likely be less specific). Typical intended effects include changes in knowledge and awareness, beliefs, and behavior.

Consider for instance the summative evaluation research of the 4-Day-Throw-Away campaign, as discussed by James and colleagues (2013). This traditional and social media campaign aimed to increase awareness and knowledge of the dangers of foodborne illness caused by unsafe leftover food practices in two midwestern states. Following the campaign, researchers conducted intercept surveys (remember this key term from chapter 6?) at local grocery stores. The results of this summative research indicated that not only was the campaign largely recognized among its target audience but also had actually affected the reported food safety behaviors of individuals exposed to the campaign. James and colleagues (2013) were able to assess through this research that the intended outcomes of the campaign were therefore met. If, however, James and colleagues wished to assess the long-term effects of increased food safety on foodborne illness, they would need to conduct an impact evaluation.

Summative Research: Impact Evaluation

Impact evaluation is much more complex in nature than outcome evaluation—even with clear objectives. An **impact evaluation** assesses the long-term effects of the campaign on the target audience and its overall progress toward larger campaign goals. Whereas the outcome evaluation asks, *Did the campaign achieve its intended objectives?* an impact evaluation asks, *What long-term impacts has the campaign had?* As such, an impact evaluation is often more appropriate to conduct for an established or repeated campaign (Centers for Disease Control and Prevention 2017). Consider, for instance, the long-term evidence provided by the National Recreation and Parks Association (2017) on the influence of safe park spaces on community crime levels: As the organization notes, the restoration of Bryant Park in New York City is one of many examples of how revitalizing parks can have a long-term impact on local communities. Once a poorly maintained park riddled with crime and drug use, the Bryant Park Restoration Cooperation (BPRC) was created in the 1990s to come up with a master plan for managing the park. The BPRC added amenities to the park including food and beverage kiosks, a restaurant, and also remodeled park entrances to create more space and openness. Results of a seven-year impact evaluation revealed that the revitalized park not only draws twice as many visitors annually but also has had a 92 percent reduction in crime. As this example indicates, whereas outcome evaluation is typically measured at the individual level (in this case, it may include an observation of park use or measurement of individuals' attitudes related to park safety), impact evaluation includes assessments of community- or society-wide changes that have occurred as a result of campaign efforts. This might require measuring changes in entire schools, communities, organizations, or the environment (Centers for Disease Control and Prevention 2017). This undoubtedly requires more resources, which your organization may or may not have. Resources are just one consideration in developing your evaluation plan—next, we will cover four other key considerations in this process.

Figure 51 Impact evaluations are vital to the improvement and maintenance of community spaces.

11.3 FIVE CONSIDERATIONS IN CREATING AN EVALUATION PLAN

A central part of the strategic communication planning process is to develop a detailed plan for evaluation. In doing so, there are five major considerations that should be included in the creation of an organization's campaign evaluation plan. In this section, will provide some detail on each of these five considerations.

11.3.1 Consider Your Objectives

The objectives of your campaign will be a crucial guide to understanding your campaign's successes and failures. We discuss developing SMART objectives in detail in chapter 5, and following these steps will certainly facilitate the evaluation process—in fact, in addressing the "M" in SMART, you are already considering how your intended campaign outcomes will be *measurable.* Suppose Harper, the museum business manager mentioned at the start of this chapter, set an objective to, "Increase children's tickets sold by 5% in the next 12 months." This objective clearly dictates what should be measured and when, making Harper's job of evaluating the museum's success much easier. In some cases, however, it may be less clear what to measure to see if your objectives are met—and what to measure in your campaign overall. We turn to this broader consideration next.

11.3.2 Decide What to Measure

As Salmon and Murray-Johnson (2013) write, measuring objectives and the outcomes related to them is not the only aspect of campaigns that should be evaluated. Rather, a more comprehensive scan of the campaign environment is often needed to determine issues related to the campaign and/or aspects of the environment affected by campaign activities. Although many of the things that you measure will be guided by your theoretical framework and research design (discussed in more detail later in this chapter), a useful interdisciplinary framework for creating an evaluation plan is to use a logic model (W. K. Kellogg Foundation 2004).

Using a Logic Model

A **logic model** is a visual way to present how your resources, campaign activities and messages, and intended outcomes are related. It can include theoretical constructs, or it can be developed without a theory if one is not being used. What is crucial to the logic model is to include campaign activities as well as the short- and long-term goals they are intended to affect. Ideally, a logic model will connect the theoretical framework to these activities and in turn the outcomes that will be affected. A logic model therefore consists of five key components: inputs, activities, outputs, outcomes, and impact (see figure 52). In the space below, we will discuss each of these five components in more detail:

- **Inputs.** The inputs include all of the resources that your organization has to direct toward the campaign. This would include money, time, employees/volunteers, and organizational and community resources. This would likely be information that would emerge in the *Strengths* part of a SWOT analysis. As such, this is likely the easiest and most straightforward analysis in using a logic model.
- **Activities.** Activities are all of the components of the campaign message delivery. This will include events, advertisements, technology, or any other aspect of your campaign intervention conducted during the implementation phase with the intention of affecting your outcomes.
- **Outputs.** Outputs represent how campaign inputs were used. This falls into the process research discussed above, in that all campaign activities are quantified. For example, how many commercials were aired? At what cost? Were all activities implemented according to plan and within the budget?
- **Outcomes.** Outcomes are the specific changes in your target audience as a result of campaign activities. This can be short-term (i.e., a few weeks or months) or long-term (i.e., a few years).
- **Impact.** Distinct from outcomes, the impact of a campaign is its broader effect on the goals of the campaign. As you recall from chapter 5, the long-term goals of a campaign tend to fall into one of two categories: task management and relationship/identity management. That is, goals may be to

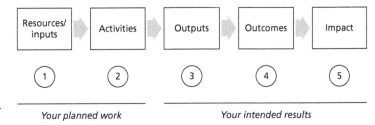

Figure 52 The Logic Model.

help an organization fulfill its mission or purpose (e.g., manufacture textiles) or they may concern the identity and reputation of the organization (e.g., responding to negative media coverage).

The logic model is intended to be read from left to right, with an "if-then" mentality connecting the five steps (W. K. Kellogg Foundation 2004). Starting on the left, you can see that certain inputs or resources are needed to start a campaign. If you have those resources, then you can use them to plan your campaign activities. If you accomplish your campaign activities, then you will produce certain outputs. If these outputs are achieved, then you will produce measurable outcomes in your target audience, and so on.

Distinguishing between Effects, Effectiveness, and Efficiency

As you can see, an advantage of using a logic model is the clarity and systematic thinking it necessitates (W. K. Kellogg Foundation 2004). Your logic model will also help you to assess three critical pieces of information in campaign assessment: campaign effects, campaign effectiveness, and campaign efficiency (Valente 2001).

> **Campaign effects** are any changes in your outcome variables that can be traced back to your campaign efforts. These might have been predicted or unpredicted (see the Strategic Communication Mentor on the unintended effects of campaigns later in this chapter) and may be positive or negative in nature.

> **Campaign effectiveness** is the extent to which the effects were consistent with previously defined campaign goals and objectives; in other words, this is the more traditional assessment of "did your campaign do what it intended to do?" If the answer to that question is yes, then you have an effective campaign. The answer is likely more complicated, with both successes and failures in your campaign plan.

> This makes the last piece of information even more crucial to assess— **campaign efficiency** concerns the balance of costs and outcomes; were the

campaign costs in terms of resources (e.g., time, money, risk) outweighed by its effects? If the answer to this question is *yes*, then the campaign will likely be received more favorably among stakeholders and supported in future iterations. If the answer is *no*, changes will be required so that the campaign is not a detriment to the organization's financial health. A simple metric for use in the nonprofit sector is the fund-raising cost per dollar raised. That is, the amount of money raised in a fund-raiser should be compared directly to how much it cost to run the fund-raising activities (Matthews 2017). If your organization has conducted multiple fund-raisers, carefully examine the patterns. Are the most expensive fund-raising activities in turn generating the most donations? If not, it might be time to reexamine the campaign strategies.

Together, assessments of campaign effects, effectiveness, and efficiency compose the evaluation process (Valente 2001). Understanding effects and effectiveness as separate constructs allows for multiple interpretations of whether a campaign was successful. Although these terms are often treated as synonymous and interchangeable, health communication scholars in particular have long argued the need to carefully consider effects and effectiveness as separate in discussing campaign evaluations (Roberto, Murray-Johnson, and Witte 2011; Salmon and Murray-Johnson 2001). Ultimately, what you decide to measure will be based on the theory that you use to frame your campaign as well as the resources you have available to you to conduct this evaluation (discussed in more detail later in this section).

11.3.3 Determine Your Research Design

If you are following the steps of the scientific method in conducting your evaluation, you will need to determine your research design. A **research design** is the general framework that you will use to answer your research objectives. Your research design will dictate how you conduct your campaign assessments as well as when you will conduct them.

Quantitative and Qualitative Research

We broadly discussed types of research in chapter 5 in distinguishing between *quantitative* (i.e., results expressed in numerical terms) and *qualitative* (i.e., results expressed in non-numerical terms) ways of measuring a campaign's objectives. As we have discussed previously in this chapter, formative research is concerned with understanding your target audience. This might be through focus groups or interviews on your campaign topic, which would be *qualitative* in nature. On the other hand, formative research might include baseline assessments and statistics that help establish your target audience's level of awareness, knowledge, and behavior prior to campaign activities. This would be more *quantitative,* as you would be relying on numbers and percentages in your results. However, research design encompasses a much more comprehensive set of choices and considerations that must be made in developing an evaluation plan. Next, we will cover one of these choices, deciding between cross-sectional and longitudinal research designs.

When to Collect Data: Cross-Sectional and Longitudinal Research Designs

In developing your evaluation plan, you will have to decide prior to campaign activities how many times and when you will collect data from your target audience. A **cross-sectional research design** measures data at one point in time from a target audience. A cross-sectional research design is very common in communication studies research, as it allows researchers to quickly examine a subsection of the population. Of course, your results must then be interpreted with the particular time in which you collected data in mind. If you were assessing people's attitudes and behaviors related to the National Hockey League, for instance, you might find that people identify more with their team and view more games during late spring than during other parts of the year, like late summer. Why? Any hockey fan will tell you—late spring is when playoffs typically occur. Fans who don't normally watch games during the regular season are more likely to turn on the TV to watch a game, wear a team jersey, and talk about hockey during playoff season. Suppose you are collecting marketing information for an NHL hockey team—this information is critical to your evaluation design. Whatever choice you make—whether to conduct research during the off, regular, or playoff season—is yours, but it should always be considered in how you evaluate your results.

Another consideration in using a cross-sectional research design is that you may be measuring variables that change—such as self-esteem, exercise behaviors, or awareness of a new cleaning product—as if they stay the same over time. The nature of this design is that you measure individual's characteristics at one particular point in time but not how they may change over days, weeks, months, or years. This is likely of particular interest to you if your objectives including assessing the long-term impact of your campaign. Therefore, to do this, you would need a longitudinal research design. A **longitudinal research design** involves multiple data collection periods and is typically used to examine changes that appear across those periods of time. This can be very helpful for examining trends in social media, marketing, political climate, or any number of variables that may change often. You can also use longitudinal designs to assess campaign effectiveness. For example, community health researchers Hull and colleagues (2017) collected data each year from 2011 to 2015 in Milwaukee to assess the impact of a social marketing campaign to reduce homophobia among black communities. Each year, the research team surveyed a unique sample of both white and black men on their perceptions and attitudes toward gay men. By using this longitudinal design, the researchers were able to offer substantial evidence that their multimedia campaign led to increased acceptance of gay men in the targeted communities.

11.3.4 Assign Measurement Responsibilities

As part of your evaluation plan, you must also determine who in your campaign team will conduct these evaluations. The evaluation of a campaign might be conducted by individuals internal or external to the organization, depending on both resources and the purpose of the evaluation. Although this may seem overly precautious to plan ahead of time, particularly if you are working with a small team where you might be inclined to think, "we will figure that out when we get there," the actual evaluation activities can be incredibly time consuming depending on your research design. As we discussed in chapter 6, focus groups require trained moderators to lead meaningful discussions—you will need to determine how many moderators you will have on your team, how they will be trained, and how many focus groups they can reasonably conduct in your time frame and within your budget. Further, a moderator will need one or two **moderator assistants,** who do not conduct the focus group but rather help set up logistics (such as audio recorders, refreshments, and name tags) to facilitate the focus group. Longitudinal surveys are by nature time consuming and require a long-term commitment from a member of your campaign team. You must also consider if your evaluators will be internal or external to your team—as this will be an important consideration in not only how your target audience perceives data collection but also how others view the objectivity of your evaluation report. Whereas external evaluators are seen as more credible, they may also be disadvantaged in that they have inherently less knowledge about the finer workings of the organization than those internal to it (Valente 2001).

11.3.5 Consider the Cost of Evaluation

The perceived cost of performing an evaluation is a central reason why organizations avoid it (Valente 2001). However, if the evaluation is built into the strategic plan for the campaign, the associated costs can be controlled and prepared for—and, as Valente (2001) notes, the benefits of conducting an evaluation to improve future campaign iterations far outweigh the typical evaluation costs of 10–15 percent of the overall budget. For the more complex and

Table 11.1 Sample Table to Organize Evaluation Plan

Objective	What to Measure?	When to Measure?	Who Will Measure?	How Much Will It Cost?

time-consuming impact evaluations we discussed previously, these costs might reach 30 percent of the overall budget. The costs of campaign evaluation can range from very minimal, even free, to significant (Lee and Kotler 2011). For instance, if your campaign evaluation only requires checking your state's organ donor registry to see if their numbers increased during your campaign, fulfilling this requirement is relatively inexpensive. Surveys are relatively inexpensive, especially if you use a low-cost online platform to design and collect responses. However, if you need to conduct advanced statistical analyses, a consultant may be required (which is typically a high cost). Whatever decisions you make, they should be based on the value that the results will have to your campaign—if you need to ensure that your surveys are well designed and analyzed appropriately so that you can request further funding, then hiring a consultant is likely a worthy investment of resources. Consider Mariana's task at the beginning of the chapter—hiring a consultant to help conduct market research is worth the cost, considering it could save her company from bankruptcy.

In sum, there are five key considerations in creating an evaluation plan (see table 11.1 for a summary of these considerations). First, you must carefully consider your campaign objectives—these will be central to determining if your campaign achieved its intended effect on the target audience. Second, determine what to measure. You might rely on logic models here and should keep in mind the differences between effects, effectiveness, and efficiency. Third, you must select a research design. You might collect data at one time in a cross-sectional design or choose to examine long-term effects in longitudinal research. Fourth, determine who will be collecting this data. As you can see, evaluation plans require a lot of time and effort—so making sure that you have dedicated staff will help things run smoothly. Finally, consider the cost of evaluation. An unfortunate truth is that your evaluation is going to be limited by the resources that you have—whether it be time, money, or staff. That isn't to say that an organization without many resources cannot conduct a good evaluation! By following the steps of the scientific method, and the principles we have discussed throughout this chapter, any organization can conduct a meaningful and useful evaluation. In the next and final section of this chapter, we will discuss a few tips for writing an evaluation report.

Strategic Communication Mentor: When Campaigns Have Unintended Effects

Unfortunately for campaign and message designers, sometimes even carefully and thoughtfully designed messages are not only ineffective but also produce outcomes that the source did not intend. In some cases, the message might even persuade the receiver to do, think, or feel the *opposite* of what the message was designed to do! This is known as a **boomerang effect** (Hovland, Janis, and Kelly 1953). If you have ever seen a frustrated parent tell their toddler to stop throwing a ball, only to have the toddler throw the ball *harder,* then you have seen the boomerang effect in action. This type of reaction actually happens frequently in response to persuasive messages among audiences of all ages.

Consider for instance research conducted by communication scholars Liang, Henderson, and Kee (2018) on messages used to encourage water conservation to reduce the ongoing drought in California. After identifying the three most commonly used messages in communication campaigns addressing the issue—namely, messages that promote conservation tips, messages that provide visual and concrete evidence of the drought, and messages that highlight the negative consequences of not conserving water—the researchers conducted a study in which residents of California were presented with these messages and completed measures indicating their likelihood to conserve water and their perception of the drought. Liang and colleagues were surprised to find that each type of water conservation message only served to decrease positive attitudes toward conservation—essentially, a boomerang effect. As the researchers note in their study, possible (but untested) reasons for this may be that participants did not trust the credibility of the message, or the message made them uncomfortable or fearful and so they chose to ignore it.

This type of reaction is in fact very common in campaigns that use messages to induce fear in their target audience. Campaigns addressing drinking (Snyder and Blood 1992) and safe sex (Cline, Johnson, and Freeman 1992) have been found to actually increase the behavior they intended to reduce, particularly when the messages present a threat without convincing the audience that they are able to overcome it (Witte 1992). However, unintended effects of persuasive messages can be broader (and even positive), as noted by scholars Cho and Salmon (2007). For instance, a school-based campaign encouraging adolescents to recycle might have an unintended effect of also influencing their parents to practice these behaviors at home.

Discuss your answers to the following questions with a peer in your class:

1. Have you ever had a reaction to a campaign message or advertisement that was opposite of what the source intended you to have? Explain the message and why you felt the way you did. How could the message have been altered to be effective?
2. What challenges do unintended effects present for evaluating strategic messages? How can researchers account for these in their evaluation? How would this change at each of the three stages of evaluation?
3. Based on what we have discussed in this chapter, how can unintended effects be avoided?
4. If the boomerang effect is positive—as we provide an example of with recycling above—is the campaign still "effective" per the definition we provide in this chapter? Why or why not?

Figure 53 Similar to effective communication in other contexts, much of writing and presenting an effective evaluation report will require anticipating the questions the readers of your report may have.

11.4 CONSIDERATIONS IN WRITING AN EVALUATION REPORT

Once you have decided what you will measure for your evaluation and when you will measure it, you must decide how you will present the results of these assessments to internal and external stakeholders of your organization. A good way to do this is by compiling an **evaluation report,** or a written summary of your campaign activities and any evidence of campaign effects, effectiveness, and efficiency. This document will describe any formative, process, and summative research conducted throughout the course of the campaign's development, implementation, and evaluation. The evaluation report should describe your campaign activities and how they linked (or did not link) to intended outcomes, how your campaign was implemented, and why your campaign should or should not be continued. Particularly for organizations seeking continued or increased funding, this last question will be crucial to answer well.

Although an evaluation report is an ongoing process for most organizations (i.e., assessing a marketing campaign takes multiple, repeated assessments), it is good for an organization to set markers defined by time or objectives to periodically assess progress. For some organizations, this timing might be obvious, such as the end of a particular fund-raising campaign or initiative. For others, such as entrepreneurial startups looking to assess the impact of their advertisements on brand equity and exposure, the timing might require more strategic thinking by organizational leaders. For many government and nonprofit organizations, the end of a particular funding period is typically a time when evaluation reports are created. Regardless of when the report is created in the life of the campaign, there are a few key considerations to keep in mind when writing your evaluation report.

The creation and dissemination of an evaluation report is an important part of the summative research process. This becomes an interactive process in which campaign findings are discussed with internal and external stakeholders, and the results can be used to reformulate campaign goals (if necessary) and restrategize for future efforts. This is therefore an important document not only in terms of summarizing past and current efforts but also in influencing the future of the strategic communication campaign for your organization.

In writing your evaluation report, there are a few key considerations that should not be overlooked. They are:

- **Consider your audience.** Before you write your report, think carefully about who you intend to read this document. Will this information be shared only with your volunteers, or will it be distributed in the monthly newsletter? Will this information be presented at the company's annual conference, or just distributed to members in administration? Once you have an intended audience in mind, it is likely helpful to state this in the report along with what you hope to be the purpose of providing this information. This might include: to increase transparency with stakeholders, to inform employees of the ongoing messaging in the organization, or to report to the funding sources how funding was used. Stating this clearly in your report will provide clarity and transparency for its eventual readers.

  For many organizations, the activity of conducting systematic evaluations will be subject to various political pressures both from organizational management and outside parties; it is up to the evaluators to resist such pressures not only to maintain the integrity of the evaluation but also to be conscious of how their report may affect organizational relationships and functioning (Lipsky et al. 2007). Consider Malik's dilemma in the beginning of this chapter—it will be important for Malik to honestly and objectively evaluate the efforts of the Office of Energy Efficiency and Renewable Energy, regardless of pressures he might face from superiors to "paint a positive picture" of their efforts. However, the data he has collected that indicate that the office is not performing well could have implications for his job as well as his employees. The consequences of a "bad" report must be carefully considered—a report that suggests an organization is not meeting its objectives could compromise the life of that program and subsequently the jobs of its employees. How will this news be delivered, and to whom? Will organizational leaders be notified first, or be allowed to be a part of framing this bad news? When organizations hire outside parties to conduct evaluations, such as consulting or research firms, it will be important to set clear expectations for what is expected from the research process and subsequent report (Lipsky et al. 2007).
- **Restate mission, goals, and objectives.** As we discussed in chapter 3, all of the strategic communication activities that your organization undergoes should be in line with your organization's mission as well as the long-term goals and short-term objectives of your communication campaign. It is important to remind your reader of these aspects of the strategic communication process, so that they can see how your campaign activities connect to these "big picture" concepts in the life of the organization. In terms of

objectives, how you have conducted your evaluation will have been strongly influenced by the objectives you set forth—so stating these early and clearly in your evaluation report helps to make sense of what you have accomplished.

- **Summarize campaign activities.** Your evaluation report should include a detailed account of all formative, process, and summative research conducted for your campaign. How much of this information and how you present it will be dependent on your intended reader—if you are preparing this report for the engineers of an architectural firm, they will likely be interested in different information than will the investors of that firm. If you are preparing one report for all potential interested readers (which may be the most time- and cost-effective option), then be sure to include all relevant information for your various audiences.

  In this section, you should also clearly state how your effects and effectiveness were measured. This includes what questions you asked your target audience (if any), analyses used, and any other source of data included in your assessments. If you used a logic model or experimental design to structure your evaluation, present it here, as well as any indicators of campaign efficiency. Visual aids and graphical representations of your work will likely be helpful in presenting your work clearly and in a way that your audience can understand, which we discuss in more detail next.

- **Provide and interpret results.** In addition to summarizing campaign activities, a significant part of your report—both in length and emphasis—should be your results and what they mean for your organization. As argued by the Centers for Disease Control and Prevention (2013), the interpretation of results is often skipped in evaluation reports—but is actually one of the most important steps of moving a communication campaign forward. What do your results mean in terms of next steps for your organization? How does all of the effort put into this campaign translate into both immediate and long-term plans? If you are conducting research using the scientific method, this will be a natural final step in the research process. Discussing how your results will improve and modify future campaign activities is important for connecting the past, present, and future of your organization.

- **Use plain language.** Plain language is communication that an audience can understand the first time they read or hear it. In 2010, the Plain Language Act was signed into effect by the US government, which requires federal agencies to use clear communication so that information can be understood and used by pubic audiences. The results of this act included the establishment of "Plain Writing Guidelines" (see plainlanguage.gov) that can be used in all contexts, by all message designers, to clearly structure written information. Although we cannot possibly provide all of these guidelines here, viewing this report will be immensely helpful as you plan your own writing. Information on the use of pronouns, active voice, everyday words, and logical organi-

Strategic Communication Mentor: Editing for Plain Language

As we discuss in this chapter, following the Plain Language Guidelines set forth by the Plain Language Action and Information Network is good practice for writing your evaluation report. Although these resources are primarily directed at government agencies, the writing principles they cover can be used in any organizational context.

The following example is provided on plainlanguage.gov. In the left column is government text on Medicaid eligibility; on the right, the same information is presented in plain language.

Medicaid Eligibility	
Before Plain Language Editing	**After Plain Language Editing**
Medicaid: Apply if you are aged (65 years old or older), blind, or disabled and have low income and few resources. Apply if you are terminally ill and want to receive hospice services. Apply if you are aged, blind, or disabled; live in a nursing home; and have low income and limited resources. Apply if you are aged, blind, or disabled and need nursing home care, but can stay at home with special community care services. Apply if you are eligible for Medicare and have low income and limited resources.	You may apply for Medicaid if you are: o Terminally ill and want hospice services o Eligible for Medicare and have low income and limited resources o 65 years old or older, blind, or disabled and have low income and few resources and: o Live in a nursing home o Need a nursing home care but can stay at home with special community care services

Examples taken from plainlanguage.gov/examples

Questions to Consider:

1. What differences do you notice between these two columns in how they are structured? How the is the language used differently?
2. What are some commercial products that could benefit from plain language editing? Find an example of such writing and edit it according to the principles outlined in the Plain Language Guidelines.
3. How do these plain language principles apply to online or social media communication?

zation are all incredibly relevant to constructing evaluation reports. See the Strategic Communication Mentor for an example of plain language.

- **Select channels for dissemination.** Just as you carefully selected channels for your campaign messages (see chapter 8), so too must you consider the appropriate and most effective outlet to distribute your evaluation report. Depending on the audience, the evaluation report might be shared in debriefing meetings, conferences, reports distributed internally or publicly published, and even peer reviewed journal articles. Ideally, the presentation of the evaluation report and accompanying materials fosters a relationship with stakeholders and generates decision-making for future campaign activities (Keegan and Rowley 2017). If your strategic communication campaign is an ongoing program for your organization—such as a marketing campaign or an annual government-funded program—then establishing feedback loops for stakeholders to offer their input and ideas for improvement will be imperative.

- **Don't forget the nuts and bolts.** Just as you would spend time ensuring that a thesis or research paper is organized clearly and in such a way that important information can easily be found, so too should you ensure that your evaluation report is properly structured. Include a title page that credits anyone involved in creating the report. An abstract or summary will be helpful as a second page, so that readers can quickly glance at the purpose, activities, and results of your campaign evaluation. Include a list of references and further readings, should a reader want to look up more information on your topic. A table of contents would also be helpful for readers to find relevant information quickly. Remember—the purpose of this report is to provide transparency in your evaluation process, so the report should be well constructed and easily accessible. You should not have to guide the reader through your report.

11.5 TYING IT ALL TOGETHER: THE STRUCTURE AND TIMING OF STRATEGIC COMMUNICATION CAMPAIGN EVALUATION

In this chapter we have discussed the importance of campaign evaluation to organizations of all types as well as how communication scholars would approach systematic campaign evaluation using the scientific method. We have reviewed the three major phases of campaign evaluation—formative, process, and summative research—as well as the considerations organizations should have at each of these phases in their campaign process. We have discussed important considerations for putting together an evaluation plan, including what information to collect and how to collect it. Finally, we discussed the evaluation report—an important document that summarizes all of your hard work in evaluating your campaign efforts. As you read the chapter, you were reminded of our friends Mariana, Harper, and Malik—each of whom work in very different fields but have the same need for effective and thorough assessment plans. As you have seen, there is not a "one size fits all" approach to campaign evaluation—the decisions that an organization makes should be based on its history, expectations, culture, and needs. Further, the evaluation process itself is fluid—at any point along the strategic communication campaign process, adjustments to the evaluation can be made to ensure that the most accurate and helpful information is being collected from and about the target audience.

There are two key points that you should take from this chapter. First, the evaluation process for a strategic communication campaign should be *carefully planned and structured.* The careful planning will require you to include your evaluation procedures in your implementation strategies, to think of what information you need to collect and when, and to assign duties within your organization so that all phases of evaluation run smoothly. A theoretical framework, a logic model, your research design or (ideally) all three should influence this structure. Second, your evaluation process *should be considered at the beginning of the strategic campaign process.* In fact, you should begin your journey in strategic communication campaigns with the end in mind. In the earliest planning stages of your campaign you should set clear and measurable objectives (as we discuss in chapter 5) and also start thinking about the way in which you will measure these objectives in terms of research design and who will conduct the measurement. In other words, evaluation is not an afterthought for campaign work—long after your campaign is over, the data and evidence you collected might be all that is remembered of your campaign—so make sure that you collect accurate, unbiased, and appropriate information along your campaign evaluation process.

CHAPTER 11 REVIEW

Questions for Critical Thinking and Discussion

1. If a campaign does not meet its goals, it is a failed campaign? Why or why not?
2. Rank formative, process, and summative research in terms of their influence on later campaign success (i.e., 1 = *The least influential* to 3 = *The most influential*). Compare your rankings to a peer in class and discuss why you made these choices. Does their rationale change how you feel about each of these phases of evaluation?
3. What is your understanding of the difference between campaign effects and effectiveness? Have you ever seen a campaign that had an *effect* but was not *effective?* What is there to learn from this campaign's successes and failures?
4. In this chapter we discuss considerations for developing an evaluation plan, ending with considerations of budget. For smaller companies or nonprofit organizations, what are creative ways

that evaluations can be conducted without high cost?
5. Who are the key audiences that Mariana, Harper, and Malik need to reach with their evaluation report? Go through each of the considerations for writing this report for each person and situation—how do they vary in what they need the report to do for the organization? Is one situation easier or more difficult than the others?

Key Terms

big data: extremely large data sets that can be analyzed to reveal trends, patterns, and associations in human behavior and communication.

boomerang effect: when a message produces outcomes that are opposite of those it intended to produce.

campaign effectiveness: the extent to which observed campaign effects are consistent with campaign goals and objectives.

campaign effects: changes in outcome variables that can be traced back to campaign efforts.

campaign efficiency: the balance of costs and outcomes in the overall campaign effort.

concept testing: when a target audience is presented with initial concepts for the visual and verbal messages of a campaign and feedback is solicited.

cross-sectional research design: a research design in which data are measured at one point in time.

evaluation: the systematic research process used to understand the effectiveness of a campaign.

evaluation report: a written summary of campaign activities and evidence of campaign effects, effectiveness, and efficiency.

hypothesis: an educated guess about the relationship between two or more variables.

impact evaluation: an assessment of the long-term effects of a campaign on the target audience as well as the campaign's progress toward its overall goals.

logic model: a visual depiction of campaign resources, activities, messages, and intended outcomes.

longitudinal research design: a research design in which data is collected at multiple points in time.

moderator assistants: individuals who help set up logistics (such as audio recorders, refreshments, and name tags) to facilitate focus groups.

outcome evaluation: an assessment of whether or not a campaign met its intended objectives.

pilot test: a small-scale implementation of a campaign.

plain language: communication that an audience can understand the first time they read or hear it.

research design: the general framework used to answer a research question or test a hypothesis.

research question: a scholarly inquiry into the potential relationships or concepts in a particular context.

scientific method: a process of conducting research that is used to test research questions and hypotheses.

summative research: any research conducted following the conclusion of a campaign or a campaign cycle.

Further Readings and Resources

Centers for Disease Control and Prevention. 2017. "A Framework for Program Evaluation." https://www.cdc.gov/eval/framework/index.htm.

Evergreen, S. H. 2018. *Presenting Data Effectively: Communicating Your Findings for Maximum Impact.* 2nd ed. Los Angeles: Sage.

Huhman, M., C. Heitzler, and F. Wong. 2004. "The VERB™ Campaign Logic Model: A Tool for Planning and Evaluation." *Preventing Chronic Disease: Public Health Research, Prac-*

tice, and Policy 1: 1–6. www.cdc.gov/pcd/issues/2004/jul/04_0033.htm.

Larkin, R. 2013. "Using Outcomes to Measure Nonprofit Success." https://nonprofitquarterly.org/2013/07/02/using-outcomes-to-measure-nonprofit-success/.

Plain Language Action and Information Network. 2011. "Federal Plain Language Guidelines." www.plainlanguage.gov/guidelines/.

Rossi, P. H., M. W. Lipsey, and H. E. Freeman. 2004. *Evaluation: A Systematic Approach.* 7th ed. Los Angeles: Sage.

SAGE Research Methods. 2018. "Methods map." http://methods.sagepub.com/methods-map.

References

Atkin, C. K., and V. Freimuth. 1989. "Formative Evaluation Research in Campaign Design." In *Public Communication Campaigns,* 2nd ed., edited by R. E. Rice & C. K. Atkin, 131–50. Newbury Park, CA: Sage.

Centers for Disease Control and Prevention. 2013. *Developing an Effective Evaluation Report: Setting the Course for Effective Program Evaluation.* Atlanta: National Center for Chronic Disease Prevention and Health Promotion, Office on Smoking and Health, Division of Nutrition, Physical Activity and Obesity.

Cho, H., and C. T. Salmon. 2007. "Unintended Effects of Health Communication Campaigns." *Journal of Communication* 57, no. 2: 293–317. doi: 10.1111/j.1460–2466.2007.00344.x.

Cline, R. J. W., S. J. Johnson, and K. E. Freeman. 1992. "Talk among Sexual Partners about AIDS: Interpersonal Communication for Risk Reduction or Risk Enhancement?" *Health Communication* 4, no. 1: 39–56.

Dillow, M. R., and K. Weber. 2016. "An Experimental Investigation of Social Identification on College Student Organ Donor Decisions." *Communication Research Reports* 33, no. 3: 239–46. doi: 10.1080/08824096.2016.1186630.

Foster, C. S., N. Graham, H. Ball, and M. B. Wanzer. 2014. "Mothers, Sons, and Testicular Cancer: An Exploratory Investigation of Health Communication." *Qualitative Research Reports in Communication* 15, no. 1: 66–74. doi: 10.1080/17459435.2014.955594.

Haas, E. J., D. Willmer, and A. B. Cecala. 2016. "Formative Research to Reduce Mine Worker Respirable Silica Dust Exposure: A Feasibility Study to Integrate Technology into Behavioral Interventions." *Pilot and Feasibility Studies* 2: 1–11. doi: 10.1186/s40814–016–0047–1.

Hovland, C. I., I. L. Janis, and H. H. Kelly. 1953. *Persuasion and Communication.* New Haven, CT: Yale University Press.

Hull, S. J., C. R. Davis, G. Hollander, M. Gasiorowicz, W. L. Jeffries IV, S. Gray, . . . and A. Mohr. 2017. "Evaluation of the Acceptance Journeys Social Marketing Campaign to Reduce Homophobia." *American Journal of Public Health* 107, no. 1: 173–79. doi: 10.2105/AJPH.2016.303528.

James, K. J., J. A. Albrecht, R. E. Litchfield, and C. A. Weishaar. 2013. "A Summative Evaluation of a Food Safety Social Marketing Campaign: '4-Day-Throw-Away' Using Traditional and Social Media." *Journal of Food Science Education* 12, no. 3: 48–55. doi: 10.1111/1541–4329.12010.

Keegan, B. J., and J. Rowley. 2017. "Evaluation and Decision Making in Social Media Marketing." *Management Decision* 55, no. 1: 15–31. doi: 10.1108/MD-10-2015–0450.

Keyton, J. 2011. *Communication Research: Asking Questions, Finding Answers.* 3rd ed. New York: McGraw-Hill.

Kreps, G. L. 2008. "Strategic Use of Communication to Market Cancer Prevention and Control to Vulnerable Populations." *Health Marketing Quarterly* 25, no. 1–2: 204—16. doi: 10.1080/07359680802126327.

Lee, N. R., and P. Kotler. 2011. *Social Marketing: Influencing Behaviors for Good.* 4th ed. Los Angeles: Sage.

Liang, Y., L. K. Henderson, and K. F. Kee. 2018. "Running Out of Water! Developing a Message Typology and Evaluating Message Effects on Attitude toward Water Conservation." *Environmental Communication* 12, no. 4: 541–57. doi: 10.1080/17524032.2017.1288648.

Lipsky, D. B., R. L. Seeber, A. C. Avgar, and R. M. Scanza. 2007. "Managing the Politics of Evaluation: Lessons from the Evaluation of ADR Programs." *Proceedings of the Annual Meeting—Labor and Employment Relations Association,* 116–29.

Maibach, E. W., and R. Parrott. 1995. *Designing Health Messages: Approaches from Communication Theory and Public Health Practice.* Los Angeles: Sage.

Matthews, K. 2017. "5 Metrics to Measure Your Nonprofit's Success." www.nonprofitpro.com/post/5-metrics-measure-successful-nonprofit/.

Minkler, M. 2000. "Using Participatory Action Research to Build Healthy Communities." *Public Health Reports* 115, no. 2–3: 191–97.

National Recreation and Parks Association. 2017. "Issue Briefs: Park Safety." www.nrpa.org/contentassets/f768428a39aa4035ae55b2aaff372617/park-safety.pdf.

Noar, S. M. 2006. "A 10-Year Retrospective of Research in Health Mass Media Campaigns: Where Do We Go from Here?" *Journal of Health Communication* 11, no. 1: 21–42. doi: 10.1080/10810730500461059.

Pai, S., S. Siddarth, and S. Divakar. 2007. "Advertising Tracking." In *The SAGE Handbook of Advertising,* edited by G. J. Tellis and T. Ambler, 233–46. Los Angeles: Sage.

Rice, R. E., and C. K. Atkin. 2013. *Public Communication Campaigns.* 4th ed. Thousand Oaks, CA: Sage.

Roberto, A. J., L. Murray-Johnson, and K. Witte. 2011. "International Health Communication Campaigns in Developing Countries." In *The Routledge Handbook of Health Communication,* 2nd ed., edited by T. L. Thompson, R. Parrott, and J. F. Nussbaum, 220—34. New York: Routledge.

Salmon, C. T., and L. Murray-Johnson. 2001. "Communication Campaign Effectiveness." In *Public Communication Campaigns,* 3rd ed., edited by R. Rice and C. K. Atkins, 168–80. Thousand Oaks, CA: Sage.

———. 2014. "Communication Campaign Effectiveness and Effects: Some Critical Distinctions." In *Public Communication Campaigns,* 4th ed., edited by R. Rice and C. K. Atkins, 168–80. Thousand Oaks, CA: Sage.

Snyder, L. B., and D. J. Blood. 1992. "Caution: The Surgeon General's Alcohol Warnings and Alcohol Advertising May Have Adverse Effects on Young Adults." *Journal of Applied Communication Research* 20, no. 1: 37–53.

Valente, T. W. 2001. "Evaluating Communication Campaigns." In *Public Communication Campaigns,* 3rd ed., edited by R. Rice and C. K. Atkins, 105–24. Thousand Oaks, CA: Sage.

Witte, K. 1992. "The Role of Threat and Efficacy in AIDS Prevention." *International Quarterly of Community Health Education* 12, no. 3: 225–49.

W. K. Kellogg Foundation. 2004. "Logic Model Development Guide." www.wkkf.org/resource-directory/resource/2006/02/wk-kellogg-foundation-logic-model-development-guide.

Index

Key Terms are denoted by **bold type.**

ability, 218, **221**
About Face, 158
Abroms, L. C., 230, 231
academic opportunities, overview, 2
action stage, 164, 165, 168*tab.* 6.1
AdExpresso, 248
advertising approach, 29
aerie brand, mission statement, 71
affinity, 286
affinity-seeking, **288**
Alder BioPharmaceuticals Inc., mission statement, 69
Alexander, M., 302
Allen, M., 209–10
American Cancer Society, 138–39
American Eagle Outfitters (AEO), 70–71
American Heart Association, 163–64
American Marketing Association (AMA), 101, 105, 109–10
analytical listening style, 283, **288**
Andersen, Janis, 285
Andersen, Peter, 285
appeals, 208–13, **221;** emotional appeals, 209–13; logical appeals, 208–10
Apple, 13, 47, 60, 82, 175
applied settings, 192, **221**
Aquino, K., 111
Arby's, 69
Aristotle, 19
Armstrong, K., 262
artifacts, 59, **63**
asking, 195
AT&T, 214
Atalay, A. S., 218–19
Atkin, Charles, 32, 229
attitudes, 131, **150,** 156, 198, **222**
attitudinal anchor, 219, 220, **222**
attitudinal objectives, 131, 132, 149, **150,** 156
attitudinal shifts, 156, 270
audience, 25, **35.** *See also* target audience
Audience Insights Dashboard, 185–86
Axiom Technology Group, 303

background research: conducting and evaluating, 123, 125–28; criteria for evaluating sources, 127; primary and secondary sources, 126
barriers, **187**

Bartkus, B., 70, 73
baseline assessments, 329
Beebe, S. A., 283
behavior, 161–62, 163, 178, 199, **222**
behavioral, **150**
behavioral intention, 199
behavioral objectives, 131–32
beliefs, 198, **222**
Ben & Jerry's, 47
benefits, 178, **187**
Bergdorf Goodman, 218
Berkowitz, J. M., 307–8
Berlo, David, 20
Best Friends Animal Society, 69
big data, 326–27, **347**
BlackPlanet.com, 231
Bodie, G. D., 282
boomerang effect, 220, **222,** 341, **347**
Boster, Frank, 206–7, 212
Botan, C., 115
Boyle, Brian, 211
brainstorming, 146, **150**
brand, 82, **89**
brand affinity, 85–86, **89**
brand ambassadors, 84–85, **89**
brand awareness, 82, **89**
brand democracy, 84–85
brand equity, 83–84, 85, **89**
brand ethics, 85, **89**
branding, 66–90; brand recognition, 13; credibility and, 82; defined, 82, **89;** governmental organizations and, 82–83; IDEA framework and, 83–87; memorability and, 82; nonprofit organizations and, 82–83; organizational identity and, 81–87; strategic communication evaluations and, 87–88; visibility and, 82
brand integrity, 84, 85
bribery, 102, **116**
Bryant Park Restoration Cooperation (BPRC), 333
budget(s), 301, 302, 303, **316;** channel selection and, 246; strategic communication and, 15–16
Buffalo Municipal Housing Authority, mission statement, 69
Build-A-Bear Workshop, 238, 241
bullying. *See* workplace bullying
bureaucratic organization, 50–52, **63**

buyer persona, 174, **187**
buzz groups, 146, **150**

Cacioppo, J. T., 219
California Air Resources Board, 173
Camenzind, Stefan, 81
campaign, 32, **35**
campaign effectiveness, 336
campaign effects, 336, **348**
campaign efficiency, 336–37, **348**
campaign evaluation, 319–50; overview, 320, 346–47; conducting research using scientific method, 323–27; evaluation report writing, 342–46; five considerations of creating evaluation plan, 334–40; funding, 321; importance of, 320–27; improvement, 322–23; morale, 322; new opportunities, 322; resources, 321; stakeholder support, 322; three phases of, 327–33
campaign evaluation phases: conducting formative research, 328–29; conducting process research, 330–31; conducting summative research, 332–33; types of formative research, 329–30
campaign evaluation plan creation: considering objectives, 334; cost of evaluation consideration, 339–40; cross-sectional research design, 338; effects, effectiveness, and efficiency distinctions, 336–37; logic model use, 335–36; longitudinal research design, 338–39; measurement decisions, 334–37; measurement responsibility assignment, 339; quantitative and qualitative research, 337–38; research design determination, 337–39
campaign implementation, 290–317, 291–317; overview, 291–92, 312, 315; matrix for campaign contingency planning, 305*tab.* 10.2; plan importance, 292–95; Principle 1: clarify purpose and objectives, 295–98; Principle 2: rely on strategic plan to translate objectives into action steps, 298–300; Principle 3: audit, mobilize, and manage resources, 300–303; Principle 4: assign responsibilities for implementing campaign activities, 303–5; Principle 5: be

prepared for contingencies, 305–6; Principle 6: pause, reflect, evaluate, 306–8; Principle 7: ensure campaign sustainability, 308–9; Principle 8: demonstrate team communication competence, 309–12; sample implementation grid, 294–95, 294*tab*. 10.1; unintended effects of, 345
Campbell, R., 171
career opportunities, 2–3
Cassell, M. M., 234
Cecala, A. B., 328
Cenfetelli, R. T., 111
census, 182, **187**
Central Intelligence Agency, 69
centralization, 55
central route processing, 217, **222**
Chan, C. M., 86
change: external changes, 305; messaging and, 203; resistance to, 200–202; strategic communication and, 14–15
"Change We Can Believe In" campaign, 230, 232
channel, 20
channel selection, 26, 226–58; overview, 228; budget, 246; campaign goals and objectives, 244; channel characteristics, 245–46; considerations in, 243–54; developing integrated media mix, 255–56; importance of, 228–43; Media Richness Theory (MRT), 248–51, 252*tab*. 8.1; message content, 245; organizational identity and image, 244; target audience, 244–45; two-step flow model of communication, 252–54
Chapman University, 59–60, 197, 298
charismatic authority, 51, **63**
Check Yo Nutz campaign, 211
Cheung, C. K., 86
Cheuvront, B., 234
Cho, H., 341
Cialdini, Robert, 207
"Clear the Shelters" campaign, 235–36
clickbait, 207, **222**
client relationships, 13. *See also* stakeholders
coalitions, 85, **89**
Coca-Cola Company, 240
co-culture, 267–69, 270–71, 275, 279, **288**
codes of ethics: AMA, 109–10; of International Association of Business Communicator's, 105; practitioners on, 101–5; PRSA ethics code provisions of conduct, 106–8
Cohen, H., 247
collaboration, 14, **35**
collegiality, 104, 104–5, **116**
commodification, 201
common ground, 202, 203, 204
communication: overview, 16; approaches to examining, 29; defining, 17–19, **35**; key components of, 20; linear model of communication, 20–23; message exchange phases, 21–23, 21*fig*. 4;

organizational features and, 62; simultaneous transactions model of communication, 23–27; study of, 27–29
communication apprehension, 143, **150**
communication channels, 178
communication competence skills assessment, 18
communication culture, 61–62, **63**
communication impacts, 56–62
communication skills: analytical listening style, 283; critical listeners, 283–84; interpersonal communication, 282; listening skills, 282–83; rapport-building skills, 284–86; relational listening style, 283; task-oriented listening style, 283
communication studies, 27–28, **35**
Community Liaison Project, 260–63, 269, 270, 281–82
complexity, 53–55
concentrated marketing, 169–70
concept testing, 329, **348**
conflicts of interest, 102, **116**
Conrad, Charles, 13–14
consumer loyalty, 250, **256**
contemplation stage, 164, 165, 168*tab*. 6.1
content analytic research, 185
context, 25–26, **35**
contingencies, 51, **63**, 292, 305–6, 305*tab*. 10.2, **316**
copyright, 103, **116**
corporate culture, 87–88
Corporate Cultures (Deal and Kennedy), 58
corporate social responsibility (CSR), 47, **63**
cost of evaluation consideration, 339–40
Coulter, Robin Higie, 212
credibility: branding and, 82; perceptions of, 197; persuasion and, 204–8
"Credo for Ethical Communication," 95
critical advisor, 143, **150**
critical listeners, 283–84
cross-sectional research design, 338, **348**
CSR (corporate social responsibility), 47
cultural diversity and stakeholder awareness, 259–89; overview, 261, 287; knowing your audience and other stakeholders, 261–65; strategic communication in diverse society, 266–81; strategies for enhancing message effectiveness, 281–87; strategies for strengthening stakeholder relationships, 281–87
cultural exclusion, 268–70
cultural inclusion, 268–70
cultural relativity, 271, **288**
culture, **187**, **288**; appeals and, 209; co-culture, 267; mainstream culture, 267; organizational life and, 56–58; segmentation process and, 161; Tylor on, 266–67. *See also* organizational culture
customer profile, 174, **187**
customers. *See* stakeholders
customization-segmentation continuum, 172*fig*. 27

Daft, R. L., 248–49, 250–51
Daly, John, 28
danger control, **222**
danger control response, 215
Dao, David, 93
Deal, Terrence, 58
decentralization, 55
decisional balance, 167
Deepwater Horizon, 93, 112
Defense Logistics Agency (DLA), 50, 51
democracy, 84–85, **89**
demographics, 160, 163
descriptive norm, 131, **150**
Desmidt, Sebastian, 75
developmental research, 329
Dick's Sporting Goods, 46–47
DiClemente, C., 165
differentiated marketing, 169
digital media, 233
Dillow, Megan, 324
discounting model, 205, **222**
diversity of perspectives, 96–97
division of labor. *See* horizontal differentiation of complexity
Doran, George T., 134
Dropbox, 242
Dukes, S., 241

EcoCleanR, 8, 33–34
Eisenberg, E. M., 63
Eisenhower, Dwight D., 230
elaboration, 217
Elaboration Likelihood Model (ELM), 217–19
e-learning, 242
email, 242
embeddedness, organizational, 41
emotional appeals, 209–13, **222**
employees. *See* stakeholders
engagement, 13, 30
equivocality, 250–51, **256**
Estee Lauder Company, 72
ethical communication, 94, 95–101
ethics, **116**; AMA statement of, 109–10; brand ethics, 85; codes of ethics, 101–8; defined, 94; ethical considerations summary, 113–14; NCA's ethical credo, 95–101; persuasion and, 206; professional ethics in practice, 108–12
ethics and ethical communication, 91–116
ethnocentrism, 268, **288**
evaluating campaigns: phases of, 327–33. *See also* evaluation plans; evaluation report writing; evaluation research
evaluation: branding and, 87–88; corporate culture and, 87–88; criteria for evaluating sources, 127; defined, 320, **348**; importance of, 320–21; mission statements and, 87–88; organizational image and, 87–88; reasons to conduct, 321–23
evaluation plans: considering objectives, 334; cost of evaluation consideration, 339–40; creating considerations,

334–41; cross-sectional research design, 338; effects, effectiveness, and efficiency distinctions, 336–37; logic model use, 335–36; longitudinal research design, 338–39; measurement decisions, 334–35; measurement responsibility assignment, 339; research design determination, 337–38; sample table to organize, 340*tab.* 11.1

evaluation report, 342–43, **348**

evaluation report writing, 342–46; campaign activities summary, 344; channel selection, 345–46; considering audience, 343; plain language use, 344–45; report structure, 346; restating mission, goals, and objectives, 343–44; results provision and interpretation, 344

evaluation research: conducting formative research, 328–29; conducting process research, 330–31; conducting summative research, 332–33; formative research, types of, 329–30

everyday ways of knowing, 193–95

Evolution Design Ltd., 81

Extended Parallel Process Model (EPPM), 210, 213–17, 217*fig.* 33

external assessment, 144–46

external challenges, 11, 15, **35**

external environments, 41–42

external members, 40–41

Facebook, 60, 185, 230, 231, 232, 247

Facebook Insights, 185

Facebook Messenger, 249

face-to-face communication, 240–41, 243

face-to-face surveys, 182

false consensus, 179, **187**

fear appeals, 213–17

fear control, **222**

fear control response, 215

Federal Highway Administration, 69

federal laws. *See* regulatory laws

feedback, 23–24, **35,** 250

The Five Dysfunctions of a Team (Lencioni), 296

flexibility, 14–15

focus group research, 184–85

foot-in-the-door, 232, **256**

Ford Motor Company, 76

formal, **150**

formal (scholarly) theory, 196, 221, **222**

formalization, 55–56

formal roles, 142

formal strategic plans, 148–49

formative research, **187;** attitudes and beliefs, 177–78; behaviors, 178; defined, 177; focus group research, 184–85; knowledge, 177; preferred communication channels, 178; reactions to message, 178–79; sample groups, 179, 182; social network analytic research, 185–86; survey research, 182–84; types of, 329–30

for-profit organization, **63**

for-profit organizations: background research for, 125; behavior and, 161–62; channel selection and, 240; coalitions and, 85; mission statements, 69; as organizational type, 45–48; strategic communication and, 11

Foster, C. S., 325

4-Day-Throw-Away campaign, 332–33

frequency, 245, 247, **256**

Friedrich, Gustav, 28

FTD, 218

full marketing, 169

Gabbott, M., 23

generation, 160–61, 163

Get a Mac campaign, 175–76

Giddens, Anthony, 63

Gilpin, Dawn, 80

Gladwell, Malcolm, 207

Glassman, M., 70, 73

goal(s), 128, **150.** *See also* organizational goals and objectives

Goldbely, 218

Goodall, H. L., 63

Google, 81

GoogleDocs, 242

Gorham, Joan, 285

government, **63**

government organizations: background research for, 125; branding and, 82–83; hometown mission statements, 76; mission statements, 69–70; as organizational type, 49–52; strategic communication and, 11

Griffin, E., 195

groupthink, 142, 142–44, **150**

growth, 14–15

guilt, 212–13

Haas, E. J., 328

Hackbarth, Kim, 180

Haley, Robert, 159

Hall, Edward T., 266

Harrison, T. R., 293

Haslam, S. A., 144

Heald, G. R., 113, 114

Healthy People initiative, 132–34

Heath, Chip, 207

Heath, Dan, 207

Heath, R. L., 71

Henderson, L. K., 341

heroes (organizational), 60, **63**

heuristics, 193, 193–94, **222**

Hewlett-Packard, 60

Hockey Fights Cancer campaign, 211

Hodgman, John, 176

Hofstede, Geert, 209, 270–75, 277, 279, 280

Hogg, G., 23

Horan, S. M., 86

Horberg, P., 308

horizontal, **256**

horizontal communication, 232

horizontal differentiation of complexity, 53

Hovland, Carl, 197, 219–20

Hubspot, 175

Hull, S. J., 339

human relations approach, 29

humor, 210–11, **222**

Hwang, Yoori, 254

hypothesis/hypothesizing, 195, 324, **348**

IBM, 75

IDEA framework, 83–87; brand affinity, 85–86; brand equity, 83–84, 85; democracy, 84–85; integrity, 84

identity, 141–42. *See also* organizational identity and image

image. *See* organizational identity and image

immediacy, 285, **288**

impact evaluation, 333, **348**

importance of research in decision-making, 127–28

improper conduct, 106–8

individualism-collectivism continuum, 271–72, 272*tab.* 9.1, 273, **288**

indulgence-restraint continuum, 279–80, 280, **288**

informal, **150**

informal roles, 143

informational, **150**

informational objectives, 131

in-groups, 266

In Search of Excellence (Peters and Waterman), 58

Instagram, 233

integrated communication, 31, **35**

integrated marketing, 31

integrated narrative, 255–56, **256**

integrity, **89;** brand integrity, 84, 85; IDEA framework and, 84

intercept, **187**

interdependence, environmental, 41

interdisciplinary perspective, 2, 31

internal assessment: groupthink factor affecting, 142–44; identity factor affecting, 141–42; of strengths and weaknesses, 140–44

internal challenges, 11, 15, **35**

internal communication channels, 242–43

internal environment, 41–42

internal management, 11–12

internal members, 40–41

Internal Revenue Service, 52

International Association of Business Communicator (ABC) code of ethics, 101, 105

internet/cloud-based workspaces, 242–43

interpersonal communication, 282, **288**

interviews with professionals (feature): overview, 4; Hackbarth (Boy with a Ball), 180–81; Jacobs (American Cancer Society), 138–39

investors. *See* stakeholders

"It Can Wait" campaign, 214–15

Jack in the Box, 114

Jackson, C., 234

Jackson, Stacy, 244
Jacob, JoAnna, 138–39
James, K. J., 332–33
Janis, Irvin, 145
Jetten, J., 144

Kantner, Rosabeth Moss, 201
Katz, E., 252
Kearney, P., 233, 271, 285–86, 310
Kee, K. F., 341
Keegan, B. J., 331
Kellermann, Kathy, 19
Kennedy, Adam, 58
Keyton, Joann, 42, 56, 94, 323
Kim, S., 247
kinesics, 22, **35**
Kraft Foods Inc., mission statement, 69
Kreps, Gary, 97, 204, 245, 260–63, 266, 268, 269, 281, 287
Kylander, N., 84, 85, 86

LaBelle, Sara, 165, 179, 197, 210–11
Langett, J., 111
latitude of acceptance, 220, **222**
latitude of noncommitment, 220, **222**
latitude of rejection, 220, **222**
laws: governing ethical behaviors, 102–3; regulatory laws, 12, **35**
Lazarsfeld, P. F., 252
leader(s), 12, 142–43, **150**
leadership: strategic communication and, 11–12; transformational leaders, 12. *See also* leader; management
Ledbetter, A., 195
Ledford, C. J. W., 234
LeFebvre, R. C., 230, 231
legitimacy, 265
LeGreco, M., 63
Leinbach-Reyhle, N., 238–39
Lencioni, Patrick, 296
Lengel, R. H., 248–49, 250–51
Lewin, Kurt, 191–92
Lewis, L. K., 265
Liang, Y., 341
Lieber, P. S., 111
linear, 20, **35**
linear model of communication, 20, 21*fig.* 4
line items, 301, 302, **316**
listening skills, 282–83
listening styles, **288**
logical appeals, 208–10
logic model, 335–37, 336*fig.* 52, **348**
Long, Justin, 175–76
long-, short-term orientation continuum, **288**
longitudinal research design, 338–39, **348**
long-term orientation (LTO), 277–79
long-term/short-term orientation continuum, 277–79
Loughry, M. L., 306–7
low hanging fruit, 170

MacNamara, S. R., 113, 114
Madoff, Bernard, 92

mainstream culture, 267, **288**
maintenance stage, 164, 165, 168*tab.* 6.1
management. *See* leadership
marketing approach, 29
masculinity-femininity continuum, 275–77, 277
masculinity-feminity continuum, **288**
mass communication, 169, **187**
mass marketing, 169
mass media, 12, **35**
matrix for campaign contingency planning, 305*tab.* 10.2
Maurer, M., 253
McAfee, B., 70, 73
McCain, John, 231
McDonalds, 60, 82
McLuhan, Marshall, 26, 229
McMurphy, S., 262
Meade, Thomas, 237
measurement responsibility assignment, 339
media: strategic communication and, 12; target audience and, 157–58
media mix, 231, **256**
media richness continuum, 252*tab.* 8.1
mediated communication, 228, **256**
medium, 228, **256**
Meloy, M. M., 219
membership goals, 42
memorability, 82
mentors (feature). *See* strategic communication mentors (feature)
message, 20, **35**
message content, 245
message decisions, 21
message decoding, 22
message dissemination: approaches, 168–72; mass communication approach, 169; strategy selection, 155; tailored communication approach, 171–73, 172*fig.* 26; targeted communication approach, 169–71
message effectiveness: communication skills and, 282–87; theory/research use and, 281–82
message encoding, 21
message exchange phases, 21–23, 21*fig.* 4
message fatigue, 247–48
message organization, 207
message perception, 22
message source credibility, 208
message transmissions, 22
messaging, focus on, 32
metaphors (organizational), 58–59, **63**
Microsoft, 47
MiGente.com, 231
millennials, 160
mindful communication, 30
mission statement, **89**; audience, 75; defined, 68; Estee Lauder Company, 72; mission taglines, 72; positivity, 76; specificity, 73; transparency, 73; updating, 75–76
mission statements, 66–90; benefits of good mission statement, 70–72; principles of

effective mission statements, 71, 72–76, 77*fig.* 12; questions for developing, 71–72; role in strategic communication campaigns, 68–76; samples of, 69–70; strategic communication evaluations and, 87–88
mission tagline, 72, **89**
mission taglines, 72
mobile instant messaging (MIM) platforms, 249–50
mobile phones, 239–40
moderator, 184, **187**
moderator assistants, 339, **348**
Montgomery, D. J., 113, 114
Moore, D. D., 306–7
motivation, 202, 218, **222**
multiple cues, 249
Mumby, Dennis, 16
Munoz, Oscar, 93, 111
Murray-Johnson, L., 329, 334
MyBO, 231–32
MySpace, 230

narrative, 210, **222**
National Cancer Institute, 158
National Coalition for Homeless Veterans (NCHV), 13, 15
National Communication Association (NCA), 94, 95–101, 113
National Hockey League, 211, 338
National Institute for Occupational Safety and Health (NIOSH), 328–29
National Parks Conservation Association, 69
National Railroad Passenger Corporation (Amtrak), 170
National Recreation and Parks Association, 333
need for cognition (NFC), 218, **222**
networking, 233, **256**
new media, 230–35, **256**
Nike, 82
Noar, Seth, 254, 328
noise, 20
nonprofit organization, **63**
non-profit organizations, as organizational type, 48–49
nonprofit organizations: About Face, 158; American Cancer Society, 138–39; background research for, 125; branding and, 82–83; coalitions and, 85; mission statements, 69; strategic communication and, 11, 12
nonverbal communication: avoiding, 287; criticism and, 147; cultural diversity and, 194; in diverse society, 266; as feedback, 23, 25; interaction rules and, 26; listening skills and, 282–83; media channel selection and, 243; media richness theory and, 248–49; nonverbal immediacy, 285; nonverbal messages, 20–22, 35, 44; organizational identity and, 71; research on, 20; selection of, 310

Norcross, J. C., 165
norms, **63**
norms, organizational, 60–61

Obama, Barack, 230, 232
objectives, **150**; defined, 129
observing, 195
Occupational Safety and Health Administration, mission statement, 69
Ohland, M. W., 306–7
opinion leaders, 252, **256**
opportunities, 144, 144–46, 147*fig.* 5.1, 148, 148*fig.* 5.2, **150**
opportunities and threats, 144–46, 147*fig.* 5.1, 148*fig.* 5.2. *See also* SWOT analysis
organization: defined, 9, 43, **63**; primary defining dimensions of, 44
organizational change, 15, **35**
organizational communication approach, 29
organizational culture: analyzing, 58–62; defined, 56, **63**; impacts on communication, 56–62; organizational life and, 56–58
organizational goals and objectives, 119–51; background research, 123, 125–28; channel selection and, 244; external assessment, 144–46; formal strategic plan and, 148–49; Groupthink factor affecting internal assessment, 142–44; identity factor affecting internal assessment, 141–42; importance of research in decision-making, 127–28; internal assessment of strengths and weaknesses, 140–44; making SWOT strategic, 147–48; organizational strategic plans, 137, 137*fig.* 20, 140; planning, 121–22; setting of, 128–40; setting SMART objectives, 134–37; SMART objectives and, 148–49; steps of planning, 123–25; SWOT analysis, 140–48, 148–49; SWOT analysis, conducting of, 146–47; types of, 130–34
organizational identity, **89**; defined, 78
organizational identity and image, 66–90, 77–81; branding and, 81–87; channel selection and, 244; distinctions between, 78–80; public relations and, 80–81; strategic communication evaluations and, 87–88; workplace structure and, 80–81
organizational image, 78, **89**
organizational life, organizational culture and, 56–58
organizational member investment, strategic communication and, 13
organizational objectives: attitudinal, 131; behavioral, 131–32; informational, 131
organizational processes, 7–36
organizational strategic plans, 137, 137*fig.* 20, 140
organizational structural features: centralization, 55; complexity, 53–55; formalization, 55–56

organizational types and structures, 37–65; government organizations, 49–52; influence on communication, 52–56; non-profit organizations, 48–49; organizations and organizational communication, 40; for-profit organizations, 45–48; relationship to communication, 62
organizational voice, 71, **89**
organizations: broad types of, 44–52; identifiable dimensions of, 40–44; organizational communication and, 40; structural features influencing communication, 52–56
outcome evaluation, 332–33, **348**
overall benefit, 171
overavailability, 201
OWN, 60

participants, 182, **187**
partnership, **35**
partnerships, 14
Patagonia, 69
patent(s), 103, **116**
peer relationships, 13, **35**
peripheral route processing, 217–18, **222**
personal identity, 142, **150**
persuasion, 190–224, **222**; appeals used in, 208–13; credibility and, 204–8; defined, 197, **222**; elaboration likelihood model, 217–19; evaluating persuasive message audience, 202–4; extended parallel process model, 213–17, 217*fig.* 33; goals of, 198–200; as key element of strategic communication, 197–98; social judgment theory, 219–20; strategic communication and, 191–92, 220–21. *See also* theory
Peters, Tom, 58, 62
Petty, R. E., 217, 219
pilot test(ing), 330, **348**
Pincus, L. B., 113, 114
Pinto, Mary Beth, 212
Pittsburgh Chamber of Commerce, mission statement, 69
plain language, 344–45, **348**
Plain Language Act of 2010, 344
Plain Language Guidelines, 344, 345
planning: importance of, 121; steps of, 123–25
Plax, T. G., 233, 271, 285–86, 310
policy makers, 158
political forces, 12
Postmes, T., 144
postmodern perspective, 200, **222**
postproduction research, 329
power distance continuum, 275, **288**
Powers, John, 28
precontemplation stage, 163–64, 165, 168*tab.* 6.1
Preiss, R. W., 209–10
preparation stage, 164, 165, 168*tab.* 6.1
pretesting, 178, **188**, 329–30
primary and secondary sources, 126

primary research, 126, **150**
primary target audience, 156, **188**
print media, 236–37
processes of change, 167
process evaluation, 307, **316**
Prochaska, J., 165
promotional items, 237–38
proofreading, 208
propaganda, 197
proprietary information, 103, **116**
PRSA ethics code provisions of conduct, 106–8
psychographics, 162, 163, **188**
psychological reactance theory: change resistance tendency, 200–202; defined, 199, **222**
Public Broadcasting Service (PBS), 69
public perception, 13
public relations: defined, 80, **89**; in organizational identity and image, 80–81; public relations approach, 29
Public Relations Society of America (PRSA), 101
Pura Vida, 85
purposive sampling, 184, **188**
Putnam, Linda, 16
Putt, M., 262

qualitative, **150**
qualitative research, 337–38
quantitative, **150**
quantitative research, 337–38
questions (feature): overview, 4; branding, 88; channel selection, 256; communication ethics, 115; cultural diversity and stakeholder awareness, 287–88; evaluating campaigns, 347; implementing campaigns, 315–16; mission statements, 88; organizational goals and objectives, 149–50; organizational identity and image, 88; organizational types and structures, 63; persuasion, 221; on strategic communication, 34–35; strategic communication perspective, 34–35; target audience, 187
QVC, 218

Raab, M., 305
radio, 236
Raposo, P. C., 86
rapport-building skills, 284–86
rational-legal authority, 51, **63**
Ravenell, K. L., 262
real world applications, 3–4. *See also* interviews with professionals (feature); strategic communication mentors (feature); vignettes (feature)
receiver, 20
receptor, 20
recorder, 143, **150**
Reddit, 233
regulatory laws, 12, **35**
reinforcement, 202
relational listening style, 283, **288**

relationship and identity management, 129, 149, 335–36
Rep Program, 85
research design, 337, **348**
research question, **348**
research questions, 324–25, 326*fig. 49*
resistance, 198, 200–202
resource audits, 301, **316**
response efficacy, 215–16
Rethink campaign, 298, 299, 313–15, 314*fig. 46*, 315*fig. 47*
revising, 196
Rice, Ronald, 32, 229
richness, 248–51, 252*tab. 8.1*, **257**
rituals (organizational), 59–60, **63**
Roberto, A. J., 329
Rocha, J., 305
roles, 142, 143, 304, **316**
Ross, J. H., 310
Ross, S., 59, 310
Rossman, Contanze, 228–29
Rotary International, 42–43
Rowley, J., 331
Ryan, M. K., 144

salient audience characteristics, **288**
Salmon, C. T., 334, 341
sample, **188**
sample groups, defined, 179
Sandy Hook Promise, 236
Saxon, Athena, 313–15
Schein, Edgar, 56–57
scholarly theory, 195–97
scholarly theory, formal, 196, 221
scientific method, 323, 326*fig. 49*, **348**
secondary research, 126, **150**
segmentation, **188**
segmentation (process), 160
segmentation process: behavior, 161–62; benefits of, 167; culture, 161; demographics, 160; generation, 160–61; key characteristics and theoretical approaches, 160–67; location, 161; psychographics, 162; transtheoretical model, 162–66
segment need, 170
segment readiness, 170
segment size, 170
self-administered online surveys, 183
self-administered paper/pencil surveys, 182–83
self-efficacy, 167, 216
Sellnow, T. L., 114
sender, 20
Sender-Message-Channel-Receiver (SMCR) model, 20
severity assessment, 215
Shannon, C. E., 20
Shannon Weaver Model of Communication, 20
Sherif, C. W., 219–20
short-term orientation (STO), 277–79
simultaneous transactions model, 23–27, **35**

single person method, 173, 173–76, **188**
size aspect of complexity, 53–54
Skype, 242
Slater, M. D., 166
sleeper effect, 205, **222**
small business owners, 12
SMART objectives: defined, 132; evaluation plans and, 334; formal strategic plan and, 148–49; long-term goals to, 133; setting of, 134–37
Snyder, L. B., 245
So, J., 247
social desirability effect, 183, **188**
social identities, 142, **150**
Social Judgment Theory (SJT), 219–20
social loafing, 294, **316**
social media, **35;** as campaign channel, 240; clickbait, 207–8; Millennials and, 161; statistic use, 331; strategic communication and, 13
social network analytic research: Facebook, 185; Twitter, 185–86
social networking sites, 233, **257**
sociocultural elements, 26–27, **35**
Sollitto, Michael, 15
source credibility, 86, **89,** 204–5
Sparks, G., 195, 263
Spears, R., 144
specialization, 246, **257**
Speech Communication Association (SCA), 95
stages of change: measuring of, 165; model, 166*fig. 25;* outcomes for audiences at, 168*tab. 6.1*
Stages of Changes, 162, 165, 166*fig. 25,* 168*tab. 6.1. See also* Transtheoretical Model (TTM)
stakeholder power, 264
stakeholders: communication skills and, 282–87; defined, **35;** divergent interests of, 263–64; legitimacy, 265; significance of knowing, 261–65; stakeholder power, 264; stakeholder support, 322; theory/research and, 281–82; urgency, 265. *See also* client relationships
Starbucks, 47, 60, 82
state laws. *See* regulatory laws
status quo, 203
Stolle, D. P., 113
Stone, C., 84, 85, 86
Stone, Romauld, 72, 76
stories, **63**
stories, organizational, 60
strategic approach: overview, 8–9; academic opportunities, 2; career opportunities, 2–3; as emerging interdisciplinary perspective, 2; organizational communication and, 10; organization process and, 9–10; strategic communication, **35;** overview, 1, 9–10; approach to organizations, 29–32; benefits of, 33–34; defined, 30; defining communication, 17; Eco-CleanR vignette, 8; engagement in, 30;

foundational assumptions of, 32–33; as foundation for organizational success, 16, 16–29; as interdisciplinary, 31; messaging focus, 32; as mindful communication, 30; need for, 11–15; organizational communication and, 44; organization defined, 8–9; real world applications, 3–4; strategic approach, 2. *See also* communication
strategic communication in diverse society: cultural and co-cultural features influencing communication, 270–80; cultural inclusion, 268–70; culture defined, 266–68
strategic communication mentors (feature): overview, 4; Big Data, 326; change resistance, 201; communication competence skills assessment, 18; communication ethics, 95; competent project management, 303; contingency planning, 306; corporate responsibility, 43; corporate social responsibility, 47; editing for plain language, 345; external and internal challenges, 15; Groupthink, 145; Hockey Fights Cancer campaign, 211; hometown mission statements, 77; individualism-collectivism continuum, 273; indulgence-restraint continuum, 280; internal communication channels, 242–43; long-term/short-term orientation continuum, 279; masculinity-femininity continuum, 277; message fatigue, 247–48; nature of communication, 19; neuroscience of guilt, 212; power distance continuum, 275; readability assessment, 74; segmentation categories, 163; SMART method, 136; source credibility assessment, 87; stages of change, 165; stories as strategy, 61; target audience, 159; uncertainty avoidance continuum, 274; unintended effects of campaigns, 341
strategic plan, 137, 137*fig. 20*, **150**
strategic planning, 122, **150**
strengths, 140–41, 147–48, 147*fig. 5.1,* 148*fig. 5.2,* **150.** *See also* SWOT analysis
structuration theory, 63
Studebacher, C. A., 113
Sullivan, P. A., 268
summative research, 332–33, **348**
Survey of the American Consumer, 163
survey research, 182–84; defined, 182, **188;** face-to-face surveys, 182; self-administered online surveys, 183; self-administered paper/pencil surveys, 182–83; telephone surveys, 182
Susan G. Komen Breast Cancer Foundation, 83
susceptibility, 215
sustainability, 308–9
SWOT analysis, 140–48, 148–49, **150;** conducting of, 146–47; contingencies and,

305; defined, 140; formal strategic plan and, 148–49; making SWOT strategic, 147–48; research and, 323
synergy, 255–56, **257**

tailored communication, 171–73, 172*fig.* 26, **188**
Tajfel, H., 142
Target, 42, 43, 82
target audience, 152–89; overview, 186–87; channel selection and, 244–45; content analytic research, 185; defined, 154, **188**; defining, 154–55; expanding of, 159; focus group research, 184; formative research on, 176–86, 182; health care perceptions of, 261–63; mission statements and, 75; salient audience characteristics, 263; selection steps, 155; significance of knowing, 261–65; social network analytic research, 185; survey research, 182–83; transtheoretical model and, 162–66; types of people in, 156–60
targeted communication, 169, 169–71, **188**
target population, 154, **188**
task management, 129, 149, 292–93, 335–36
task-oriented listening style, 283, **288**
Taylor, David, 73, 75
TED, 69
telephone surveys, 182
television, 235–36
testing, 196
text messaging, 242
T-groups, 192
theoretical saturation, 185, **188**
theory: defined, 193, **222**; as everyday ways of knowing, 193–95; Lewin on, 191–92; as scholarly frameworks, 195–97; usefulness of, 192. *See also* persuasion; psychological reactance theory
theory-based segmentation, 162, **188**
Thompson, Eddie, 61
threats, 145, 145–46, 147*fig.* 5.1, 148, 148*fig.* 5.2, **150**, 306
TopNonprofits.com, 72
TOWS analysis, 148
tracking, 331
trademark(s), 103, **116**
trade secrets, 103, **116**
traditional advertising, 236–37
traditional authority, 51, **63**
transformational leaders, 12, **35**
transmitter, 20

transparency, 73
transtheoretical model, 162–66
Transtheoretical Model (TTM), 162, 162–67
trends: opportunities and, 144; strategic communication and, 14–15; trending, 240
Trethewey, A., 63
Trevino, L. K., 249
Truth campaign, 254
Tseng, F. C., 249–50, 250
Tumblr, 233
Turner, J. C., 142
Turner, Lynn, 196
turnover, 13
Twitter, 13, 80, 81, 185–86, 233
two-sided message with refutation, 206, **222**
Two-Step Flow Model, 228, 252–54, 253*fig.* 38
tying it all together (feature): channel selection, 255–56; communication ethics, 115; cultural diversity and stakeholder awareness, 287; implementing campaigns and programs, 312, 315; mission statements and organizational identity, 87–88; organizational goals and objectives, 148–49; organizational types and structures, 62–63; persuasion, 220–21; strategic communication perspective, 33–34; target audience, 186–87
Tylor, Edward B., 266–67
Tyner Construction Company Inc., mission statement, 69

Ulmer, R. R., 114
uncertainty avoidance continuum, 273–74, **288**
undifferentiated marketing, 169
unintended effects of campaigns, 345
unique selling proposition, **150**
United Airlines, 93, 111
urgency, 265
US Army, 69
USO, 69

Valente, Thomas, 323, 339
values (organizational), 58, **63**
Vangelisti, Anita, 28
vertical (communication), **257**
vertical communication, 232
vertical hierarchy (of complexity), **63**
vertical hierarchy of complexity, 54–55
Victor, Ronald, 159

video conferencing, 242
vignettes (feature): overview, 3–4; channel selection, 226–28; communication ethics, 92–93; cultural diversity and stakeholder awareness, 260; evaluating campaigns, 319–20; implementing campaigns, 291–92; mission statements and organizational identity, 67–68; organizational goals and objectives, 120–21; organizational processes, 8; organizational types and structures, 38–40; persuasion, 191–92; target audience, 153–54
visibility, branding and, 82
vocalics, 22, **35**
VoIP (Voice over Internet Protocol), 242

Waldeck, Jennifer, 59, 192, 233, 263–64, 269, 271, 284, 285–86, 301–2, 310
Walmart, 55
Walt Disney Company, 60; mission statement, 69
Waterman, Robert, 58, 62
weaknesses, 147–48, 147*fig.* 5.1, 148*fig.* 5.2, **150**; defined, 141. *See also* SWOT analysis
Weaver, W., 20
web conferencing, 242
Weber, Keith, 324
Weber, Max, 50–52
Webley, P., 144
websites, 238–39
West, Rich, 196
WhatsApp, 249
Whole Foods, 80
Willmer, D., 328
Witte, Kim, 213–15, 329
workplace bullying, **35**, 105; strategic communication and, 13–14
Workplace Bullying Institute, 13
workplace structure, in organizational identity and image, 80–81
World Wide Fund for Nature (WWF), 238, 241
Wounded Warrior Project, mission statement, 69

Xu, D. J., 111

Yelp, 234; strategic communication and, 13
YouTube, 230, 231, 233, 304

Zenefits, mission statement, 73
Zuckerberg, Mark, 60

Founded in 1893,
UNIVERSITY OF CALIFORNIA PRESS
publishes bold, progressive books and journals
on topics in the arts, humanities, social sciences,
and natural sciences—with a focus on social
justice issues—that inspire thought and action
among readers worldwide.

The UC PRESS FOUNDATION
raises funds to uphold the press's vital role
as an independent, nonprofit publisher, and
receives philanthropic support from a wide
range of individuals and institutions—and from
committed readers like you. To learn more, visit
ucpress.edu/supportus.

Milton Keynes UK
Ingram Content Group UK Ltd.
UKHW030401170724
445591UK00008B/210